kansas city public library
kansas city, missouri
Books will be issued only
on presentation of library card.
Please report lost cards and
change of residence promptly.
Card holders are responsible for
all books, records, films, pictures
or other library materials
checked out on their cards.

Duel of Wits

BY PETER CHURCHILL

G. P. Putnam's Sons
New York

This book is based on the author's two volume work, *Of Their Own Choice* and *Duel of Wits*, previously published in England by Hodder and Stoughton, Ltd.

Library of Congress Catalog
Card Number 55-5773

MANUFACTURED IN THE UNITED STATES OF AMERICA

DEDICATION

This book is dedicated to my beloved Arnaud, the late Captain Alec Rabinowitch, a violent, difficult, devoted, and heroic radio operator, and through him to all "underground" men and women of his supreme caliber who died, as they lived, in solitude. Their feats are legendary and beyond all military awards Their words, their bearing, and their acts are proudly handed down from father to son in the French homes which they endangered, enriched, and also helped to save by their presence in the hour of darkness.

AUTHOR'S NOTE

THIS is a true story. Every man and woman who appears in these pages is, or was, a living person. In some cases code names have had to be used, but in the main, correct names are revealed.

It is the story of my four secret missions to wartime France, which I entered twice by submarine and twice by parachute. It begins in July 1941 at the Sabotage Training Schools of the French Section of the War Office and ends in April 1943 with the betrayal and capture of my courier—now my wife—and myself.

Resistance movements took a larger share in World War II than is generally realized, the French losing in the region of 200,000 people in the concentration camps and the heroic Poles topping the tragic list with a death roll twice as great as the total losses incurred by the combined Armed Forces of the United States for the whole war.

PETER CHURCHILL

Contents

Operational maps will be found on pages 57 and 142.

PART I

Of Their Own Choice

CHAPTER I

GENTLEMEN!" began Major Roger de Wesselow, addressing the fourteen recruits assembled for their first course of sabotage at Wanborough Manor, "you will be given three weeks' intensive instruction in this school of subversive activity. There will be lectures and practical exercises in map reading, demolitions, weapon training, the Morse code, fieldcraft, and close combat. French will be spoken at all meals. You will be worked very hard, and I think I should warn you in all fairness that your reactions and progress during the course will be carefully noted There is no limit to the number of candidates acceptable for the tough and solitary life of this organization for which you have volunteered, but the requirements of physical endurance, patience, technical knowledge, and security are high. Not only will your lives depend on these qualifications, but also the lives of your comrades in the same group I cannot sufficiently stress the importance of security. Nobody outside this school knows what goes on here, and nobody must know. All letters written from here, or received, are carefully censored. The telephone must not be used. When the course is over, those of you who have passed—and I hope all of you do—will be sent up to Scotland for the second course of advanced training. There will be no leave between the courses; only after the parachute course, which comes third. In conclusion," said Major de Wesselow, putting on his well-fitting service cap, picking up his gloves, and adjusting his impeccable Sam Browne, whose leather shone as only old leather can, "you will find the food here to be good and plentiful, the canteen well stocked, and the beds excellent. That's about all. Are there any questions?"

Dead silence spread over the assembly. Not that there was

any shortage of questions; on the contrary. But nobody felt strong enough to voice them.

In the absence of any query, the Major went on:

"My staff and I are always at your disposal for any problem you may have. And now, as you would no doubt like to get acquainted with one another before lunch, I will leave you. A ring on that bell will produce the corporal who handles the drinks. That's all."

Having delivered his welcoming speech in the best traditions of the Brigade, this elegant and self-composed Coldstream officer turned and walked smartly out of the room.

A temporarily speechless group of junior officers, of all ages, some of whom had never worn a uniform before, gaped at his departing form.

"Well," I said, getting up and pressing the bell long and hard, "at least we know where we are. I spent four months in 167 O.C.T.U. being mucked about from morning till night, but nobody took the trouble to explain what it was all in aid of. Here, at least, the old man makes it perfectly clear that the pudding can be eaten or left. It's over to us."

"Very little treacle on this particular pudding," murmured someone, as they all gathered round to order drinks from the corporal, whose swift response to the bell made it appear as though he must have anticipated it from past experience of these courses.

When he had left the room with his orders, an elderly student, aged about fifty, said, "It looks as though the days of Olga, the beautiful spy and all that exotic stuff, were things of the past. A pity, in a way, as I can hardly see myself parachuting or trudging across the Pyrenees at my age. I'm sure to be fired after a couple of days of this high-pressure training."

"I shouldn't think so," answered someone else. "They'll probably land you by aircraft. Much more comfortable way of traveling. They wouldn't have let you come here unless they'd something in mind for you."

After the drinks had been passed round, we formed ourselves into small groups, introduced each other by the Christian name we had been given at Headquarters before joining the course, and presently a general hubbub of conversation filled the room.

I found myself in a small party of three with Robert and a pleasant young man called Philip. Robert was the Conducting Officer who knew all the "gen" about the S.O.E. (Special Operations Executive) courses, and whose duties consisted of appraising the character of each student, which he would ultimately hand over to Head Office in a written report. He explained to us that he would accompany us on all the courses, including the parachute training, in which he would take part himself, for the simple reason that he really enjoyed parachuting.

"Quite a job," I suggested.

"Oh, not really," replied Robert. "It's a job kept for those who have been 'in the field' and who are waiting for their next assignment. It keeps one in good condition, while allowing one's brain to take a rest."

"Is it very nerve-racking over there?" asked Philip.

"You can never really relax," replied Robert. "The actual operations are all right. In fact, they're the high spots. It's the waiting for operations that becomes a bind Whether you're in a flat, a house, a hotel, or deep in the country on a farm, it takes something out of you each time there's a knock on the door. You're always thinking of your cover story, altering it to fit fresh circumstances, and thinking up what you hope are foolproof reasons for being wherever you may be."

"Are there any snap controls on the trains?" I asked.

"Yes. But you get quite *blasé* about them because the papers they give you at Head Office are perfect. Anyway, you'll hear all about it at the finishing school, where you get all the dope on security," said Robert.

We all trooped in to lunch. I was amazed not only by the meal, but also at the high standard of the French I heard at my end of the table. Only one person appeared to regret that French had to be spoken at meals, and that was none other than the School's Commandant.

Immediately after lunch we started in on the course. The first hour was spent laboriously learning how to tap out the alphabet on the Morse buzzer. Every student was convinced he would never learn it. In this depressing state of mind we were handed over to an instructor who taught us the rudiments of map reading. To me this was easy, as I had been through it all before. Then we were taken out of doors into the warm sunshine of a July afternoon and shown by a sergeant how to put a detonator into a primer and how to put the primer into a "six-inch brick" (a gun-cotton explosive).

At five o'clock there was tea, and this was followed by an hour's practical demonstration of how to bring down a tree so that it fell in the direction in which you wanted it to fall. Each student was required to apply a six-inch brick to a different tree and bring it down himself. At the end of this hour of destruction on a selection of rather seedy old trees, everyone began to feel much better.

A swim in the private pool that nestled among some pine trees in the grounds rounded off the first afternoon's activities. However, a glance at the notice board was sufficient to change anyone's plans for staying up late after dinner, for it stated that reveille was at 0600 hours, and that the customers were requested to parade for P.T. shortly afterwards.

I was in a dormitory for six. Philip was in the same room, occupying the next bed on the left. On my right was a tall young Frenchman who went by the name of Raymond, and the three beds on the other side of the room were occupied by John—a cheerful regular officer in the Coldstream Guard, whose fair hair, typical English features, and schoolboy French made him as conspicuous as the Rock of Gibraltar—Gaston, a placid man of about forty, and André, whose father was French and mother English. André was about twenty-five. Conversation flowed easily, now in English, now in French.

As the six of us lay chatting and waiting for "lights out," Robert came in to see that all was well. As Conducting Officer, he had the privilege of a room to himself. His confidence and ease made themselves quickly felt among the newcomers. Although not a day over twenty-six, his manner reflected the poise that comes from facing reality and overcoming fear.

After a few moments of conversation, I said:

"Robert, couldn't you tell us something about your last operation?"

"Why?" asked Robert.

"Well, to hear what it's actually like from someone who's been there seems to me worth all the courses."

"I felt just the same way when I was doing my training," said Robert, "and no doubt if I were to tell you all you'd like to know it would be of some assistance, but it would compromise several people and put the lid on my returning to France."

"How's that?" I inquired.

"Supposing I were to tell you of my meeting with Jean Dupont, the stationmaster at Quimper, and how we arranged to sabotage the trains in Brittany. One of you might accidentally talk about the incident to a friend in whom you had the utmost confidence. This friend, not having learned the vital importance of security as you will have it drummed into you during the next three month, might innocently tell the same story in his own Officers' Mess, and so it would spread around until the wrong person overheard the information. The enemy would be delighted to learn that the author of all the railway damage in Brittany was none other than the genial Monsieur Dupont. That is why I am glad to tell you that I have never been to Quimper and that there is no such person as Jean Dupont"

"I see it all now," I said.

"But what about yourself?" queried Philip. "How would it stop you returning?"

"Well, the very fact that you know I've been in France is bad enough in itself. If any of you were captured and shown my photograph, you might accidentally give a sign of recognition. If, then, under torture, you were made to tell them where you had seen me, the Germans would know I belonged to this organization. What you may not realize is that my cover story claims that I am a Frenchman who has never left France. So, you see, if you could connect me with other people as well, they would rope them all in and pin me down as a British agent."

"Even this short explanation," said John, "makes it abundantly clear to me that the less you know, the less they can get out of you."

"That's about what it all adds up to," agreed Robert. "But you'll learn it all in the days to come. All the points of interest gathered from the stories of those who have returned from operations and from other sources of intelligence have been carefully and cleverly woven into various sections of your training. When you pass out, you'll know everything there is to know."

"Do many people fail?" asked André.

"Quite a few. I think you'll agree that they're right in setting a high standard in this branch. It means that those who go to France have a comfortable feeling that any other chap in his neighborhood who was trained over here must be as reliable as he is. But," went on Robert, seeing the faces around him lengthening somewhat, "there's no need to be downhearted. The standards can't be unattainable, since I managed to pass myself." He smiled round the room and said, "Good night."

Long after he had left the room, we six newcomers lay pensively digesting the Conducting Officer's words. Robert well knew that he had loosed off a shaft that would be passed on to the rest of the recruits, and he had no regrets for having done so. He was proud of belonging to the French Section. The new intake might just as well realize from the start that this was no convalescent home. From his own experience he knew that those who were keen would now be all the keener; those who had no stomach for a hard life had been fairly warned. Later on I learned that Robert's first impression of the six men he had just left, and whom he had known for only twelve hours, was that John was probably being shown the ropes so as to give him a job in the organization somewhere in the United Kingdom. His French barred him from "underground" activities abroad; Raymond was all right, but they would probably have trouble with him, as he seemed undisciplined; Philip was sure to pass. Head Office had told him that they liked the look of him, that he was intelligent, although pretending not to be, and that he seemed a good mixer. André was the right type; I seemed all right; Gaston would not stand the pace—a sleek and altogether unprepossessing type.

All in all, Robert's own guess, as I also learned later, was that about six of the fourteen would pass. Time alone would show if he was right.

Six-thirty the next morning found the fourteen of us, rigged up in P.T. kit, in two lines facing our instructor, a sun-tanned Adonis of about twenty-four. Having spaced out his squad, he put us through a few minutes of limbering-up exercises. Presently, added to the pleasant chirping of the birds, came the dismal groans of those who up to that moment had quite successfully managed to hold their own in a competitive world without wearing themselves out before breakfast. They now began to wonder how they had done it. But even in the absence of groans, the young athlete whose job it was to exercise this motley crew, and who was waving his arms about entirely for his own pleasure, had weighed up each man with a professional eye. Three were distinctly good; seven of them would improve under treatment, and for the remaining four there was, to his mind, simply no hope

Sergeant Smith swung our arms about, upwards, forwards, sideways, downwards, and backwards. He made us breathe deep and long. He raised our squad onto its toes, brought it down on its heels and then tried to raise it to its feet again. He gave us press-ups with legs raising alternately, and made us lie on our backs and pretend to bicycle upside-down. He ran through several of the simpler exercises he had himself so easily mastered at Aldershot, and he kept his thoughts to himself. Major de Wesselow had made it clear to him that during P.T. instruction at Wanborough Manor he would not tolerate any reference to the recruits' parents, that if some of the pupils did not appear to be born athletes, they had other qualities, and that any comparison between their movements and those of a crippled washerwoman would be strictly frowned on.

After an exciting but somewhat unorthodox game of netball the class came to an end. Our squad, many of whom were aching from head to foot, straggled back to the showers, the last six being speedily overtaken by Sergeant Smith, who covered the hundred yards between the lawn and the Manor on his hands. A few of us who were only just capable of walking the right way up hoped he would break his neck on the six steps that he was rapidly approaching, but Sergeant Smith took them at a run, and his body—beautiful whichever way you looked at it—swayed gracefully past some shrubs and disappeared from view.

"Dreadful exhibition," groaned Gaston. "As though one didn't feel bad enough as it is."

"I suppose he hopes we shall all be able to copy his example by the end of the course," said Raymond testily.

"I think I shall end up in hospital tonight after he has shown us the rudiments of all-in wrestling this afternoon," said André.

After breakfast, at which appetites were unusually good, there followed a succession of classes. The first of these was weapon training.

Being a hot July day, this was held out of doors in the shade of some copper beeches. Here we found our sergeant instructor surrounded by every known type of revolver, automatic and light weapon then in existence. Having been in the Commandos, I immediately spotted my old friends the Tommy gun, the L.M.G., the Colt automatic, and the .45. Besides these, however, there was a Browning, a French light machine gun, a Schmeisser, two different sizes of Luegers, a small Belgian pistol, and a handful of lesser-known weapons. The sergeant gave each of these its correct name and then proceeded to take each to pieces and put it together again. He required us to follow suit.

"We shall be firing with every one of these this afternoon and every day," he explained, "so you'll soon get used to them, even if they appear a little confusing to begin with."

The second class was held a few yards away. Here a corporal demonstrated the art of signaling with an Aldis lamp.

The third class was a lecture on bridge demolition, which included certain formulas which gave the saboteur the precise amount of explosive required to demolish a bridge of any given size.

The fourth and last class before lunch was French platoon and arms drill, given by a French officer, to accustom the students to the words of command, in case any of them whose cover story claimed that they had seen service with the French Army should be required to prove it.

After lunch there was a demolition class, during which the "time-pencil" and "instantaneous fuse" were introduced, as well as the "pull switch" and the "press switch."

This was followed by shooting practice, and lastly came the all-in wrestling. Sergeant Smith, wearing a minute pair of swimming trunks around his slim waist, looked an even more perfect specimen of manhood than he had in the early morning. With every movement his muscles seemed to smile as well as ripple.

He gently threw the fourteen students around the grass as though they were as light as paper bags, and when it was their turn to throw him by a simple hold, he fell softly as a cat or bounced back onto his feet, as though made of rubber. All the time he kept up a steady flow of patter, explaining the art of falling "soft," or rolling backwards, forwards, and sideways. By his continued demonstrations of rolls and holds, he had the whole class interested and doing them after him. Those who had misjudged him in the morning now realized that he was nothing but a healthy panther enjoying himself, for all were aware that he never used even half his strength.

My Commando training I thought made me almost as fit as Sergeant Smith, and I along with a few others were rash enough to pit our strength against his vast experience. To our surprise, we merely found ourselves falling rather harder and a good many feet farther away from our expert instructor than before.

"You've got to learn the holds first," said the sergeant, smiling at our crestfallen looks. "In any case, it's a hundred to one that if you ever have to apply any of the tricks you'll learn here, you'll take your man by surprise, and even if he's ready for you, he won't know as much about it as you will."

We left the battleground tired but happy. Together with Sergeant Smith, we spent a leisurely hour swimming in the pool. Then it was time for dinner.

"Well, how did you like your first day?" asked Major de Wesselow in execrable French of those who happened to be sitting anywhere near him.

"I think we're all rather stiff, sir," I said, sitting on his left.

"That'll wear off," said the Major. "But you'll be glad to get to bed every day as the course becomes progressively more strenuous. It has to be done that way in order to cram into three weeks what should normally be taught in as many months."

"I don't suppose Sergeant Smith ever gets tired," said André, somewhat enviously.

"No," said the Major. "But Sergeant Smith only does one job. By the time you've finished all the courses you will be almost as good and as tireless, not only as Sergeant Smith, but also as knowledgeable as the instructors in demolition, fieldcraft, the Morse code, weapon training, map reading, canoeing, parachuting, bomber receptions, security, and the general organization of an underground circuit The amount of usefulness of a properly trained saboteur to the war effort is something that you may one day be proud of."

The days now followed in an ever-increasing tempo, and each student settled down according to his make-up. Little by little the speed of the Morse buzzer increased, the night compass marches became more intricate, more devices for igniting explosive charges were introduced. We learned how to approach a guarded house noiselessly and surprise the sentry. On these astonished men we applied the latest and most deadly grips so patiently taught by Sergeant Smith. All this we did with gusto, and did not relinquish a strangle hold until the sentry tapped on the ground to show that he was exhausted. We practiced shooting regularly, and the results were noted down. After each exercise there was a discussion at which all mistakes were explained by the umpires.

When a week had passed and the candidates were considered fairly well grounded in map reading, fieldcraft, compass marching, and explosives, more complicated exercises were set including all these subjects, and each man, in turn, was placed in charge of an exercise. We were marked for the way in which we gave orders to our colleagues, the way we split up the party into various groups for the final attack on the objective, and the speed and efficiency with which we blew up the target. All this gave each of us a chance of demonstrating our powers of leadership.

By the time the three-weeks' course had come to an end and Major de Wesselow had sent in his report on each student, based on the individual reports of every single instructional officer and N.C.O. at Wanborough Manor, four men were turned down out of the original fourteen.

The ten remaining men then left their first Training School and, accompanied by the untiring and faithful Robert, we entrained for the west coast of Scotland.

After a long and weary journey, changing at Glasgow, we left the train at a little station near Mallaig. Two three-quarter-ton trucks sped us over narrow and bumpy lanes at breakneck speed to a small country house near the sea. Here we were welcomed by the genial and handsome Major Young, of the Argyll and Sutherland Highlanders. Six of us were put into one small room with three double bunks, and the rest into another. When Robert had been allotted the last tiny room to himself, I wondered what they would have done if all fourteen had arrived. In my room with the five others there was hardly enough space to unpack our kits.

As Robert put his head round the corner and witnessed the turmoil, I said, "I suppose this is part of the system to discover how patient we can be in times of stress." To this sally Robert found no reply and beat a tactful retreat. It was his first visit to this particular house, and it was obviously never intended to be crammed with so much humanity.

When he went downstairs, Robert saw Major Young and said, "They're a bit crowded up there, sir."

"I know it," answered the Commandant. "There's simply nothing we can do about it. The whole district is teeming with saboteurs of various Country Sections. Within three miles there are Poles, Czechs, Dutchmen, Norwegians, and Belgians. With the usual courtesy of Great Britain, the best houses have been allotted to these chaps, and we're just left to get on with it."

"Changed a bit since I was down the road at Arisaig a few months ago," said Robert.

"Yes. They have to concentrate them all in one zone, so that the same instructors can drive round and give them the same course."

"At least it's good to know that business is looking up in our line," commented Robert.

"It's the one consoling factor," agreed Major Young.

It rained almost incessantly throughout the entire course, and for those of us undergoing arduous training and returning worn out, wet, and muddy to our tiny rooms, life was a great trial. Here, if there was no need to speak French at meals and no previous warning as to what to expect in the way of training, we soon discovered that the ways of a Scots Commandant, however genial, contained little unnecessary talk but a great deal of action. Prodigious exercises took place every other day, entailing treks over the mountains of at least twenty up to twenty-five miles. Here there were no crossroads, or even roads, churches, post offices, milestones or rivers to assist the map reader. It was all done by means of the compass, by following the contours on the map and finding the same contours up the mountains. This was real map reading, and we who had survived Wanborough Manor were truly grateful for the knowledge we had gained there.

Tommy-gun and revolver practice, as well as the throwing of hand grenades and the exploding of high-powered charges, were done to such an extent that they became second nature to the ten remaining hopes of the French Section. Yet there were still a few of us who got lost in the mountains, who could not sufficiently master the Morse code to receive at the required minimum rate of twelve words per minute, and who lacked imagination and leadership when taking charge of an exercise. The Training Staff gave their time and encouragement to the weaker links, knowing that the others could look after themselves.

Apart from the repetition of our advanced training and the added impetus brought to our close combat and all-in wrestling by the presence of a professional all in wrestler who bore the rounded scar where a broken bottle had been jabbed into his forehead, the only real difference between our present activities and those at Wanborough Manor consisted in canoe practice and learning to swim with a "clam" or a "limpet" (magnetic bombs attached to the steel hulls of ships). Only a few of us were able to accomplish this rather strenuous feat.

When the last day of the course came round, John was seconded to another unit, and of the nine remaining people, four more were turned down.

My four fellow surviving candidates and myself proceeded with Robert to the Parachute School at Ringway, near Manchester.

Apart from myself, there was Raymond, Philip, André, and Gustave.

Here we were put through an intensive physical-training course which taught us to do Japanese rolls to right and left with both hands in our pockets, not to mention backward and forward somersaults. All this was to fit us to land naturally in whatever position we fell with our parachutes. Then we went through the drill of jumping through the hole in the floor of the aircraft from a stationary fuselage installed on the ground for that purpose, and every day we swung on a giant trapeze so as to get the feel of landing. Nothing was omitted to prepare the student for the real thing, and if he measured up to the P.T. instructor's requirements, he would then be amply qualified to apply for a job as a circus acrobat. In point of fact, my companions and I were now so fit that we were not very far from such a standard. At long last came the five terrifying jumps. If I live to be as old as Methuselah, I am sure I shall never forget them. To me the business of landing was of no particular account, for so great was my delight at getting down to mother earth that I would roll, and even bounce like the rubber ball that I was, but the idea of leaping through the hole of an aircraft at over 100 m.p h. was, for me, just as terrifying at each jump.

Owing to the presence of other prospective jumpers and instructors I had, of course, to put a good face on it. As for the instructors, I thought they were all raving lunatics. They jumped all day whenever they could, and would go about the camp with long, sulky faces if it was not their turn to go up. How well I remember the extravagant remark of a certain sergeant whose head had suddenly appeared through the hole in the aircraft a few moments before the plane was due to take off. Beaming round at our green faces within, he said, "You lucky people!" The weak titters that met these words merely covered up a general desire to beat his brains out.

Robert told us that nobody was ever rejected for bad parachuting, for being medically unfit to parachute, or for refusing to do it. They could always be infiltrated by submarine, by felucca, by M.T.B. (Motor Torpedo Boat) across the Channel, as well as by bomber or by Lysander—the light Army co-operational plane that could land in a much smaller field than that required by a bomber. Lastly, they could always get as far as the British Consulate in neutral Barcelona and either cross the Pyrenees with a guide, or take the train with false papers. The swiftest and safest method, however, was always the parachute.

My four companions and I all passed our jumping test, and were much relieved to turn our backs on Ringway.

As we sat in the train we felt as if we had really accomplished something and that we had earned our leave. As the express slowed down through the outskirts of London, Raymond turned to Robert and voiced the thoughts of all five of us when he said, "Can one still be turned down at the school where we shall be meeting again?"

"To be quite candid with you, one can," said Robert. "This is the toughest school of them all. Not because the physical effort is any greater. It isn't, and the place is very comfortable. But they're absolute sticklers for security, and you'll find the place is full of traps and pitfalls."

"What exactly do you mean by traps and pitfalls?" inquired Raymond anxiously.

"I can't explain, but you'll find it's the nearest thing to being on the actual job. I wish you luck."

At Euston, we separated and went our various ways.

By the time we were due to reassemble at the Finishing School—a modern villa hidden in the depths of the New Forest some twenty miles north of Bournemouth—we had had plenty of time to reflect on all the possible snags we must now expect to encounter. The station wagon that drove us through the pine-forest approach carried five very sober and alert young men.

*

the gift of making people feel at home. After showing us to our rooms and allotting us batmen, we reassembled downstairs to discuss our work before dinner.

"You'll be quite comfortable here," said Captain Harris. "We have a staff of ten men to look after you. Over the way, deeper in the forest, is another house where the instructional staff live. There are about fifteen of them, each for a different subject. You'll meet them all in time."

"Fifteen!" I echoed, somewhat taken aback. "Could you give us some idea what subjects they specialize in?"

"Well, first of all, there's the Security expert, who'll give you tips as to how to behave inconspicuously and tell you what to expect in the way of local curfews and customs; then there's the code expert, who dreams in code; the German uniform expert for recognition purposes; the man who shows you how to bury your parachute without leaving any trace; the expert on how to build up a circuit on the basis of cells of six independent people, only one of whom is allowed to contact your number two—without ever knowing who you are; the cover-story expert; one of the King's gamekeepers, who'll teach you everything there is to know about snaring, poaching, marking trees in a forest so that you can find your way out again, skinning a rabbit or cooking a fowl, putting dogs off the scent and making a bed from branches, et cetera." Taking a breath and continuing to tick off the various people on his fingers, he proceeded: "Then there's a specialist in the art of railway sabotage; an expert on how to find the weak points of huge factories, who'll explain his advanced wrecking theories; the Piat-mortar instructor; the interrogator who'll tell you what to expect and how to tackle Gestapo methods, and to end up with, there are the inevitable strong men for P.T. and close combat, not to mention those who will help you revise various subjects with which you are already well acquainted."

"A good time should be had by all," suggested Gustave.

"With twenty-five people to take care of your physical and mental requirements, I promise you there'll never be a dull moment," agreed Captain Harris. "By the way," he added, "I forgot to mention the disguise expert."

For André, Raymond, Gustave, Philip, and myself, the days

rushed by, and did not seem long enough to digest the many new subjects which were crammed into us at the Finishing School. We began to see that ten weeks were barely enough to turn us into Agents. Moreover, as none of us would know if he had passed until the last day, we felt as though we were constantly under the sword of Damocles.

Among our new exercises we were taken to Bournemouth and told to look for various spots of interest, such as the gas works, the central telephone exchange, and so forth. We would be followed, and our task was to shake off our followers without showing any sign that we knew we were being shadowed, make a full report with drawings of the place we had investigated, and hand over the report to one of the instructors at a certain hotel at a fixed hour and in a manner unnoticeable to anyone else.

Outings such as this very soon distinguished the man who could carry out his operation with a poker face from the one who went about his business looking like a stage villain.

The five of us were plied with drinks to discover if we stopped of our own accord, and beautiful women belonging to the organization—but of whose origin the students had no notion—were produced in order to see how much information they could extract with their feminine wiles.

We were roused in the middle of the night and questioned for hours on our cover story.

Exercises, led by each of us in turn, were watched by the entire staff, from the Colonel-in-charge downwards. All the batmen, N.C.O.'s, and O.R.'s took part in each exercise as troops to be ordered about by the leader of the day. Particular attention was paid to the way in which that leader explained the plan which he had drawn on the blackboard to the assembled men.

Out of the fourteen original candidates in our group, only three were accepted: Philip, André, and myself.

The three new saboteurs then separated, I being sent on a kind of post-graduate course in specialized railway sabotage. I followed this up by visiting a sixth establishment, where I learned the art of arranging bomber and Lysander landings in the dark. Philip and André were "dropped" in France on two separate missions.

With all these courses behind me, I was now fully equipped to start anything from a whispering campaign to guerrilla warfare. My only prayer was that I might avoid capture for as long as possible, so as not to waste all this knowledge. I also hoped I might remember a great part of it.

CHAPTER II

"Well, Michel, here is your French identity card with your new French name, Pierre Chauvet. You will be known to us and amongst our contacts in France as Michel and you had better forget your real name. Wipe it completely out of your mind."

Major B.*—forty-five, alert, and bilingual in English and French—paused for a moment to let his words sink in. He lit his pipe and smiled at me through a cloud of rising smoke. He had seen me three or four times already, had read my reports from the four training-school Commandants and the Conducting Officer. If only more than three could pass out of fourteen; there was so much to be done. He knew it was a mistake to allow any kind of sentiment to enter into the relationship between himself as Commanding Officer and the men who undertook this vital work. At the present early stage of the war—December, 1941—there might only be a handful of these saboteurs, and he could get to know them intimately. But when their ranks swelled—as he had every hope that they quickly would—these men would literally become the ciphers by which they were already known, and it would never do to add

* Now Colonel Maurice J Buckmaster, O.B.E.

to the increasing burden of his work the wear and tear on his own personal feelings as the news came in that one or other, or maybe a whole batch of these highly trained experts, had been captured. God knows, he may have thought, it had been difficult enough in the 50th Division to find experts, but here they not only had to be experts, they also had to speak French like natives and act like Frenchmen into the bargain. It was fairly safe to say that there could not be more than about four hundred such oddities in the country, and it was an even safer bet that not half of them could be enrolled for such lonely and dangerous work as this. If it was a temptation to take a liking to some of them, it was not one to which he must give way. He no doubt hoped I would prove to be the right man for this job.

There was certainly nothing about me to attract attention; in fact, I could pass as a native in any European country except Scandinavia. Aside from my uniform of a Lieutenant in the Intelligence Corps there was really little else that was remarkable about my looks—unless perhaps that I appeared somewhat younger than my thirty-two years.

Major B. continued: "And this scruffy bit of paper is your demobilization certificate from the French Army. Just stick your thumbprints in these two squares, and then you can wash your hands in the bathroom."

I pressed both thumbs onto a purple pad before applying them to the spaces on the sheet.

"There we are, sir," I said, and went to scrub off the stains.

The bathroom, which was next door to the chief's office, was in keeping with the rest of the luxurious flat at Orchard Court in which the French Section of the War Office interviewed and briefed the men who had been selected for various secret missions to do with sabotage and the French Resistance. There was a black bath and basin with shining chrome taps, and the walls were inlaid with black tiles. Thinking back, I realized that it had been like this throughout my training. Although the courses had been tough and exacting, the private houses and estates that had been requisitioned for their purpose had, except for the house in Scotland, all provided more luxury than I had ever hoped to meet in the Army. I was proud of belonging to this young organization and fully realized what I would be up against on entering France.

"Now, *mon ami*," said Major B as I reappeared from the bathroom, "I have something important to tell you. You were chosen for this delicate and tricky mission because you passed out of the Training Schools quite well. But before I ask you to repeat the instructions I gave you to learn, I want you to understand quite clearly that if you think we're asking too much of you, you needn't accept the operation. Should you cry off at the last moment, no one will think any the less of you. Everyone in this business is a volunteer, and every job is of his own choice."

I looked at my superior smilingly.

"I'm quite happy about the whole thing," I said, "and although it means finding a guide and crossing the Pyrenees on the way out—which is rather a bore—I still think the exercise will do me good."

"Very well, Michel. But remember, if you should get caught, there is very little we can do for you. As you will be operating in the South, you will be in the Unoccupied Zone. Should you get picked up by the French police, the papers you've just received should keep you out of trouble, because they're perfect in every detail. If, however, you should get into *real* difficulties —but only then—you may tell them your English name and explain that you were an interpreter with the 50th Division, and that you joined them so late that you can only remember the names of two of your fellow officers, Captain Acott and Lieutenant Stevenson. Both of these chaps escaped and are back in England, so you're safe in quoting their names. Say that you got away after being captured and that you are trying to pass through Spain. Is all that clear?"

"Perfectly, sir."

"All right. Now let's have the details of your mission."

I took a deep breath, then began the recitation of what I had painstakingly learned off by heart from my typed instructions.

"I am to take two million francs in a belt which I shall wear under my clothes and hand this money out to the following people: Laurent, 400,000; Charles, 300,000; Olivier, 300,000.

The other million is to go to Colonel Deprez in Marseille for the purpose of bribing lawyers of rather doubtful integrity to get ten French patriots out of the Fort St. Nicholas prison in that town. I shall have 100,000 francs for my own use. On my return to Gibraltar I am to account for these transactions and give anything left over to Captain Benson of Joint Intelligence. On the way there I go by boat from Glasgow to Gibraltar, and then on by submarine to a spot I know west of Cannes. My first contact is Louis, whose real name is Dr. Lévi. He lives at 31, Boulevard Maréchal Foch, Antibes. If I arrive too late in the day, I am to spend the night at the Nouvel Hotel. When I get into the doctor's consulting room I am to give the following password, so as to let him know I am a friend from London: '*René de Lyon vous envoit ses amitiés.*' He will then reply, to show that he has understood: '*Vous voulez dire René la Salle?*' After this introduction I am to ask him for a report of the local situation and give him money to pay for all his activities. He will introduce me to Laurent, who works in Cannes. They are to share the money. Then I proceed to Lyon by train.

"In Lyon I stay at the Hotel de France near the station, and then call at the Grand Nouvel Hotel, where I contact Brigitte le Contre. She is known as Germaine,* and once I have proved my identity by saying, '*Je vous apporte des nouvelles de votre soeur Suzanne,*' she will put me in touch with Charles,† who can't be approached in any other way. Here again money, information, and certain instructions. But the main point is that he will produce a ration card for my own use as well as samples of every type of current ration card in France, which I am to bring back with me. I am also to arrange for R.A.F. 'pick-up' grounds.

"Next, I go to Marseille and contact Olivier‡ at the Hotel Modern in Cours Belsunce. Money, report, instructions. Afterwards I call at the Glacières Réunies, where Colonel Deprez works. I am to try to persuade him to help in the matter of the ten Frenchmen now in jail. Their names are Dubois, Erlanger, Jeanville . . ."

* Miss Virginia Hall.
† Captain Dolan.
‡ Lt. Coppin

"All right, all right, Michel," broke in Major B. "For someone who claims to have spent his school days in the bottom form, your memory isn't half bad. If you promise me that you know all the rest, we'll let it go at that."

"I do, sir," I said. "It's all photographed in my mind from the typed sheets I've been studying for the past ten days in the next office."

"Very well, Michel. I only hope the negative doesn't fade. You will be catching the nine P.M. train for Glasgow, where you'll board the S.S. *Batory,* which is going to Gibraltar. You will then proceed by submarine to the particular creek you want. Everything's laid on with the Admiralty."

We both rose. Major B. reached out his hand to shake mine, and put his left hand affectionately on my shoulder as we moved toward the door.

"Good luck," he said, *"bon voyage,* and we shall be waiting for you with our fingers crossed."

CHAPTER III

THERE WERE still a few details to be settled with Captain de G.* at the office, but in the meantime I was free until the afternoon. I ran lightly down the stairs and into the street.

It was a cold, bright December day in 1941. Despite the general havoc wrought by air raids, Portman Square was untouched, and looked very solid and homely to me. I walked along by Selfridges, turned right along Oxford Street, and entered Hyde Park. It was only twelve o'clock, and since my next engagement was lunch with friends in the West End, there was plenty of time for a stroll.

* The late Major Jacques de Guélis, M.B.E., killed in a motor accident in Germany, 1945.

As I strode along toward the Serpentine, life seemed very good to me.

I though of my parents, with whom I had just spent my ten days' leave, and was glad of the brave way in which they had accepted my statement that I might not always be able to write regularly. The leave-taking had not been too easy, for we were a devoted family. My elder brother was a fighter pilot,* and I looked forward to the day when I could present myself at his Fighter Station after my return. It did not occur to me that I might never return, or that my brother might not be there to meet me.

My thoughts switched to my younger brother, Oliver.† He had been a Company Commander in the 7th Worcester Regiment, and when we had met on a previous occasion, he had sensed that my Intelligence Corps badges and buttons had little to do with being an I.O. at company or even brigade level, and had pestered me, under a promise of silence, until I had given him an insight into my real work. Thereafter he had not left me alone until he could transfer to similar activities. Thanks to his excellent Italian, it had been child's play to get him into the Italian Section of the War Office. The only delay in the matter had been due to me as I spent several tormented nights weighing up the question as to whether or not I ought to switch my brother's path toward a destiny of untold dangers and pitfalls. Oliver had subsequently vanished into the blue, and was probably fighting with the Italian partisans somewhere up in the hills.

Now all three of us would be away, and my parents, like so many others, were entirely alone.

Then my thoughts returned to my coming mission. I wondered, as I had so often done, what it would really be like to land on that coast of France with which I had become so well acquainted in happier times.

By now I had passed the Serpentine and was turning left out of Hyde Park Gate. I caught a number 9 bus, and jumped off it as it swept out of Piccadilly down the Haymarket.

* Group-Captain Walter Churchill, D.S.O., D.F.C., killed in action.
† Major Oliver Churchill, D S.O., M C.

After lunch, I returned to one of the War Office hide-outs where I had been staying, and checked up on the contents of my suitcase. It contained a badly cut, inconspicuous, dark French suit, a pair of stout walking shoes, a hat from South America—all designed to be part of my cover story. My sleeveless woollen sweater, shirts, vests, pants, handkerchiefs, and one suit of pajamas were all French. I also had a French razor, shaving brush, soap, toothbrush, etc., and ten packets of *Gauloise* cigarettes—made in London. I could wear the raincoat which completed this modest outfit over the uniform which I would have to travel in as far as Gibraltar. There I would leave my uniform in a suitcase, and the small attaché case that lay on the bed would be large enough to carry the articles I would not be wearing. I put the attaché case inside with the rest of my things and squashed down the lid. Then I drew out my wallet. It contained my French identity card, my War Office card—to be given up in Gibraltar—my demobilization card, a half-used book of Marseille tram tickets, my railway voucher to Glasgow, a couple of faint photographs of the man and woman who were supposed to be my parents—now in South America. Even their identity could never be checked, as the town from which their fictitious names had been chosen was one whose archives had long ago been bombed to ashes. I scrutinized my money. In the bank-note division were several pound and ten-shilling notes. I would leave these in Gilbraltar —if there were any left—and transfer to their place some of the French currency provided for this venture. Slipping the wallet back into my pocket, I walked over to the house phone and dialed WEL 7381.

"Park speaking," came the well-known voice.

"Michel here Can I speak to Captain de G.?"

"One moment, please." Then, after a slight pause, "Here you are." A genial voice spoke:

"Hullo, Michel. When are you coming to be fitted for that truss?"

"I was just ringing about that. Can I come over now?"

"Certainly. I'll be expecting you."

I left the room and called back at 6 Orchard Court. I was shown straight into Captain de G.'s office.

"Hullo, Michel. Well, here's the large belt and your smaller one. Let's see how much they show under your uniform."

I slipped off my belt and jacket, pulled out my shirt, and strapped on both belts. I then did myself up, patted my jacket, and said, "Well, now I know what it feels like to be a millionaire more than twice over. How do I look?"

"Not bad. In fact, if I hadn't seen you before, I should never have known the difference."

"I can't quite make up my mind," I said reflectively, "whether to buy a liner or the Albert Hall."

"Both rather vulnerable to bombs, I'm afraid. I'd settle for a gold mine, if I were you. Well, Michel . . . I shall be counting the days. And, by the way, Major B. informed me that when you reeled off your stuff to him this morning, there's one thing you forgot. That was to send us the three telegrams I told you about, the first from Antibes, the second from Lyon, and the third from Marseille—each to different business addresses in England. Speak from Antibes about the health of your Aunt Annabelle, about your sister Leonore from Lyon and about your brother Marius from Marseille. Since postal and telegraph services still function between the Unoccupied Zone and the rest of the world, we shall be able in this way to follow your movements a little and warn the Consulate in Barcelona that you are on your way there. Do you still remember the three addresses in England?"

"Yes, fortunately they're quite simple," I replied.

"There's just one more thing. You may possibly have a slip-up with those guide contacts, and if you do, you can follow the same course as I did when I came out alone last summer. You'd better follow it on this map. As you leave Port Vendres the road runs beside the railway on the left and, after two hundred yards or so, it bears right under this bridge, and then starts climbing up to the lowest summit of the Pyrenees, almost hugging the coast. You'd have to do this at night, and walk very quietly, because the French and Spanish Customs patrols are in the habit of waiting in the hedges and pouncing on people whose approach they can easily hear. Do it slowly and quietly, and you will usually hear them talking behind their hedge. They always hunt in couples. From the top you'll see the lights of Llansa. Walk down to the station and catch the workmen's train for Barcelona at two A.M. Germaine would find you some Spanish money and, as you speak the language, Bob's your uncle."

"Sounds too easy."

"We're counting a great deal on you, Michel. Yours will be the first landing from a submarine in this part of the world. It can be quite rough down there at this time of the year, but knowing the way you handle a canoe, we feel pretty confident you'll manage all right. We shall continue or cancel this method of arrival on the results of your experience. Best of luck, old boy."

CHAPTER IV

S.S. *Batory* was a Polish ship manned by a Polish captain, officers, and crew. Thanks to the Captain's resource, this fine, medium-sized liner had slipped its moorings at Gdynia during the German occupation, and ever since had done yeoman service as a troopship.

I was somewhat coldly received by the Adjutant on board, and the explanation came from a colonel in the 60th to whom I was introduced

"The Adj has been hopping mad," he said, "because we've been kept waiting here at least six hours for you. You must be a very important person," he added, half humorously. "But what really interests *me* is that now we have three Army officers on board and you will be able to share in the supervising of the ship's gun crews. There are twenty-one guns and they're manned day and night by naval officers and Army gunners. By the way, I hope you know something about these weapons?"

"I'm afraid I don't," I replied, never having seen any guns except the four which proudly looked upwards in Hyde Park. "But I'm perfectly willing to learn, sir."

"All right. Leave your gear here for a moment and we'll go on deck and have a look at them." With that he led me to the nearest companionway. As he put his hands on the rails he turned his head saying, "I didn't quite catch your name."

"Churchill, sir."

"Right, Churchill. Let's have a look on deck."

Being in uniform, I naturally kept to my real name as shown on my War Office identity card. Up on deck, he showed me the various guns. There were Bofors, Oerlikons, Pom-Poms, and a big four-inch gun on a platform in the stern. He explained the various duties and said that he would tell me later how he proposed splitting up the night watch.

It was not long before the *Batory* slipped her moorings and began to make her way unobtrusively down the Clyde.

The seven-days' trip passed without incident, and each day very much resembled the last. Early on the seventh morning when I woke up I could feel that the ship had slowed down to a crawl. I looked out through the porthole, and there stood Gibraltar, with its massed houses bathed in the early morning sun. It all seemed very peaceful. Behind the breakwater was a battleship, an aircraft carrier, a cruiser, and several smaller ships. An Aldis lamp blinked incessantly from a tower, but as yet I could see no submarines.

The *Batory* dropped anchor just outside the breakwater, and there was some delay before tenders came out to pick up the officers and men. During this time my friends and I had breakfast, packed our gear, tipped our respective stewards, and went up on deck. We exchanged addresses, and arranged to meet later on in the day.

At long last a tender picked us up and took us alongside the pier. No sooner had we landed than I was approached by an Army officer, who took me to one side and, after inquiring my name, said, "I'm Benson. We were expecting you. Everything's laid on. We have a special flat in a quiet street where you are to stay. For security reasons, we should prefer you to drop any acquaintances you may have made and spend your time either with us or on board the *Maidstone* over there." He gave a nod in the direction of the submarine Depot Ship, beside which I could see four submarines. "Now if you're ready, we'll go straight to the flat in this car."

The car bounced over the uneven cobbles along the quayside. At the dock gates we were stopped for passes and then proceeded through the narrow, twisting streets. I took it all in, occasionally exchanging a word with Benson. I had expected to see thousands of troops and sailors, but what surprised me was to discover that the traffic was controlled by ordinary English policemen.

Presently the car came to a halt outside a squalid-looking house. Benson told the driver to wait, and then led me through the front door and into a dim passage which led to a shabby hall. Here I was introduced to a woman of uncertain age who could speak only Spanish. As this happened to be one of my languages, my *"Muy buenos, Maria,"* produced quite a cheerful effect on the landlady. Benson said he would come and fetch me for lunch and left me in the hall.

Maria led me upstairs to a room where she hoped I would be comfortable. She asked no questions.

As soon as she had closed the door, I, having slept little on the previous night, and being besides one who invariably demanded a solid eight hours, threw myself onto the bed fully dressed and was immediately unconscious. Benson found me there three hours later, still sleeping. He grinned and gave me a gentle nudge.

"Sorry to disturb you, chum. But if you want any lunch we'll have to get a move on."

I groaned and groped my way to the wash stand, where I threw some water over my face. We then drove up to the Rock Hotel.

I was introduced to a captain in charge of the hotel billeting arrangements. I also met a colleague of Benson's, and by the time we had all had a glass of excellent sherry, I had forgotten all about my tiredness.

The three of us, who were in the same racket, lunched together. At last I was free to talk a little shop. Benson told me that the Admiral wanted to see me about the submarine. He supposed that as this was the first time a Gibraltar-based submarine had been used for landing an Agent, the Admiral might want to know some of the details. He explained that the Admiral was universally known as the "Giant Panda," and that I would see why when I saw him.

After coffee on the terrace, during which my new friends pointed out the various landmarks of La Linea, Algeciras, and far-off Tangiers, we all went back to the offices of Joint Intelligence. The same car was turned round to take me to the Admiral's H.Q.

"Come back afterwards and give us the 'gen.' "

"Right," I answered, "and you might offer up a small prayer, because I have a feeling I shall need it."

CHAPTER V

THE CAR swung out of the Fortress yard, and I was given a smart salute by the M.P. on duty, which I returned.

We had not far to go before the car stopped beside the watchtower.

"This is it, sir," said the driver. "I shall be out here waiting."

"Thanks, Corporal," I said, and started climbing the steps of the building.

" 'Afternoon, sir," greeted a naval orderly. "Who do you wish to see?"

"I've got an appointment with the Admiral. My name's Churchill."

"One moment, sir," and he picked up a telephone to check with the Admiral's office. Putting back the receiver after the words "Right away, sir," he asked me to follow him. Knocking reverently on a door, he walked in announcing, "Lieutenant Churchill to see you, sir."

I saw before me a man of gigantic width and thickness with a most imposing head on top. It was this head that quelled any mirth that might have been evoked by the term "Giant Panda." I could not gauge the Admiral's height, as he was sitting on every spare inch of an enormous armchair covered in black leather—or, at least I supposed so, from what I could see above his back.

I produced the finest salute I had learned in 167 O.C T.U., and was immediately told to sit down there, my boy, where I can see you.

The Giant Panda then picked up a piece of paper in one colossal hand, and as he peered with open amazement and obvious distaste at its contents, he spat out:

"Well, T.17—or whatever your name is—so you want a submarine, do you?"

"Well, yes, sir," I murmured apologetically, beginning to fear that I might be lucky to get away with a rubber dinghy.

"Where do you want to go, and what's it all about?" spluttered the Admiral, twisting up his face and narrowing his eyes into mere slits.

"I would like to be dropped somewhere near Cannes, but with the deepest respect, sir, I am not at liberty to talk about the operation."

"All right; I quite understand that. But what you probably don't realize is that my submarines are working overtime in the Mediterranean and, since the Germans have control in the air—a matter which I trust the Air Ministry are applying their mighty brains to put an end to—even supplies of petrol have to be carried in submarines to Malta to make sure that it gets there instead of being sunk on the way. In the light of this knowledge, do you still consider that your operation is more important than the delivery of several hundred tons of petrol for the R.A.F.?"

"I don't really know what to say, sir, unless I might make a suggestion."

"Speak up, my man!"

"I should be very pleased, sir, to lie on top of any cargo that may be going to Malta, and when I've been dropped near my destination, the submarine could then proceed to Malta without very much loss of time or distance."

"An excellent suggestion, my boy," roared the Admiral. "But let me warn you. My submarines are valuable, and as I am certainly not going to risk losing one in any jiggery-pokery business, you will be dropped five miles from your objective, and you'll paddle your own canoe."

"Thank you, sir. Thank you very much, sir," I gasped, both relieved and delighted.

I got up, stood rigidly to attention, and saluted. Then I walked smartly out of the building, hoping to goodness that the Giant Panda would not have time to change his mind.

A few minutes later I was telling Benson about the interview, and my account of it was met with a good deal of raucous laughter.

"When do you think I shall get away?" I asked.

"That depends on Captain S.,* as the commander of the *Maidstone* is generally known here. It doesn't matter what his real name is. If you should discover it, just keep it under your hat. Everything's frightfully hush-hush in Gib, owing to the presence of some five thousand Spanish workers who come over from Spain and work on the Rock every day, leaving every night. Most of them work in the docks, and there's obviously a percentage of spies amongst them. It's too easy for these chaps to give the latest dope to their German friends, who are as thick as ants in Algeciras, and sit up all night writing Intelligence Reports for their masters in Berlin." He picked up a phone as he was speaking and said, "Give me Captain S., please."

Presently I heard him say, "Hullo, sir. Benson here. You remember the 'bod' we were talking about yesterday evening? I've got him here. Could you see him?" There was a slight pause and then, "I'll ask him, sir." Benson turned toward me and asked, "Six o'clock on board suit you?"

"Fine."

"He'd like that very much, sir. Right, sir," and put down the phone.

I smiled, "All so simple."

We were having a cup of tea when Benson pushed over a plate of biscuits, saying, "You'd better pile into these. You'll find the hospitality on board the *Maidstone* from six P.M. onwards needs something more than blotting paper to counteract it, not to mention the fact that it's New Year's Eve."

After tea we went for a walk in the Fortress gardens. Benson showed me round the beautifully kept flower beds, and told me something of Lord Gort, the Governor of Gibraltar, whose gardens these were. He spoke of the war as it was seen through the eyes of those who lived in this small garrison, of the occasional air raids and of the many rumors of German attacks through Spain. He put me into the picture with regard to the Spanish situation since the end of their long civil war, and told me of the vast numbers of Poles, Belgians, and Frenchmen who kept filtering through Spain to arrive somehow on the Rock—their first contact with a British outpost. He spoke feelingly of their first refuge from defeat and oppression, and of that tiny rest camp from which they were sent to some spot in Britain to join the Free Forces of their own country and help to prepare for the mighty Allied assault in Europe that would, one day, put an end to the Nazi oppressors.

It was a delight to listen to Benson. I had heard the same sort of thing from Major B. and Captain de G. I had heard it on the French programs of the European Services of the B.B.C. I had heard the Queen's moving broadcast to the women of France, and I had not missed a single one of the inspiring words uttered by that immortal Briton, Mr. Winston Churchill. Whenever I thought of Winston it was with awe and with profound affection, proud to be one under the shadow of that mighty wing.

Very soon now I would be able to see for myself the effect of Winston's words on a defeated France. As one of the first half-dozen men to enter that country since the war, the going would not be easy. There was constant German propaganda and the inevitable sapping of energy from a people who had known even temporary defeat. But I considered it a privilege even to be an "underground" ambassador in the country which I so deeply loved.

We returned to the yard. I picked up my cap in Benson's office and said, "So long."

Within seven minutes I was on the quayside by the *Maidstone*'s gangway. I told the driver that he could go, planning to find my own way back later. Then I climbed up on the *Maidstone*'s quarter-deck. A sailor piped me on board. My salute included the quarter-deck—which I had been told always to salute whether boarding or leaving—as well as a young lieutenant who was on duty.

"Good evening," I said. "My name's Churchill."

"Oh, yes. Captain S. is expecting you. Will you follow me?"

We went down a steep companionway, and at the after-end of that deck level I was introduced to the Captain's semi-circular cabin. A tall, fair-haired man was leaning over a table with his back to the door. Four gold rings ran round the arms of his uniform. As he swung round and caught sight of me he smiled and said, "Surely we've met somewhere before? Of course. You're Churchill."

"Yes, sir. You were a Commander in submarines in 1936 during a courtesy visit of four submarines and a Depot ship to Oran where I was bottle washer and office boy at the British Consulate. And you're Captain S., sir."

"Correct. Well, this is a happy coincidence. I was wondering what sort of a mysterious visitor to expect."

He poured out two glasses of sherry from a decanter and picked them up from an engraved silver tray. Handing me one—"So you've seen the Admiral. What did he say?"

"He said I was to be dropped five miles from the coastline."

"Five miles," repeated Captain S. in tones of considerable surprise. "Between you and me, Churchill, I think we can safely reduce that to two, but don't tell the Admiral I said so."

"You bet I won't, sir."

We raised our glasses. Captain S. smiled at me, saying, "This is well met, Churchill. God bless!"

"Cheers, sir."

We drank

"Well, now, I think you'd better meet the Captain of *P36*," said Captain S. "He's a quiet chap with hidden depths. You'll like him."

He rang a bell, and to a Petty Officer who came in he said: "Give my compliments to Lieutenant Edmonds, and ask him if he would kindly come to my cabin for a moment."

During the wait we skimmed briefly over the events of the years since our last meeting.

Presently there was a knock at the door, and in came Edmonds.

Captain S. stood up, and I walked over to shake Edmonds' hand.

"Edmonds, this is Churchill," introduced Captain S. "He's going with you to the South of France."

He offered him a glass of sherry.

"Now let's have a look at this chart." The three of us moved toward a table upon which was already spread a naval chart that showed the coastline around St. Raphael and Cannes. "You might show Edmonds exactly where you want to go."

This was the first time I had looked at a naval chart with its unusually large scale, but I saw the Pointe de l'Esquillon at the western tip of the Bay of La Napoule. I knew all this part intimately, and let my finger run west an inch or so to the next promontory, and then brought it to rest about a quarter of an inch farther west, where the coastline turned slightly north.

"That's the spot," I said. "There's a tiny bay just here at the back of which lies the Hotel St. Christophe. I spent a couple of summers there, and the hotel grounds are hidden from the coast road by a wall. It couldn't be a better spot for landing."

"Right. Let's put a mark there. You'd better take this chart, Edmonds. Are you all shipshape to leave?"

"Yes, sir."

"Very well. Churchill can dine with me and then sleep in one of the spare cabins. You'd better return to your boat and lay everything on for six A.M. tomorrow."

"Right, sir."

Captain S. walked over to the decanter and returned with it, saying, "Have the other half?" He poured out three full glasses and said, "Here's luck." Edmonds murmured a pious "Amen."

As the cabin door closed, I looked at Captain S., smiled, and said, "That's easily the quickest arrangement I've seen so far in this war. I wasn't expecting to be so lucky as to be off tomorrow. Had I known I should have brought my stuff over from the hush-hush house where I'm staying."

"If that's your only worry I'll soon fix it. I'll get Benson to send it along and take back anything you won't want with you. As far as your departure is concerned, it's just a lucky coincidence. It might not happen another time."

CHAPTER VI

I WAS wide awake long before I was called. I was glad that I had declined Captain S.'s invitation on the previous night to stay up and see the New Year in. Much as I would have liked to do this, I knew myself well enough to realize that I would have had the greatest of difficulty in being fresh on parade bright and early on the following morning. I was excited by the thoughts of all that lay ahead. My knowledge of submarines was limited to one short visit on board Captain S.'s boat as it had lain peacefully beside its Depot Ship inside the breakwater at Oran That was six years ago. I remembered how appalled I had been by the cramped space below and how I had edged my way closer and closer to the open conning-tower hatch so as to avoid the feeling of claustrophobia. I began to wonder what my reactions would now be when I got inside and they clamped down the hatch and let the mighty ocean swallow me up with all the other entombed men. I supposed one got used to it in time.

I looked at my wristwatch. It was 5:15. Getting out of bed, I drew aside the blackout curtain that covered the porthole and looked out. It was pitch dark. Quickly I redrew the curtain.

From my wallet I extracted my War Office identity card and a few banknotes. Then taking a few thousand- and hundred-franc notes out of my personal money belt I arranged these in the vacant spaces of the wallet.

I then shaved, strapped on both belts, and dressed in my civilian clothes. After putting the English papers into one of the breast pockets of my uniform, I sat down at the small cabin table and wrote on a sheet of paper:

Dear Benson,

Thanks for everything, blotting paper included. Papers in l.h. breast pocket. Please keep buttons bright for my return and place trousers under mattress.

C.

I laid this note on the top of my uniform and closed the case. At that moment there was a knock at my door, and an A.B., carrying a cup of tea, popped his head inside.

"Morning, sir. Cup o' tea, sir," he said. "You're up bright and early in 1942. Or didn't you go to bed, sir?"

Somewhat surprised, I took the proffered cup, but before I had time to reply to any of these comments the other babbled on:

"Oh, no. I forgot, sir. You wasn't in the wardroom last night. Hell of a party—beggin' your pardon, sir—didn't stop playin' the pianner till four o'clock."

"How do you know I wasn't there?" I inquired.

"We know everything on board this ship, sir. We never leave it, but we know all the officers and their little 'abits as well as the crews. They're always comin' and goin'. Last night *P36* all 'ad their 'eads down good an' early. Yes, sir, we know quite a lot, them as stays aboard the *Maidstone*."

"What else do you know?" I asked, strongly suspecting the worst.

"Well, sir, as you ask me, I 'appen to know that you're going aboard *P36* in a few moments, that you're leavin' at 0600 hours, and that you're goin' for a little cruise somewhere down the west coast of Africa."

"You're a very smart man," I said, hiding my relief.

"I wouldn't 'ave told you, only you did ask, sir. I promise I'd never breathe a word of this in the town, sir. And now I'd better be leavin' you to get on with your tea."

I was very glad to see him go, and the reasons for security began to strike me rather forcibly. I drank the tea and wondered why the man thought we were going to West Africa. I shrugged my shoulders.

Presently there was another knock at the door.

"Come in," I said.

The door opened, and in came Edmonds. He was wearing an old uniform, above the collar of which protruded the top of what had once been a white sweater With him came a strange smell of oily rags. It was the submarine smell, with which I was to become very familiar.

"Sleep well?" inquired Edmonds.

"Fine, thanks."

I put on my raincoat and hat and, picking up my attaché case, followed Edmonds.

We went down to the lower deck, over the side of the ship and down a gangway to where the four submarines lay.

It was pitch dark, but under the electric lights I could clearly see the outlines of the *Clyde,* whose deck we were crossing, and then the *Thunderbolt*—in reality the salvaged *Thetis,* with all its gruesome and tragic memories. The next submarine was *P36.*

Placing his feet in the small recesses that had been put there for the purpose, Edmonds climbed up the outside of the bridge, with me close behind. We then lowered ourselves through the conning-tower hatch.

Once below, I took a look round the control room. An incredible mass of pipes ran in every direction, and the floor was covered almost roof-high with kit bags. The officers' ward-room was situated just away from this guards' van along a small section of corridor. It was curtained off like a palmist's tent, and in here the Captain introduced me to the rest of his officers. There were six of them, but three of these did not belong to the ship's complement and were merely being conveyed to Malta to join another boat If they appeared very young to me, at least it was consoling to think that, as they had probably only just left the submarine school, they could hardly have had sufficient time to forget what they had learned there.

Harry Edmonds looked an experienced and solid type. He was a dark, quiet, handsome individual, with large brown eyes and strong teeth. He had a complexion that not even this crazy tomb could alter.

The introductions over, he turned to the navigating officer and said: "Sub. Get rid of all those West African charts lying on the chart table and put these there instead," and he handed him a fat roll of Mediterranean charts which he had brought on board. "Sorry they're all rolled up like that, but S said it was to be done that way so as to keep the chaps off the scent."

"Well, well," I thought to myself, in admiration.

Turning to me, Edmonds said: "Churchill, your bunk is on top of the kit bags in the control room. I'm afraid it's the best we can do in the circumstances. You'll find a mattress up there."

"That'll suit me perfectly." I smiled back.

Edmonds seemed glad to see that his Army passenger would be no handicap to himself or the others.

Then, turning to his First Officer, he said, "All set, Number One?"

"Yes, sir," answered the other.

"All right, Sub.," said the Captain, addressing his Navigator, and the two men got up to leave the wardroom.

Looking across at me, Edmonds inquired, "Like to go above and see us cast off?"

"Thank you, sir," I said, delighted at the opportunity of seeing all I could.

It was still pitch dark on the bridge. "Let go forward!" said Edmonds quietly through cupped hands, and a wire hawser was detached from the rail of the *Thunderbolt*. "Group down, slow ahead port, slow astern starboard. Let go aft Stop together. Group up. Slow ahead port," and *P36*, with one propeller turning, moved gently away from its sleeping neighbor.

The stern wire was released and *P36* began to move slowly forward. When she was clear of the *Thunderbolt*, came the order "Slow together"—and the submarine now glided gently away from its sister ships.

Harry Edmonds steered the unlighted *P36* amongst all the warships that lay moored behind the breakwater. When he came abreast of each ship, whistles sounded from the quarter-decks as the mighty battleships, cruisers, or aircraft carriers answered the salute of this unit of His Majesty's Submarine Fleet going out on patrol.

Calling out his orders through the voice pipe, Edmonds steered his boat through the boom and, turning to port, gave "Half together." Shortly afterwards we were cutting our way at full speed into the Mediterranean.

"Well, Churchill," said Harry Edmonds, "we're off, and as dawn will be breaking in about half an hour, we shall have to dive so as to stop any prying eyes from reporting our position."

"Right," I said, and made my way down through the conning-tower hatch.

From below I now heard the Captain's voice calling through the voice pipe, "Diving stations!"

The duty watch swarmed into the control room and took up their respective positions. There was little space left for me, and, since my retreat was cut off from the wardroom by the constant comings and goings of seamen in the narrow passage that led to it, I climbed up onto the pile of kit bags.

The klaxon sounded.

"Out pipes," called the First Lieutenant—and the Captain, preceded by the two lookout men and his Navigating Officer, came down the ladder, closing the hatch above him.

At that moment the diesel engines were cut out, owing to the sealing of the air intake, and the electric motors switched on, and in the strange and sudden silence the men swiftly carried out their orders, announcing their actions when completed.

To me they all seemed tense and alert. The orders and repetitions came to me in a muffled jumble of incomprehensible jargon as the ritual followed its well-ordained and age-old sequence.

"Open one and two main vents." "Five feet." "Open three and four main vents." "Number one and two main vents open, sir." "Half together." "Three and four main vents open, sir." "Ten feet." "Fifteen feet." "Slow together." "Down a bit, stern."

The final order by the First Lieutenant, who was in charge at the time, was: "Shut number four Kingston Main Ballast Tank."

At this command a seaman made a dive at my eagle's nest, capsizing everything, including me, onto the floor. He then began turning a huge wheel as though he were taking avoiding action in a steam roller.

P36 was down, and but for an almost imperceptible buzzing sound, a heavy silence filled the boat. With the exception of four men on duty, everyone had vanished.

We remained submerged at about twenty-six feet throughout the day, and speed was reduced to a mere crawl. I slept most of the time. At sunset we surfaced, and the salt air was sweet and cool to breathe.

On the following morning, when this diving operation was being re-enacted, I was ready for it and, handing off my bed-wrecker, shut the Kingston tank myself. Having wound the handle tight to the end of its thread, I announced the fact like a guard commander reporting to the Duty Officer, closing my remarks with a very loud "Sir." I then settled down to continue my sleep. This performance met with great success and was repeated every morning, and accepted with the usual good humor by the seamen, who, like music-hall audiences, are more pleased with an old joke than the unfamiliar, which requires mental effort before the laugh.

I soon accustomed myself to the ship's routine and, being adaptable, I even came to like the life.

In the officers' wardroom we talked, read, or played bridge, and the next officer for duty always wore dark glasses for about half and hour before taking his watch in the dark. The "Sub," as the Sub-Lieutenant was commonly called, crossed the passage from time to time and marked *P36*'s position in the Mediterranean. Every twenty-four hours he reported the distance covered to the Captain.

The ship's company were, of course, well aware that they had been fooled by the clever ruse of the West African charts. Once out to sea, Harry Edmonds informed the crew that I was being dropped somewhere, but he warned them that no mention was to be made of the fact in Malta, or the culprits would be severely dealt with.

The general opinion of the officers and seamen with regard to my coming venture was fairly summed up when the First Lieutenant said. "I don't know how you can face the idea of wandering about in France all alone, Churchill."

"It's not so terrifying as all that when you know the language," I said. "And, anyway, I shan't be alone all the time."

"Nevertheless I'd just as soon not be in your shoes, and I'm pretty sure everyone feels about the same."

"And I'd just as soon not be in a submarine when it's being chased by a pack of angry destroyers, and the depth charges come closer and closer"

"I *don't* know," countered the First Lieutenant. "It's different, somehow, because we're always together"

"By the way, Churchill," cut in Harry Edmonds, changing the subject, "you remember there was some talk with Captain S. about dropping you two miles from the coastline?"

"Yes, why?" I asked.

"Well, now that we're on our own, I thought I'd let you know that I shouldn't consider making you paddle all that distance if the sea is as rough as this It's like dropping a man by parachute from thirty thousand feet in a high wind You might strike the beach at an impossible spot, if you ever got as far as the beach."

"It's very good of you, sir," I said, "but I don't really mind this paddling business. Thanks all the same."

"Are you sure I can't land you nearer the first house or the first contact you have to make?"

"As a matter of fact you could, but it would be too much of a gamble for me to land near my first contact, because the beach is open there and I should be visible for miles. To make sure of being hidden from curious eyes, I specifically chose this spot because from the road it's impossible to get a view of the sea It'll mean a long walk, I'm afraid, but it can't be helped."

On the ninth day, Harry Edmonds showed me through the periscope the spot I had marked on the map in Gibraltar. The navigation had been perfect, for what I saw was the clear picture of my chosen hotel—twenty kilometers west of Cannes—rising up behind its own private little bay.

Having confirmed that this was my objective, the Navigating Officer took a bearing on it and began cruising slowly to and fro below the surface, waiting for nightfall.

At 5 P.M., I shaved off my beard and had a wash. I knew that this shave would last the whole of the following day, because experience had taught me that when you let your hair grow for several days, the first shave always lasts longer than when the process is a daily one.

The gun layer had prepared me an enormous sandwich that looked like a manhole cover. He also topped up my pint flask with rum. All was set for zero hour.

P36 surfaced at about 6:45 P.M. It was a pitch-black night. Giving a breezy all-in wave to my friends in the wardroom to accompany my farewell of "So long, chums," and hardly waiting for their good-luck wishes, I climbed up through the conning-tower hatch to the bridge. The submarine was already well under the lea of the Maritime Alps, toward which it was still moving at half speed. This proximity to the shore made me smile when I thought of the Admiral's five-mile limit and Captain S.'s reduction of it to two miles, for here was Lieutenant Edmonds taking me in so close that the headlights of the cars on the coast road were quite dazzling as they turned round the Corniche bends and came in line with *P36*.

The submarine was now within about eight hundred yards of the rocks, and I turned to Harry Edmonds and said, "If it's all the same to you, I think I'd like to get off here."

Edmonds put his mouth into the voice pipe and told them to stop the engines. All was still as *P36* slowly coasted to a standstill.

The First Lieutenant was on the outer casing supervising the launching of my canoe. He and a handful of seamen were just visible from the bridge.

A moment later the Captain did something that gave me the creeps. Seeing that *P36* was riding fairly high, and wanting to avoid his passenger having to climb down the rope into his canoe, he muttered something into the voice pipe which sounded like "Open one main vent," then "Shut one main vent." Before I knew what was going on, there was an appalling groan of submarine thunder, as though *P36* were a dying whale issuing its final resounding gasp. Phosphorescent water billowed up around the bows and must have been visible for miles. It was a pretty sight, no doubt, but at that moment my artistic sense was subordinated by an overpowering desire to arrive unseen and unheralded. The waves of electrified water spread out all round, marking *P36*'s position as though she were floodlit.

As it was perfectly obvious that Harry Edmonds was not trying to be funny, but only helpful, I said nothing about this froth-blowing episode. All I said, in a rather plaintive voice, was: "Captain, sir. When I climb down onto the outer casing and get into my canoe, will you promise me to stop your chaps singing 'Auld Lang Syne,' or anything of that sort, because as far as possible, I should like to arrive unheard—even if not unseen." Harry Edmonds smiled his gentle smile and stretched out his hand, for it was now time to go.

"Good hunting, Churchill."

"Thanks, Captain. And . . . many thanks for everything."

"It's been a pleasure to have you on board."

I climbed over the ledge and down the outside of the bridge to the outer casing.

Halfway between the bridge and the bows, I saw the true size of the waves I would have to negotiate. From the bridge I had not noticed the heavy seas. Fortunately there was no wind.

"Here's your rope, Churchill," said the First Lieutenant. "Think you can make it all right?"

"Too easy," I replied, climbing over the rail.

The submarine was rising and falling a distance of some three feet. I hung on to the rope in a squatting position, waiting for the swell to bring the canoe up to me. When it did, I let go my hold and settled into it with my weight evenly divided.

Someone pushed me off, saying, "Your attaché case is by your legs. Good luck, chum."

I started paddling gently to get away from the heaving bows of *P36*. It was an odd sensation to find myself amongst these giant waves, and as they seemed to come from every angle, it was all I could do to keep my balance In order to do so, I had to look straight in front of me, and yet I was longing to turn my head to see what the submarine looked like from sea level.

In the distance, when I was on the crest of a wave, I could see the light which the Captain had pointed out as coming from the hotel. When it had come into view three times and I was more accustomed to the canoe's behavior, I gave way to my curiosity and turned my head. *P36* had vanished, or in the darkness I could not see her. I swiveled the canoe round so that it faced out to sea. There was no sign of her whatsoever. I swung it back. The hotel light had also gone.

CHAPTER VII

I PADDLED toward the outline of the Maritime Alps, whose peaks, varying between two and three thousand feet in altitude, I could faintly distinguish against the starry sky.

It was only 7:15, so there was no particular hurry. I foresaw a difficult landing on the rocks on account of the waves, and decided not to exert myself now by strenuous paddling.

As I approached the shore, I could see the waves curling into breakers before dissolving into a creamy foam on striking the rocks. This was not only a beautiful sight but a most satisfactory thought, for I knew that the sound of the breaking waves would drown any noise I might make getting ashore.

Peering through the darkness, I suddenly realized that this was not at all the place for which I was aiming. I should have kept my eyes on the light, and not bothered with what the submarine might look like. This was going to complicate matters considerably. My objective was a good deal farther to the west.

I made off to the other side of the bay, keeping up a steady paddle. Owing to the startling and dramatic illuminations caused by tampering with the forward tanks, I had instantly decided against spending the night at the hotel, an idea I had previously considered. There was always the chance that people might put two and two together. I therefore decided to walk to Cannes instead

The two-odd sea miles across the bay did not take very long to cover, and as I again approached land, I saw that this time the waves were crashing onto a sandy beach. I recognized the spot, and knew that the exact point at which I wanted to land was only a few hundred yards back.

Having turned about and covered this small distance, I then found the narrow inlet to the hotel's private bay It was at this very moment that the light which I had previously seen and then missed came on again. It helped me considerably to negotiate this tricky passage, and I murmured a low-voiced "*Merci bien.*"

Keeping fairly close to one side, I turned into a little cove on the left and began to look anxiously for the rock on which was the hotel's private springboard. Due to the blackness of the rocks, which were out of the white beam of the hotel light, it took me a little time to find the place. This was particularly irritating for me, as I was certain of its location, having dived from it a hundred times in better days. Finally, when I was only three feet away, I saw the iron steps up which swimmers had climbed after diving.

I faced the canoe out to sea and, backing up to the iron ladder, waited for the right moment. As it was fairly deep just here, the swell did not crash against this rock, but merely rose and fell some four feet at a time. I studied this very carefully, then planned to get my left foot onto the highest possible rung so that, once there, it would not be swamped by the next wave. I waited for what seemed an interminable time, plunging up and down, and then grabbed the highest rung with my left hand and thrust my left foot onto the next rung but one below. Slipping the paddle down the front of the canoe and holding my small attaché case in my right hand whilst steadying the canoe with my free foot, I slithered my case onto the flat top of the rock.

All was well. I hauled out the canoe easily with one hand; it could not have weighed more than twenty pounds.

I took a deep breath. I had successfully landed in France.*

After hiding the canoe accessories in different places, I pulled at my flask and leisurely smoked an excellent French cigarette —made in England. I laid out my raincoat and saturated gloves and changed my socks. My Commando training had taught me the value of dry socks on the march. Looking at my watch, I saw that it was 9:15. Two hours had already passed since I had quitted the submarine.

But now there was work to be done. I made my way down the steps to the cove and, with my knife, ripped half the bottom out of the canoe. Then I held it up like a spear and pressed the slashed end into the water. When the pressure was even, I gave it a good push and it disappeared from view. Hardly had I turned away before I heard a little splash behind me and, looking round, saw that the cursed thing had resurrected itself like Venus from the deep and was floating upside-down. A wave carried it farther out to sea, so I shrugged in the pious hope that the hotel people, if they discovered it, would imagine that whoever had been in it must have been drowned because of the slit canvas. This seemed fairly reasonable so long as they failed to discover the paddles.

I turned to the highway and went up a long, winding hill with the sea on my right. The first thing was to find a safe place for rest and sleep. I decided on a spot some three miles farther along. Then, in the morning, I would catch an early bus to a place just beyond Cannes, on the Route d'Antibes. There I intended to break my journey before tackling my first contact in Antibes.

Soon after 11 P.M. I reached a hairpin bend just short of Théoule. As I would have to pass through the main street of this village, I decided not to risk being questioned for being out after curfew, but to spend the rest of the night here. I crept through the gate of a property on the left and sat down beneath some trees out of sight of the road. Here I smoked another of the Firm's cigarettes, while pondering the chances of getting some sleep. It was a cool, windless night, and except

* See map on p. 57.

for a good deal of distant lightning and odd rumblings of thunder, conditions were not bad.

I wrapped myself up in my raincoat and made up my mind to sleep. But the excitement of the last few hours, the stimulus of the benzedrine tablets, and the absence of air-raid warnings kept my mind and my brain alert. And by now the night had turned colder. Definitely!

I took off my suit and put on pajamas beneath it. I pillowed my head inside the open attaché case and let the lid cover what it could. I rolled myself up into a ball and wrapped myself completely inside my raincoat. It was of no avail. The cold crept through everywhere, and seemed to stroke me with icy fingers. I stuck it, shivering, until 2 A.M., when my teeth began to chatter. Then in a desperate search for warmth I got up and cut some branches with which to cover myself. If anything, the branches made me even colder.

The freezing night forced me to get back onto the road and risk passing through the village. There was no other way except by the railway line, behind which rose sheer rocks. If I were seen on the line at the level crossing a mile farther down, it would look odd, to say the least of it, and might call for an explanation which my numbed mind was in no state to invent. I took a deep breath, closed my attaché case, and left the shelter of the trees.

At this very moment, by a stroke of tremendous luck, a hailstorm descended from the heavens. It was a thumping performance, with huge white pellets bouncing on the tarmac, such as one seldom sees in the course of a lifetime. Before I had walked a hundred yards the ground was completely white. If anything would keep the Vichy police off the roads, this was it.

There was not a soul to be seen in the narrow thoroughfare of Théoule. Even the dogs seemed unaware of my presence, since my footsteps were now muffled.

Once through the village, I felt that most of my troubles would be over. The brisk walk was making and keeping me warm. By now the hail had turned into snow, but it was only a powdery variety that could easily be shaken off whenever I liked. I shifted my case from one hand to the other and moved silently along.

Then I came to the level crossing, and just as I was carefully negotiating the line, the whole area was floodlit in a flash which startled me considerably. It proved to be merely the result of wartime economy. The little station was only illuminated a few moments before and after the arrival of goods trains, and was in darkness for most of the night. This system helped to maintain a sort of intermittent blackout.

Half an hour later, I had reached the bridge that crosses the line. At this point one road goes to Cannes along the shore and the other does a long detour by La Bocca.

As the Cannes airport lay beside the coast road and might be patrolled, I decided to go round the long way. This meant covering some twelve kilometers instead of five. There would soon be plenty of workmen along this road on their way to the steel and other factories, and in the crowd I would be less visible. The snow was six inches deep, and in the general misery I could not have hoped for better conditions.

Having reached La Bocca, I turned off right to the coast road. It was four inches deep in water. Cyclists were plentiful, as it was now broad daylight. They squelched along slowly through the slush and water. The time was nearly 9 A.M., and as I had been plodding through the entire scale of nature's foul weather, I began to feel the effects of weariness.

After another two sopping kilometers I reached the outskirts of Cannes, and in order not to be seen in the vicinity of the Port looking like someone who had just been hauled out of the water, I made my way through the town by the back streets. There I saw endless queues of people in the market squares and outside the food shops. There also seemed to me to be a large number of police about, although that was perhaps just an impression.

After passing through the town, I splashed along the Antibes road for another two kilometers or so, then took a little side track up to the left in a district called La Californie. By then I began to hope very much that my caretaker friend would be at home.

On the gate I saw a very pleasing notice which read: *Joseph is in the 1st Lodge.*

I pushed open the gate and walked into the grounds and up

toward the first small cottage. Joseph was standing under his porch behind a curtain of rain that fell off the ledge, and he looked at me as though he were seeing a ghost. I walked up to him slowly and stopped beside him, with water dripping off my hat. For a few moments we eyed each other without saying a word, and it was quite plain to me that my visit was causing Joseph no great pleasure.

"Good morning—" I said—"if you can call it that."

"I don't remember ever having seen you before," said Joseph sourly.

Now, this old ruffian was an Italian, but he had lived so long in France that his nationality did not count any more and, anyway, if he had been an enthusiastic Italian, he would certainly have returned to his homeland a long time ago and got himself a uniform so as to join in some of the wars that Mussolini always kept going in one place or another. But Joseph was not such an enthusiast, and he never had been one. Three years before, he and his wife were acting as cook and gardener for some English friends of mine, whose large villa stood at the highest point in the grounds. They had been doing this for years, and knew me perfectly well from my past visits. Consequently, when Joseph claimed he did not know me, my opinion of him fell to zero. Obviously I was not looking quite at my best, but my face had not changed all that much, although Joseph's was as narrow as the front of an icebreaker and his eyes had sunk so far back, owing to the starvation diet, that I would have had to look twice to see them, had it not been that they were temporarily bulging with surprise and fear.

"For God's sake, man, can't you see I'm soaked to the skin?" I said.

Joseph never budged. Nodding his head in the direction of a nearby house, he said nervously, "It may interest you to know that that is where the head of the local Gestapo lives."

Seeing my look of surprise, he continued: "Yes, we even have them here in the Unoccupied Zone. And, believe me, they would more than disapprove of my harboring an Englishman. Over there"—and I followed his gaze to a large villa some two hundred yards away—"is the house in which none other than General Weygand lives—if you can call it living—with an ever-changing guard of twenty Vichy police. What you're doing is very dangerous," he concluded.

"You're telling me!" I agreed. "But let's talk it over inside, for old times' sake."

Looking round like a stage villain, Joseph at last opened the door, and I entered a dark and squalid kitchen. As I stood there looking round at the empty stove and broken-down fittings, a pool of water began to form at my feet. I was disgusted with Joseph's reception, and wondered if everyone was going to receive me in a similar way.

When at length Joseph had closed the door behind us, I explained that I was an R.A.F. bomber pilot who had had to bale out and that there could be no particular danger in my dropping in, as Joseph had only to say that he had always known me as a Frenchman, as could be seen by my papers, which I then produced for his benefit. At sight of these, Joseph calmed down a little.

Seeing that things were going the right way, I said, "Besides, Joseph, unless you knew it, you would certainly never take me for an Englishman by my face or accent."

"You're taking a terrible risk," said Joseph. "Thank God my wife is out marketing. You know what women are. . . ."

"It's all right," I replied. "I have no wish to spend a month here. All I want is a chance to dry my clothes and push on this very afternoon."

"Very well," he said. "I'll dry them and iron them at the same time. Take them off."

I stripped down to my shirt, but as I did not want to expose the money belts, I retained my shirt and hoped it would dry on me.

Just then the garden gate creaked and slammed. Joseph looked through the window and saw his wife come trotting up the path. He warned me again to be careful what I said in front of her.

Francine was a local girl, and as she opened the door and saw me with a towel that I had hastily snatched up and draped around my middle, she came straight over to me and gave me a big hug. She would not listen to her husband's mutterings and merely said:

"I don't require any explanations for his presence If the British Government have sent him here, they know what they are doing."

This young woman had masses of white hair, although she could not have been a day over thirty-five. It soon became obvious which of the two possessed spirit in this household.

Francine immediately started juggling with pots and pans, and before Joseph had a chance to get a word in, she rounded on him for not having offered me anything to eat.

"Do you mean to say you've kept this man standing about without offering him a cup of coffee or anything?"

"It's all right, Francine," I chipped in hoping to avoid a family squabble. "I've only just come in, and anyway, I'm not at all hungry."

"Get along with you," snapped Francine, not unkindly, while taking in the ironing process and the pools of water lying on the floor. "One doesn't get as wet as that from a short walk in the rain. You must have been out all night. Nothing very edible could have grown on the trees in the snowstorm you must have passed through."

Joseph continued silently with his ironing, thankful that attention had been drawn away from him, and perhaps a little ashamed of his chickenheartedness.

Meanwhile, Francine had produced her daily ration of brown bread—375 grams—and was cutting it into thin slices, which she laid on a plate, and then she prepared me a bowlful of something that looked like bill-stickers' paste seasoned with brown glue. It emanated from a tin marked *Cocoa*. I had the greatest of difficulty in swallowing the stuff, and would have been prepared to wager twenty to one that there was not two per cent nutrition value in it.

When I had finished eating, Francine said, "You look as if you could do with a good sleep."

"Francine, you know everything," I replied.

"There's still the same bed in the next cottage and, although there are no sheets, there are plenty of blankets to keep you warm, and nobody will disturb you. Come along and I'll turn it down for you."

She left the room, and I got into bed. I was asleep in no

time. Almost at once, it seemed, I felt a hand shaking my shoulder. I murmured: "O.K., O.K. Come back at three." But the hand kept on shaking and a voice repeating, "It *is* three. It *is* three, and you *must* wake up. I never saw a man in such a coma unless he was drunk as an owl."

I shook my head violently. I had been dead to the world.

I found all my clothes as dry and clean as they had been on the first day I had put them on. Even my shoes, which I considered ruined for good, were polished and in very passable condition. In fact, I was as good as new once again, and much refreshed by my heavy sleep. The only fly in the ointment was that the quantities of water that had fallen on my attaché case had penetrated the locks and one of these had jammed. Fortunately, I could open one side and force things out.

I said farewell to Joseph and Francine, and thanked them for their hospitality. Joseph, who must have received no mean pep talk from his wife, accompanied me to the bus stop five hundred yards down the road. This place was just opposite the local police station, and Joseph did not seem to be the least worried by the inquisitive looks of one of the gendarmes who was then on duty outside. I figured that Francine's talk was something I would have given up those four hours of sleep to have heard.

This was a request stop, but no amount of requesting would stop the first bus that passed in a cloud of vapor. It was crowded to bursting point, and the driver took no notice of our signals whatsoever.

"I don't think there's much hope here, Joseph," I said.

"Oh, there'll be another in half an hour. You're sure to get on to that one. Let's pop into the *bistro* and have one while we wait."

I wondered if this was wise, with the policeman eyeing us at such short range. Yet I felt drawn on by his very presence. We crossed the road and entered the gloomy café.

"Deux grenaches," ordered Joseph, catching the waiter's eye.

"What the dickens is that?" I asked quietly.

"On non-alcoholic days there are only three drinks worth having—*Grenache, Banyuls,* or *Muscat.* I prefer *Grenache,* and I think you'll like it," said Joseph. Then, peering inquisitively into my face, he said, "But what have you been drinking on your way across France?"

"I've spent my time in farms where they gave me red wine," I answered promptly.

Just then the café door opened, and in came the policeman. He went up to the bar and spoke to the proprietor. On his way out, he passed by our table and stopped.

"If you gentlemen think you can catch a bus here, you're mistaken They're crammed to the hatches. The only way to get a place is to queue up at the terminus "

"Merci, monsieur," I said, with much relief.

I paid for the drinks, shook hands with Joseph, and made my way back through the town.

I walked up to the terminus shelter and joined the queue. It was a silent and abject crowd, the very antithesis of the normal gay, chattering, argumentative people of the south.

A dirty bus was standing outside the shelter and when, finally, the unshaven driver pushed open the door, with the expression of a besotted farm hand opening a gate for a herd of cattle, the mob advanced sulkily between two serious-looking gendarmes, whose eyes were on their parcels, as though on the lookout for black marketeers.

I was lucky to get the last spot of standing room before the door was slammed behind me. The bus started immediately, and went as fast as the driver could make it go along the Croisette. Its wheels squelched through the slush, and amply splashed the passersby. In normal times the driver would have been flooded with abuse from the indignant passengers, but now nobody paid the slightest attention.

The spirit of Cannes had sunk to a low level. It was a blow to me to find my beloved France in such a sorry plight and, as the bus splashed implacably onwards, I hoped it was only a local complaint.

CHAPTER VIII

THE BUS reached Antibes at about 7 P.M. I got out and took a stroll around the main square. It was getting a little late to call on the doctor. He might have guests for dinner. You could hardly drop in at the eleventh hour in these days, not even if you were the bearer of two or three hundred thousand francs. Anyway, it would require a morning's shopping to cope with the appetite that I now had. So I made my way to the Nouvel Hotel, a small, unassuming place that had been recommended to me by the London Office.

I decided to clean up and have some more sleep before calling on Louis on the following day At the reception desk I filled in the necessary form, copying down the requirements from my identity card.

I was then shown to a little bedroom, where I washed with my own soap and put on a clean shirt. Having put everything away, I locked the door and made my way back to the big café in the main square.

There were very few people sitting at the tables, so I was able to pick myself a quiet spot where the lighting was not too strong As I looked around the place, I could hardly recognize it. But after my experience of Cannes I was not at all surprised.

I ordered a *Grenache* and settled down to study the local paper. It was full of insidious German propaganda and was clearly controlled by the enemy. I then asked for the telephone directory and made doubly certain of Louis' address. Then I paid for my drink and walked out.

In the town I came across a shop that sold artificial sweets. Entering it, I bought myself a box of this saccharine confection. It set me back about a week's normal pay, and with this under my arm I returned to the hotel and feasted off the remains of the *P36* sandwich, finishing off with the sweets.

It was a very cold night, and there was neither heating nor hot water in the hotel. I undressed as far down as a thick jersey which covered two other vests. Around this I retied my money belts before slipping on my pajamas. Then I put on a clean pair of socks, and with my jacket and raincoat spread out on top of the bedclothes, I disappeared from view.

I woke up twelve hours later, feeling properly rested and ordered some coffee, but nothing to eat, as that required coupons. When the coffee arrived I dropped a saccharine pellet into the bowl and tasted the result. It was so appalling that I took my revenge by shaving in it. I then washed, dressed, packed my few belongings and paid my bill.

I well remembered that the French Section had told me the correct procedure for contacting Louis was to swallow a stomach-ache powder (which they provided), ring at the door, and queue up for very legitimate medical treatment. The idea behind this was that neither the servant who opened the door, nor anyone else, could possibly suspect such a caller of being anything but a very sick and miserable individual. However, as I understood that these tablets had a guaranteed four hours' duration, and from another source I had gleaned the interesting information that the Doctor's meals were practically an international gastronomic event, I decided to give these a miss, because I had every intention of crashing the family lunch. So I decided to use an old parachute accident as an excuse, although, of course, I would find another reason for the fact that one side of my chest had been slightly pushed in. It was midday when I set off for this first encounter.

As I ambled down the Boulevard Maréchal Foch it was not long before I reached No. 31. I mounted the steps and rang the bell. When the maid came, all the words I had to say were lined up on a spring. I slipped the catch and said: "I know it's Sunday, but I've come a long way on special recommendation, so I hope the Doctor will see me."

"I'm afraid the Doctor is out," replied the maid. "But he'll be back at twelve-thirty. Would you care to wait for him?"

"No, thanks," I said. "I'll come back later."

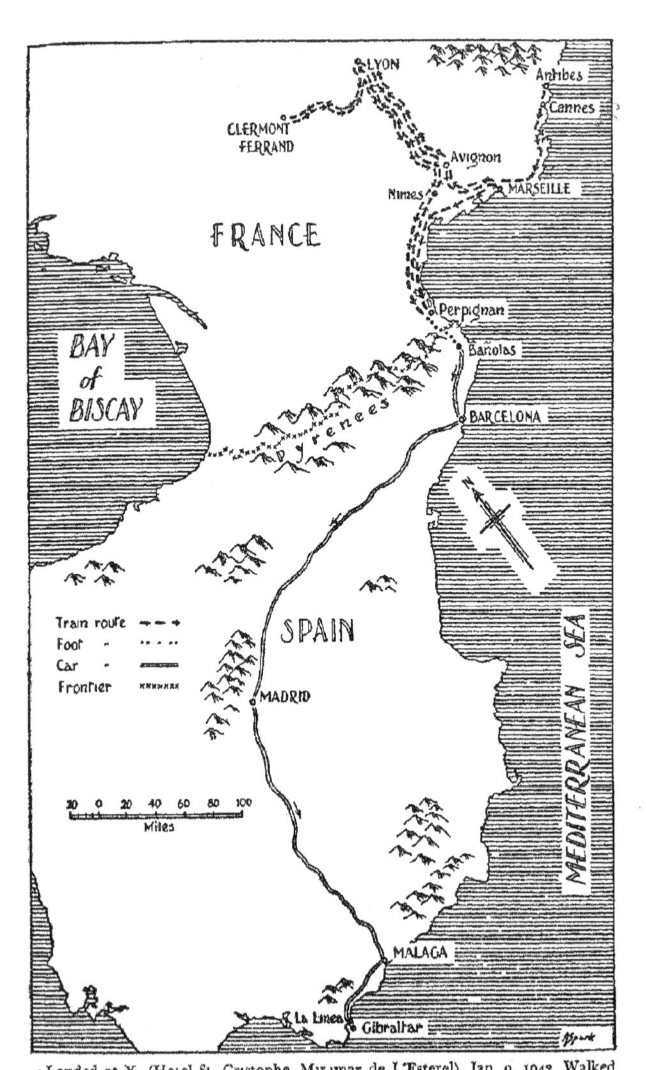

→Landed at X (Hotel St. Cristophe, Miramar de L'Esterel), Jan 9, 1942 Walked east to Californie district of Cannes, via La Napoule and La Bocca

TRAIN JOURNEYS—January 11 to February 2

Antibes to Lyon; Lyon to Marseille, Marseille to Perpignan, Perpignan to Lyon, Lyon to Clermont Ferrand, Clermont Ferrand to Lyon; Lyon to Perpignan

I walked down the road toward the sea. It was a peaceful road bordered by small villas. There were no cars to be seen, only an occasional cyclist and a new wartime contraption called a vélo-taxi, whereby a cyclist towed his passenger in a kind of gocart.

At the end of the boulevard was a circular Public Gardens around which ran a road; beyond this was a circular pavement bordered by a wall two feet high. I put one foot on the wall and looked over.

The first thing that met my gaze was a flight of concrete steps built into the rocks and running from sea level up to the point where I was standing.

I lit a cigarette and looked at the steps pensively. Looking over my right shoulder I saw the Doctor's house, three turnings up the avenue and not four hundred yards away. This spot was a gift from heaven. If ever I came back by submarine I would save myself a lot of trouble by landing here at a very late hour. I took special note of some low-lying rocks just out to sea, and taking in the rest of the bay with a photographic sweep, I locked it all up in my mind for future reference. Looking at my watch I saw that it was almost 12:30 so I made my way back up the road I thought the Doctor's temporary absence might one day prove to have been a godsend.

On my return to the house, the maid informed me that the Doctor was back, and led me into the waiting room. She left me there, and after exchanging a few words with the Doctor next door, she returned to fetch me.

The man whom I saw seated behind his desk was Louis right enough. Headquarters had described him perfectly. Bald, clean-shaven, around forty-eight, and of stocky build. As he rose briskly to shake my hand, I could see that this man was not wilting from undernourishment.

"Bonjour, Docteur," I said. *"René de Lyon vous envoit ses amitiés."*

A twinkle came into the Doctor's eye in recognition of the first part of the password, but as he had obviously forgotten his cue, he merely replied:

"I forget what comes next, but between you and me, I thought London had forgotten us altogether."

I smiled and introduced myself. I briefly told Louis my cover story—that my name in the field was Michel—and showed him my identity card with the name Pierre Chauvet upon it, Louis nodded his head, being accustomed to this sort of thing.

"There's a man in the next room whom I'd like you to meet," said Louis, getting up. "He's a Baron, but his war name is Bernard,* and he's the Head of a large Resistance Movement. Just excuse me a moment while I fetch him in."

He was back again after a moment and introduced a tall, good-looking man wearing a beard.

"Bernard—Michel," said the Doctor briefly.

We shook hands.

"I'll leave the two of you to your conversation," said Bernard. "I promised to spend the afternoon with my wife before catching the evening train to Lyon."

He prepared to leave, and as he was shaking hands once more with me, I said, "I've got to go on to Lyon, too. Do you mind if I join you?"

"Not at all," said Bernard. "In fact, I should be delighted to have your company on such a long and boring trip. I shall board the train at Cannes, and you'll find me opposite where the first second-class coach pulls up."

"Good," I said. "I shall look out for you."

Then the Doctor produced a typed sheet, which was his latest report to London. It was to have been sent by courier through Spain and Portugal. The gist of what I read was that the organization on the coast was in dire need of a trained radio operator with a short-wave sending and receiving set to communicate with London. The other item of interest was that if someone did not produce some money for them within the next ten days, the organization would not be able to continue to function.

Having read the report, I handed it back to Louis.

"I'm only sorry Laurent† isn't in Cannes at the present mo-

* Baron d'Astier de la Vigerie Head of Lyon group known as *Résistance.* Brought out of France by the author in another submarine in April 1942 Was thus able to report to General de Gaulle. Later became Minister of Interior in Algiers government under General Giraud, and is now (1952) Deputy in the French Parliament

† Captain Bazin.

ment, or he would have confirmed all this," he said. "He and I work together. When are you going to see him?"

"I was told in London that you would be able to contact him, that we might all have a meeting together, but that, in any case, whatever you and I said would be passed on to him."

"That is so, but unfortunately he's gone up north somewhere, and goodness knows when he'll get back."

"Ever heard of a man called Olivier?" I asked.

"If you mean the man who works in Marseille, I certainly have."

"Yes, that's the man. I just wanted to make sure that you were supposed to know him."

"Don't they tell you anything in London?" inquired the Doctor, rather sarcastically.

"They prefer to keep things in watertight compartments as far as possible," I explained.

"Well, Laurent and I are in constant touch with Olivier by means of a weekly courier," said Louis. "When we have something urgent to pass to London we send it to him, and he gives it to the captain of a fast motor launch that plies regularly between Marseille, Gibraltar, and Penzance. Don't ask me how he gets through He just does and, moreover, in very urgent cases, he is willing to take someone on board. But Olivier has got to be convinced that it is a question of life and death before recommending such a course; otherwise everybody would want to return to England by the speedboat in preference to the slower monthly fishing boats, or walking the Pyrenees."

"Then that solves the problem," I said. "I shall be spending a few days in Marseille, and I'll get Olivier to contact Laurent and arrange a meeting there, if he thinks it necessary."

"I'm sure he will. After all, he's one of your chaps, and he'll want to see you personally. Besides, my wife will get some of your linen washed, and Olivier can bring it along when he goes."

"Now, as to the financial question, I think I can solve that. How much do you want?" I asked, to see if the figure tallied with what London had mentioned.

"A good deal more than you could possibly be carrying on

you at the moment!" said the Doctor, with a twinkle in his eye.

"Well, how much, anyway?" I went on, without twitching a muscle.

"Four hundred thousand francs is what I asked London for, six weeks ago."

"You shall have it," I said, remembering that this was the figure given me in London, besides the intimation that they were not fussy to 100,000. "Where can I undress? I've got it round my waist."

"Pop into the operating room. It's just through that curtain."

I went through to the next room, laid my jacket and sweater on the operating table, and pulled up my shirt and several layers of vests to unveil the money belts. I took off the big one and extracted 450,000 francs. I then reshuffled the notes so as to balance the weight of the belt and was surprised to feel that there was practically no difference in its bulk. In a few moments I was dressed again.

Returning to the consulting room, I laid the notes on the table, saying, "There you are, Louis. Would you mind counting it?"

The Doctor did so in about half the time it had taken me, and he looked mightily pleased.

"You've given me fifty thousand francs too much," he said.

"Glad to get rid of the stuff," I said.

"Like to get rid of any more, while you're at it?"

"Sorry, but Father Christmas has several other calls to make," I replied, with a laugh.

Having completed my business with Louis, I then wrote out a telegram in French which read: ANNABELLE QUITE RECOVERED AND SENDS LOVE AND KISSES. Handing it to the Doctor I said, "Could you have this sent as soon as possible to the address I've given below?"

"Certainly," said Louis.

Opening the door he shouted out:

"Micheline. Viens ici."

Presently a small, fair-haired girl of about fifteen came into the room.

"Micheline," said the Doctor, "this is Michel. He's just arrived out of the blue from England."

The girl held out her hand, and the expression on her face indicated quite clearly that she was well accustomed to the odd assortment of people who passed through her father's house. Her handshake and manner were those of a woman of thirty.

"I want you to see that this telegram gets off soon after two o'clock, when the Post Office reopens And now go and tell your mother we have a guest for lunch."

"Oui, Papa," said the girl, and left the room.

"Yes," went on the Doctor, handing me a cigarette, "I have no secrets from my family, and they are my best Lieutenants. You may speak freely at lunch."

We then settled down to a tremendous meal, beginning with hors d'œuvres washed down by a bottle of white Châteauneuf-du-Pape that tasted like a liqueur. The Doctor apologized for the fact that the cork had already been drawn from this bottle before my arrival, on the insistence of one of his patients who had brought this elixir in appreciation of services rendered.

It was a lunch fit for a king.

What there remained of the afternoon was spent playing *belotte* with the family and some friends who had dropped in. The Doctor had introduced me quite simply as Monsieur Chauvet, and I, who was an adept at this typically French card game, could not help deriving a certain satisfaction from the obvious fact that the only essential difference felt by the visitors toward me was one of slight envy for the way I kept winning.

Presently it was time to go, and Raymonde, the elder daughter, offered to accompany me to the station.

Having accepted a small bag in the place of my attaché case, whose lock was still jammed, I took leave of the rest of the family and thanked them for their kind hospitality.

It was dark outside, and a hard frost had set in, making the going rather slippery.

While waiting for the train, Raymonde told me some of her father's exploits and of his reputation in Antibes based on his war record, both in the 1914–18 conflict and the recent fiasco of 1940. In both he had been awarded the Legion of Honor and the Croix de Guerre. He had lost no time in forming resistance cells all along the coast, and all he now required in order to fit into the overall plan as seen from London was wireless communication.

Noticing that she was wearing the Cross of Lorraine under the lapel of her jacket, I said, "Isn't it a little rash to flaunt your allegiance to de Gaulle so openly?"

"My sister and I both do it, and so do many of our school friends. Some of the staff get livid about it. But those are the collaborators, and fortunately there aren't many of them. The good ones daren't approve of the Gaullists for fear of losing their jobs."

"Perhaps they're wise," I suggested. "Maybe under the cover of being teachers they are doing the same sort of job as your father. In that case it would be a pity to draw attention to themselves."

"Maybe you're right. I hadn't thought of it that way," said Raymonde.

A distant clatter announced the arrival of the evening express. Raymonde shook my hand and walked away toward the exit. Some of the passengers getting off the train might know her and ask a lot of questions about her new friend.

I took in her proud and confident bearing as her figure receded along the platform. A few more families like that, I thought, and the occupation of France would prove to be no picnic for the invader.

CHAPTER IX

THE TRIP to Lyon with Bernard was uneventful, and my identity card successfully passed the scrutiny of the three plainclothesmen at the ticket gate in the Lyon station. After an unsuccessful attempt by Bernard to get us breakfast and me some food coupons, I returned by tram to the square in front of the station.

Walking east, I made for the Rue de la Charité, which I knew to be the next turning to the left. According to Captain de G's information, the Hotel de France was situated about a hundred yards down the street.

I found it immediately, and saw that it was a small, unpretentious place outside which hung a modest sign.

I took a room, filled out the registration form, and went upstairs. It was an identical room to the one I had occupied in Antibes. There was no hot water, no heating, and no pillow. The bolster, over which the lower sheet had been passed, took the place of the pillow.

Having emptied my bag of its contents and placed my toilet articles on the washstand, not forgetting to hide my soap, I was now ready to track down Germaine.

Not knowing the tram routes, I walked down the Rue de la Charité into the Place Bellecour and straight on to the Place de la République, all of which were located in the narrow central strip of Lyon banked by the Saône on one side and the Rhône on the other.

Here I turned right, passing the Carlton Hotel, which I knew to be Gestapo Headquarters. A handful of Vichy police were guarding the entrance.

A hundred yards farther along I turned left and entered the lobby of the Grand Nouvel Hotel. I walked straight up to the desk and asked the reception clerk if Mademoiselle Le Contre was in. The clerk ran his eye along the pigeonholes and, seeing her key still on its ring, he said:

"Mademoiselle is not in, Monsieur. She is usually out all day, and returns at about six o'clock in the evening."

"Thank you," I said. "I'll call again this evening."

This was a slight setback, for it meant no lunch for me that day. I had no food tickets, and could therefore not order a meal in a restaurant. Then it occurred to me to try the Café de la République, on the off-chance that Bernard might be there, as en route to Lyon he had mentioned that I could probably find him there at lunchtime or in the evenings if I ever needed him.

First of all I made for the bar of the Grand Nouvel Hotel so as to acquaint myself with the geography of the place for future reference. Here I ordered a drink and spent half an hour reading the paper. Then I got up and left.

A watery sun was peeping through the winter sky as I emerged into the street. I took a turning to the right and then to the left and followed the Rhône along the *quai*. Pity there was so much wet snow on the ground, I thought. A walk would have solved the question of how to fill in the rest of the morning. I did not want to return to my desolate and icy hotel room. It was too cold to tramp round a museum or look at an art gallery; besides, you had to be in the mood for that sort of thing.

There was nothing for it; I must just make the best of it and drag my damp feet from one café to another until I could reasonably be seen inside Bernard's suggested rendezvous.

Having read every morning newspaper in the country, I finally made my way to the Café de la République and hoped that Bernard would show up.

Walking through to the far end of the room I sat down at a table facing the door and ordered my fifth apéritif. I left the drink on the table for a good quarter of an hour before sipping it slowly and distastefully.

It was half-past twelve. I would give Bernard another twenty minutes; not that I could wait no longer, but simply because most of the tables between me and the door were occupied by people having lunch, and I could not bear to watch them for more than that length of time.

I began to think that my pride in refraining from asking Bernard to lend me some food tickets, when we were on the train, was a little stupid. I had hoped to contact Germaine quickly, and then the question would not have arisen. Also, Germaine was attached to the British circuit, and Bernard had nothing to do with it. I knew that everyone was short of food tickets, particularly people like Bernard, who were always providing for others.

At ten minutes to one there was still no sign of my friend, so I got up and left the café. I took a tram back to the station and walked to the hotel.

Setting the alarm clock for 5:30, I lay down and, feeling confident that I would see Germaine that evening, I managed to get some sleep.

When my alarm woke me I felt much refreshed, although it was cold and dark in the room. I switched on the light. Then, dipping my face cloth into the icy water that came from the only tap, I dabbed my eyes and squeezed the cloth onto the back of my neck.

In five minutes I was outside the hotel, making my way to the tram stop by the station. When the same number 3 tram that had brought me back previously appeared, I hopped onto it. Five minutes later I had left it in the Place de la République, and presently found myself outside the Grand Nouvel Hotel. Six o'clock was striking as I entered the hall. I went through the same process as I had in the morning, only to learn from another receptionist that Mademoiselle Le Contre was not yet back, although she generally returned at about this hour. I thanked him, and said that I would go into the bar for a while before inquiring again.

I had one or two glasses of what they had got in this bar, and also killed time by reading the paper. Every half-hour or so I went out to see if Germaine had arrived, but without success.

All I knew about Brigitte Le Contre was that she was a tall American girl of about thirty-three, whose occupation was that of a newspaper correspondent. At the War Office they did not seem to know whether she was a blonde or a brunette. However, they did know that she had one brass foot owing to some hunting accident, but this fact was said to be well concealed and to handicap her walking so little that her infirmity was neither a hindrance to herself nor a help to anyone trying to find her, unless that person went to the lengths of stamping on the feet of every girl in town who seemed to be around thirty-three years of age.

By the time I had spent about two hours in the bar, I was

prepared to stamp on anybody's feet, for I was a very hungry man. I was also beginning to get really worried. There was still just time to try Bernard's place, but if I did, I might miss Germaine. If I left a note asking her to come over to the Café de la République she might very properly not wish to be known by Bernard and reprove me for lack of security. In the end I wrote her a note, giving the hotel address and telephone number, explaining that I had to see her urgently. Having deposited this with the reception clerk I returned to my hotel.

By the time I had reached my room at the hotel I was ravenous, and began to work out how long I could last on the monotonous national diet of acorn juice and sleep as alternatives for food. As I was lying on my bed considering all this, I was suddenly called to the telephone. To my great relief I found myself talking to Mademoiselle Le Contre. It was a simple matter for me to express my pleasure at hearing this young lady's voice, especially when on hearing I had news of her sister Suzanne, she asked me if I would care to join her for supper. There could be no doubt I was speaking to the right person, because the accent that came over the wires had little to do with the French Republic.

I was soon back in the Nouvel Hotel lobby, shaking hands with Germaine. She did not waste any time before hustling me through the snow to a little restaurant conducted by a Greek. This man welcomed Germaine like a loving daughter, so I presumed everything would be all right, even if it was after nine o'clock.

"Germaine," I said as we sat down in the warm restaurant, "I'll make no bones about it. I'm simply delighted to see you. I've had nothing to eat for twenty-six hours. My inside contains about seven pints of *Grenache*—whatever that may be. I hope the *patron* has enough food for a herd of elephants, because I shall need it. If you can produce the food tickets, I shall be pleased to pay for anything he can provide."

"You can have as much as you want, so don't worry. As for the food tickets, we have a friend who works in the Food Office and brings out just as many as we require. But how is it that you haven't brought out your own?"

"Well, you see, I'm the first person to have come over this year, and as the color changes every year, they're waiting for me to bring back this year's samples to copy."

"You poor devil! How have you managed so far?"

"I haven't been here many days," I replied.

The proprietor came up to our table and handed us two giant menus. Seeing at a glance that everything was available that one could possibly dream of, I had the courtesy to ask Germaine to order what she liked, first suggesting we start with a dozen oysters each. We then chose various other dishes, and when the proprietor had written it all down and disappeared into the kitchen, I said, "I thought there was no food in this country."

"Lyon is better provided than most places," said Germaine. "But you can't eat like this anywhere. This is a black-market restaurant."

"Isn't he taking rather a risk?" I asked.

"No. He bribes the right people."

"Does he expect food tickets?"

"Only if you happen to have any."

"Could anybody drop in here?" I inquired.

"Yes. But he wouldn't get much of a meal unless he had been introduced by a well-known customer first."

"What would happen if he pointed out that other people were getting the dishes he was refused?"

"People over here just don't do that sort of thing. They know the form."

"Sorry to ask so many questions, Germaine, but I too want to know the form."

"Fire away," said Germaine. "The night is still young. But remember, although you may have three quarts of *Grenache* inside you, I haven't had a drink all day."

"I'm most dreadfully sorry," I said. "What shall I get you?"

"A gin and Italian, please," replied Germaine archly, waiting to see the effect of this seemingly impossible fantasy.

"Do you really mean to say you can get that, too?" I gasped.

"You can get anything here; even English cigarettes."

"Garçon," I said, *"deux Cinzanos gin."*

"Germaine," I said, turning to the girl again, "I won't bother you with anything more after this, but while we've got time, would you explain how the food tickets work?"

"But of course," said Germaine, pulling her food card out of her bag and placing it on the soft leather seat between us. "If you take a look at that under the table, nobody'll notice that you're a learner."

"Right," I said, "I've got it open at the first page. It says *Matières grasses.*"

"Those are the fats. They're divided up into 20-gram tickets. You give one of those at lunch or dinner. It goes towards the cooking fat in which the food was prepared. If there's macaroni on the fixed menu, they require an additional ticket for that dish. Now turn over."

"Here it says bread."

"These coupons are divided up into 25-gram tickets. Each slice of bread in restaurants is cut to that weight. You can have as much as you like, so long as there are tickets in the book. It's worked out on a basis of 375 grams per day."

"I see," I said, turning over to the next page. "This says *Fromage.*"

"Well, that's easy enough. The tickets are for 20 grams. If there's cheese on the menu, they give you a tiny slice weighing that amount, and you have to give up one ticket. Now the one over on the last page is for meat, and they're in 90-gram divisions—about the weight of a fair slice of meat. When you're in a restaurant, never hand over your book, but tear out the tickets according to the meal."

"I've got it," I said, handing back the food card.

Germaine tore out a few tickets from each section and passed them to me. "You'd better have these to tide you over until Charles provides you with your own card," she said.

When our drinks had been set out on the table, Germaine turned to me and said: "News of your arrival reached Charles by courier last week, so he told me to expect you. I'll fix up a meeting between you and him tomorrow. By the way," she continued, leaning closer to me, "I'm not an inquisitive person, but it's my turn to ask questions now. Your French is so perfect that I take it you are French."

"It doesn't really matter what I am," I replied, inwardly

delighted at the compliment. "All you need know, in case we're ever grabbed together, or if you're ever asked to explain your association with me, is that my name is Pierre Chauvet, that I was a French Liaison Officer with the 50th Division who escaped capture at St. Valéry and made his way to Corsica. I don't have to bother you with the address of the friends with whom I've been staying ever since. That's my headache, and it's not a particularly bad one either, for the War Office went to the trouble of communicating somehow with a friend of mine over there who is prepared to back the story if inquiries should ever reach that point. As far as you're concerned, I've only just come over via Marseille and, because I was running short of money I'm approaching you—who are a newspaper reporter—with a view to cadging a little free-lance work."

"Well, that's one of the best cover stories I ever heard," said Germaine. "Short, sweet, and to the point As far as I can see, it also holds water in every respect. They must have got somebody with a real brain back home."

"You know how it is," I said; "they simply love playing these games in England."

"Michel," interrupted Germaine urgently, "we never name that place when we wish to speak of it. Instead we say *chez nous*—at home. The other word is apt to attract attention."

"Sorry. I'll remember that in future," I said, lowering my already quiet voice by another tone.

We had a splendid meal, and left the restaurant around 11:30. Afterwards Germaine showed me the café where I was to contact Charles at eleven o'clock on the following day. Then I accompanied her to the street that led to her hotel and walked back to my own, as the trams had stopped running.

I slept soundly, and rose late the next day. I ordered the *petit déjeuner complet* for the first time, having got some bread coupons at last.

I then went to the café on foot, to study the names of the streets and see what they had in the shop windows. Although I had often previously passed through Lyon by car on my way to and from the south coast, I could hardly say that I knew the town. Nor had it ever been my idea of a place in which to linger. There were still a few cars about, but in the main the taxis consisted, as elsewhere, of tandem bicycles drawing single- or double-seater wheel chairs in which the passengers looked like overgrown babies.

Having reached the café, I sat down at a table at the far end and ordered a cup of hot synthetic meat bouillon. I had several of these to keep out the cold. I read the paper, but it was so full of poppycock about the "New Order" that I soon gave that up. I wondered what the half-starved French people thought of all this propaganda piffle, as they saw one large trainload after another taking away the rich fruits of their soil and vineyards to the Fatherland. It was not surprising that at home they concentrated so much on instruction in railway sabotage. I thought what a great day it would be when in due course the French had learned these tricks from us and, when they could get their hands onto some of the precious plastic explosive, they would at last succeed in preventing many a trainload from reaching the instigators of the "New Order," or rather the gangsters of the biggest pillage racket ever seen in the history of the world.

Presently I saw Germaine enter the café. She came straight up to my table, and we shook hands like old friends. I ordered her a cup of bouillon, and within five minutes Charles joined us. He was a tall, slim, and quietly dressed young man. I had heard good accounts of him from London. He lived on the outskirts of Lyon in a modest house, and carried on his activities without attracting any attention.

Charles seemed very pleased at meeting me, so I presumed that he, too, must be running a little short of cash. In any event, I was the first man he had seen from the old country since his arrival, six months before.

Soon after introducing us, Germaine found some tactful excuse for leaving.

Charles and I discussed everything concerning his district: the fields at his disposal for parachute and aircraft landing, his connections with the railwaymen, bargees, police, magistrates, and so forth—in fact any and all persons and departments that were of help to our work. There was nobody in this part of the café, and we merely changed the subject when the waiter came to refill our cups.

Charles confirmed what Germaine had already told me about

their friend in the Food Office, and he promised me an authentic food card, stamped and signed and bearing my false name.

After lunch we took a tram out to Charles' house. Here I again disrobed to produce some money. Charles' organization was not quite so large as Louis', or perhaps it would be better to say that it was more modestly run and included many older men with established positions, whereas most of Louis' cells consisted of the younger element who required a salary to keep going, as they were of no fixed abode and had to travel anywhere. Charles only required 200,000 francs, so I gave him fifty per cent more from the treasury belt that never left my waist and which had helped me considerably in withstanding the bitter cold.

I then passed on to my own requirements.

"They told me at home that I could count on you for a sample of every type of ration card issued in France, as well as the personal one you've promised me."

"Yes," said Charles, adding, "I'm delighted to see that my reports are getting through all right. When I heard from Germaine that you had arrived I made arrangements for the ration books to be ready by tomorrow at lunchtime. You will also have a 1942 tobacco and textile card."

"Excellent," I said. "Now the second important point the Section mentioned was that they want you to study the countryside just north of Lyon and close to the banks of the two rivers where the ground seems made for aircraft landing strips. The rivers would be a great help to the pilots as a guide to find the fields by moonlight."

"How many do they want?" asked Charles.

"Half a dozen or so," I said.

"What sort of size?"

"For bombers they should be at least 1,600 yards long by about 800 wide. There are some other essential details to remember as well. The fields have got to have a good, hard surface, and they should be as flat as possible. The R.A.F. aren't terribly fussy about the unevenness, but they do insist that there should be absolutely no sort of a ditch anywhere in the field, and neither telegraph posts nor trees at either end of the runway. They don't mind water at either or both ends because that doesn't in any way reduce the actual 1,600 yards of runway. For Lysanders only 800 yards by 400 is necessary. These, of course, should be easier to find. According to the maps, this district is simply swarming with flat meadows, but, then, maps don't exactly show irrigation ditches and so forth."

"As a matter of fact," put in Charles, "in this case the maps are right. I've been along part of the Saône in a barge with some pals of mine, and now, I come to think of it, many of the fields I saw were so large that you could hardly see where they ended."

"Well done," I said. "That's the sort of thing that will suit the R.A.F. literally down to the ground. You might have a look at them from the land side and see if there are any country lanes leading up to them. Transport will have to come up to within reasonable distance to take people to the field and fetch passengers and material back to safe houses."

"Who's going to handle these operations?" asked Charles.

"You are, chum," I said.

"Suits me. But how's it done? They must want a flare-path, or something, don't they?"

"Exactly. We're just coming to that. Have you got a pencil and a bit of paper?"

"Yes, here you are," said Charles, opening a drawer and pulling out these articles.

With a few strokes I drew a plan of the flare-path and

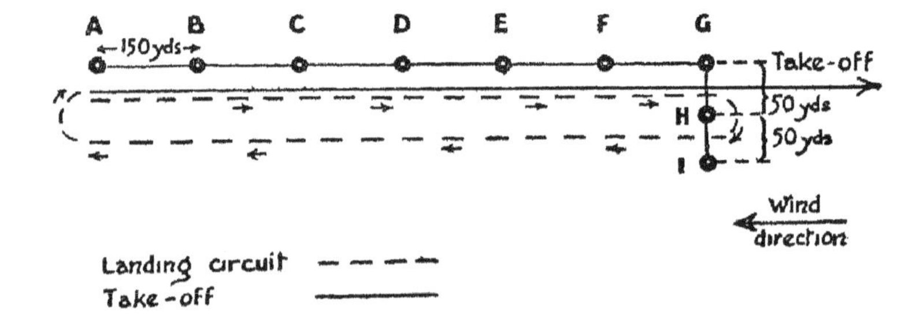

then began to explain: "The rectangle AGI is your flare-path, and the nine dots indicate the places where nine men have to be posted with bicycle lamps From A to G they're spaced out at intervals of one hundred fifty yards; but from G to H and H to I the distances are only fifty yards each. You have to place this lot in such a way that when the pilot sees the letter L with the base line inverted he will know that the wind is blowing from G to A. He will then know he is safe to put his wheels down at A and run into wind up to G. When he gets there, he'll turn round H and come back to A, like this," and I drew it for Charles on the plan.

"He'll then turn again, and only stop at lamp A when he is facing into wind for the take-off."

"I begin to see why he needs all that space," said Charles. "He needs it at one end to come in and at the other to get off the ground."

"You've got it," I said. "Now as to the signals: When you've sent in the position of your fields by code the chosen ground will be agreed by the R.A F. after they've taken aerial photographs of it. Then London will tell you what B.B.C. message they'll send out at seven-thirty to show that the plane's coming on the night of the message. They'll also give you the letter to be flashed up in Morse to the pilot by you, who are running this operation from lamp A. The pilot will flash back another letter of which you will have been informed. When you recognize the pilot's letter, you shine your torch along the flare-path so that your team see it. They must then light their torches, shine them at you to show that they've cottoned on and then shine them upwards at the aircraft, following it wherever it twists on its ways down to the ground. When it passes you on the ground, keep following it with your torch—and get the others to do the same—while it is turning round in the field. Only when it stops beside you can you afford to put out your light and approach the plane. However, the others must keep on shining their torches until the machine has passed them on its take-off run past lamp G."

"That's all straightforward, but it's surely going to be a little slow arranging this sort of thing by courier through Switzerland. My chaps always risk being caught on the frontier."

"You find the fields first and by the early spring you'll have your own private radio operator," I said.

"Three rousing cheers!" exclaimed Charles. "Without a radio one feels absolutely hamstrung; it makes our parachute operations very complicated, and doesn't help our relations with the local patriots who wonder what we're playing at."

"That's the worst of being a pioneer," I said. "But you'll have the satisfaction of seeing things change."

In the later afternoon, Charles' Number Two returned to the house from his banking job at the Crédit Lyonnais. George* was a Frenchman whose work at the Bank was an ideal cover for his underground activities.

I had seen a photograph of a young man of about twenty-five in the room where I had undressed to get at my money belt, and Charles had told me about his friend and warned me of the change that had come over him after spending eighteen months in a German prisoner-of-war camp from which he had just escaped. It was a sensible warning, for I would never have connected the pale person with watery eyes with the handsome youth I had seen in the photograph.

"I was captured in 1940 with about two million other Frenchmen," explained George. "The camps were flooded with prisoners—far beyond the Germans' most optimistic hopes, or capacity to deal with. Consequently, the rations were a little on the thin side. But I shall soon pick up," added this optimist.

The three of us then went off to dine in the back room of a black-market restaurant known to Charles and George. We were joined by Germaine, who was accompanied by Laurent. He was on his way back to Cannes from Chateauroux, and had stopped at Lyon to see her. Hearing of my presence in the town, he elected to stay the night in order to meet me.

The room was fairly small, and Charles had previously sent George to arrange with the proprietor—one of the best lieutenants he had in the district—that they were not to be disturbed.

Laurent and Charles were the first two British officers to have been landed in the Unoccupied Zone since the war had begun. The majority of the early members of the French Section had been planted in the Occupied Zone.

* Lt. Marcel Fox.

It was an odd state of affairs that I should be sitting at the same table with these pioneers. This getting together was one of the things that London had always warned me against most strongly. It had been pointed out to me that in the event of anyone of such a gathering being captured he might, in a moment of weakness under torture, admit that he had met and known the others. Once this admission had been extracted, it would only be a matter of time until the group's entire conversation was divulged as well as the date and place of their meeting. With the subsequent arrest of the restaurant proprietor, who would be suspect, another piece of the jigsaw puzzle would fall into place to help the Gestapo catch each one of them in turn. That, of course, was painting the picture in its blackest form. At best, the captured man would refuse to talk, but he would not have had to suffer torture if they had not met. The ideal way of operating was to accept a solitary life, to meet only when absolutely necessary, and to know as little as possible about everyone else.

But the temptation for the others to meet me was very great. For six months or so they had been working hard at their lonely tasks, and here was someone straight from home. I brought them news of fresh activity, increased supplies. My disposition was naturally a gay one and I would know all about life in London and how they were taking the bombing. I would know how the war was going and all Winston's latest quips. I would recharge their dynamos, which were not deflated, but rather stale.

I could sense all this. Though I was a stickler for form and capable of hardening my heart against those whom I suspected of swinging the lead, I knew I would be a pompous ass to throw ice into the warm atmosphere which my friends created. These people were doing a dangerous job. Their smiling, inconspicuous faces were like my own. A trace of weariness behind the smiles was the mark of those who had known fear and faced reality, whilst knowing that there was more to come. I felt a bond between myself and my companions, so I let go the brakes and joined in with their mood.

The next day I found Charles sitting at a small table in a good and discreet restaurant where we were due to lunch. I sat down beside him. After greeting each other and agreeing that the weather was not fit to be discussed, Charles picked up the menu, glanced at it, then, leaning forward as though suggesting a variety of dishes, he said:

"If you were to take that folded newspaper on the table into the toilet just behind you, you'd find it contained the answer to all your dreams."

"How thoughtful of you!" said I, putting my hand on the paper and getting up. "Whatever you choose will suit me."

Locking myself into the toilet, I opened the newspaper. Inside were three ration books, one for an adult, one for a heavy worker, and on the cover of the third was the name Pierre Chauvet, on the next line appeared an authentic address in Lyon, and in the bottom right-hand corner was an official stamp and the signature of the Mayor. Inside my ration book I found the textile card and tobacco card that Charles had also promised me. I slipped these into my wallet and put the other two into my empty left-hand breast pocket. Then, taking out a pencil, I wrote down on a piece of paper the name and address of someone in Leatherhead. Below the address I wrote in capital letters the words: LEONORE NOW FLOURISHING Putting this note inside the newspaper, I folded it twice and returned to my table.

Charles had ordered, and we had an excellent meal together, sharing a bottle of Côtes du Rhône burgundy. It made all the difference when you knew the ropes, and this was obviously the case with Charles. He was a man of the world. He had good manners and a quiet and commanding way with him.

During our conversation I thanked him for producing the ration books so quickly and asked him to get Germaine to send the telegram which he would find inside the same newspaper. Charles said he would see to it that afternoon before exploring the countryside on his bicycle with George, who had the afternoon off from the bank.

We parted after lunch. I, having nothing to do, went to a cinema and saw an old favorite of mine, "Carnet de Bal."

Afterwards I went to a small café for a drink. I then dined alone in a modest way and read the paper. I gave the correct coupons out of my own ration book as though I had done it a thousand times. I was delighted to see that no one, not even the waiter, looked at me as though I were anything other than another Frenchman. I was beginning to feel my feet. I ordered an Armagnac, and as I warmed the glass between my hands I thought of my parents and of my brothers. Maybe, I thought to myself, they're doing the same thing—for it was my birthday.

CHAPTER X

THE LYON–MARSEILLE morning express was gathering speed. From my second-class corner seat that George had reserved for me, I surveyed the wintry scene. The train was passing through the manufacturing district in the south of Lyon, and above the vast silk warehouses, factories, and petrol refineries hung the same foreboding curtain of clouds as on the previous day. The snow lay thick on the ground, but even this white carpet was unable to reflect much light into the compartment. There was no heating, every seat was occupied, and the corridor was packed with humanity. The atmosphere was charged with chilly gloom and suspicion. Nobody talked. The few faces that were visible behind their protective newspapers were grimly set, as though to face an unpleasant ordeal. From what I had read of the German-controlled Press, I imagined that there could be little escape or distraction for a good Frenchman in the papers. Every article was biased and written with a Nazi Lueger pointed at the author's head.

I supposed that owing to the presence of the millions of surplus people who had fled to the Unoccupied Zone, and to the almost total absence of cars and buses on the roads, the trains would always be overcrowded. In a way this would be an advantage for people like me, as there was a greater chance of being lost in the crowd. This was about the only consoling thought I could muster up in my drafty corner, for even when the four-hours' journey was over, the trickiest part of my program would still lie ahead of me. Fortunately Germaine—who had left in advance—would be there to introduce me to Olivier. She had struck me as a woman who would overcome any obstacle, and if I was inclined to shudder at her accent, I thought it was perhaps preferable that it was so obvious, otherwise it might have aroused suspicions through a state of near perfection.

I began to think about Colonel Deprez. All I had to work on was the knowledge that he was the manager of a large ice factory and also the leader of the local ex-Service Men's League. The organization's main activity was the recruiting of men for the French Legion that was being trained by order of the Germans to fight with them against our Russian Allies on the Eastern Front. And yet, paradoxically, Deprez had a soft spot for Britain, which was evident from the fact that he had been awarded the D.S.O. for services rendered in the 1914–18 war. The prospect of interviewing this man with a view to asking for his help in the release of ten imprisoned men—even if they were French—was not exactly inspiring. I ran over the men's names once more. Then I closed my eyes and slept fitfully.

At Marseille I found Germaine waiting for me on the platform. To avoid the inquisitive reception committee at the barrier, she took me into the crowded buffet and out by a side door.

She told me that Marseille was one of the worst towns in which to operate. Being a port of considerable consequence, with a mixed population of over a million—much of it of a rather low order—it came in for a great deal of attention from the Gestapo, who were everywhere in civilian clothes and in force at the station barriers.

"Lucky they haven't discovered the buffet exit yet," I said as we descended the wide steps that led down to the town.

"Yes, but anyway our papers are in perfect order. They might have been a little stuffy about me, although they can't do much to neutrals. As for your being with me, we've got our answer to that, too."

We walked past the Hotel Splendide, which Germaine pointed out as being the headquarters of the Gestapo, and then down to the Canebière—the main street which leads from the port right up through the town. Here we turned right, and also took the next to the right into the Cours Belsunce.

There was no snow in Marseille, but it was bitterly cold and the pavements were thronged with people. They looked thin and hungry and many of them very poor.

I was struck by the speed and ease with which my companion walked. I said to her, "Is it true about your foot, Germaine?"

"Yes," she replied, smilingly, "it's actually made of aluminum, and there's an opening where it fits round the heel."

"Good heavens!" I exclaimed. "A walking ground-floor letter box that nobody would ever find. Hermes had nothing on you, Germaine."

"You're right. You'd be surprised at what goes into my aluminum puppy."

She led me into one of the many cafés in the square, past the crowded tables in the glass veranda and into the main room. She stopped by a corner table, and shook hands with a young man who was sitting alone. She sat down and motioned me to follow suit.

Olivier was a fair-haired youth whose clothes and manner were sober. When I heard him speak I found it hard to realize that the French Section's admirable choice for Marseille was actually an Englishman.

"The town's crowded out," he said to me, "but I've managed to fix you up in a tiny room at the hotel where I stay. It's quite close by. I think it must have been a box room in better days. Its only window opens up onto the garbage shoot. If you close the window there's no air, and if you open it I'm afraid it's rather like sticking your head into a dustbin full of dead chrysanthemums. Anyway, it'll be quiet, which is some compensation. You have to look for compensations in this sort of life, but so far I haven't found many in this town."

"Never mind," I said. "I'd rather sleep with the dead chrysanthemums than spend a night at the Splendide. I wonder if you'd mind looking after my case, as I've got to see a man this morning. By the way, do you know the Rue Montgrand?"

"Cross the Canebière and you'll find it about five streets up. If you're free for lunch let's meet in the next café up. You'll find Germaine or me there."

"Splendid!" I said. "See you both later."

Just before 11 A.M. I found the Ice Works. Deprez was in, according to the clerk, and would see me in a few moments.

I was very glad to have been given a description of this man beforehand, for when he came in I knew that it could not be anyone else. I told him, without any hemming or hawing, that I had come from England, where I had left Captain de G. a month previously, and that the latter had told me that he had been one of his—Deprez'—Liaison Officers in the French Army; that they had been stationed at Rennes and Caen, among other places; that their last meal had consisted of *bouillabaisse* and two bottles of Moselle at Basso's restaurant, and that they had discussed ways of getting through the Pyrenees.

Deprez nodded, and expressed his satisfaction on hearing that his friend had managed to return safely to England. Before saying anything further, he got up and went to the door. He opened it as though about to go out, closed it again, and walked back to his chair, satisfied that nobody was listening in the passage. Then, placing both hands on the table, he leaned forward, looking me straight in the eyes.

"Monsieur," he began, "I am perfectly satisfied with your bona fides. What can I do for you?"

"*Mon Colonel,*" I replied, "there are ten men imprisoned at St. Nicolas, and my Chiefs feel that their release is of paramount importance. If you were prepared to use your influence, they would consider your help in getting them out as a war service worthy of high recognition. As far as money is concerned, there is practically no limit, and if you could agree to handle this delicate matter, I can produce the sum required for purposes of bribery in a matter of hours."

My words were followed by a moment of deadly silence. I had imagined this situation at least a dozen times before. I wondered if Deprez would press a bell and have me thrown out, or call the cops, or fly into a tearing rage. I felt as though I were sitting with my feet over the hole of an aircraft ready for "action stations." Only in this case my eyes were on the telephone, the bell buttons, and the man opposite. Whatever he chose to do, I was quite decided to silence the Colonel in one way or another and get out of the building as fast as possible. I was pretty sure I could vanish in the crowd with a safe lead from any pursuer.

"What are the names of these men?" came Deprez' voice at last.

The thumping in my ears died down and I ran off the names as though calling the roll from a printed sheet.

Deprez gave no hint of recognizing a single name. He said, quietly, "I sympathize with their lot and your anxiety to get them out, but I cannot afford to associate myself with such a deal, as I am far too well known in Marseille, and the news would get around at once if I touched it. However, there is one man in this group—Ritner—who used to be a junior officer on my staff and, unofficially, I will do everything in my power to save him. In fact, I am obliged to you for the information."

Deprez got up. The interview was obviously at an end. But for Ritner it was a complete failure. Due to Captain de G.'s close wartime connection with Deprez, I shot my last bolt.

"*Mon Colonel,*" I said, "would you do me a personal service?"

"What is it?"

"Would you be prepared, if ever confronted with me, to say that you remember having seen me once on a visit to 50th Division Headquarters? My name is of no importance."

"Yes. That I am prepared to do."

We shook hands, and I left the office. As I wove my way through the throngs in the Canebière I ran over the conversation, trying to discover where I had failed. I had dangled a decoration under Deprez' nose and given him a big peek at the money, but all to no avail. If he had not even nibbled at this bait, there was no point in returning to offer him a directorship on the Suez Canal Board, or a seat in the House of Lords. I could not understand it. If his integrity was so unassailable, he could not possibly have hitched himself to the Pétain wagon for the sake of the money he was getting for sending the same men who had fought against the Germans to fight with them against the Russians. It did not seem to make sense.

And why was he prepared to confirm an important detail in my cover story?

I found Germaine writing postcards at the café table.

Looking up at me as I sat down opposite her, she said: "What's eating you?"

"Is it as obvious as all that?" I asked.

"You look like a crowd I once saw when they heard they'd lost the Ashes."

"I didn't know you'd ever been to Australia," I said.

"I haven't. But some day I hope to go there and meet some real athletes," cracked Germaine. "Why don't you tell me what's happened, or is it a State secret?"

"I suppose they intended it to be in London. Personally, I'd hoped to bring it off on my own, too. But since you're on the spot, two heads are sure to be better than one."

"I'm all ears," said Germaine.

"I was supposed to get a local man to help in springing ten men out of prison, but he won't play."

"Is *that* all?"

"Isn't it enough?"

"Depends."

"On what?"

"The size of the bribe."

"Anything up to a million," I quoted.

"Child's play," mocked Germaine. "What do they think we do out here? Consort with princes and high society? Why, there isn't one of us who hasn't got at least a couple of unscrupulous lawyers up his sleeve who would jump at a crooked assignment like that. If these prisoners are held in Marseille, Olivier will handle it for you. He's an expert at such transactions, and I'm a little too busy on a similar proposition in Lyon to take it on just now."

When Olivier joined us, I put the proposition to him. He undertook it without hesitation.

"If only you'd told me about this before, I could have spared you this morning's goosechase," was his only comment.

I knew that London would have preferred this question to be settled without Olivier or Germaine knowing anything about it, but seeing that it had not worked, I had no option unless I merely reported a failure and left those men to languish in prison.

Having handed this task over to Olivier, the two of us went into the café toilet and locked ourselves in. When we emerged a few minutes later, Olivier was a millionaire. I arranged that the entire balance of money was for him after he had settled the question of the ten men and, having done this, my mission was over.

On a piece of paper I wrote the name and address of someone living in Colchester and below it these words: MARIUS FIRST TOOTH ONLY VISIBLE AS YET. I gave this to Germaine, and asked her to have it telegraphed when she had a moment. I knew that in a very short time, when this wire was redirected to my headquarters, they would guess what I meant and then warn Barcelona to expect me.

CHAPTER XI

THE FOLLOWING DAY, Olivier's courier brought my attaché case plus laundry from Antibes. Wrapped up in my underwear was a small bottle of *Marc*. After lunching with Olivier, Germaine and I set about the next problem, which was "how to get back to England."

I had been given the name of a man whose brother was said to run a small fishing fleet at Port Vendres. This old bandit had apparently been an influential smuggler for the past twenty-five years, paying his dues to the Catalonian Civil Guards and the French Gendarmes with punctilious regularity, and he was therefore considered a good bet His name was Tomas, and he would not look at anyone who did not come with a note of introduction from his brother in Marseille, who, in his turn, was quite a big pot on the waterfront.

We found the man finally, but it was no soap, and I resigned myself to crossing the Pyrenees on foot. Luckily, I had carefully studied the mountain route which Captain de G. had shown me, so I was not completely unprepared.

After hearing the bad news I caught a tram that took me close to my rendezvous with Germaine.

Cutting through a narrow side street to reach the "Vieux Port," I found my way barred by two men, one of whom wore the official white armband bearing the letters S.O. (Service d'Ordre) of a new branch of the Vichy Government police instigated for the repression of the black market.

Realizing their significance and that I had nothing compromising on me (unless they emptied every single pocket, one of which contained the sample ration cards), I decided to bluff it out with them. Besides, it would only prove that I was hiding something if I made a dash for it and were caught.

"Your identity card!" said the man with the armband. I brought out my wallet and produced my card.

"Nice lot of bank notes tucked away in that wallet," said the man, with a suspicious leer.

"What about them?" I said, still supposing I was dealing with officials. I then noticed the second man stiffen and push something forward in his overcoat pocket

"We're looking for likely people to volunteer for work in Germany, but I think we could come to terms. After all, one must live and let live, Monsieur."

"How much do you want?" I asked.

"Let's see," said the man, looking at my identity card. "Age: twenty-nine. Profession: Free-lance journalist Not exactly a reserved occupation for a healthy young man, is it? If we were to take you along to headquarters you wouldn't get very far on that. I think, on the whole, if you were to empty that bulging compartment we might call it a deal."

"But that's all I've got in the world," I said, trying it on.

"Monsieur, you still have your freedom," said the man skilfully extracting the notes.

"Charming!" I said, moving off with a shrug.

As I made my way to my rendezvous with Germaine, I did not know whether to be furious or relieved at the outcome of this venture. Twenty-five thousand francs down the drain. Was this a holdup or the real thing? I still had my own private belt containing 65,000 francs. Lucky thing, I thought, that they had provided me with so much money. And yet I hated the idea of losing any of the Treasury's supply almost as much as if it had been my own. I wondered if I should have fought my way out, but then remembered the significant bulge in the other man's pocket.

"Well, I'll be damned!" I muttered to myself, as I hurried along the Canebière.

The pavements were crowded with people. In this town of a million inhabitants it seemed to me as though they must all be out of doors. I spotted a man with a Leica camera some fifty yards ahead, aiming at the passersby. Automatically I crossed over to the other pavement. I did not want my picture in any rogues gallery.

Presently I reached the chosen café. Germaine was not there, so I sat down at the far end facing the door and waited. I ordered a Cinzano and took a good gulp of it to calm my nerves. Then I lit a cigarette from a packet that Germaine had procured for me, lifted down one of the café newspapers which was hooked to a nearby rack, and pretended to read it.

I wished Germaine had been there. It was not like her to be late. She had said she would be waiting for me. There was a nasty atmosphere in this town, and I would be glad to see the back of it. I wondered how Olivier could have stood it so long. Then I thought of what Bernard had once told me: "One can get accustomed to almost anything " Yes, I thought, provided one has nerves of steel. Always on the alert, always on the defensive, always in the wrong. One could not afford to get into trouble even in a back-alley affair such as I had just experienced. The inevitable inquiries would be a waste of time, as well as dangerous, and were to be avoided at all costs. The thing was to be patient and always under control. I finished my drink and ordered a second.

I left this glass untouched, but lit another cigarette Drawing on it deeply I let my mind wander off into the mysterious labyrinths and complications of this weird and dangerous mode of warfare. I smiled at the thought of Laurent's nerve in throwing his London-made identity card into the fire and calling at the Town Hall for a new one, complaining bitterly that his had been stolen. Olivier had told me this story and how Laurent's indignant protestations had made him known as a respectable citizen with the authorities, not to mention his success in obtaining genuine papers. I wondered how many stories Laurent could tell about Olivier.

"Think of the devil," I said to myself as Olivier came striding up to me between the tables. Catching a glimpse of Germaine just inside the entrance, I knew something was wrong.

"Let's go," said Olivier quietly, shaking hands with me. "There's a flap on."

Throwing down a note beside my untouched drink, I got up and we went out, preceded by Germaine.

Olivier took us both by an arm and hurried us up a side street. When we turned into the Rue du Paradis I said, "What's it all about?"

"They're raiding the cafés," he replied tersely, leading us up a flight of stairs to his small flat.

As he closed the door behind us, Germaine exclaimed:

"*Bon Dieu,* what a town! Lucky thing you knew that inspector, Olivier."

"What is all this?" I inquired.

"It's a long story. But in short, it's this. Every now and then the police cordon off a road and grab all the people they find sitting in the cafés for slave labor in Germany. We've just escaped from one of those traps."

"What happened?" I asked.

"When they'd got everyone in our café lined up and passing in front of the District Police Commissioner on their way to be packed off in locked trains to Germany, I caught the inspector's eye, while hanging onto Germaine's arm to show that she was with me. The inspector, who's an old prewar friend of mine, said to one of his men:

" 'Take those two into that back room. I want to see them privately. When you come out, lock the door behind you.'

"Well, of course, we just got out of the window, and here we are."

"Do you mean to tell me that French police are doing this sort of thing to French citizens?" I asked.

"Good heavens, yes!" said Olivier. "It's like this. Pétain has been forced to open offices in every town in France for the purpose of recruiting voluntary labor for Germany. But although the people are tempted to go there with promises of good food, good pay, concerts, and regular paid holidays, very few seem to enter these offices. As a result, the Germans come down on the Vichy Government like a ton of bricks, and they, in turn, relay the threat to the prefects of police in large towns such as Marseille that if they don't produce, say, three hundred workers by such and such a day, the Germans will either collect policemen for the work or have to consider occupying the whole country."

"I still think it's a bit steep that the police should accept the carrying-out of those orders."

"They thought so, too, at one time," said Olivier. "But they were very soon brought into line."

"How?" I inquired.

"Some time ago they flatly refused to undertake one of these raids. I think their wives shamed them out of it."

"Good for them!" said Germaine.

"It wasn't so good, as you'll see. The Germans were hopping mad, and shortly afterwards, at a Police Sports' meeting in the Marseille Stadium, they grabbed the whole lot as they left the ground. They were driven to the station in their own Black Marias and bundled unceremoniously into a waiting train."

"Weren't they allowed to pack a bag?" asked Germaine.

"Not on your life. They got the full dose of the New Order, and were yanked off to Germany under guard, without even being allowed to say good-bye to their families."

"Good Lord!" I said. "What lovely people! What a cozy little spot! Oh, you almost made me forget"—I interrupted myself—"I've just survived a two-man raid myself."

"What do you mean?" they inquired.

"Couple of spivs with an S.O. armband between them held me up for the same purpose, or so they said. . . . I didn't even have to think of bribing myself out of it—" I broke off the sentence.

"They thought of it for you," concluded Olivier.

"The stinking gangsters!" said Germaine. "Those weren't S.O. cops."

"Not that they're much better," observed Olivier.

"What did it cost you?" asked Germaine.

"Twenty-five thousand."

"Judas! What a day!" cried Germaine.

"It's consoling to think of my gangster's philosophy," I said.

"What philosophy?" asked Germaine.

"He put it all in a nutshell when he said, 'Monsieur, you still have your freedom!' "

"How right he was," said Olivier. "After each narrow escape, freedom becomes more precious than ever. It's our greatest compensation; our highest reward."

"Talking of freedom," said Germaine, "how did you get on with old Tomas?"

"Nothing doing. His brother's 'in' for the duration for smuggling."

"Better and better," came Germaine's comment.

"Doesn't matter. I've got another address up my sleeve for Perpignan. If that fails, I can walk it on my own. I've been shown a route," I said.

"You're probably crazy enough to do that," said Germaine. "But my advice is that if your Perpignan contact fails, just stick around the Hotel de la Cloche. Charles and Laurent spent a couple of nights there after they were landed, and I know the proprietor is a sympathizer."

"Thanks for the tip," I said, already aware of this hotel.

"I'll have one of my chaps reserve you a second-class ticket for the nine-thirty tomorrow morning, if you like," suggested Olivier. "It'd be dangerous for you to go near the station this afternoon."

"It'll be a humming hive of hatred," put in Germaine.

"Thanks, Olivier. I'd appreciate that," I said, with feeling.

"I don't think it's safe for him to go to Perpignan alone," said Germaine, after a moment, with a glance at Olivier.

"What *do* you mean?" I said, looking at the girl a trifle pompously. "It can't be any worse than this stinking hole."

"That's what we all think when we first arrive in a strange

place," she said, as though addressing a five-year-old. "The atmosphere takes a little time to penetrate our thick skulls. But it's there, nevertheless. It hasn't been waiting for us to arrive before maturing. If you don't believe me, ask Olivier."

"She's perfectly right," corroborated that witness. "But far be it from me to try to teach my grandmother to suck eggs."

"Don't mind me," I said. "I'm still in the kindergarten, and I confess I can hardly wait to become a grandmother in this business."

"Very well, then," continued Olivier. "On arriving in a place like Perpignan you imagine you're in a pleasant small town of a semi-Spanish aspect, miles away from the turmoil and strife of espionage, counterespionage, informers, traitors, and racketeers. But, of course, you're dead wrong. It's only after a day or two that it suddenly begins to dawn on you that the man with the lizard's face, hanging around the hotel lounge, is a guide tout who'll presently try to squeeze you dry before producing a guide; the slimy-looking specimen sitting alone at the opposite table in the restaurant, and who is never short of cigarettes, is an informer whose face you suddenly remember having seen at the station bookstall. And as for . . ."

"All right, all right," I chipped in. "What's it all leading up to?"

"Just what I said," observed Germaine, stifling a yawn "Someone ought to go with you."

"Who, for instance?" I inquired.

"I could spare two or three days," said Germaine. "Besides, there's no better cover to be had in this country than to be seen in the company of a girl. A seemingly carefree couple, on holiday, is just the right sort of impression to give in a place like Perpignan."

"They even recommend it at home," I said. "And personally I should be delighted to have your company, if you can really spare the time "

"Then that's settled," said Olivier. "I suggest you both lie low this afternoon, and that we foregather tonight at the Angleterre, by which time I should have two reserved tickets for Perpignan."

"Better make them both 'returns,'" suggested Germaine. "It'll make our cover even better."

"Top marks, Germaine," said Olivier.

CHAPTER XII

THE NEXT DAY I was up early and went to fetch Germaine at her hotel. We walked slowly up the hill to the station.

Though there were ordinary taxis in Marseille, Germaine said few people ever took them, for it meant giving your name and address to the foreman on the taxi rank, who put it down in his notebook. Not that this was more dangerous than having to fill out a hotel register, she said, but simply because of an impression that the less you wrote down your name the longer your lease of life.

On reaching the station barrier we were stopped and asked for our papers. I handed mine to a man on the opposite side of Germaine so that there could be no question of our being together. After a long scrutiny my identity card was handed back with a scowl.

I caught sight of Germaine fifty yards up the platform and followed her slowly. After joining forces we found our reserved seats.

It was something to have passed the barrier. It was even better to have reserved seats on the Perpignan express.

When at long last the train started, it was a great relief to the two of us to be leaving Marseille and to be going in this direction.

After many hours and two changes, we reached Perpignan. It was bitterly cold, as it had been everywhere else. In fact, if there was one thing that I would remember better than any other about this whole venture, it was that I had felt like an icicle most of the time, except when I had some liquor inside me, which was fairly often but not often enough. Germaine was only half so affected, owing to her false foot. This, however, did not prevent her from being the most genial of companions, and she never complained about anything.

After passing through the ring of police and other armed gentry at the station, we boarded a tram which, as usual, was overflowing with humanity. Germaine managed to find a seat inside, while I stood guard over our two suitcases on the back platform. As the tram started getting under way, a sportsman suddenly boarded the rear platform with a pair of skis and sticks, and many of the outriders were poked about the head and body by this advancing windmill. One of his skis rammed the upper suitcase of my heap, and as there was no gate, this case shot out into the road. I quickly opened the door and told Germaine at which stop to get out and then, after a few warnings from the public to be *prudent,* I jumped off the platform and raced back up the hill.

Fortunately, the case had fallen at the feet of an honest man, and this rare godsend was actually running in my direction to help me in the relay race. I thanked him in a breathless sort of way and, turning round, raced back after the tram. I did quite well for the first eight hundred yards, and actually closed to within twenty yards of the rear platform. From here I could clearly see the passengers watching this one-sided contest with about as much interest as one might vouchsafe to the sight of a bluebottle crawling over the body of a dead kipper. Even the man who had been responsible for my undignified plight had not the gumption to press the bell and give me a chance. I tried a final spurt—but so did the tram. . . .

I had to give it up, and followed the tramlines for a mile or so until I caught up with Germaine, who was sitting on her suitcase in the dark street.

We then made our way to the Clock Inn, where Olivier had been wise enough to make reservations in advance. The manager showed us to our rooms, and although he was obviously surprised at our requiring so much space, he made no audible comment, for he was a businessman as well as a Frenchman.

We found a first-rate restaurant nearby with a correspondingly good cellar. It was warm inside, and the walls were covered with vivid posters advertising the bullfights and cinema programs. In this atmosphere it was possible to work up a good laugh over the suitcase fiasco.

On the morning after our arrival, I noticed an unscrupulous-looking character hovering about the hall of the hotel, and without overstraining my imagination, it was fairly clear that this vulture must belong to that class of crook who lived off people like myself by selling them an introduction to a guide. I asked the manager who he was and what he did to keep the wolf and the gendarmes from his door. The manager said that he was a Russian Jew who went by the name of Popofski and confirmed that his occupation was precisely what I had imagined it to be. How right Olivier's warning had proved.

The manager of the Clock Inn was indeed no friend of the Axis, and he spoke warmly of Charles and Laurent whom he had harbored on their arrival in France six months previously when they had walked in from the nearby shore where they had been deposited by one of the Navy's feluccas. He went on to explain that Popofski had already done an eighteen-months' stretch in the local cooler, and was now an adept at keeping out of trouble with the gendarmes. Besides this, he added, his prices were quite reasonable. I asked him how many noughts there were in Popofski's spelling of that word, but as the manager did not appear to see anything very humorous in this crack, I supposed he must be an active partner in the setup.

As I was not at all in favor of Popofski's face, I decided to call at the address of my final contact where, if things went right, I would be provided with one of the organization's personal guides. It was a very complicated address, or so it seemed to me, and perhaps I only remembered it on that account. This was it: Madame Guiauchain, 45 Faubourg Carnot, Eaux Vives.

After some inquiry I managed to find this place. It was a poky little shop with a few sacks containing goodness-knew-what lying about the floor. I entered, and asked a man who was pumping up his bicycle inside if Madame Guiauchain was in. The man went through to the back regions and returned saying that she would be along in a moment. Then he left.

Shortly afterwards a dark woman of anything between thirty and fifty, wrapped in a soiled kimono, emerged from the recesses. She asked what she could do for me.

I gave her the "open sesame" phrase which was a simple affair—*"Bonjour, Madame, je suis de passage"*—but instead of encouraging me, her only reply was "So what!" A trifle nonplussed, I gave her part two of the password according to my repeated and well-rehearsed instructions—*"Je viens de la Suisse et je vais aux Etats-Unis."* She merely gaped at me. My orders in these circumstances were to retire gracefully, explaining that there must be some mistake. However, as this woman was entirely alone and did not look a very dangerous kind of scorpion, and in view of the complicated address, and this and that, I did not feel inclined to drop the matter quite so easily.

I threw out the opening gambit concerning the weather. I had noticed at home that this was as useful a way as any of warming up any kind of proceedings, whether it be to introduce an appeal for charity, a request for someone's hand in marriage, or the declaration of war, and I hoped that it might possibly lead to some signs of thawing in this monosyllabic pelican.

However, Madame Guiauchain was not interested in the weather, but perceiving that I was still in her shop, she asked me pointblank:

"What do you really want?"

"A guide to take me across the Pyrenees," I replied in a flat voice, and watching closely for her reactions.

"I have absolutely no connection with anything of that nature," said the woman, looking down, and I was fairly certain that this was untrue, since a real grain merchant whose husband was not a guide would have been more likely to say that this was a grain shop and that she was completely baffled by the mention of the words "guide" and "Pyrenees."

As it was perfectly clear that something had gone wrong, I raised my hat and wished her a very good day. Just as I was leaving the shop she called me back and asked:

"Where are you staying?"

"What does that matter?" I retorted.

"If you come back at six tonight," hedged the woman, "I shall have given this matter some heavy reflection."

"So shall I," I said, walking out.

By the time I had gone a hundred yards I decided there was something very fishy in this business, and that I would not take any unnecessary risks at this stage in the proceedings.

So now there was nothing for it but to confide in Popofski, which was an idea I hated from head to foot. While discussing it all with Germaine, I said I would prefer to do the thing alone rather than have dealings with such a shark. Germaine thought this was nonsense, and repeated that there was no longer any future in solo trips. Besides, she added persuasively, the War Office would not mind how much it cost so long as they got their hands on those ration cards.

As there was unquestionably a great deal of sense in what Germaine said, I made an appointment with Popofski. The Russian beamed ingratiatingly as he shook my hand and heard what I wanted

"I have won a small bet with myself that you were a prospective client, and I assure you that I shall provide you with the best guide in the place as soon as he has returned from his last trip," he said.

"I sincerely hope that's very soon," I replied.

"I will contact you the moment he gets back," said the other.

Three days passed and nothing transpired, which was not to be surprised at, for Popofski was no mean psychologist and knew all about the sliding scale of charges that he could automatically increase in ratio to the impatience and anxiety of his customers.

This anxiety was accentuated in my case, for the continuous cold and the many nerve-racking events of the past twenty days had taken their toll of my sun-loving system by giving me the added discomfort of acute gastritis. So when I decided I would fox Popofski at his own game it was probably because desperation and pain had mastered my natural patience. It was in this state of mind, therefore, that on the fourth day of waiting I cornered Popofski and said,

"If you don't find me a guide by midday tomorrow, Monsieur, I shall move off without one."

"But this is madness," said Popofski. "The Pyrenees are a death-trap, and I shall have the man I promised tomorrow morning "

"Midday," I repeated. "Otherwise I need hardly point out that there will be no walnuts for your wallet."

It worked like a charm. At 11 A.M. on the next day Popofski found me and said:

"Monsieur Chauvet, by an unaccountable stroke of good fortune I have unearthed the king of all guides. He will come round with me to your hotel room immediately after lunch."

"Good," I said. "Now can I give you something in advance?"

"There is no need, Monsieur. The usual procedure is for the client to place four thousand francs in an envelope and leave it in the hands of a neutral person whom I suggest, in this case, should be the hotel proprietor. In the event of your going I shall claim the money. If for some reason you do not go, you get it back. This measure," he said, rubbing his hands, "is always adopted so as to create an atmosphere of confidence."

As this talk had taken place in Germaine's presence, I felt fairly satisfied, so I placed the sum in an envelope and we trooped off to give it to the stakeholder. I was now quite convinced that Popofski and the hotel proprietor were partners.

"It looks as if this might come off, all right," I said to Germaine on our way back to the hotel.

"Yes, something tells me that it will, too," she said. "I'd better start looking up a train or they'll be wondering in Lyon if we haven't both been picked up. I must also wire Barcelona that you're on your way."

"There's only one snag now," I said, as much to myself as to Germaine. "That is, that Major D. should have arrived in France in the meantime. I'd almost forgotten about him. He's from H.Q., and I was told that if he came he'd want to contact me to hear my news, so as not to go over the ground I'd covered. If he's arrived, he's sure to contact you. He may have arranged for me to be picked up by Lysander, but in the circumstances I wouldn't miss the Pyrenees for anything. Remember to call me back only if he says so Don't stop the crossing for any other reason."

"All right, Michel," answered Germaine.

Having looked up a train, we found that there was one leaving for Lyon at 12:20. Germaine packed her few belongings and together we boarded a tram for the station.

When it was almost time for the train to pull out, I took her hand and said:

"I don't know what I should have done without you, Germaine. What with your cheerful company, your good judgment, and your visits to the chemist's shop to cure my jittery innards, these five or six days have been raised from their bare grimness to a period for which I shall always be grateful to you."

"Give them all my love at home, and tell them how beautiful the mimosa looks at this time of year."

"Is that a new password, or something?" I asked.

"No. Just a parting nonsense."

"Well, thanks for everything, Germaine. And *au revoir.*"

The train started to move. The whistle blew and she climbed the steps, pulled down the window and looked out.

"Au revoir," waved Germaine.

There was gratitude and affection in my answering wave.

I went back to our favorite restaurant for lunch, then I returned to my room and waited for the guide's visit.

At exactly 2 P.M. there was a knock at the door. Popofski entered with the guide, and a youth who turned out to be a Frenchman from Alsace. Popofski introduced me to the guide —Cortez—and said that the Frenchman would be joining the party.

The Alsatian boy was very excited at the prospect of getting away after spending three weeks in Perpignan. He was delighted at the knowledge that I was English, because the British Consulate would now be child's play, with me around to hold his hand. On hearing me speak Spanish with Cortez his joy was almost complete, but not quite. He could not believe that anyone speaking Spanish and French could really be English, so he asked me naively to say a few words to prove it.

This request immediately drew from me the opening lines of "Sam, Sam, pick up tha' musket," which I laid on in my best Yorkshire accent, at which I was not considered to carry any extra weight. The boy's face became more and more puzzled, and it was quite clear that he thought the whole thing was nothing but a huge swindle.

Cortez was a very handsome Spaniard of about twenty-five. He and I proceeded to discuss the expedition in detail, agreeing on a price and arranging to meet at 5 P.M. at a little café near the bus terminus on the following afternoon. Having explained this to the French lad, they left.

Shortly afterwards, Popofski returned and asked me for another thousand francs and gave me a long explanation for the reason for this. He said that his total charge was always five thousand francs for these operations. I handed it over, and he went away satisfied.

I then left the hotel and went hunting for cigarette ends, but the afternoon bag proved to be a very scruffy lot

The next day I took a satchel out of my attaché case which Captain de G. had given me for this trip and filled it with food which I had stored and the minimum amount of my belongings. I paid my hotel bill and told the manager he could inherit my attaché case and other belongings in the event of my departure.

CHAPTER XIII

AT 4:30, Popofski showed up with the Alsatian and the guide, and we checked up on our kit before leaving for the café. The Alsatian was in a prodigious state of excitement, and little wonder, after lying low for so long, not to mention the months he must have spent pounding the highway before reaching this point.

As for me, I was a person who never imagined anything was ever going to come off until it actually had, although this feeling never prevented me from doing everything possible to see that it did. So far, I had had all the luck, but that this should work smoothly into the bargain was too much to anticipate.

My philosophy was well founded, for just as we were on the point of leaving my room there came the sound of hurried footsteps outside in the corridor. We all turned round and listened. The footsteps stopped outside my door and there was a knock. I opened up and it was the hotel porter. He handed me a telegram.

Now, as Germain was the only person who had my address and as she was not the kind of person to waste time and money on sending me the season's greetings, I knew that this was the red light as far as the Pyrenees were concerned.

After reading the telegram I handed it round and in silence the others read the words: HOLD EVERYTHING STOP MANAGING EDITOR WISHES TO SEE YOU TOMORROW STOP SIGNED LE CONTRE.

When the Alsatian had read it he looked at me with perspiration all over his forehead, and said:

"*Merde, alors!* Another five minutes and you would never have received this wire Why don't you pretend you never got it? Who's to know? You might easily have left before it arrived. If you don't come, the guide won't take me alone."

"Well," I said, "I'm just as disappointed as you are, but the telegram means that the captain of my aircraft has been found, and as he doesn't speak a word of French, I'm sure you will agree that it's rather natural that I should give him a hand."

"Oh, I see," said the unhappy youth.

Popofski took it very well, and assured the Alsatian that it was a case of *force majeure* and as Cortez was quite unmoved, the meeting closed.

When they had all gone, I walked up to a small piece of furniture beside the bed and gave it an almighty kick. The thing collapsed like a house of cards, accompanied by the sweet music of the shattered chamber within. That penalty goal cost me seven hundred francs, and it represented about the best value of any item on my expense account. I wondered if the War Office would write it off, later, as a free kick.

I then went out to visit several drinking establishments, where I drowned my disappointment in a good quantity of alcohol that was full of headaches. I was glad of one thing, and that was that there were no crazy closing hours in this country, and I almost pitied any German agent who might be trying to console himself anywhere in England about 5 P.M.

Toward seven o'clock I made my way to my favorite restaurant, and after giving myself some more encouragement in the form of a Châteaux Margaux 1929, I went to a cinema to see what the dubbing was like in a splendid double feature showing "A Slight Case of Murder" and "You Can't Take It With You." It proved excellent.

It must have been 11:30 before I closed the hatches on this evil day. I could not have slept very long before there was a heavy hammering close by, which I clearly recognized as coming from the bedroom door and being in no way connected with the fiend who was breaking stones like a Stakhanovite inside my head.

I quickly prepared myself for anything as I opened the door. Happily it was only the night porter announcing that some uncivilized person wished to have words with me on the telephone downstairs. Putting on my dressing gown, I followed him down to the desk, where I picked up the receiver. Very far off I could just make out George's voice saying, "Germaine is in a coma and keeps repeating your name."

"I'll be on the first train," I replied, "if she's as bad as all that."

"Good man!" said George. "And in case you don't know it the first one pulls out of Perpignan at exactly four A.M. Can you get it?"

"Certainly," I said. "Tell her to keep her chin up and that I shan't be long."

Now that I knew the next move, I started making a plan of action. My first stop was at the hotel manager's bedroom, where I had to make a considerable noise before he would open up. Finally his door opened about an inch, and a sleepy voice asked what in hell it was all about. In a few words I told him I was leaving for the interior by the next train, and that I had come to collect the money he was holding.

I was prepared to apply any one of a series of lowdown attacks to enforce my claim, but there was no need for any unpleasantness, for the proprietor walked straight over to a vase and produced the envelope. I shook hands with him, apologized for disturbing him at such an ungodly hour, and said that I would be glad to recommend his hotel to other airmen who were walking home. Then, after getting the night porter to promise to pull me out at 3:15, I settled down to a short sleep.

The porter did not forget to rouse me, and within a very short space of time I was downstairs with my attaché case, the satchel being wrapped up inside for later use—I hoped. I tipped the porter a hundred francs and made my way through the dark streets to the station on foot, since it was too early for trams.

When I got off the train at 6:15 that evening and had passed the barrier with its tireless reception gang, I found Germaine in her favorite place beside the newspaper kiosk, and by the expression on her face I could see that something was very wrong. I imagined that this visit was nothing but a red herring, after all And that is precisely what it proved to be.

Germaine informed me that one of our biggest operators from another zone had heard that I was in France and wanted to see me urgently. She said that he would be waiting at 5 A.M. in the Clermont-Ferrand rest room for the arrival of the train that left Lyon in exactly fourteen-minutes' time. Charles was to accompany me on this trip, and our seats were already reserved. Germaine said that this visit was none of her doing.

I was simply furious at having been dragged back all this way just as everything was set for crossing the Pyrenees. Charles arrived in the middle of this, and also tried to impress me with the importance of meeting this man. I knew this was all nonsense. If everyone wanted to see me, there would simply be no end to it. But as I had come so far, I decided that I might as well do the rest.

We walked toward the crowded train, and Germaine handed me a hamper, which she had somehow managed to fill with a magnificent picnic. I thanked her for this kind thought. Charles and I then boarded the train just as it was moving out. It took us a good hour to find our reserved seats, wading past the masses of people who were crowding the corridors as usual, and by that time we were quite ready to open up the hamper.

It contained bread, butter, chicken in aspic, and a bottle of wine.

It was quite evident that nobody in the compartment had the foggiest notion that Charles and I were British officers, and indeed, after all this traveling around, I did not feel very much like one, although if anyone were to have asked me what it felt like to be a British officer, even when I was in full fancy dress, I would probably have been unable to tell them. As for Charles—Lieutenant J. Dolan—even I would have put him down as a Frenchman.

At about 5·20 A.M. we reached Clermont-Ferrand. Charles and I got out and went straight to the restaurant, where our man was already waiting for us.

After a putrid cup of coffee we made our way to the rest room, which lay between two sets of tracks, and it was extremely cold in this drafty refrigerator. I was so worn out by the endless journeys and lack of sleep that what I generally used to think with was quite clogged up. However, I managed to gather that our friend had made me come all this way merely to explain that he was rather surprised that the Section had not included his zone amongst my ports of call. He also told me a great many things that did not concern me or my mission. I was simply delighted when he got up and left, and so was Charles.

I was not at all amused over all this foolishness, and could not help thinking that by now I would probably have been in Barcelona if I had followed the Alsatian's advice and ignored the telegram that had arrived two days earlier.

Charles and I went off to the largest hotel in the place, and while waiting for some people to vacate their room, we had some coffee and bread-and-jam in the dining room, where we saw the German orderlies carrying off the best victuals to their Lords and Masters upstairs.

The rest of the day I spent sleeping, while Charles pottered about the town and made sleeping-car reservations for the same evening back to Lyon By the time we had reached Lyon once more, I had just about caught up with my sleep, although in my view loss of sleep was almost as serious as losing the family jewels.

There was a foot of snow on the ground in Lyon, and I spent a dismal week end at Charles' house. However, there was good news from Germaine. She had been so upset at the stupidity of my forced and unnecessary return from Perpignan that she had gone round to her two friends at the American Consulate and more or less laid her cards on the table. When she had told them about me and asked them if they catered in traffic leaving the country in an irregular manner, they replied that they had a very good line in this sort of thing and would be only too glad to oblige her. They added that they had been helping R.A F. personnel to get back for quite a time and enjoyed the work enormously.

I was invited to call on these gentlemen with Germaine, and they showed me that hospitality for which their country is justly renowned The younger man of the two told me that after hearing Germaine's story he had immediately gone to Perpignan himself and seen their "number-one" guide, who would be expecting me at 11 A.M. on Tuesday at the second café below the station on the left-hand side. I was to sit at the table farthest from the door laying a torn postcard in front of me to prove my identity.

My American hosts explained that this guide was a kind of superman who conducted only emergency cases who had to get through at all costs; he never took batches of people, for fear of a slipup. They also asked me not to give them any publicity at the War Office for what they had done. I quite understood about the guide, and as for the second part I said: "Sure, sure," but all the time I had my fingers crossed. Obviously the French Section would not write to the papers about this event in wartime, but, when I told them the story—as I wholly intended to—they would merely hang up this friendly gesture on the records for future reference once the bells of Democracy got clanging again.

CHAPTER XIV

ON THE NIGHT of the first Monday in February I took the express that was due in at Perpignan just before eleven the next morning. Germaine saw me off at the station. I was feeling very pleased at the way things were going, for the news had just reached us from Marseille that one of the ten men was already out of prison, and that for the rest it was only a question of time. Germaine also told me that London would be informed from another source that I ought to be in Barcelona by the end of the week, and I had promised to send her a postcard of the Christopher Columbus monument on arrival. I also told her to get herself a large apartment and stop living in an hotel room, and said that I had no doubt I could persuade the Section to confirm this move. Finally, I thanked her for all the help she had given me.

The flat country around Lyon looked quite pleasant under its blanket of moonlit snow as it flew past the window next to my corner seat, but, then, anything would have looked pleasant to me at that moment. Yes, it had been a lucky trip so far. Charles, George, Laurent, the Doctor, Olivier, and Germaine were all set for months to come. They had received instructions and plenty of money, and they knew that they had not been sent out here to be forgotten. Also, they knew that their activities would be spoken of at home and that messages of theirs would reach loving and anxious families.

In my attaché case was another small hamper and a bottle of Armagnac that Germaine had given me for the Pyrenees. I drew deeply on my Lucky Strike cigarette, and felt the two packets in my pocket with satisfaction. Then I went to sleep.

When I woke, the sun was shining and the snow had vanished. Eventually the train pulled into Perpignan.

Two gendarmes were checking up on the passengers' papers, surrounded by the usual armed guards at the barrier. My papers passed their scrutiny without comment. Walking on air, I went to the station bookstall and bought the February railway timetables of the whole of France for my department. I knew what a feather it would be in their caps when briefing a new man to be able to say: "When you have buried your parachute walk east three kilometers up to the main road, then follow the road due north until you come to within two kilometers of the station of La Férté-sous-Joir. Spruce yourself up a bit and then catch the 5:14 train for Paris. You won't have to bother with timetables or have to ask any awkward questions." I also knew what a feeling of confidence such precise instructions would give to a man or woman who was setting out on one of these solitary, nerve-racking ventures, for there was no getting away from the fact that the first days in enemy-occupied or even unoccupied territory were enough to give anyone the jitters.

Then I set off to my rendezvous. The café in question was quite close to the station. There were very few people there at this early hour, and if any one of them was the guide, it was most certainly the young athlete talking to the café proprietor at the bar. At all events, he ignored my entry.

I sat down and ordered a drink. When I had been served I placed a postcard torn three-quarters of the way across the middle upon the table and waited to see what would happen. I did not have to wait very long before the young man at the bar made his way toward me. Stopping at my table and smiling broadly, he held out his hand and said, "My name is Pasolé," to which I truthfully replied, "I am very pleased to meet you. Won't you join me?"

Pasolé was unquestionably a magnificent specimen of manhood. He was perhaps twenty-eight years of age. He had fair hair, small strong teeth, and a fair complexion tanned by the sun. He was about five feet nine inches tall, and his tailor had had to use several meters of cloth to cover his broad shoulders.

He was dressed as though he were a subscriber to *Men Only.* He had on a pair of gray flannel trousers, a tweed sports jacket of excellent cut, with a dark-toned shirt to match. His tie was in faultless taste, and he wore a pair of heavy brown shoes. In fact, if Pasolé had been sipping a champagne cocktail in Piccadilly, his appearance would have marked him down as a 'varsity man just having one for the road before stepping into an ancient three-liter Bentley and going off to do whatever people do do who have such automobiles.

"You'll have no time to waste here, for we're off this evening at six-thirty," said Pasolé. "A taxi will take us the first twenty-five kilometers, then a short walk brings us to the frontier, where we shall spend the night in a barn belonging to a friend of mine. We'll rest there throughout the following day, and complete the trip on the next night. In the meantime you'd better rest up for the day in my room."

I got up, paid for my drink at the bar, and followed Pasolé up to his room. I found the place full of kit for the journey: a bulging rucksack, a huge parcel, loaves of bread, sausages, tobacco, etc.

"Perhaps it would help if I paid something of what I shall owe you, in advance," I suggested.

"Thanks," said Pasolé. "As you're a friend of my friends in Lyon, I propose taking you for twelve thousand francs. Is that all right with you?"

"Suits me fine," I said.

"If you'd let me have a thousand now, it'll pay for the black-market taxi. The rest will do on arrival."

I gave him a thousand-franc note.

"I'll give you a call at lunchtime," said Pasolé, taking the note and leaving the room.

I lay down on the bed with my hands clasped behind my head, gazing emptily at the low ceiling. An indefinable feeling of security pervaded the smuggler's untidy room. I had taken to Pasolé immediately.

Thanking my lucky stars that things had taken such a swift turn for the better, I rolled over on my side, dismissed all thoughts from my mind and, like a good soldier, went to sleep.

A little over an hour later Pasolé woke me.

"How about some lunch?" he said.

I jumped off the bed and uncorked my sleepy eyes in some cold water.

"Downstairs," said Pasolé, "you'll meet a Spaniard who's paying his way by helping me carry some of this junk across the frontier. He's a good chap, and I've known him for years. Like myself and the remnants of the Republican Army he was chased out of Spain by Franco's men. Since that day he hasn't seen his wife, who lives in Barcelona."

We went down to the café, and in a quiet corner I saw a ropey-looking individual who was introduced to me as Manuelo.

At first sight I found him a most unprepossessing scoundrel and felt sure he must be suffering from chronic consumption. However, if that were true, I concluded, then it only went to show what a spirited person he really was to undertake such a strenuous and risky excursion.

After they had exchanged a few words, Pasolé turned to me and said:

"Have you any objection to lunching with a young gendarme?"

"If he's a friend of yours it's all right with me," I said, not wishing to appear stuffy.

"He's my co-back in the Perpignan football team, and he tips me off so as to avoid snap controls."

"Let's lunch with him by all means," I urged.

The party was most agreeable and, as though by tacit and mutual consent, no leading questions were asked by anyone. Being something of a footballer myself, I was able to join in on the discussion of the merits of various French and Swiss teams, and this took our minds off the food, which was definitely not worth discussing.

After lunch I had a shave, and spent the afternoon sleeping in order to be fresh for the main event at 6:30.

A quarter of an hour or so before zero hour all our packs were ready. I had transferred my few possessions to the light hunting bag that I had kept rolled up in my case. At last it was to prove handy. I made a present of the case to Pasolé. A piece of string was found for the cardboard parcel that

Manuelo was to carry, and Pasolé's pack was further crammed until it must have weighed a good thirty kilos. As I raised it with both hands, Pasolé said:

"Radio parts. Four hundred per cent profit on that stuff. On the way back it will be stuffed with articles you can't get in France. It'll be waiting for me at my father's farm. All this weight on my back keeps me in training and doesn't do me any harm financially either."

I reckoned there must have been about twenty-five thousand francs in the round trip for Pasolé and that he earned every cent of it.

"One day I shall be able to buy a small villa for my wife and children," he added, producing a photograph of an astonishingly pretty girl smiling at two fine-looking children.

"Where are they now?" I asked.

"In hiding," said the guide.

Manuelo and I went downstairs and played French billiards to pass the time until Pasolé turned up with the taxi. He was punctual, a quality which augured well for the coming trip.

We all piled into the taxi, and it was almost dark when the driver began fiddling with the taps and lighting up the charcoal in the wartime stove attached to the back, which he used to fuel his cab. It took him three good clips before there was any spark of life from the motor. Finally it gave a dull splutter, and soon we were hiccuping painfully along the side streets. Bicycles overtook us in a most disconcerting manner, and I held my breath and prayed that the gas cooker with its little flame of hope would not drop off the stern or flicker out.

After a while the motor settled down to its work, and soon we were clear of the town and moving along with the trees swishing by. It was an agreeable sound for anyone who had not been in a car for some time.

Pasolé told us that if a patrol held us up he would do the talking, the story being that we were going to our factory for the night shift, having missed the last bus. He told us that the probabilities of any such holdup were very slight, as the gendarme with whom we had lunched had assured him that the road would be clear until 8 P.M.

It was slightly uphill all the way, and the old cab groaned along as best it could. Yet the idea of riding in the right direction, even in this ancient hack, was well worth a thousand francs. Eventually the driver turned off to the left up a small country lane and then pulled up in the middle of nowhere. Pasolé said this was the terminus, so we all got out.

CHAPTER XV

By now it was pitch dark, although there should have been a full moon, it being the third of February. But the sky was blotted out by a high, solid wall of cloud and, for our trio, the darkness was ideal. As Pasolé had placed me in the middle of the safari, I tied a white handkerchief to his rucksack, since I was quite incapable of seeing him even at a distance of two yards. I then placed another one on my own pack so as to help Manuelo follow me—for Manuelo was not the sort of character to own any white linen himself—and in this manner we moved silently forward through the night and up the foothills.

We followed Pasolé blindly and implicitly. He kept up a fast, steady pace, and it was just like the old days training in the Highlands, only this game was played for higher stakes and not just for a blister on your heel. We passed over fields, through hedges, small streams, and undergrowth. We took short cuts to find tracks known to Pasolé, and all the time we came back to the gap in the dim silhouette of the mountains away in the distance.

We passed through a village as silently as cats, then down some steps, across a stream, and away again up the side of the hill. Then began some serious climbing up a slope that was thick with cactus bushes. It became blacker than the inside of a coalpit, and as there was no path, we got utterly lost. But Pasolé was not in the least worried. He just trekked around in circles like a hound that has temporarily lost the scent, and eventually he hit the trail again with Manuelo and me close behind.

Pasolé often led us straight up some mountainside in order to avoid a detour, only to find it impassable, and these episodes were very tiring—especially for Manuelo—whose condition could not be compared to mine. Nevertheless, Pasolé found his way out of every maze.

The pace was soon too hot for Manuelo. I was sweating all over, as I was wearing everything I possessed except for a pair of pajamas. Over my clothes I wore my raincoat as a protection against the prickly pears.

The first slow-up was caused by two explosions that sounded like revolver shots fired just behind me. I dropped down flat and looked back. Then I heard Manuelo blaspheming in Catalan. When I returned to him I found that his cardboard box had come to pieces and two of the radio tubes had come into contact with nature's knitting-needles, causing them to explode. This merchandise was certainly never meant to put up with such a rough-and-tumble. When we reached a clearing, the clouds obligingly parted for a moment to allow the moon to shine on them. In this sudden illumination Manuelo's parcel appeared as nothing but a heap of twisted scrap that looked as though it would not have fetched a nickel in the Caledonian Market, but Pasolé said they were tough tubes, and Pasolé was always right. He retied the string and we set off again.

After about two solid hours of this killing pace we seemed to be getting higher up in the world, and then we came to another village.

"You must keep very quiet going through here because of the dogs," said Pasolé.

"Why don't you go round the place?" I asked.

"Have a look for yourself. We've got to take some risks or we'd never get there," said Pasolé.

My eyes had been glued to the ground so I shouldn't fall in the dark, and I looked up and saw two peaks rising sheer beside the village to a height of about eight hundred feet. In the narrow gap, between. lay the village.

"I see what you mean," I said, then, "How do you cope with the dogs?"

"If there's a hullaballoo we run. I've got some pepper, but if that fails, then I use this," he said, smacking a long knife that hung from his rucksack.

Silently we crept between the houses, but not silently enough for the vigilant dogs. First one started, then the warning was picked up by every dog in the place until the night was made hideous with sound. Lights flashed on here and there and the gruff tones of men's voices, disturbed in their early sleep, could be heard giving orders.

"Come on!" said Pasolé, and he began running with Manuelo and me at his heels. Slowed up by his heavy pack he was unable to outstrip us.

Having got through the village, he led us through some trees and up to a stream. We splashed our way up this for about three hundred yards. The going was painfully slow.

I was merely intent on following Pasolé in the dark, and deaf and blind to all else. Presently, however, I could not fail to notice the barking form of a large dog, smarter than the rest, who had followed us on the right bank.

Pasolé saw it, too, and shouted:

"Up here! Wait for me in that gap," and pointed at a low ridge in the skyline.

Manuelo scrambled past me, but since my hands were free, I thought I would stay by the guide and give him a hand if necessary.

Seeing us clamber out on the opposite side, the baffled animal plunged into the water and, half swimming, half scrambling along the rocky bed, it closed with the other bank.

I saw Pasolé reach for his knife. At the last moment he merely kicked the dog back into the swirling stream and it had not the stomach for a second attempt.

Hearing the rest of the pack gaining on us, Pasolé poured some pepper on the spot where we had been standing, and both of us made off through the trees as fast as we could go.

After a ten-minutes' climb we found Manuelo sitting just below the crest of the gap he had been aiming for. We stopped and listened. So still was the night that the sounds of distant barking and conversation came to us clearly over the trees and above the rushing of the stream. The retreating voices and spasmodic barks told us we were clear of the hunt.

Although Manuelo had reached the spot well before us, he was breathing painfully after his spurt. Owing to his bad lungs and the awkwardness of his ungainly parcel, whose shape had not been improved by its recent splashing in the stream, he was sorely handicapped, yet uncomplaining.

Looking at his compatriot, Pasolé said, "All right, Manuelo?"

The other nodded and got up.

Presently we emerged from the trees onto a mountain road. Pasolé gave his instructions.

"Don't drag your feet on the road. We'll walk at a two-hundred-yards' interval, with Manuelo in the middle. If I walk into a trap I shall talk loudly enough to warn you to get into the bushes. Should that happen, wait for an hour to allow me time to give anyone the slip and return. After an hour, if I don't come back, walk straight on to within three hundred yards of the Customs barrier at the top. Turn right up a steep hill, keeping the French and Spanish Customs sheds in view. They'll be a guide for your next move. Probably none of this will happen; it's only in case."

With these words Pasolé hitched up his enormous rucksack and set off along the road.

Manuelo and I watched his powerful form until it was swallowed up in the dark.

"What a man!" gasped Manuelo.

"You'd better go now," I said, realizing that Manuelo could never keep up Pasolé's pace.

When Manuelo had gone, I waited for a while and then brought up the rear.

The going was easy on the road, and, although I was not in good health, I felt I could go on forever in this direction.

Presently I saw Manuelo's slim form ahead and the parcel, tied round his back with a piece of string, wobbling from side to side. I slowed up to keep my distance, and noticed how slowly Manuelo was moving. A hundred yards at this pace, and I realized that Pasolé would get miles ahead and far out of earshot.

I closed rapidly with Manuelo, and placed one hand on the swinging parcel, adding a little pressure as well.

"You needn't push me. I can manage," said Manuelo, breathlessly.

"I'm only steadying the scrapheap," I said, agreeably, continuing to press lightly.

We moved on in silence.

After about half an hour we caught up with Pasolé, who was smoking a pipe behind a hedge by the road.

"Our troubles are practically over now," he said, coming out to meet us. "The barn we're aiming for is only two kilometers ahead. We'll leave the road here and take this short cut."

We stepped out with renewed heart. I found myself walking beside Pasolé with Manuelo about twenty yards behind. For a while it was not too steep to talk.

"If it isn't too indiscreet a question," began the guide, "what have you been doing in France?"

"Why, didn't my friends tell you?" I hedged.

"They just said you were a friend of theirs," he replied.

"Well, it's simple enough," I said. "I was a bomber pilot until I was brought down by flak."

"I've met plenty of them," said Pasolé. "But none of them spoke French like you do."

"I admit we're not very good at languages on the whole, and I believe most of the linguists are in the Fighter Squadrons."

"What squadron were you in?" asked Pasolé

"The number wouldn't mean anything to you, Pasolé."

"You'd be surprised."

"How many R.A.F. men have you taken to the other side?"

"Well over twenty, I should say."

"Well," I said, picking out a squadron in which my brother had trained, "I was in 605."

"It used to be 605," said Pasolé.

"What do you mean?" I asked, amazed.

"A Birmingham Auxiliary Squadron that no longer exists."

"How the devil do you know?" I asked.

"When people are tired and miles from anywhere and they trust you, they sometimes tell you interesting anecdotes. One remembers certain details, for no apparent reason; others one forgets. So far, with you it'll be the French. But we've hardly started yet."

"I'm considered more than a raw hand at Spanish, too," I said, avoiding the topic of the miles that lay ahead.

"You're lucky. I was born in the mountains, where we spoke only Catalan, and I didn't pay much attention to Spanish. They taught it in the schools, but somehow I never seemed to remain in any school for very long. I started work at fourteen."

I turned round and saw that there was no sign of Manuelo. We waited for him to catch up.

"Keep on the move, Manuelo. It's not much farther," said Pasolé.

We kept in a bunch and slowed down the pace to Manuelo's rate—or rather, just beyond it, so as to keep him going.

The path wound through the trees, and we staggered against roots and boulders in the dark. The gradient was always steep, but occasionally it seemed to go straight up the side of the mountain. Pasolé was in his element, but Manuelo and I were well-nigh done.

After an hour we were back on the road once more, having climbed about one thousand feet. By now Manuelo was staggering and half asleep on his feet.

As we plodded along the smooth surface, I turned to the guide and said. "Pasolé, why don't you tell us how far it really is? It's much easier to distribute one's strength over a distance one knows than to have to keep stretching it again and again."

"It's a curious thing," said Pasolé, "but during the Civil War I found that the soldiers in my battalion never liked the whole truth as to how far we were going, and my methods of understating distances proved so successful that it has become a habit with me, so as to encourage people to keep going. Anyway," he concluded, confidentially, "our farm is only two jumps around that bend up there."

After about half an hour's steady walking we reached the

bend, and from there on the two jumps proved to be about a kilometer in length. Only then was the barn in sight.

By the time we reached the barn I was in no condition to complain; as for Manuelo, he simply crumpled up on the straw and went fast asleep.

CHAPTER XVI

PASOLÉ AND I huddled up for warmth, but Manuelo's coughing spoiled our night.

At about 9 A.M., on February 4, the barn door creaked open, and in came the farmer with a pot of steaming coffee and three plates of eggs, which just went to show that "Pasolé's Guided Tours" were no kind of a slapdash enterprise.

It rained hard all day, so we spent the time huddled up over a little stove which was brought in, and Manuelo told us how he had worked in the mines from the age of fourteen and how the dust had got into his lungs. But this did not prevent him from entertaining us with Spanish songs, which he delivered in a husky but very pleasing alto voice.

Pasolé said his family consisted of four sisters and three brothers, besides himself, ranging between the ages of nine and thirty-two, who all lived happily in Bañolas with their father and mother—under the régime they had helped to bring into power. He said that his family was not very keen on the English, but would nevertheless see me through to the British Consulate in Barcelona.

During the afternoon the rain stopped, and it was agreed that we should set out to do the last lap of the journey at nightfall

We duly set off at 7:45 P.M. in the pitch dark, and the farmer's son led us up to the top of the Pyrenees, a distance of only eight hundred yards. Here, after seeing that the coast was clear, he left us. The view from the top was quite sensational. Down in the valley on our left shone the lights of Llansa. In the far distance Pasolé pointed out the lights of Figueras, the town that spelled disaster to so many Allied airmen and to countless others who tried to reach Barcelona on foot or by train and were caught and imprisoned there.

Pasolé said that we would be giving this place a wide berth on our march to his father's farm, which lay eight kilometers northwest of Bañolas—Bañolas being already southwest of Figueras.

As I looked at the distant lights of Figueras, I began to realize more fully the extent of the prodigious journey that lay before us, and I suggested that we get a move on straight away. It would also have been too stupid to be caught admiring the scenery right on the border, for Spanish Civil Guards and French Customs men patrolled the whole frontier.

Pasolé then gave us our marching orders.

"We shall walk all through the night," he said. "There will only be one stop of a quarter of an hour for a short meal and a smoke. Apart from that neither of you must stop, or you will not be able to get up again, as stiffness will set in. It's slightly up and down for the first half of the way, but afterwards it's fairly easy going. Watch your feet carefully and don't sprain an ankle."

Manuelo and I said the program suited us all right.

For the first two hours we made our way along a stony track down into the valley. We all had long sticks and Pasolé led us at a very sharp pace We slithered and tripped down incredible slopes, sometimes going between the trees to meet the winding path below. Pasolé took everything straight, and it was a wonder to me that neither Manuelo nor I twisted an ankle on these rough tracks. It was almost as dark as it had been on the previous night's climb.

We followed one another at close intervals, and at one point Pasolé went over the edge and disappeared from view, making noises like a landslide. I just managed to stop in time. A moment later Pasolé's voice came up from some twenty feet below, saying, "Don't follow me," to which I replied, "I've no intention of doing so, *hombre*."

He came scrabbling back, and this slight delay gave us two-minutes' rest. Laughing, we set off again.

As we proceeded, I took out my identity card and demobilization paper and tore them into little pieces, dropping bits here and there at intervals. I did this so that if I were caught I would not be mistaken for a Frenchman and sent back across the frontier and placed in the custody of the French police.

We carried on like this without seeing a living soul or hearing a dog bark until 1:30 in the morning. I was still feeling in fine shape, and Manuelo was doing very well, though he was quite beyond speech.

Then Pasolé called a halt in a little gully beside a stream, and the moon came out, as if it had all been arranged for our benefit. We had a welcome meal and drank some of the Armagnac from Germaine's bottle, finishing up with a smoke. Pasolé did not touch the clear water in the stream, and told Manuelo and me to go very easy with it, if we must drink at all. When our time was up we set off again, feeling much revived.

At about 4 A.M. Pasolé got us all entangled in a maze of terraced vineyards, and getting us out of this meant climbing over endless walls in every direction, and this wasted half-hour was more tiring than two hours of straight walking.

We only had one more lot of trouble from dogs, but this time they began barking when we were still a mile from the Civil Guard's hut, so Pasolé could easily give it a wide berth.

By now we had broken the back of the journey and had reached the flatter portion. My feet were so tender that every stone I walked on seemed to send an electric shock through my entire body. What Manuelo must have been going through I could well imagine, for he was wearing black, thin-soled pointed town shoes.

From 6 A.M., Pasolé, who knew that his charges must be getting tired, began telling his customary bedtime stories about the short distance that now remained to be covered before reaching the farm. The nonsense he spoke could hardly be credited. He pointed out a landmark—dawn having broken—and said, "My father's property begins there." On reaching the spot a fresh gigantic stretch of country spread itself before our weary eyes, representing a distance of perhaps ten kilometers to the horizon. Having spent two hours covering that distance, even Manuelo said· "For God's sake, man, don't do that again. I'm doing the best I can to make my remaining strength last out, but you're cutting the guts right out of me with your phony distances."

Poor Manuelo! His ashen face was pitiful to see. The string of his parcel must have been gnawing into his flesh at every step. I tried, for the umpteenth time, to yank it off his shoulders, but the proud Spaniard just turned round and gave me a savage look.

"Good old Manuelo!" I thought. "What a man you proved to be!"

It was only at 9 A.M. that we reached the farm. I was practically dead on my feet. Pasolé still looked as fresh as though he had just emerged from a cold shower. I could not bear to look at Manuelo.

When we were five hundred yards from the farm we let Pasolé go ahead to spy out the land, and followed him at about two-hundred-yards' distance, approaching the farm over a ploughed field. The reddish earth was soggy, and came up over our shoes. I kept my eyes on Pasolé. Suddenly I saw him signal to us to lie down. I pulled Manuelo down beside me in a gully, and we lay in the furrows, our faces cupped in our hands. Manuelo fell asleep, or maybe he was unconscious.

For half an hour we lay thus, and then Pasolé returned and said to me, "The Civil Guards had to choose this very moment to come round scrounging for eggs at the farm. I nearly walked slap into them. As an exile from this country they would have been only to glad to put the arm on me."

I woke Manuelo, and, together with Pasolé, we dragged the half unconscious man with difficulty over the last three hundred yards. A terrible stiffness had spread itself through my limbs and aching back Manuelo was almost dead to the world Slowly we revived him beside a water trough.

At the farm we were given an enormous breakfast of potato omelette made with a dozen eggs and washed down with a light *rosé* wine served without glasses in a Spanish flask with a long pointed spout. The food did Manuelo good, and he demonstrated how one should drink from the flask by holding it at arm's length and allowing the thin stream of wine to pass between his almost touching teeth. I tried this with much gusto, but only succeeded in disgracing myself.

We spent the rest of the day hiding in a silo, as the Civil Guards were expected to return. When darkness eventually came we went back to the farm, and were treated to another colossal meal.

We then went upstairs, and Pasolé and I shared a double bed while Manuelo had one to himself. We slept like the dead for twelve hours, and woke up much refreshed.

As we were shaving, one of Pasolé's brothers entered the room with another man of maybe fifty. They spoke to Pasolé in a businesslike way without any greeting or sentiment. Pasolé's brother looked the spit of Ronald Colman, even down to the mustache and voice. The other man's name was Garcia.

They said they could not take Manuelo, as it was too risky to hide him, but they would take me, since that was part of their contract. Their conversation was carried out in Catalan, and I only got the gist of it. Manuelo did not say anything. Perhaps he was used to the disappointments of life.

After breakfast I went up to collect my things, and found Pasolé in the room. Pulling out my wallet I paid him the eleven thousand francs I still owed him, throwing in an extra thousand.

"How many kilometers would you say we'd covered, Pasolé?" I asked.

"From where we left the car it must be twenty-three to the barn," he replied. "And from the barn up to here's about another fifty-five. Yes, by the zigzag route we followed it must be just about eighty kilometers in all."

"When are you going back?" I asked.

"I shall rest here all day, and start back tonight. That'll get me into Perpignan on Saturday morning in time for a short rest before our League match against Toulouse."

"What do you do when it's an away fixture?"

"In the winter it's easy enough because the nights are long and I can go straight through with one stop of half an hour.

But then, of course, I go rather faster when I'm alone," he explained.

"What happens in summer, then?" I continued.

"I leave on Mondays instead of Tuesdays."

"What'll happen to Manuelo?"

"He'll stay here and build up his strength on the farm, and I'll take him back next week."

"Poor devil!" I said. "Coming all the way here only to find he can't go on to Barcelona. I feel sorry for him."

"Between you and me," said Pasolé, "I think my father's manager on this farm will do the best he can to bring Manuelo's wife up from Barcelona. But don't tell him I said so, as we'd like it to come as a surprise. If something goes wrong he won't be disappointed."

"Nice of you to have fixed that, Pasolé," I said.

"I never saw a man who deserved to reach his goal as much as Manuelo," stated Pasolé.

"He's in a bad way, isn't he?"

"I hardly expect to find him alive when I come back."

"I didn't think he'd ever reach the farm."

"It was sheer guts that brought him."

"I'd like to help," I said, producing my wallet.

"No. It's our affair. We can manage," said the proud Catalan.

"Maybe it is your affair, but it's become mine, too, since we did the trip together," I said firmly. I thrust a five-thousand-franc note into Pasolé's hand, adding, "If you don't take that for Manuelo, I'll give it to him myself."

"You've been a gay companion, but you mustn't do this," said Pasolé slowly and firmly.

"Then please accept this flask as a personal token of my appreciation," I said, handing him the French Section's gift to me.

"That I will do with pleasure," answered the guide. "But what can I give you of mine in exchange?"

"There is no call for an exchange, but if you can spare it, I've had my eye on your tobacco pouch with the zip fastener."

"At your disposal," said Pasolé, fishing it out and stuffing it full of tobacco from a tin in his rucksack.

We shook hands and I left the room.

Downstairs I found Manuelo. I put my left hand on his shoulder and took his right hand in my own, but no words would come—only "*Adios, chico.*"

"*Adios, amigo,*" said Manuelo.

I turned and joined the two men. We walked toward their car.

CHAPTER XVII

GARCIA had no notion of how to drive. He left that to the car, and simply talked away, keeping his eyes on his companion and gesticulating, with both hands off the wheel. Both men talked hard and fast and at the same time. It was very difficult for me to understand much of these long duets of machine-gun fire. Nevertheless, I gained the impression that neither man gave so much as two hoots where they hid me until I could be passed on to Barcelona, provided they got rid of me somewhere.

I waited for the right moment, and when Garcia was doing most of the wrong things in negotiating a particularly dangerous hairpin bend and both men were taking a breath before the next burst of conversation, I opened up innocently in flawless Spanish:

"What a lovely country this is!"

Both men turned right round and gazed at me. For several seconds the car drove itself, like a horse returning to the stable. A rather severe clout from the grass curb reminded Garcia that the steering wheel had been placed there for a purpose, and for fully fifteen seconds he deigned to look at the road.

"I'm glad you like it," observed "Ronald Colman." "Where did you learn Spanish?" he asked, as though suspecting I would have to confess I had been an enemy of the Franco regime by fighting in the International Brigade during the Civil War—a Brigade that was allied to the Republicans.

"In Madrid," I answered. "I was there in 1932 and 1934."

The simple statement temporarily stemmed their flow of words. The natural prejudice felt by all fascist Spaniards against Englishmen for the sanctions applied by the British Government at the time of the Franco rebellion was appeased by the sound of their own language emanating from the mouth of this particular one.

After perhaps half a minute's silence, Garcia again abandoned the car and its occupants to the will of fate by turning his head to address me.

"We are political enemies of Pasolé," he began. "And our association with him is merely a business one."

"Pasolé told me that even his own family holds different political views from his own," I said. "But I still think Pasolé is a splendid guide."

"Pasolé is a remarkable man," said Garcia. "His only mistake is that he is on the wrong side."

Fortunately the car did not meet a single soul on the road, and after a quarter of an hour's very frightening drive we were circling the beautiful lake of Bañolas.

Garcia turned through a private gateway, ran up the drive, and stopped his car with an unnecessary jerk outside a pretty country house overlooking the water.

His friend went off on his own, and Garcia led me into the house.

Inside we found Garcia's wife doing the housework in a dressing gown and bedroom slippers. Helping her was their fifteen-year-old daughter. I was introduced to Carmen and Carmencita.

Garcia then began talking to his wife, and I assumed the dazed look I always found so useful when trying to follow a dialect of which I understood the gist while pretending to understanding nothing. Carmen seemed to be saying something like: "You're not going to let this young man stay in that beastly hotel all by himself, are you? Why, he might be our own son. Haven't you noticed the likeness? Just imagine our boy in similar circumstances. I bet you no English family would fail to take him in."

I could have hugged this unknown Lady of Spain.

Garcia turned to me and said.

"Señor, which would you prefer: to go to the hotel or remain here with us?"

Without hesitation or preamble I replied:

"Stay here with you."

"Then it's settled. He stays," said Carmen.

After a colossal lunch with *hors d'œuvres* assisted by a dishful of eggs, and then huge slabs of steak freshly bought on the way out from the bullfight on the previous Sunday, I was taken over to the Pasolé household and introduced to the parents and the rest of the family—all handsome and with an obvious resemblance to their brother. I was on the lookout for animosity either toward myself or Great Britain from this family, but I met only with kindness.

An enormous spread awaited us, consisting of platefuls of cream cakes and bottles of choice wines. Courtesy demanded that I should hold my own at this feast, and I was as courteous as my recent lunch would permit.

During my visit, I wrote a letter to the Consul General at Barcelona, and in it was a code phrase whereby he would know who I was. I had also to sign myself Sqn/Ldr. Edwards.

"Ronald Colman," who was present at the party, said he would be driving into Barcelona on Monday morning and would deliver this letter in person.

I spent a very agreeable week end in Bañolas, being taken around everywhere and enjoying myself thoroughly. My greatest treat, however, was to wallow in hot baths, have my clothes cleaned and repaired, and be able to put on fresh linen.

On the Monday—true to his word—"Ronald Colman" went to Barcelona and delivered my letter. The same afternoon D. of the Consular Staff drove out to Bañolas. Garcia led me to his V-8 Ford, which was parked beside the lake with the bonnet open and the chauffeur pretending to look for some fault in the engine.

I had already said good-bye to Carmen and her daughter

and thanked them for their marvelous hospitality, and now I expressed my gratitude to Garcia, who then walked away so as not to be conspicuous.

D., with a pipe in his mouth, was leaning against the door of the car with the unselfconscious ease of someone who does this sort of thing frequently. While pretending to watch the chauffeur, he was really sizing me up.

It was a great moment when I shook hands with this countryman, and a greater one as the car raced down the main road to Barcelona.

My arrival was celebrated in regal manner. Boxes of English cigarettes lay on every table.

Half an hour later, the Consul-General came in. He was an ex-Guards Major, of stimulating personality, a man of quick decisions, whose military manner gained my immediate respect. He seemed to me the very epitome of what a senior Consular Representative of Great Britain should be in wartime. Having been attached to the Consular Service myself, and having had a father, three uncles, and grandfather who were all Consuls-General, I believed I was qualified to judge.

The C.G. took me into the next room. He had brought a score or so of photographs of men who resembled me to some extent. These he laid out on a table, saying:

"Pick out the one you think looks most like you. We've got to have a photograph on your temporary pass, and there's no time to have one taken of you. I've already made my choice."

As I scrutinized each face, I supposed that D. had already given his Chief a rough description over the telephone when anouncing my arrival, that the Consul-General had then picked out a handful of passport photographs of Spaniards who, on producing evidence that a grandfather was born in Gibraltar, had been issued British passports, and that these photographs were actual copies from those very passports.

"How about that one, sir?" I said, pointing to the photo of a man who might have been my twin brother

"That's the one all right," replied the Consul-General. "I'll have a *salvo conducto* made out right away, and my car will return to fetch you in about an hour. I should like you to dine with me and afterwards I have a room prepared for you.

We shall have to get up early tomorrow morning, as I'm driving you and O. to Madrid."

"Thank you very much, sir," I said.

"I may as well tell you that the Foreign Office cabled me some days ago advising me that you were on your way here and that you were to be sent on to Madrid urgently. However, I should imagine you could do with a square meal and some sleep, so I shall expect you presently."

"It's very kind of you, sir," I replied.

After he had left, I returned to the other room. As I stood beside D., who was mixing me a drink, I said:

"What a man your Chief is!"

"Yes," nodded the other. "Nothing much grows beneath his feet. In fact, he leaves a trail of scorched earth behind him."

"From what I've seen, you don't do so badly yourself," I said to my host, no less admiringly.

A pleasant hour with the D.'s and Lt.-Cdr. O.,* a Belgian officer in civilian clothes whom I had met upon my arrival in D.'s home, passed all too quickly. The Consular car was at the door.

I had an excellent dinner with the Consul-General. It was served by a Spanish butler in white jacket and gloves on a mahogany table with a glass top, and my host's manner made me forget the rather shabby suit I was wearing and the scratches on my shoes where the rough going had left its scars. It was very pleasant to be made to feel that I was an honored guest and to be received with such courtesy by an exalted member of my country. We spoke of the war, and the C.G. was really interested to know what the actual feeling was in France.

After dinner, I was led to a magnificent bedroom. There was whisky-and-soda and a bowl of fruit on the bedside table. I had a private bathroom. A pair of silk pajamas lay folded on the turned-down bed.

The Consul-General asked me if I would be all right in this room, and I had some difficulty in finding an appropriate reply.

Within five minutes I was fast asleep.

At 6:30 in the morning I was awakened with a breakfast of boiled eggs, toast, marmalade, and coffee served on a tray.

* Lieutenant-Commander Pat O'Leary, G C

At 7:25 the Consul-General took me downstairs, and we came out into the brilliant early light of a perfect Spanish morning. At the door stood a brand-new black V-8 (30) Ford saloon with Union Jacks on both front mudguards and a C.D. plate back and front. A uniformed chauffeur stood beside the car.

In the back was O., and for the first part of the trip I rode in front with the Consul-General, who was driving, while the Belgian chatted away with the Spanish chauffeur behind.

We were off on the four-hundred-mile run to Madrid. The car carried two extra petrol tanks in the luggage boot, thus enabling it to do the whole journey without refueling.

The first part of the trip was very dramatic, and we wound our way through canyons above which the sky was a deep blue. The C.G. was a perfect driver, and kept the car at its maximum speed for safety. I was aware of the soft and easy contrast of these moments compared to my experiences of the past twenty-eight days in France. I allowed myself to relax, but knew full well that it was merely a brief, if welcome, interlude.

At 12:30 we stopped and picnicked by the roadside. The only other cars that passed the spot were large Mercedes-Benzes full of Germans going about on their nefarious ways.

After lunch we passed through Guadalajara, where the Italians had taken such a pasting in the Civil War, and many other battlefields, before reaching Madrid at 6 P.M. The Consul-General had driven all the way.

The whole trip down to the details of the picnic, the carton of two hundred cigarettes, the car, the chauffeur, and everything else had been in keeping with the C G.; efficiency, organization, punctuality, and power. All the things I had always admired about my own country had been turned on for O.'s and my benefit in the last twenty-four hours; things I need not necessarily take part in myself so long as I felt they were there; things I would have been sorry—as, I supposed, most of my compatriots would—to see disappear.

CHAPTER XVIII

We had now reached the outskirts of Madrid, and scars of the bombing in the Civil War could be seen on every hand. It was a different Madrid from the one I had known in its heyday of 1932, when I had first gone there to study Spanish, and where my first *novillada* had turned me into a bullfight fan.

Poverty and gutted buildings met my eyes in place of the wealth and glamour of a mere decade ago. No longer did shining cars glide up and down the wide Castellana—Madrid's elegant Park Lane—showing off the proud youth and beauty of the capital.

Now we were entering the imposing gates of the British Embassy. The C.G. parked his V-8 and told the chauffeur to refuel and be ready to leave in half an hour. Passing through the courtyard, he led his two charges into the building and introduced us to our contact.

With the Consul-General's departure came the feeling that another step had been accomplished toward my goal.

O. and I were put into the same room in the Embassy. Our only anxiety was to get home quickly. Both of us had important information to hand over to London, and we could not relax until our missions were completed Our only safe topic—on which both of us heartily agreed—was that even if the forced rest might do us good, it was in no way to our liking, to put it mildly.

As nothing materialized on the following day, my request to see a tailor was granted, and I was fitted out in the Embassy with a pair of gray flannel trousers, a sports jacket, two silk shirts, a tie, two pairs of socks, and a pair of pajamas. Wearing some of this new outfit, I felt slightly less embarrassed at approaching the impeccable personnel of the Embassy.

I was introduced to one of these demigods, who listened sympathetically to my tale. Unfortunately, as his chief was away from Madrid that day, his manicured hands were tied. I realized that as I was in all probability the first specimen of my type to pass through Madrid, I presented a thorny, unprecedented problem not to be tackled lightly or, indeed, swiftly, much as they would, no doubt, have liked to get rid of me. I felt an intruder in this well-ordered society of distinguished diplomats. To them my impatience was unintelligible and distasteful, and my temper was not improved by the encounter. I left hoping I would not be dependent on help from this quarter again, and so indeed it proved.

Next day I called on a Naval Commander, and found him talking to an Army officer. To my surprise and delight, it turned out to be a friend whom I had met in Gibraltar, Captain Coburn.

"Well, if it isn't my old friend Churchill! I heard there was a strange 'bod' around tearing his hair to get away from the very place where everyone wants to go."

"Where have you sprung from?" I asked.

"I've just come up from Gibraltar in the courier car. If it's all right with the powers that be, I'll take you along with me. The car's going back this evening."

"I'm your man," I said eagerly.

I rushed off in search of O., and broke the news of my imminent and incredible departure. The latter, having long ago judged me to be all right, confided in me.

"As it's fairly obvious that I shan't get away from here for quite a time, I wonder if you'd do something for me, Michel?"

"Anything you like," I replied.

O. opened his dispatch case and drew out a sheet of paper and a postcard.

"The names, addresses, and passwords on this paper refer to the new points of departure for the R.A.F.'s escape route," he explained. "With what they've already got at Bomber and Fighter Commands, these complete practically every Department of France. A pilot who is shot down has only to go to the nearest house to where he finds himself, and once he has said the password his troubles are over, for each safe house is linked to the next, and they all lead to the Pyrenees, and ultimately to this haven of rest. Each house provides a guide who will accompany the airman to his next safe point. I want you to see that this reaches the proper quarter as soon as possible. Please make a point of stressing that when the pilots are briefed they should only be given the addresses and passwords of places on their particular route. This will avoid their having to learn more than the bare necessity for that one flight. Above all, they must never write down any of this information. If any member of the crew were killed by flak or night fighters the Germans would ransack their pockets, and not only would the whole game be given away, but the French people who are on this list would all end up in Buchenwald."

"A piece of cake!" I said. "My brother, who is at Fighter Command, is one who will give three cheers when he gets his hands on this. In any case, my H.Q. will see that it reaches the right people immediately, and I'll have your special recommendation sent out with this 'gen' wherever it goes. What's on the card?"

"This card shows a rough plan of Calais. As you can see, it's dotted with numbers. On the back," he added, turning it over, "is the key to the plan. It even gives the times when various Germans are gathered at the different spots. A friend of mine in the area thought it might be a good idea for the R.A.F. to save up their pineapples for these interesting landmarks, and so hit the jackpot every time."

"Crippins!" I exclaimed with admiration, "this is the real McCoy."

I picked up O's "dynamite" and placed it carefully among my own papers. Then I packed my belongings. When I was all set, I walked over to O., who was lying on his bed gazing vacantly at the ceiling.

"So long, chum," I said. "I hope that you and I will meet again."

O. turned his head toward me and, giving me a friendly smile, he answered quietly:

"That goes for me, too. *Bon voyage.*"

I could hardly believe that I was actually sitting in the powerful Humber that was gliding slowly out of the Embassy gates. It felt as though I had been there for months, and yet it was only three days.

Coburn told me I might have had to wait three weeks until the next lorry convoy took its load of British military personnel away from Miranda Prison, where they were regularly confined after having been captured escaping through Spain.

"Three weeks!" I echoed. "Holy smoke!"

But I refrained from speaking my thoughts any further, for they were that I hoped to be back in France by then.

"It's a tricky situation for our Ambassador, with all these chaps who get themselves caught and stuck in Figueras and Miranda," said Coburn. "He has to keep old Franco sweet so as to get them out. You can imagine the Germans know all about it, and put the squeeze on him to keep them in. We'd lose a packet of experienced blokes if the Germans forced the Spaniards to have these prisoners transferred to Germany. Yes," he repeated, "you're lucky all right to be off so soon." And he added, as an afterthought, "You must have been quite a problem child in that outpost of Empire."

Besides Coburn and myself, there was a taciturn Spanish chauffeur and a most agreeable Gibraltarian called Albaran who had a military post on the "Rock." I was introduced to him as Squadron-Leader Edwards. Albaran, who spent his time on the roads between Gibraltar, Lisbon, and Madrid, and who knew these roads intimately, shared the driving with the chauffeur.

We stopped for supper at one of the national roadhouses, and I got better acquainted with the others over an excellent meal. Afterwards we drove until 11 P.M., and spent the night at another similar roadhouse.

The next day we were off early, as we intended to cover the rest of the journey by nightfall. It was a pleasant run, with many twists in the road down to Malaga, where we had lunch. The car then made a short halt at the British Consulate. Diplomatic bags were exchanged, and then we proceeded toward La Linea, the frontier town, beyond which rose the Rock of Gibraltar. It was on this stretch that Coburn began to worry seriously over the problem of getting me through the frontier barriers. Coming out, there had been three names on the official pass, and now there was a fourth party to be accounted for.

Coburn and I talked it over in the back of the car while Albaran was driving with the chauffeur asleep beside him. We discussed the chances of my getting through on his *salvo conducto*. This was ruled out because there would certainly be a flap whoever the fourth person in the car might be, despite my papers being in perfect order. We then worked through the possibilities of my staying with the British Consul at La Linea and swimming across on the following night, or being fetched in a double canoe or by a party of the Independent Company in their landing craft at a given spot. These propositions were equally ruled out as being too far-fetched. In the end I said:

"How about packing me into the trunk of the car? Can you get away with pretending to have lost the keys?"

"That's a nifty dodge," replied Coburn, "although I wouldn't exactly care to be locked up in that stifling hole myself. You'd probably pass out cold."

"What if I do? A mugful of brandy would soon fix that."

"Maybe," said Coburn, rubbing his chin thoughtfully. "I'd hoped to wangle this without having to explain to Albaran who you were. Now I'll have to tell him, because we shall have to stop at his villa to get you into the trunk unseen."

"Can't you stick to the R.A.F. story?" I suggested.

"I'd thought of it, too; but as a pilot's priority is not quite so pressing as yours, our friend might boggle at the trunk idea, and then we should only get ourselves into a long discussion that would get us exactly nowhere."

"Go ahead and tell him, then," I said.

We stopped the car on a pretext and walked down the road with Albaran. When he had been told the situation, he merely asked why we had not confided in him sooner. Coburn made some suitable excuse. Albaran shrugged his shoulders and said, "We'll stop at my *estancia* and work this out inside the palisade."

It was not a very long drive to his place, and presently the car came to a halt outside a high, solid wooden stockade. A peep on the horn and the gates were opened by a servant. A few moments later the car and its four occupants were inside and hidden from the public view.

Beside the entrance to the villa we had the trunk cleaned out and dusted. All the petrol cans were removed and two cushions replaced them to serve as a pillow.

First of all I got inside and tried it for a minute. As there was nothing very terrifying about that, I got my friends to let the motor run and shut me up in the trunk for five minutes so that I could test the effects of the petrol fumes I would encounter on the road. They gave me an orange with a hole bored into it, and this I held to my nose like smelling salts. They then closed the lid and, at my request, returned to the house for the testing period.

On their return after the allotted time they snapped the boot open with great haste and found me quite unperturbed by the experiment. I was soon roaring with laughter at the white, disconcerted faces peering in at me. The rehearsal had proved more successful than I had imagined, for it had not only got me accustomed to the idea, but my friends were also quite happy about the whole thing, and would not now panic at the frontier from fear that I would be asphyxiated during the delay.

We then went indoors to have a glass of sherry before the departure. I was warned that the car would have to stop outside the British Consulate at La Linea, but that we only had to deliver a mailbag there. The second stop would be at the frontier, and Albaran promised he would do his best to get through as fast as possible, that if there were any questions about inspecting the trunk he would say that he had mislaid the key and that anyway there was nothing in the trunk except the usual petrol cans, to which the frontier guards were quite accustomed.

I said that all this was most satisfactory· that they could drive as fast as they liked, and that if I passed out it would be quite simple to bring me round again.

They then went out to the car, and I was locked into the trunk and we were off.

It was an odd sensation for me to be riding locked up in this box. I thought of my submarine experiences, and chuckled when I remembered my previous fits of claustrophobia. I kept the orange close to my nose and got no smell of the exhaust fumes. That I could not move a centimeter in any direction did not worry me in the least. It suddenly occurred to me that my mother would let out a very large yell if she were to open the lid and find her ever-loving son in this biscuit tin. I wished the people inside the car would stop calling out and asking how I was. There was not sufficient air for me to keep on putting their minds at rest. It was rather hotter than I had anticipated. I felt lightheaded.

After a quarter of an hour we came to our first stop, and while the mailbag was being deposited at the Consulate some little boys came and scribbled with their fingers in the dust on the paintwork outside the trunk about a quarter of an inch away from my head. They chortled with merriment as they went about it, and I had quite a job not to join in, for I was having much more fun and being even less visible than they.

Three minutes later the car moved on its way again and went racing up to the frontier. When it stopped, I could hear the conversation between the Civil Guard and the chauffeur and the sound of many feet coming from the teeming nightly exodus of Spaniards leaving Gibraltar and regaining their homes in Spain.

"Señor Albaran," came a voice. "Here are your car papers and passports. What have you got with you this trip?"

"Nothing but the usual mail," came the answer.

"Nothing to declare?"

"Heavens, no! We can get everything we want in Gibraltar."

"Do you mind if I have a look under that rug in the back seat?"

"Go ahead."

There came the sound of the door opening and a hand rummaging among the mailbags. Then the door was closed.

The voice proceeded, "Anything in the trunk?"

My throat went dry. I was too anxious to think of squeezing some of the orange juice into my mouth.

"The usual empty petrol tins."

"All right. You may proceed. *Muy buenas.*"

"Muy buenas," came the reply, and the car glided away as

though the driver had already engaged low gear and was merely waiting to release the clutch.

And now the rest was easy. I recognized each turn of the road; the humpbacked iron bridge before turning sharp left under the old arches, followed by a sharp turn right to avoid the narrow main street which would be crowded at this hour with troops off duty.

Within thirty-five minutes of being locked in, the Humber reached her journey's end inside the Fortress courtyard. She was backed up under the small covered way at the end on the right. The lid was unlocked, and I was able to get out under my own power, feeling little the worse for the lack of air. I thought I must have been so cold in France that this was just about what I needed. Nobody saw me enter Gibraltar that night.

While the luggage was being removed, Coburn called at Benson's office and returned with a message for me. Opening the envelope I read:

> DEAR MICHEL,
>
> Expecting you any moment. Ask orderly for car. Call at flat. Get into uniform whose buttons are shining. Trousers under mattress. Expect you any time Rock Hotel. Have news for you.
>
> B.

I stuffed the letter into my pocket, wondering what the news might be.

A driver was soon whistled up and one of the cars put in readiness. I shook hands with Albaran and Coburn.

"I can't thank you enough for all your help and kindness," I told them.

"Wouldn't have missed it for anything," said Coburn.

"Glad it all came off so well," put in Albaran.

They waved me off the premises, and the chauffeur stood beside them and actually broke his long silence with *"Adios, Señor.* May God be with you."

It was a treat for me to wash off the dust of my journey and get back into uniform. It fitted me rather loosely round the waist. No doubt this was partly due to the absence of the money belts and partly to the loss of a few ounces of weight over the past week. I felt in terrific form, and counteracted the slackness of the jacket by pulling in the belt two notches.

By 7:30 I was making my way through the Rock Hotel toward the bar.

In a corner stood Benson with his eye on the door. He was surrounded by Polish naval officers. Catching sight of me, he signaled me to come over. I weaved my way through a mass of service uniforms up to the group.

"Hullo, Churchill," said Benson, smiling. "You're looking well. Let me introduce you to some friends of mine from the *Maidstone*." Then, turning from one to the other he said:

"This is Lt. Kraiewski and Jan Buchowski. They run the feluccas. And this is Boris, who drives a submarine."

The Poles shook hands, and each in turn made a very slight bow. Then all of them asked what I would like to drink.

Jan, a fair-haired, slim youth with a row of decorations, got his order in first, then, putting a hand on my shoulder and with his mouth close to my ear, he said in execrable English:

"I see you on *Maidstone* maybe one month ago. I see you today. I ask no questions. But maybe one day we travel together. I think you and me capture German U-boat in our fingers. We talk about it sometime."

"Pay no attention to Jan," said Boris. "He says that to all the girls."

Benson then interposed and excusing himself, he drew me over to an empty corner of the bar.

"Good trip?" he inquired.

"Fine," I said.

"Not too groggy after your ride in the trunk?"

"How do you know about that?"

"I know more. Sorry to bother you with details now, but I've got to dine with my Poles, and you won't be here long. Have you any French money left?"

"Yes," I said "Thirty-seven thousand francs. Can you take it?"

"Let's go into the card room. There's no one there at the moment."

In the deserted card room I took the money from my wallet

and handed it to Benson who, in turn, gave me a chit as receipt for it.

"How about some English money?" he asked.

"Could do," I replied.

"Here's twenty pounds for you. Hand me that chit, and I'll chalk it up."

Having concluded these matters, Benson looked at me for a while in silence, then he said, haltingly:

"I'm sorry to tell you that the Captain of *P36* . . ."

"Not Harry Edmonds?" I said, without much hope of denial.

"When he reached Malta," Benson went on slowly, "he docked, and then he and the crew spent most of their time in the air-raid shelters. The Germans plastered the port. It was as though they were aiming at *P36* and its stores of petrol. In the end, of course, they got her, and the duty crew on board naturally had it. In due course Edmonds and some of the others were shipped back here on another submarine. Well, they struck a mine just outside Malta."

"God, how awful!" I said.

"Yes. That's the way it goes. Three of the officers of *P36* came back on another submarine. I dined with them on the *Maidstone* yesterday. They told me all about your trip. After they'd dropped you, Edmonds, who didn't exactly waste words, apparently said to the others, 'It seems quiet without Churchill. Wonder what it's like doing his job. Something tells me he'll get through all right.' "

"What are the chances of seeing these chaps?" I asked.

"None, I'm afraid," answered Benson. "You see, in another corner of the bar is one of your Cloak-and-Dagger pals. He's returning to England tonight, and he's made room for you in the aircraft."

"Very well. Let's get weaving," I said, glad at the thought that activity would keep my mind from brooding over what could never be altered.

It was a pleasant surprise and an almost incredible piece of luck for me to find Major V. in the bar. The last time we had met had been in Scotland, where he was one of the chief instructors. He told me that he had just returned from Malta by air and was going to fly back to England that very night, subject to the engines being serviceable after the pranging they'd received in Malta. When I asked him if there was room for me, V. said:

"Of course. There's a non-priority crate of stuff on board that can go on the next plane. You can take its place and join the eight men who are already traveling on this bomber."

So all was teed up for the departure, and Benson could return to his guests, while I joined V.'s party.

It was Friday, February 13—not a particularly good day for traveling if you happened to be at all superstitious, but nevertheless one that had done me no particular harm so far. At 10 P.M. we reached the airport, only to find that the Whitley's starboard engine refused to fire. The captain of the aircraft was in no way put out by this, and got the ground staff to make the necessary repairs. Only at midnight were these experts able to bring it to life, and by that time it was no longer Friday the thirteenth.

There was not a breath of air on the ground, and the C.O. of the airport told the pilot that his departure was ill-advised, and that if he took off it would be entirely at his own risk.

The Gibraltar airport, built on the old racetrack, was at that time only about one thousand yards long, and pilots were not over-fond of it.

The captain of the aircraft, having got his passengers on board, taxied down to the water's edge at the western end of the tarmac, turned on one engine to face the flare-path, and with brakes hard on he revved up. When he was satisfied with their performance and had checked his temperature, he opened up both throttles wide and released the brakes. The heavily laden aircraft surged forward like a thoroughbred, but this was more exciting than the start or finish of any race ever held on that one-time racetrack, and it was a weird kind of start, for there was no competition and the ghosts of dead horses must have watched us with their ears well back.

One or two sleepy mechanics and the duty officer were the only living people attending this event, and at the back of their minds must have been the ever-present knowledge that anything might happen, for they had seen plenty of aircraft fall into the sea.

All the passengers were required to congregate as near the pilot's cabin as possible to get the weight well forward for the take-off. Through a small lateral window I could see the torches of the flare-path flashing by in ever-quickening succession, but still the pilot kept the nose down.

Then I saw the last two flares and nothing but the blackness of the night merging into the Mediterranean beyond. At the last flare but one, having reached the maximum ground speed attainable in that short distance, the captain pulled back the joy-stick very gently, and we were airborne. Passing by the last flare the plane could not have been more than three feet up, but three inches would have been enough.

Our eight-hours' night flight had begun. The rest of the passengers and I settled down to sleep in the pitch-dark interior of the plane. It was terribly cold, and drafts rushed along the floor from front to back, making sleep impossible.

I huddled up beside my neighbor, who introduced himself in the dark as Major M., also of the French Section of S.O.E.

The hours dragged by.

After a long night the gray light of dawn began to filter slowly through the cracks of the blacked-out window slits.

At about 8 A.M. there was a sudden spluttering from the motors and the starboard engine went dead. The Whitley began to dip like a winged bird, and the captain had to do some quick thinking to check this, and then keep the aircraft level, powered by its port engine alone.

Those of us in the dark interior of the plane could see absolutely nothing of what was going on. We were like rats in a trap, and could only hope that the coast of England was not too far off. The aircraft kept losing height and bumping along unsteadily. I scratched some of the blacking off the window-slit and breathed more freely. The coast was well in sight. I spread the news around.

How stupid it would be to be written off within a mile of home by anything so ignominious as engine trouble! But I realized that this sort of thing could and did happen. I could not refrain from thinking how true was the Chinese contention that "He who has ten paces to make and who has done nine of them, can only claim to have accomplished half his journey." My thoughts were interrupted by the appearance of one of the crew, who told us to assemble close to the pilot's cabin. It was with great relief that we then saw, through the open door, the cliffs on which Portreath airport was situated and toward which the aircraft was valiantly staggering. I prayed that our luck might hold and that the pilot could bring us down safely to earth.

With the rest of us holding our breath, the captain executed a masterly landing. The aircraft slithered round to a standstill, and its only working engine was switched off.

A great silence filled the machine. We were in England.

Presently the door was opened and the much-relieved passengers climbed down onto the tarmac, forming themselves into a little group. Feeling very chastened, I stood among them, watching the pilot get down from his cockpit and approach us. After the abundant baptism of fear I had undergone in the past six weeks I had hoped, at last, to be immune to this enemy, only to discover, with a slight pang of disappointment, that the fight would have to be made all over again at each fresh encounter with danger.

"Phew!" gasped the captain, wiping the perspiration from his brow despite the cold morning air. "I'd just as soon that didn't happen too often."

His passengers made various appropriate remarks of appreciation and relief. Then our attention was distracted by the appearance of a small party of officers coming toward us across the airport; among them I spotted the tall figure of my friend Captain de G. from Headquarters.

He came up smiling and greeted me.

"Well done!" he beamed when we had got out of the crowd. "You've broken all the speed records. We followed your movements from your telegrams, and then Barcelona, Madrid, and Gibraltar signaled your passage. I only just had time to get down here before your plane arrived—and that was some sight viewed from the ground. But we'll talk about all that later. Instead of having breakfast in the R.A.F. mess, I thought we'd sneak off to a good spot I noticed on the way down in the car."

I allowed myself to be led off, only too glad to be able to relax at last.

Beside the car stood a pretty Canadian F.A.N.Y. driver whom I recognized. She stood smartly to attention and came up to the salute.

I put out my hand and the girl grasped it, saying:

"It's awfully good to see you back, Michel."

My smile spread from ear to ear.

"It's awfully good to be back," I said.

PART II

Duel of Wits

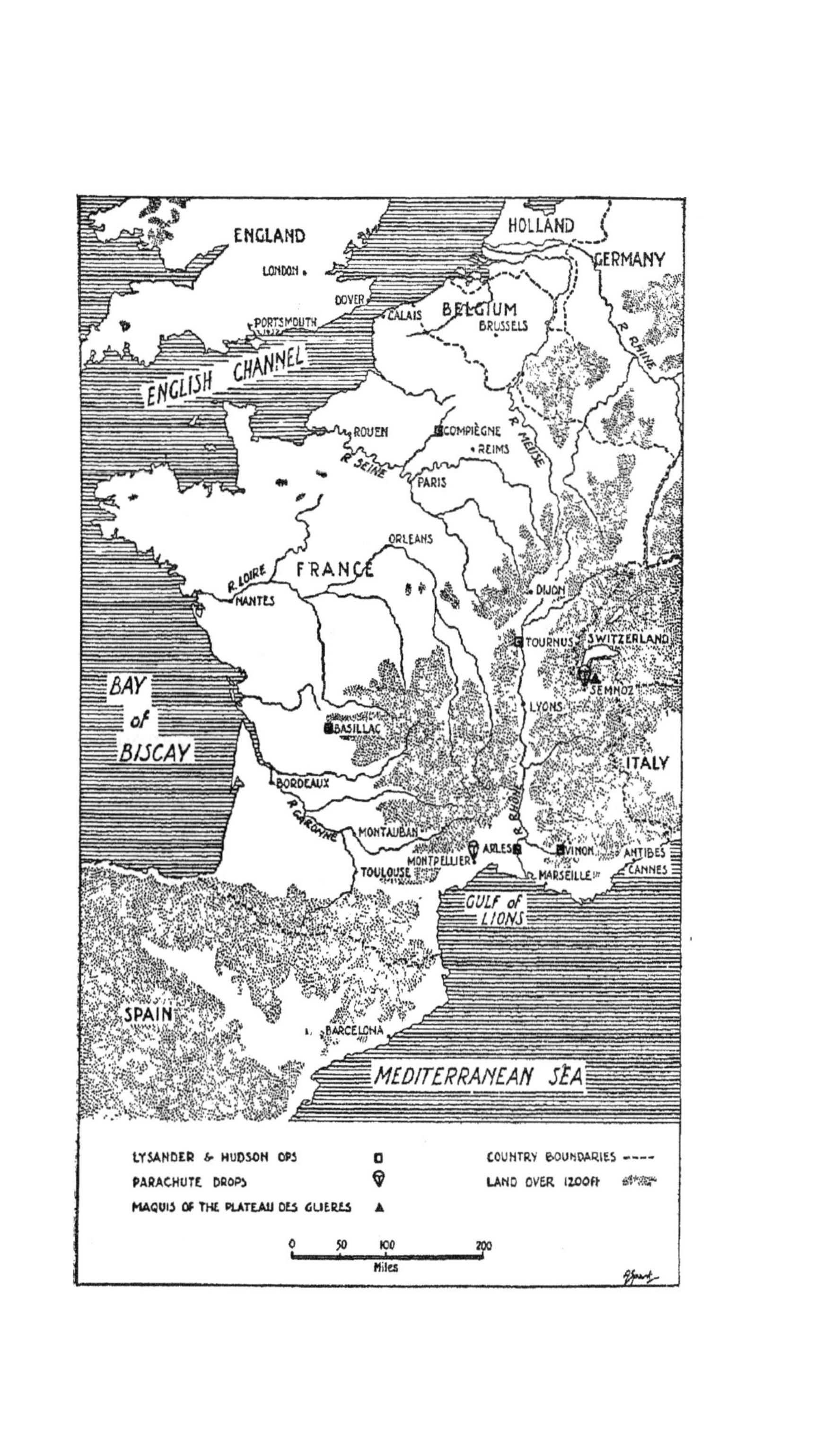
ENGLAND
LONDON
DOVER
PORTSMOUTH
ENGLISH CHANNEL
HOLLAND
GERMANY
BELGIUM
BRUSSELS
CALAIS
R. RHINE
R. MEUSE
ROUEN
COMPIÈGNE
REIMS
R. SEINE
PARIS
ORLEANS
FRANCE
R. LOIRE
NANTES
DIJON
TOURNUS
SWITZERLAND
SEMNOZ
LYONS
BAY of BISCAY
BASILLAC
ITALY
BORDEAUX
R. GARONNE
R. RHÔNE
MONTAUBAN
ARLES
VINON
ANTIBES
CANNES
MONTPELLIER
TOULOUSE
MARSEILLE
GULF of LIONS
SPAIN
BARCELONA
MEDITERRANEAN SEA
LYSANDER & HUDSON OPS
PARACHUTE DROPS
MAQUIS OF THE PLATEAU DES GLIERES
COUNTRY BOUNDARIES
LAND OVER 1200ft
0
50
100
200
Miles

CHAPTER I

THE POWERFUL Humber limousine slid quietly under the archway and drew up at the entrance to Orchard Court. Major de G. and I thanked the F.A.N.Y. driver for bringing us up from Port Reith. With her salute went a gracious smile, and nobody watching this simple exchange would ever have suspected that the elegant chauffeuse, now heading away her mud-spattered charge for a refueling, had just come off a sixteen-hour shift, or that she would have given a month's pay to have overheard the conversation that had taken place behind the glass partition during the long drive up from the coast

As we crossed the hall and made for the stairs, I felt a sudden weariness behind the exhilaration of having accomplished an exciting mission crammed into two short months. The near-misses during those thousands of miles by ship, submarine, trains, cars, aircraft, and on foot had sobered me. I felt much older, somehow. The flowers in the hall were as fresh as ever, the porter unchanged. It might have been yesterday, and yet it seemed years ago.

We walked up the two flights and rang at the doorbell of No. 6. It was instantly opened by the faithful Park, as though that guardian had been expecting us. He had hardly time, in his characteristic singsong way, of getting out the words, *"Oh comme ça fait plaisir,"* before we were joined by the tall, gaunt figure of Major B

I saluted rigidly and then my hand was grasped and warmly wrung by my Chief.

They led me triumphantly into the main office with Park in close attendance, rubbing his hands with joy. Park knew what was cooking and followed us as far as the door around which he put his head to watch the officers lead me up to the open bathroom door. The three men then watched my face as I looked in at the super black bath. It was full of water and a cloud of steam met my astonished gaze. I turned my head inquiringly toward my Chief, who nodded and said, "Help yourself. I'll be back in a moment."

In a daze I undressed and got into the bath. Presently Major de G. came in with a bottle and three glasses. Then Major B. appeared. Thus, with my two superior officers sitting on various commodities that one finds in such a room and poring over the papers and chuckling over the French ration books for 1942 which I had brought back, I, with a piece of soap in one hand and a glass in the other, gave them an outline of my trip.

I told them of the urgent request for radio sets and operators from Louis of Antibes, of my suggestion that Germaine should take a flat in Lyon. I gave my impressions of Charles, her chief, Laurent of Cannes, and Olivier of Marseille. I told them about my visit to Deprez in Marseille and subsequent action, of the grain shop in Perpignan, of my return to Lyon, and the trip to Clermont-Ferrand. I related my good fortune in being helped by the American Consulate and underlined their request for silence on that score. I glossed over my crossing of the Pyrenees and asked that a cable of appreciation be sent to the Consul-General in Barcelona.

At this point, fearing that the water would get cold if I started on the subject of Madrid, I got out and began to dry myself. The others got up and went into the office to let me get dressed. In a few minutes I joined them and concluded my story.

When I had finished, my Chief, who had been taking rapid notes, began his comments:

"We've just got time before dinner to run over a few points. Let's start with the radio sets. We've got the sets and the trained operators, but we're still working on a method of dropping them together by parachute. At present they are dropped on separate 'chutes and either the operator can't find his set in the dark, or some of the tubes get broken in landing. Soon we hope to attach them in thick felt padding above the operator's head. But it will take some time before this comes into operation."

"I've got the answer to that," I said.

"What?" inquired Major B.

"Let me take out two chaps and their sets by submarine."

"And have them carry their heavy sets twenty-six kilometers? No thank you!"

"Oh, no," I said, "that's old stuff. I've got some concrete steps in Antibes Bay about four hundred yards from Louis' house. Drop in at two A.M and bob's your uncle."

"Not bad. Not bad at all," said Major B., tapping the table with a pencil and considering the matter.

"The only thing is that we should have liked you to have had a good spell of leave—say a month or so—and I doubt if anyone but you could find those steps in the dark."

"Give me ten days' leave and I'm your man. Can you imagine anyone else using my steps?" I said in a proprietary manner.

"No, I can't," said both men in unison.

"If ten days aren't enough," went on Major B., "we'll make it up to you the next time. I'll see to it that our two best men are in this office waiting for their guide on the twenty-fifth of March." Then, turning to de G., "Make a note of that date, Jacques, and lay on a flight for three to Gibraltar and contact the Admiralty for a submarine."

"Right," said de G., noting it down.

"Well, that's settled," said Major B., anxious to get on with the next points. "Now, as to Germaine's flat, I quite agree and will send her confirmation by the next courier. By the way," he branched off, "your three telegrams reached us in good time and we understood the innuendo about Marius' first tooth. We heard later that Olivier had picked up where you'd left off and we approve of your decision to hand the matter over to him. Those chaps in prison will be taken care of and you can forget all about them henceforth. It was a cute move to ask Deprez if he would vouch for you, if asked, and that ties up your cover story beautifully. As time goes by, you'll develop even more roots."

"It won't be long before we shall discover what went wrong in the grain shop. Are you sure you remembered the correct passwords?"

"Certain," I answered.

"What were they?" asked Major B.

"Bonjour Madame. Je suis de passage."

"That's right," he said, looking at a typed copy of my instructions. "Anything else?" he asked, looking up from the paper.

"Yes. If she didn't play on that I was to say, *'Je viens de la Suisse et je vais aux Etats Unis.'*"

"Sainte Mère!" ejaculated de G., who was looking at the printed orders over the C.O.'s shoulder, "What a memory!"

"All right, go on and give him a swollen head," said his superior. Then, turning to me—"You know, Michel, on this Barcelona question, we don't usually send greetings telegrams to all the departments who help to make a good show of what, thanks to all the Services, becomes a combined operation They don't expect it and it clutters up the lines. What we do is to go on using every means toward success while trying to avoid the dead spots. One thing is absolutely certain, and that is that you must never return to Madrid where you caused such a stir, because we need all the help the Foreign Office can give us."

"Yes, sir," I said, looking at the housetops through the window and trying to suppress a smile at the suspicion of a wink from de G.

"We shall see to it that all this important information from O'Leary reaches the R.A.F. tonight. There's a shorthand typist waiting for us by the dinner table. You can dictate the special instructions about pilots memorizing the safe houses and so forth to her. Dispatch riders are waiting in the kitchen and, by the way, four of my colleagues—and you know them all—are waiting for us now, so if you're not too tired I know they're anxious to hear the whole story from the submarine trip right through to the very end."

"Very well, sir," I said, and we all got up.

Park was left to lock up after us and we trooped off and found a taxi. The cab took us somewhere in Mayfair. It was pitch dark in the blackout, and as we went down some stairs to a basement flat the sirens sounded their warning wail.

As the front door opened, a blaze of cheerful light met us, and I was pushed forward into the midst of four officers who gave me a warm reception. We all sat down round the table which was heavily laden with dishes of cold chicken, vegetables, and salad, besides two decanters of claret. The dancing light from two candles in their silver holders added the final touch of elegance and dignity to the setting. Outside, the bombardment raged closer, until a resounding crash put out the electric lights and shook the house to its foundations. The candles quivered uncertainly before their flames rose up once more as bright as ever. By their light, this little band of pioneers heard the story of the returned wanderer. They would not spare me a single detail and well knew when I was hedging. By the time I had got as far as extricating myself from the trunk of the courier car in Gibraltar, the night was far advanced. The raiders had passed, the lights come on again. Dispatch riders had come and gone, forgers were already at work on the ration books, and my every word had been taken down in shorthand, for they did not want to keep me from my leave with endless reporting at the office.

As Major B. led me to the outside door where a taxi was waiting for me, he said:

"You've done a grand job, Michel. Tomorrow you can put up your captain's pips. I'll have it put in Orders. Furthermore, I'm making out a recommendation that you be decorated for this operation. We're very proud of you."

I could find no words to answer my commanding officer. I just stood there gaping.

Seeing my embarrassment, Major B. pushed me smilingly through the door, saying, "Go on. Off you go!"

As I sat back in the taxi I knew that I had just lived my finest hour. Beyond the satisfaction of higher rank and pride at the thought of a possible decoration was the knowledge that during that hour the greatest honor had been paid me, for I had been made to feel that I was a prophet even in my own country. I was well aware that no man could hope for more than that from life.

CHAPTER II

DURING MY LEAVE the French Section made arrangements with the Admiralty for the submarine and also advised Louis of Antibes, through a courier, to expect a knock at his back door between the hours of midnight and 4 A.M. between certain dates. Louis was informed that one of the two radio operators due to land was assigned to Laurent's circuit in Cannes and he was asked to allow the other to rest for a few days after the tiring experience of being cooped up for ten days and nights inside a submarine, before proceeding to his allotted post.

When my leave was up, an appointment was made for me to meet the two selected radio operators at headquarters. Major B. introduced them.

"Michel, meet Julien and Matthieu." Then looking from the new men back to me, "This is your guide, he is going to take you to within four hundred yards of your 'safe house' in Antibes. He is one of our old hands, and thanks to him you should avoid many of those anxious moments usually felt during the first few hours in the field."

I shook hands with the two men, sizing them up. Julien was tall, dark, and in his early twenties, Matthieu short and middle-aged. Both were English but spoke faultless, rapid French, and their appearance was such as to make them pass unnoticed in any French crowd, train, or restaurant.

The two expert radio operators were all set for their first venture. With French clothes and all accessories, down to the last detail, packed away in their suitcases, they were ready and, indeed, anxious to get under way. Each man was provided with a money belt containing one hundred thousand francs and in their wallets they carried some small notes, their identity cards, and various other French identification papers such as photographs, an odd newspaper clipping, local tram tickets, etc., to implement the cover stories which had been indelibly impressed upon their minds.

For this landing operation I was given a replica of the identity card that had served for my first mission and which I had destroyed while crossing the Pyrenees.

It was not imagined that this identity card, bearing the name Pierre Chauvet, would serve any better purpose than a British passport with my real name, if I were caught red-handed on the beach, but it had been given to me in addition to some money in order to help me make my escape overland in case, for some unpredictable reason, I should miss the submarine in the pitch-black night.

On February 26, I and my party entrained for Bristol. Here we boarded a CW 20 aircraft, apparently standing by in our honor, and were flown to Gibraltar in style and comfort. This was to be our last experience of being treated like V.I.P.'s for quite a long time.

Captain Benson of Joint Intelligence who represented—among other things—S.O.E.'s interests in Gibraltar, met us on the tarmac and drove with us up to the Rock Hotel. Owing to the presence of the driver we were unable to speak of anything but the weather and our flight. However, once Julien and Matthieu had been given their rooms, Benson followed me into the privacy of my room, and we could get down to business.

"They're keeping you rather busy, aren't they?" began Benson.

"Someone had to bring these chaps," I said, "and as I've only recently returned from the area I thought I might as well do it myself."

"You won't get a submarine as easily as you did last time. Captain S. got the Admiralty order for this landing operation through our old friend the Panda. Things are changing for the worse here, and all submarines are packed with supplies for Malta these days. The percentage of surface craft getting through is negligible. The Malta situation is giving everyone the jitters and S. is afraid you are going to make a habit of using his meager brood of submarines for cloak-and-dagger stuff. I warn you, S. is after your blood."

"Well, now, isn't that just dandy?" I spluttered. "Why don't they sort this out at Admiralty level and let the common people fight in peace? How's an Army captain supposed to persuade a Naval four-ringer to hand over one of his pet toys? Personally, I can't blame him for wanting to get on with his own job. What's to stop me and my two chaps going by felucca, anyway?"

"Only the fact that the feluccas are jammed to the hatches with other agents being landed at various places in the South of France," said Benson.

"Are they here now?" I inquired.

"No. But they're due any day"

"Where'll you park them?" I asked.

"In our special house down in the town."

"So that's why we're being kept up here."

"Precisely."

"Funny how we're all kept strictly segregated at home only to meet in this holiday camp," I said.

"Unavoidable," replied Benson.

"How do I tackle S.?" I asked, getting back to my major headache.

"My advice would be to let yourself be used as a punching ball You'll get your submarine eventually. After all, you were no trouble to them on your first trip."

The difficulty over the submarine was, as Benson had intimated, quite considerable; so was the delay before one was available. During the interval of waiting, the other members of the French Section had arrived, and this party consisted of two more men than were expected. How I managed to wangle these extra men into the small submarine on which I and my original party of two had been somewhat ungraciously accepted, I never understood The extra men included another radio operator and an agent on a special mission. It was decided to land them at the Pointe d'Agay after the Antibes operation.

There was plenty of time for practice with the foldboats. This was done beside the airport on a strip of coastline adjacent to the Spanish frontier, which was defended by the Independent Company. The major in charge was most helpful and resourceful. He devised a contraption whereby a compass could be quickly fitted into recesses which were made in the board that covered the front of my canoe. This would help me to return to the submarine in the pitch dark by following a back-bearing. The major had a sling made for my torch, to which he also fitted a blackout funnel, so that only a thin shaft of light could be seen by the submarine's lookout men while following my return course through their powerful glasses When these accessories had been made, they were tried out at a full-dress rehearsal at night from a landing craft off the east side of the Rock. Owing to a strong current, I had to paddle for several hours trying vainly to reach the coast. On the way back I had to be rescued by the landing craft, whose lookouts, having followed the pinprick light from my torch, were able to pick me up after I had drifted two miles in the direction of Tangiers. As a result of this trial, senior officers of the *Maidstone* (Depot Ship of the submarines) judged that the real operation would prove a failure. However, I was not impressed by their forecast, since I knew from experience that the currents in the South of France were nothing like as strong as those I had encountered during the trial.

The next step was my introduction to the submarine which was to take us to Antibes. The captain of H.M. Submarine *P42* was a young lieutenant of about twenty-six and his name was Alastair Mars. This was to be his first patrol since bringing his submarine from the Clyde to Gibraltar. He had been instructed not to attempt any sinkings until after the four men had been landed at two different points. Only then was his offensive patrol to begin.

Before leaving Gibraltar we had a night practice to show the four new men how to climb down from the bridge into their canoes without upsetting them. This was no easy matter, even in a flat calm, for the canoes were very light and needed gentle handling. On the night of the practice, which was held in the center of the harbor inside the breakwater, a squall made things very difficult, but fortunately all four managed to perform their task without mishap.

It was early one morning at the end of March when we finally embarked on what was to be known as Operation A.

P42 was a small submarine never intended to carry five extra passengers, but the hospitality of the officers and petty officers included giving up their bunks at certain hours and this allowed my four companions to be comparatively comfortable during the ten-days' voyage. I took up my old position on the control-room floor, which was not a busy thoroughfare after dark, for the submarine would then be surfaced and making its highest speed on the diesels while charging the enormous batteries for the next day's slow progress underwater.

Eventually we reached the zone where the first part of Operation A was to be conducted. On the ninth night we sighted St. Raphael and the light above the Bay of Agay where the couple on Operation B were to be set down later on. We passed the Hotel St. Christophe with its own little bay, where I had landed in January. Then the Bay of Napoule lay before us, followed by Cannes, the Ile Ste. Marguerite, and Golfe Juan where, as dawn was about to break, we dived. During the early morning, Mars kept *P42* cruising back and forth off Antibes and let me have a good look at it through the periscope.

After what seemed a very long day, the darkness came at long last and we could surface. The half moon, which would later go down over the Maritime Alps, now cast its pale reflection before us. I was standing on the bridge beside the captain and *P42* was about four miles out of Antibes.

Suddenly my arm was nudged and Mars said: "Look at that confounded boat over there, floating about without lights. I don't want any snooping patrols to report our position. God knows what it is. I think I'll ram him."

"Hold on, sir!" I said. "It may be a harmless French fishing boat doing a spot of black-market fishing and, not wanting to give his own position away, he's doused his lights."

Then it suddenly dawned on me that it was more likely to be one of the Spanish feluccas, manned by Polish crews. I recalled a conversation I had had a fortnight back when I had been asked by Major de G., then in Gibraltar, to help settle the transport question, where the felucca should land the rest of their men who could not go by submarine. I had given them a spot near the Pointe de l'Esquillon, about halfway between Antibes and Agay. This had been agreed to; but before leaving the conference I remembered saying: "Above all, don't let the felucca come to Antibes and get mixed up with the submarine, or else everyone will get the jitters."

I quickly explained all this to the captain, whose instant comment was, "Why the hell didn't they tell me about it?"

"Goodness knows," I said.

The felucca, which is what it proved to be, must have seen the submarine at about the same time as Mars saw it. After several seconds of apparent hesitation it made off as fast as it could. I never afterwards found out why my friend, Jan Buchowski, had brought his felucca here, but at all events he had succeeded in gumming up our plans for that night, because by the time we had dived, surfaced, and got off course for a few moments chasing him, we found ourselves about half a mile from the Ile Ste. Marguerite instead of entering the Bay of Antibes.

We had to give up the landing project for that night and Matthieu and Julien got the jitters, a thing I had hoped to avoid.

On the following day we cruised up and down as before, and that night there were to be no mistakes. To help make the time pass, I explained the lay of the land to my two charges so that they would know exactly what to expect on landing. I drew them a plan showing the circular gardens which they were aiming for and which they would reach by climbing the concrete steps I had already inspected during my previous visit to Antibes. I told them in detail how I had stood with one foot on the low wall looking at the steps and how, by turning my head, I had seen all the way along the Boulevard Maréchal Foch to the third turning on the right, past which lay Louis' house, Number 31.

"You say you can remember all that so clearly, Michel, without even having had a definite plan in mind at the time," said Julien, somewhat doubtfully.

"Yes, I can and I do," I replied. "In fact, this was the plan I had in mind."

"But what if there should be some slight discrepancy in what you imagine you saw. Perhaps it's the fourth turning to the right and not the third," suggested Matthieu.

"Tell you what I'll do," I said, to put them both perfectly at ease. "I'll leave you both with your luggage in the gardens and go and check up that the house is really where I left it. How's that?"

"I shall feel better if you do that," said Julien. "One would feel an awful clot floating around Antibes with a radio set and suitcase in the small hours of the night during the curfew. What do you say, Matthieu?"

"Well, I feel an awful clot already asking Michel to do this, after all the nanny work he's been put to already. It'd be different if he wasn't here. Then we'd just have to do the best we could."

It was our longest day of inactivity, but like everything else it came to an end and again *P42* surfaced. We waited for the town to put out its lights and for the population to go to bed. The operation was to start around midnight.

At about 11:30 P.M. Mars began to close with his objective, and from about two miles distance he and I caught sight of some powerful lights moving slowly to and fro along the front, but neither we nor the lookouts had any idea what they could be.

As we slowly cruised in to within about a mile of the steps, I peered at these lights intently. I had hoped it would all be so easy and quiet doing it in the dark. Although I was almost certain I had recognized the unlighted boat of the previous night as being the felucca, it had nevertheless given me a jolt, for I knew Jan intimately. He was one of those Sten-happy, grenade-throwing young Poles and I distinctly remembered that our last conversation had been a one-sided affair during which this twenty-one-year-old "Virtuti militari" holder had suggested we should team up and go U-boat hunting together. For a few moments while both boats were eyeing each other I feared that the temptation might be too great for Jan. Here, like a gift from heaven, lay the dream surpassing all his dreams, and what did it matter that there were eight agents to be landed? They could be landed afterwards. My imagination had gone on to watch the noisy, fruitless battle that would inevitably have taken place between these allied hotheads if either had given rise to a suspicion of aggressiveness. All that was last night and now here were these blasted lights cluttering up the very spot where I hoped to perform in peace. It was going to be tricky enough to find the steps in the dark and still trickier to rediscover the whereabouts of the submarine at this distance on a back-bearing. These moving lights were certainly not going to make things any easier. I knew Mars must be anxious to get rid of all the agents as soon as possible, so as to get on with his own war, the real war. So there was no question of postponing the landing for a few paltry lights. I could hear the captain's muffled tones in the voice pipe ordering the canoes to be brought up through the forward hatch.

Presently he spoke

"Well, Michel, you'd better get cracking. God knows what those lights signify I'll keep you covered and my chaps will be on the lookout for the pencil light coming from your torch on the way back. Good hunting"

"Thank you, sir," I said, as I moved away and climbed over the rail, feeling for the slots on the outside of the bridge that led down to the outer casing.

My canoe had already been lowered into the water, and a suitcase and radio set belonging to one of the operators lay neatly stowed in the rear seat. I slid down a rope from the outer casing into the foldboat's front seat. My Colt was in its shoulder holster, the torch round my neck, and the compass, which was set on the correct back-bearing from the ship's compass, was in my pocket. When I left *P42* she was lying about 1,500 yards from the concrete steps.

Before leaving the bridge I had suggested to the captain that one of the men due to land on the following night might be posted on the bridge so that if any fishermen became inquisitive he could tell them in French to move away for their own safety, using the pretext that they were on a mine-laying exercise from Toulon. Mars had agreed to this ruse. The two machine guns on the bridge were manned and in one way and another it was quite clear that he was determined to make a success of the enterprise.

I paddled off toward my destination and, as I drew closer to it, I discovered that the lights came from powerful acetylene lamps attached to the bows of big rowing boats. What I did not know was what those boats were up to. There were three of them, and they seemed to be patrolling the entire bay. I waited until there was a suitable gap and then spurted toward the steps. It was my intention to unload the luggage, take it up the steps, and hide it under a tree in the gardens. I was then going to return for Matthieu and Julien, who would follow me in a second canoe, when I would also land the second and last lot of luggage.

But at the very moment that I was about to put a foot on the rocks, the place became illuminated by an acetylene lamp. I did not have to look round to realize that one of the boats was coming in my direction. Quickly settling myself back in the canoe, I turned about and made off as fast as I could in the general direction of North Africa. Out of the corner of my eye I could see that the boat with the dazzling head lamp was catching up with me. In the same glance I took in the fact that three oars were dipping and pulling with the precision of a practiced crew. When I registered the fact that blue lines ran along glittering white paint around their bows, I was certain that I was being chased by coast guards, and that all these boats were on the lookout for me.

Fortunately, the night was ideal, and not a ripple disturbed the smooth waters in the bay. I turned on all the power I possessed, and with long sweeping strokes began to outdistance the boat. When I felt comparatively safe I lit up my torch. Then, with a hundred yards between myself and the sizzling light, I pulled out the compass and laid it in the recess before me. As I followed the hairline I hoped that the first few hundred yards had not upset my back-bearing. A thousand yards would not take long to cover in one of these canoes, especially after that racing start. I could see absolutely nothing. Then, to my relief, *P42* suddenly loomed up before me.

Someone held my canoe as I climbed out. On the outer casing there was dead silence and I could see precious little.

"I must speak to the captain," I said.

"I'm standing beside you," came a deep-sounding chuckle from Alastair Mars.

I started to relate my experiences in gasps, as I was somewhat out of breath from my exertions, but Mars broke into my recital, saying:

"We saw you clearly all the way there and back. It was like Henley Regatta. Those weren't coast guards, chum. They're just fishing boats, freshly painted, out on the night shift. One of them nearly bumped into us as you were about to land, and your pal told him the tale and also discovered that they're due to pack up at any moment now."

"So they are," I said, somewhat abashed at having wrongly suspected, as so many do who are up to no good, that everyone must be looking for me. "They seem to be making for the entrance to the harbor."

"You were wise to buzz off, Michel," said Mars consolingly. "A little difficult for you to explain that you were a pearl diver, or some such nonsense at this hour of the night. However, as well as the machine guns, I've got men manning the three-inch gun down here. If there's any trouble I'll soon settle their hash."

"Don't forget," I said in a still, small voice, "that I'm out there, too."

The captain laughed. "Your two lads are already waiting for you in their canoe a cable's length off the starboard bow."

"Well, this'll take rather longer, sir. So don't get impatient and go away."

"Don't worry. I'll come in a little closer on the same bearing so as to make it easier for you."

"Thanks," I said and lowered myself back into my canoe.

I soon found Julien and Matthieu waiting for me some two hundred yards away in the inky night. In the absence of the acetylene lamps, the bay was now in complete darkness and it was only the sound of our paddles being occasionally dipped that indicated our position.

"Follow me closely," I said, "and only talk in whispers."

Hardly waiting for a reply I paddled off slowly toward the land. After a minute or so I looked round only to discover that the second canoe was nowhere in sight.

"Holy Mother!" I muttered to myself, pulling up and reversing along the way I had come. A hundred yards brought me alongside my ghostlike companions, who were creeping along with a special feather action of the paddles at a speed that was almost imperceptible.

"For God's sake, step on it, chums!" I whispered. "Don't forget I've another trip to do. I couldn't land the first lot of luggage owing to those blasted fishing boats."

"You ought to see the phosphorescent wake you're leaving behind at that bat," came the reply.

"All right, I'll slow up," I said, swallowing back my impatience. I reduced the speed of my valuable convoy to under two knots.

It was quite difficult to find the steps now that there was no light whatsoever, and at one moment I ran aground on some submerged rocks. However, there was no damage to my foldboat, and after clearing the obstacle we reached the steps without further trouble.

I climbed out of my canoe, lifted the cases onto a rock, picked up the canoe, and placed it on another rock with the bows pointing seawards. Then, holding the second canoe, I helped Matthieu and Julien to land and told them to rest while I pulled out the second canoe and attached its bows to the stern of my own.

Next I carried the suitcase and the radio set up the steps separately so as to leave my right hand free for any unfriendly welcome, but there was not a soul about, and the gardens beyond seemed blacker than the night itself. I put the cases under a tree and fetched up the two men.

Before leaving them I said, "I'm going to the house now to make sure where it is. You're well hidden and you've got nothing to worry about. When I come back I'll whistle the tune 'La Madelon.' So long."

I was just about to move away when the lights of two bicycles came into sight down the road. The three of us automatically ducked while two policemen whirled by, the dynamos of their lamps singing against the front tires as they went.

Now I got up and moved off to see how well I had remembered the place. First I looked for the street sign of the wide avenue leading straight up from the circular gardens. Having seen it before, I supposed that its absence on either side meant that this was not my street.

I then went west along the coast road looking for the avenue I knew so well, but could not find it. What I could see in this inky darkness made no sense to me at all. How different it had all seemed in daylight—and how easy.

As I had to return to the gardens to reconnoiter the eastern side I whistled "La Madelon" and, coming up to Matthieu and Julien, said, "It's all Greek to me in this light. After last night's efforts I'm not even sure it's the right town."

"Never mind," said Matthieu, who was feeling a lot better now that his feet were once more on mother earth. "It's the right country, all right. I can smell garlic somewhere."

"You're right there," I said, delighted with this optimism. "I'm just going to snoop around in another direction. I hope I shan't be too long."

I walked down the road on the other side of the gardens and saw the fort which I knew of old, but still could not recognize any of the roads. The houses seemed larger somehow and I began to get a little worried, for it was already 3 A.M. As I retraced my steps toward the gardens and my eyes became more accustomed to the night, I suddenly realized that the road leading up from them into the town was, in fact, the one I was after. Ignoring the absence of its street sign, I went quickly up the right-hand pavement, counting the three turnings of which I was certain, and there, sure enough, just beyond the third turning, was Louis' house, No. 31.

I peered at the name on the plate to make doubly sure. There it was: Dr. A. Lévi. I chortled to myself, thinking what the local Gestapo would give to know the sort of fishy underground activities that centered round this innocent-looking abode.

I then hurried back to the gardens. My footsteps did not make a sound, for I had changed my gum boots for black plimsolls. Whenever I heard anyone approaching I kept out of sight. I now felt sure that the worst part of the operation was over. The chances of missing the submarine no longer seemed to worry me. I knew that it would take a great deal of opposition before Mars would be forced to leave the bay without me. My great satisfaction lay in the fact that I had fulfilled my promise to my two friends.

Again I whistled "La Madelon" as I approached their tree in the gardens.

"I thought you were never coming," said Matthieu.

"Everything's O.K." I announced. "Sorry to have been so long."

"You mean you've found the road?"

"Yes, and the house too."

"Oh boy, oh boy!"

"It's exactly as I showed you on the plan. Straight up this road. Count three turnings on the right and the house is on the far corner of the third turning. You pop up there now while I get the rest of the luggage I'll leave it here. Come and fetch it before dawn. In the meantime, I'll be thinking of you boys, and maybe we'll meet again before you know it."

"Well, so long, Skipper," said Julien. "You certainly brought home the bacon"

"Thanks a million," said Matthieu.

We all shook hands. It was a strange farewell. Nothing was said, but there was a world of feeling in our handclasps.

I watched until they were swallowed up in the darkness. Then I went over to the parapet and down the concrete steps. I placed both canoes carefully into the water, laid my compass on the board, and paddled off on my back-bearing. I switched on the flashlamp and looked around for any signs of dawn. It was nearly 4 A.M. but still pitch dark. I paddled on for several minutes, feeling the second canoe tugging at my stern like a sulky mule. There were no signs of the submarine. I felt I could paddle on all night—probably due to the benzedrine tablets.

Odd thoughts crossed my mind. I saw myself lying on the sunny beaches as I had done around here so often in peacetime. Such an expedition as tonight's would never have occurred to me then. Little did my parents realize, as they financed those pleasure trips, that they were giving me the key to this venture.

Suddenly I saw three blue flashes over to the right. I turned my flashlight in their direction and altered course. There was no doubt in my mind that those flashes came from the submarine and that the current must have pushed her toward the rocks after all. There was also no doubt that Alastair Mars was more than co-operating with me. He knew very well that there was another load of luggage to be taken and that his Aldis lamp—even if dimmed—would give his position away, if it were seen. I decided that it was a treat to work with the Royal Navy.

In a few moments I was lying alongside and, without any fuss or unnecessary chatter, Lt. Haddow put in the two cases, cut the painter between the canoes, and turned me round, saying, "For Pete's sake make it snappy. We've been here four hours already and three more boats were nosing around in your absence."

"You've moved northwest at least seven hundred and fifty yards," I said. "I nearly lost you."

"The current shoved us in," said Haddow.

"There are some bad rocks around here," I warned.

"You're telling me," came the reply. "We're having quite a game standing clear of them. The captain's bringing us up still closer to the steps for a quick getaway, as dawn is only just around the corner."

"O.K. Shan't be ten minutes on this trip. I'm getting to know the way. So long."

With only some seven hundred yards to do, I was soon back close to the shore My eyes were now thoroughly accustomed to the dark and I easily avoided the submerged rocks that had surprised me before and which, at my present speed, would have ripped the thin bottom of my canoe, like paper. When the rocks were only thirty yards away, I noticed several shadowy forms moving about at the top of the steps. I instantly stopped paddling, zipped open my jacket, and pulled out my Colt automatic, laying it, still attached to its lanyard, on the board in front of me.

What was all this flap about? A dozen suppositions flashed through my mind. If I did not deliver the second radio set it would take months to get another one out here. If I gave it to one of the remaining two who were landing elsewhere and asked him to deliver it, he would have to know this address—a thing I wanted to avoid.

I turned the canoe round and paddled gently backwards, so as to be able to make a quick getaway if necessary.

Now the figures started bounding down the steps, led, I noticed, by a bald man. I breathed more freely, for this could be none other than my old friend Louis, who had probably come to collect the cases and might also have something to say to me. When I was sure it was he, I slipped my Colt back into its holster and put out a hand to steady myself on the rocks.

Louis hopped over from rock to rock like a two-year-old and shook me warmly by the hand. Wasting no time, he said, "What about those faked baptismal certificates you promised for my two daughters when I last saw you?" *

"Aren't you ever satisfied, Doctor?" I said. "I've just brought you two real live radio men and you buzz me on the certificates. We can fake Protestant papers easily enough, but Catholic ones seem to be more difficult. You shall have them when they're ready." Then peering round I added, "What's all this mob doing, Louis?"

"Your two chaps come to help with the luggage and some of the gang come to watch the fun."

"Louis, have you ever heard about security?" I asked.

"No, you must tell me about it some day," laughed the Doctor.

"One of these days the cops'll put the arm on you, Louis," I warned.

"Well, if they try it tonight they'll get an awful surprise."

"They won't try it tonight. They'll do it at three in the morning when you're alone and very sleepy," I said.

"I know what I'm doing, Michel," said Louis in a good-natured tone, then added, "By the way, would you do something for me?"

"Name it, Louis," I said with similar good nature.

"I'd like you to take a friend of mine back to England in the submarine."

"Who is it?"

"You won't know him. His name's Bernard."

* Dr. Lévi had bought a house in his daughters' name, but being Jews they were liable to have it confiscated by the Germans This false certificate would prove that they were not Jews and save the house The certificate was later dropped by parachute and had the desired effect

"Don't be a chump, Louis. You introduced Bernard to me in your own home three months ago, if it's the same one."

" 'Course it's the same one."

"Well, why all the mystery? I've had a bad night, Louis, I'm in a hurry. Tell him to get in. They're impatient out there."

"Sorry, Michel. Just my way of fooling. It's so nice to see you and meet people who carry out their promises. It's all so short. Come back soon." And with that he hauled out the two cases, and Bernard loomed up from behind to get into the vacant seat.

To my horror I saw my six-foot friend aiming one foot at the floor of my canoe as though about to step onto the bridge of a liner. Like lightning I moved the canoe out of reach while Bernard was neatly rescued from taking an early morning plunge by the ever-alert Louis.

"In heaven's name, Bernard," I muttered, "sit on your foundation and slither in or you'll go right through this paper bag."

Bernard obliged, but I had plenty of perspiration running down my face before he was finally settled into his seat. Hanging onto a rock with my left hand, I shook hands with the crouching Doctor and waved to Matthieu and Julien before slipping away for the last home run.

Bernard announced that he had been waiting ten days for me to come and that he was still in a daze, having been pulled out of bed by Louis only ten minutes previously. I tried to explain that it was only thanks to the fishermen that I had made the third trip which had enabled this meeting, but Bernard was in too great a stupor to understand what I was saying, and I could feel the canoe trembling as my friend, new to this mode of transport, tried desperately to keep his balance.

I did not have to bother much with the compass, for by now *P42* was only about five hundred yards out and she soon came in sight As we drew alongside I balanced the paddle in the crook of my arms and, cupping my hands to my mouth, announced quietly in the direction of the birdge, "I've got a pal with me."

But they could not have understood very well, for I distinctly heard the voice of Buck Taylor (the first lieutenant) in the stillness of the night saying to the captain: "He's got a dame with him." And the captain's reply: "I don't give a row of dead

Huns if he's brought Cleopatra or Mary, Queen of Scots, so long as we get cracking out of this ruddy bay."

Bernard and I clambered up the rope, helped by willing hands. As we climbed up to the bridge the canoe was raised and taken in through the forward hatch. Before we had reached the top of the bridge, *P42* was already under way.

Seeing that the captain was fully occupied, I showed Bernard down the hatch and led him to the wardroom. It was empty, the four officers of *P42* and most of the crew being at duty stations for the swift getaway.

I handed Bernard a cigarette and took one myself, drawing deeply on it. The sound of the diesel engines turning over at full revs was sweet music to my ears. I was sure that Mars would have no objection to this extra passenger when he heard who he was Through the wisps of smoke we smiled warmly at each other. Destiny had made us the forgers of a real Entente Cordiale, and this was a moment we were not likely to forget.

The shrill note of the klaxon shattered the silence. I stubbed out my cigarette and Bernard followed suit. A clatter of many boots tripping down the vertical ladder from the bridge to the control room, mixed with staccato words of command, told me that we were going to crash dive.

In a matter of seconds Mars was beside us in the wardroom. We both rose at his entry, but he looked at neither of us. With his head slightly cocked to one side and one hand resting on an upper bunk, he seemed to be listening for something. Then we all heard it. It was like an express train heard first in the distance of a still night With its rapid approach the sound grew louder and louder and then diminished as it passed. Not until dead silence had been restored within the submerged submarine and the faint hissing sound from the electric motors again reached the ears, did Mars relax his tension; for those were the fatal seconds in which the depth charges would do their deadly work.

"Phew!" he breathed, wiping his brow and coming down to earth. "That was quite close enough. Lucky he left no visiting card. I made a wide turn leaving the bay and, at the last moment, we sighted a French destroyer sweeping round head-on toward us at full bore. All his lights were out, but I don't think he saw us."

"I feel I owe you a double apology," exclaimed Bernard in fluent English, holding out his hand toward the captain. "In the first place, I was responsible for holding you up a few minutes, and secondly, that my compatriots in the destroyer should be your enemies. I, too, used to be a French destroyer commander, and I confess it is a new experience to pass so close to the keel of such a ship in these circumstances."

"Don't apologize," said Mars. "You are welcome on board my boat, particularly if you are in the same business as Michel. It won't be a pleasure trip exactly, because after landing two other men tonight, we're proceeding to the Italian coast on patrol."

"I'm afraid I kept you for four and a half hours on that job, sir," I put in. "No doubt one of those fishermen reported our presence. They must have telephoned Toulon. It seems stupid merely to say thank you for all you did."

"That's all right," said Mars. "I enjoyed every minute of it and so did everyone else."

Cups of excellent cocoa were brought in and the night's work was discussed from every angle. A first successful page had been written in the records of *P42*. Their Jolly Roger, a flag bearing the skull and crossbones, which submarines hoist on returning to port to show the score, could now boast a single dagger—the sign for landing agents on foreign soil. Another dagger would be added the same evening, if that event were also successful.

Throughout the day we had a well-earned sleep.

During the afternoon I confirmed the position of the Bay of Agay through the periscope and slept again while the submarine moved slowly back and forth inside the bay waiting for nightfall.

When the time came we surfaced. Again it was a perfect night and once more we saw the acetylene lights on the fishing boats. But this time it was a simple operation. There would be only one trip on which I would carry the luggage and then tow back the second canoe. There was no exact spot for setting down these two. Their luggage was not heavy, the radio operator having a light, compact set, and neither of the men was fussy about anything. After landing they would approach the nearest railway station on the coast and catch the first train to their respective destinations after daybreak.

The captain did not waste any time by making us paddle a long way. Once the last fishing boat had cleared off, he ran in to within two hundred and fifty yards of the rocks and set us down at 11 P.M. The two men were as cool as cucumbers. They had been ideal passengers all the way. They were also glad to be able to get on with the jobs for which they had been trained. I took all the typewritten pages from which they had been memorizing addresses and destroyed them before leaving.

We set off in two canoes, and this time I carried no compass. The sea was absolutely calm. On reaching the rocks I handed them their luggage, wished them good luck, and then towed back their canoe. I never saw them again.

The submarine was visible all the time. Within half an hour I was back on board, the canoes stowed, and *P42* was on her way for the Italian coast at full speed.

CHAPTER III

"WELCOME HOME, Michel," said Major B., coming over with outstretched hand. "You've brought it off again in traditional style. The three radio operators you landed have all been in constant touch with us ever since. We're really getting somewhere now. Nice fellow, Bernard. We've had some interesting conversations in the past week. Told me something rather odd about his first meeting with General de Gaulle. When he learned you'd brought him back in a submarine he snarled:

'Kidnapped by those British.' Bernard tried to explain that, on the contrary, he was in your debt, but the General would have none of it. At least, that's Bernard's story."

"Well, I'll be damned if I understand anything any more," I shrugged.

"Never mind. It's a political misunderstanding which we're faced with every day. How do you feel after it all?"

"As fit as a fiddle, now. The return trip in the sub had its moments, but I spent most of the time afterwards sleeping it off and lying in the sun while waiting about for the aircraft that finally brought me back. The combination of sleep and sunshine for an entire week was like a month's holiday to me."

"I'm rather glad to hear you say that . . . because there's something rather big on, and I hadn't forgotten my promise to make up for the very short leave you restricted yourself to last time."

"Never mind about that," I smiled. "Can you imagine me lolling about under a parasol and missing something big like the Second Front?"

"I hardly think we're quite ready for anything on such a large scale as the Second Front yet. What the chiefs of staff had in mind for you was something of a more intimate and specialized nature," he hinted.

Major B. then proceeded to outline my new assignment. It was an exciting job, but to my intense disappointment it never came off. The Nazis were using a powerful radio transmitter near Paris called Ste. Assise to direct their U-boat campaign, and it was so powerful that the U-boats could pick up its messages without having to surface. Sabotaging this transmitter would deal a crippling blow to the German undersea campaign. My partners in this enterprise were to be two brothers, Henry and Alfred, whose peacetime occupations as circus acrobats equipped them beautifully for the job. The section had a scale model of the transmitter, and our training for the operation was characteristically thorough. Only at the last minute as Henry, Alfred, and I were waiting to take off were all the signals called off. A brave but foolhardy Frenchman had apparently taken it on himself to attend to the job. He had failed, alerted the Germans, and Ste. Assise was swarming with Wehrmacht guards. Our frustration and disappointment can only be imagined.

May, June, and July passed. Headquarters sent me on one course after the other, keeping me in the U.K. in the hope of sending me to France on the sort of solo mission for which they considered me best fitted. There was talk of sending me to Switzerland, but that fell through. An idea of sending me to plot the position of ideal landing grounds for aircraft in France was put aside because such activities could be done just as well, if not better, by men already in the areas concerned.

Although consulted from time to time by the Admiralty as to the feasibility of landing agents at various points and despite keeping my hand in as a saboteur and parachutist, I was bored to distraction. Events which hitherto had run like clockwork seemed to have come to a full stop.

Like everyone else, I had to face the situation and try to develop some patience. I had to learn that things were not always going to fall into my lap like ripe plums. Had I already forgotten the eleven lean years since I had scraped through Cambridge with a very lucky degree in Modern Languages and wandered from job to job in search of my vocation? Could two successful war missions rub out all that frustration? I had hoped that the seven ripe years had, at last, come my way, but now I knew that they had not.

A large cross had been put on the Ste. Assise operation, the model in the office was broken up, and everyone except me was busy with other matters. Major B. told me that I ought to consider myself a lucky devil that S.A.D. had got their information through in time, or I might well have landed slap in the midst of all the commotion. I was asked to consider what I would have thought of Headquarters if such an eventuality had occurred. It would not have been their fault. It was all a part of the risks of this business. Thanks to working in watertight compartments there was always an outside chance that two lots of people might be attending to the same job at the same time in the same place. Little could I suppose that I was to be a witness of such a dangerous and unlikely coincidence in the not-too-distant future.

It was the second half of August, 1942, before I was finally called to the office by my chief and offered a job.

"I've got something for you at last, Michel. It's not exactly up your street, but it's something you could do well, if you'd like to consider it."

"At the moment I'd even consider scraping barnacles off the bottom of the feluccas with a putter," I said.

"Those plums are kept for our 'plus two' men, Michel."

"Well, sir, I'm all agog. What sort of a street had you in mind?"

"It's a wide and winding road that has no end."

"The permanent way of those who are left behind?" I queried.

"Yes, if you like to put it that way. But seriously, this is a big job, Michel. I want you to get out as liaison officer to a man called Carte who works the southeast zone. He's got hundreds of men working for him and his area includes some seventeen towns. They're building up a vast organization. We thought of you because you met Carte through Louis on your first trip. Cannes would be your headquarters, so you wouldn't feel strange there."

"How long has Carte been running the local show?" I asked.

"For a month or so."

"Any of our chaps with him?"

"I'm afraid the last man has just been caught."

"Oh!" I exclaimed. "Do I happen to know him?"

"Yes. I'm afraid he's your old friend, Laurent. Part of your job would be to try and get him out."

"I see," I said slowly. "What's the rest of the setup?"

"Besides joining the Carte circuit, I want you to contact Laurent's cells. They'll be lying doggo, naturally, and they'll fight shy of anyone claiming to replace their old boss. I leave it to you to see what you can do about them."

"Now, here are the general lines of this job," went on Major B. "You'll be dropped by parachute somewhere near Montpellier and will catch a train for Cannes. You shall have the train times. You stay for a while with Antoine, whose address you'll get later. Our friend Pierrot from H.Q. is holding the fort until a new man comes. He asked Carte if he'd like you to be that man and the answer was yes. You'd have to organize parachute landings of arms and explosives, reception committees for felucca landings, find 'pickup' grounds for Lysanders and Hudson bombers, and, above all, prepare the sabotaging of all the railways in your area. Before leaving you'll be given the B.B.C. message that will be broadcast in clear every half hour throughout the day, and that will mean that the lines must be blown up late that night—after all French passenger trains have ceased running—and that night, for your especial ear, will be two nights before D-day. You will be responsible for the financing of this group. It comes to about a million francs per month. The three hundred-odd men of the group only get three thousand francs per month each. It's a pittance for chaps to live on. The top men don't get anything. We'll send you money regularly. As this is the unoccupied zone of France we want to keep it that way. So no bangs in the night, please. You'll be told soon enough if there are any specific targets we want you to attend to. Is this clear so far?"

"Perfectly," I said. "Sounds about as exciting as a glass of stale beer."

"There is an instructor out there," continued Major B. ignoring my flippant remark, "by the name of Gervais. This ace, who passed out top in all the training schools, will come under your aegis as 'organizer.' He trains the local amateur talent and turns them into experts. There's a commando instructor, Robert, who teaches ambush tactics and works on his own in Antibes. Your wireless operator is your old friend Julien. Your number two is Porthos. He'll tell you all about the Laurent situation. There's no courier so far. You'd better find one from local talent. At the present we're training women over here for those jobs, and you shall have one in due course if you need one. The second major point, besides the railway sabotage, is for you to inform us of the whereabouts of gatherings of French youth hiding away in the mountains to avoid forced labor in Germany. Where you consider these groups are sufficiently large and officered by men of caliber and determination, give us their position and we'll arm them by parachute and turn them into guerrilla bands."

"Fascinating," I interposed. "Any chance of joining these irregulars, one day?"

"Shouldn't be surprised . . ." Then to my beaming look, "Let's find them and arm them first."

"When do I go, sir?"

"This very moon period. But, Michel, don't forget what I said at the beginning about this possibly not being your cup of tea. You see, as an organizer, you must delegate the work to others and keep out of sight yourself. In practice, as well as in theory, your orders go to your 'number two' who sees to their being carried out. In theory you shouldn't really come into contact with anyone else at all. Of course, we've discovered that this is hardly possible, but that's the general line to follow as rigidly as you can. Remember, Michel, that if you can't stomach this thought you needn't accept the job. It's really a kind of Diplomatic Post. Above all, you must keep the peace. Harmony is an essential to this job."

"I'll take it," was my prompt reply, influenced by the possibilities implied by the words D-day and guerrilla bands.

"By the way, there's some paper work attached to this sort of job. I want situation reports to enlarge on the W/T messages. This shouldn't be such a bind as you imagine, particularly as Vera Atkins tells me that some story you wrote in Runyonese stopped all work in the office recently. Write your reports in that style, using your own code for names, and if these reports fall into the wrong hands they'll never unravel them. Sign yourself Ramon."

I was reissued with my old identity card bearing the name Pierre Chauvet, a demobilization paper from the French Army, a set of French clothes, a packed money belt, and a full set of ration tickets and tobacco cards. A small suitcase with shirts, handkerchiefs, shaving tackle, and a change of underwear was to be attached—just above me—to the parachute by which I would land.

Once again, on August 27, 1942, I entered the charming grounds of Tempsford House. Despite the great disappointment that had followed the last visit and the resultant brakes that I applied to my normal zest for action, I was aware that the standard of hospitality was just as high in this station, and I could not altogether repress a thrill at the unknown prospects that the future held in store for me.

It was a beautiful late summer evening as I was driven across the tarmac, with the sun's rim poised on the distant horizon. In the blastproof bay stood the giant Halifax, like a fabulous prehistoric bird. In a moment its four engines would shatter the peaceful silence that now reigned. The idea that in a few hours I would be dropping behind the lines into the turmoil of stricken Europe gave me a sudden stab. "Here we go again!" I thought to myself.

The arrival of a small car containing the crew of the Halifax put an end to a spell of jitters that I had felt coming on like a lump of hot lead in my stomach.

The casual manners of the crew had an instant contagious effect.

"We ought to have a perfect flight," said the captain, "and my navigator will drop you on the exact spot he showed you on the map. I shan't be able to leave my controls so I'll wish you the best of luck now." He shook hands with me.

The navigator then introduced the dispatcher, saying, "This is Janek. He doesn't speak much English but he knows the form backwards. When it's time he'll give you some sandwiches and a thermos of hot coffee with rum in it. He'll tell you when to move over to the hole. When we're doing our run up I shall switch on the red warning light beside the exit hole. Janek will raise his hand and when the light turns to green he'll shout 'Go' and drop his hand. He will also hear my instructions over the intercom. If you chuck yourself out at the precise second you'll drop within thirty feet of the spot we looked at on the map."

I shook hands with André Simon who had accompanied me.

One of the motors now burst into life and it was time for me to enter the plane. Putting my mouth close to Simon's ear I shouted "Thanks for coming to see me off," and climbed up into the aircraft.

I dozed off for a while. The heat from my zipped-up parachute overalls coupled with the regular droning of the motors had made me drowsy. There was no need for me to resist sleep The dispatcher would wake me in plenty of time, and it was pointless to worry about possible mishaps. And yet I could not drop off properly. My mind kept on being alert and following the movements of all the cogs that went to make up the machine of this operation.

I undid the buttoned pocket on my leg, drew out a packet of cigarettes, and pulling one out, raised it inquiringly in the direction of the Polish dispatcher. The latter nodded his head and I threw it over to him; he stuck it on the aluminium ledge beside him. I lit one for myself and inhaled the smoke deeply into my lungs.

We were well over the Channel by now and flying high to avoid flak. The countryside far below looked very peaceful and innocent to me. I settled down and had a good sleep.

When I woke up, the dispatcher was standing over me with a thermos and a small parcel containing a few sandwiches. The coffee was delicious and well braced with rum. I drank two cups of this elixir and munched away at the sandwiches. This light supper meant that my time was almost up. Wiping my hands on my overalls, I then lit another cigarette, put on my helmet, and began to tie the tapes under my chin. Then I leaned back once more, smoking the rest of my cigarette while the dispatcher busied himself opening up the trap doors of the parachute hatch. When the hole was open he signaled that all was ready. Holding onto the side of the thousand-pound bomb rack, I made my way up to the edge of the hole. The dispatcher pulled out the end of my parachute strap and clipped it firmly onto a strong static line running the length of the interior of the plane. Nudging me, he pulled on the strap to show that the clip was properly attached. I nodded. I then sat down on the edge of the hole and peered down. We had lost considerable height and were still going down. Then I saw the lights of a town. That must be Montpellier. I must still have about a minute and a half to go. My watch showed the time to be 1 A.M. Maybe the navigator would circle round the dropping spot once before expecting me to jump.

The aircraft kept losing height and the dispatcher seemed intent on what was reaching him through the intercom. His eyes kept turning toward the lighting panel, but the red light was not yet on. My eyes never left the panel.

Suddenly the warning light flashed on. I tensed myself and looked out of the corner of my eye at the dispatcher's raised hand. I felt them reduce the speed of the aircraft and supposed they must have lowered the flaps. There was obviously to be no circling of the area.

This was it, then. The old panic seized me in the guts and tore up into my throat. I swallowed hard, quelling it, and tightened my stomach muscles. I wished I was not so aware of the horrors of the unnatural act I must now perform in cold blood. It had been all very well practicing these jumps at home with nothing but friends waiting for me below. This was something quite different. I must launch myself into the night over unknown territory with nobody to receive me. All the best wishes in the world were of little use to me now, for I would be alone out there. These thoughts raced through my mind in about one second. Thank God, I thought, the dispatcher was a Pole. Had he been English I might have asked him to shove me out with his foot during the split second of my worst moment. It was better this way. I must put up a good show. I simply must.

"Go!" shouted the dispatcher, flashing his hand down before my face.

I clenched my teeth and shot myself through the center of the gap as stiff as a ramrod. I closed my eyes and held my breath as the slip stream caught and threw me back horizontally under the tail of the aircraft with all the power of its 150 miles per hour. For three of the longest seconds in my life, I was swept through the air like piffle before the wind, until suddenly a jerk from the canvas webbing round my crotch told me that the canopy had opened.

The first horror was over. Then, to my dismay, I found myself spinning round and round. I reached up my hands and clutched the two main braces, ready to stretch them wide apart at the moment they untwisted themselves, to prevent them overlapping the other way as they always did. From three hundred or four hundred feet I would be down in about fifteen seconds and from the way the moon kept winking at me the revolutions did not seem fast enough to disentangle the coil I could see above my head. Keeping my feet locked together I raised my knees slightly to take the first bump, hoping that this would send me sprawling onto my back. Looking up I saw the last fold uncross, and quickly jabbed the braces apart. Simultaneously I felt a bang on my head, saw a blinding flash before my eyes, and passed out cold.

The first thing I knew on waking up was that my head was in great pain. I thought someone must be sawing bricks inside it. Slowly I opened my eyes, but all I saw were hundreds of spots going round and round. I closed them again but the spots were still there. I felt sick and lay back for a moment. Then, rolling onto my side, I was violently ill. I lay still for a while, then slowly began to recover.

Presently a sound came to me above the banging and clanking in my head. I wondered what it could be. Holding my breath I listened carefully. Mosquitoes. Yes, that's what it was; the buzzing of dozens of mosquitoes.

Raising my eyelids a millimeter or so, I discovered that the spots were disappearing. They made a ring round what I saw and danced unpleasantly in an ever-widening circle. I had known this before and knew they would eventually vanish altogether. The moon was playing in some vines immediately in front of my face.

Now I could feel the insects biting me. I raised myself on one elbow and felt a stab of pain in my coccyx. I was thankful for the inch-thick rubber spine pad without which I would have broken my back. I was not yet certain that I had not.

Pulling back the left-hand sleeve of my overalls, I saw the luminous hands of my watch pointing to the hour. It was 1:15. I must have been out for some ten minutes. This would never do. What a piece of luck there was no one about, I thought. Better snap out of it quickly in case anyone had seen me emerge from the plane and start drifting down in this direction.

I now saw that I was sitting on a large rock with my legs dangling over the side. So that was it. My feet had never taken the first bump. Instead, my backside had struck the rock at twenty miles an hour; enough to shake up anyone's foundation. No wonder my head was reeling after my spine had tried to jump through it. I let myself roll off it onto the soft earth of the vines.

I twisted the chrome clasp on my chest and smacked it open. The four clips dropped out. I pushed them aside and zipped open the overalls. In sweating agony I then dragged my limbs free of the clinging material.

This effort left me gasping. Weakly I rolled over on my left side and pulled out my hip flask. Unscrewing the hinged cap I dragged the flask toward my face and let the liquor spill into my mouth: most of it dripped down my face onto the ground. The rum revived me with a jerk and I took two or three big gulps of it before screwing back the cap.

Leaving the flask on the ground I put both hands round my knees and pulled them up under by chin. Apart from the pains in my spine, and head, there was nothing broken. I stretched out my legs and took a good look round. I was at the edge of a large vineyard fringed with olive trees, and the rock I had struck was the one and only rock in sight. If I had come straight down, an expert parachutist like myself would have had nine chances out of ten to avoid crumpling up like an old sack of potatoes. I wondered how the devil the strands of my parachute had got themselves entangled like that. I had not come out of the hole like a corkscrew, but perfectly straight. It was not conceivable that the girls who packed these 'chutes should have plaited the strands while chanting "This year, next year, sometime, never!" or any similar drivel. If they wanted to sabotage the saboteur all they had to do was cut the strands and be done with it. I could not make it out.

Extracting my small suitcase from its thick felt envelope I rolled up the parachute with the overalls inside and stowed the bundle inside the square of felt. Then I looked round carefully, picked up my flask, replaced it in my hip pocket and seeing nothing else lying about I carried this single bundle of compromising evidence into a thicket among the olive trees. Pushing my way in as far as I could, I then poised the heavy bundle on one hand, like a waiter carrying a tray, and threw it three or four yards into a small clearing where it fell out of view.

During this short walk I realized that my left leg was dragging painfully and that either the muscles or tendons in that groin were not performing their normal duties. No doubt, I thought, it would wear off in time.

Now I must get a move on. If the R.A.F. had dropped me correctly, I ought to be about halfway between a road and a railway some ten kilometers west of Montpellier. Looking up into the peerless night sky I spotted the north star. Then letting my gaze drop to the horizon I knew that must be the road. Presently the sounds from a passing motorcycle confirmed that this was so. I hobbled back to my suitcase and set off. My head, lower back, and leg were giving me such trouble that I did not know which was the worst. Above all, I must clear my head. In my present dopey condition I was liable to walk into trouble.

CHAPTER IV

ON REACHING the road I looked both ways. There was no one about, and the only sounds came from the chirruping of crickets, occasionally interrupted by the croaking of a frog. I walked east to have a look at the first signpost. I came upon it almost immediately and scanned its face beneath the moon.

It read: MONTPELLIER 10 KMS. An involuntary smile crept over my face in homage to the R.A.F.

I pulled out the compass for which I no longer had any use and pressed it down deep between the stone and the long grass. Perhaps, I dreamed vaguely, the day might come when I would step out of my own car, with a G.B. on the back, and retrieve this souvenir.

Looking east I saw a faint glow rising from the lights of the town. I decided to leave the road, which seemed to meander off to my left, and aim straight for the glow across the vineyards. It would be wiser during the curfew.

In a semicoma I dragged my way through the vines, and after some painfully slow progress was halted by a wide stream. The very ticket!

I tested the depth with a long stick. There was about three feet of water. I undressed and let myself in gently from an overhanging branch. When I felt the hard bottom I let go the branch and submerged myself completely. Then I stood upright and shook my head lightly. The pounding was definitely on the wane. I ducked again several times and tested the result. The icy water was doing the trick. The gods be praised, I thought. The other pains were as nothing so long as my head was clear.

I climbed out gingerly. There must be no mistakes; no sudden shooting pains to send me splashing back into the water and set every dog barking within a radius of twenty miles. I wiped myself off with my hands and dressed quickly.

Tingling all over, I set off like a new man in search of a bridge or steppingstones to cross the stream.

My direction took me still further away from the road and I walked slowly, assessing the damage to my left groin. Whatever it was that normally brought a leg forward for the next step was certainly not functioning. The pain had diminished to a numbness and by rising up on my right foot and helping the left leg forward with my hand I managed to make excellent, if somewhat unorthodox, progress.

It was easy along the path that followed the stream, and I soon got the hang of the new rhythm. I fancied that this handicap would, if anything, increase my confidence in making my daylight entry into Montpellier.

At every bend in the stream I looked as far as the eye could see for a possible bridge. I was going too far south and it was already half past two. I gave myself another two bends and then, if there was no bridge, I decided to wade across.

There was no bridge, so I scanned the water for any signs of stones or shallowness. The best place had a steep rise on the far side. I would do it here.

Taking off my shoes and socks, I hung them round my neck. Then, with great care and concentration I began to negotiate the tricky passage. At the halfway mark I took a good stance and flung my suitcase onto the far bank. With both arms free, the rest was easier. On reaching the far side it took all my remaining strength to drag myself up the verge. I lay panting beside my suitcase for quite a while, unable even to reach for my flask.

I rested for perhaps five minutes; then, pulling out my flask, took a good gulp and swallowed a benzedrine tablet at the same time. When I felt the glow from the alcohol taking a hold I made my way slowly up the rise.

At the top I beheld the rolling vineyards sweeping gently down toward the town—some six miles distant I plodded on across country, intent on covering as much ground as I could before lying up for a spell. The vine leaves were dripping with dew and the soil cloggy. I made slow headway and my trouser legs were soon sopping wet. None the less, I must have covered over two miles before I was exhausted by the heavy going.

I curled up finally on my mackintosh in the middle of a vineyard, miles from anywhere, and went fast asleep.

At five-thirty the rising sun woke me up. Birds were singing all around me. There was a cloudless sky and under the rising temperature the night dew was curling up into silvery drops on the vine leaves.

I now saw that my shoes, socks, and the bottom of my trousers were covered with brown earth. I opened my case and took out some blue cotton summer trousers, a fresh pair of socks, and a pair of sandals. I quickly changed into these and repacked the muddy articles after scraping the mud from the shoes.

Shouldering my case, I sauntered down to a narrow road which, to my surprise, led to the railway line on the left. I was just in time, for laborers were popping up everywhere in carts, on bicycles, and on foot. Soon the vineyard was swarming with men beginning another day's work.

About a mile further I came across tram tracks. A few minutes later I was clanging along comfortably in the first tram, toward the center of the town. In what was obviously the main square, I alighted and made off to a modest-looking café. Sitting near the window I ordered a bowl of coffee, a hundred grams of bread, and some jam. I tore out four August bread coupons—bread being cut in twenty-five-gram slices—as though I had been doing this sort of thing all my life. With a look of utter boredom on my face and yawning from the night's exertions, my dark, bespectacled, unshaven and incongruously dressed person fitted the picture to a *t*.

Behind this bohemian façade, my mind was ticking over just as it might if I had been dolled up in cap and gown on my way to sit for a university exam; and from what I could remember of those painful incidents, I would have said that it was ticking over a good deal better now. I was running over the train times which they had given me at the office, and it struck me that I might just as well catch the seven fifty-three as wait for a later one.

I paid my bill and went out into the sunshine. Following the tram lines that led out of the square, I saw a blue-and-white sign that read: A LA GARE. Two corners farther, and I was there.

I bought a third-class ticket to match my getup, and sat on a bench in the sun reading a newspaper while waiting for the express. The station was already crowded and I guessed the sort of journey I was in for. Nor was I wrong. Jammed between two fat gendarmes in the corridor, I stood like an upright sardine all the way to Marseille.

The train slowed up before the Cannes tunnel and I prepared to get out. Mixing with the crowd, I passed under the subway that led to the exit. I perceived that the crowd was hardly moving at the gates and instantly realized the cause. Two gendarmes in khaki uniform were examining all papers. It was a snap control; the second that I had experienced. Once again I would know how good or how bad were the French Section's forgers.

I followed the crowd, remembering a previous fright when a man in front of me had been grabbed at Lyon. It had been a cold, snowy day in January. Here, at this moment, under the blazing sun, the whole thing seemed unreal. The crowd was muttering its disapproval and I joined in for good measure. The sulky looks of the passengers had a salutary effect on the gendarmes, for there were many passengers and only two gendarmes, and being French they were stung in their pride at doing this for the Germans. A cursory glance was soon sufficient to conclude this odious imposition and get away from their abusive compatriots.

Assuming the same air of bored contempt when my turn fell due, I held up my identity card without even bothering to open it. A fumbling gesture to read its contents wasted more time and drew a wave of groans from the impatient crowd. After two seconds of simulated concentration—more probably an act of defiance—it was handed back to me. I was of the opinion that I would have got through that control with a homemade pass for the Kremlin.

I walked up to the first free vélo-taxi—the only form of transport—and gave the cyclist an address on the Route de Fréjus. Then I sat down in the trailer seat and began to observe and sniff the atmosphere of Cannes at the end of August, 1942.

CHAPTER V

AT THE GATE of Antoine's villa, I bumped into Pierrot who was on his way to the town. Our meeting was matter-of-fact, as though we had seen each other every day. Together we walked up the drive to the house. Antoine was on the porch and I was introduced. I was shown to my room and there left to unpack my modest possessions and have a much-needed bath.

Without any waste of time Pierrot, who was anxious to leave by the next felucca, gave me an outline of the situation.

"Laurent is being held at present in Nice. Carte has sent someone to see him with a parcel of food and to discover when the police are transferring him to Lyon. When that takes place they'll put a team of rescuers on the train and get him away. We'll call on Carte tomorrow.

"Julien is coming here to dine tonight. He's tickled pink at the idea of working for you. 'Fraid he's not very keen on the local setup, and it's a tricky business to try and explain to Carte that radio operators aren't supposed to beat up the keys all day long with lengthy reports.

"Laurent's lieutenant is away on his rounds of the area. He'll contact you through Carte when he gets back.

"I've instigated a courier service between Arles, Marseille, and Cannes. It's run by a girl called Gisèle. You meet her on Wednesday at the Café des Allées. She's expecting a dark man of medium height wearing glasses and with an unlit cigarette in his mouth. She'll come over to your table and ask if she may take a look at the latest food-regulations column in your paper, so 'verb sap.' When she's given you the latest dope from Arles and Marseille, you give her a different rendezvous for the following Wednesday. If she doesn't find you there, she'll suspect that something serious has happened. She'll make a further call on the next Wednesday and look for you at the time and place you agreed for the previous meeting and she'll take another peep at the Allées Café. This is a mutual aid and information stunt. Gisèle is about thirty-five, shortish, inconspicuous, and has masses of graying black hair.

"There's about three million francs in Antoine's combination safe. He'll give you a spare key and when you've used that up, plus what you may have brought, there'll be more forthcoming.

"Carte's men bring in the parachute grounds for the railway sabotage. All you have to do is send the coordinates of the pinpoints they mark up on the Michelin maps in our code. When the B.B.C. messages for each accepted field are sent back through Julien, you give them to Carte, who sends them to the right people by his couriers.

"Since you're here more or less permanently, Antoine has found you a tiny flat which he'll rent for you in someone else's name. He's only been waiting for your arrival before closing the deal. It wouldn't do for you to remain in his villa for very long."

I questioned Pierrot on various points and then, toward six o'clock, Julien joined us. A warm reunion took place with my old friend. It appeared that Julien had only one house from which to work his set, and he confirmed his distaste for transmitting copious reports. He felt confident that I would soon put an end to this sort of thing.

As for me, I felt that the first hook in the grappling irons of my coming responsibilities had not been long in coming. But it was only a small sample of what lay ahead.

We dined at Antoine's exquisite table and shortly afterwards I arranged to meet Julien on the following day. I handed him a message for H.Q. containing all my news. It ran: R.A.F. PERFECT—CONTACTED PIERROT—ENDS. I then excused myself on the grounds of having had a longish day.

Next morning, Pierrot and I cycled into Cannes on two of the machines hanging up in Antoine's garage. We stopped outside the Casino Theatre and Pierrot led me through the "Entrées des Artistes." Above the stage on a plank between two trestles stood an artist wearing a white coat belted at the waist. Various figures were taking shape under the sweeping movements of his brush upon a canvas that was patently to serve as the background for some future play.

An odd assortment of men and women—mostly men—of all ages crowded the stage at the foot of the plank. A few conversed together, but the majority were looking up at the central figure as though all were seeking his advice at the same time.

I took this group to be the cast of some play and the man on the ladder some kind of producer-cum-scenepainter. A uniformed Casino official, possibly the stage-door man or someone responsible for the antifire regulations, who was strolling up and down the aisles with his hands in his pockets and the ragged end of a homemade cigarette in his mouth, paid no heed whatever to the clamor that issued from this gathering. To my mind the scene was perfectly normal in every respect. I supposed that Pierrot would bypass this assembly and lead me round to some private office. But in this I was quite mistaken.

Climbing onto the stage, he pushed his way through the mob toward the foot of the plank. Then, tapping the artist's leg he called out simultaneously, *"Bonjour, Carte,"* and on meeting his eyes he indicated my somewhat timid approach with a wave of the hand: *"Le voilà!"*

"Bonjour," sang out the genial chief of the southeastern Resistance Movement, waving his brush and other arm outwards in an all-embracing gesture. He got down from his plank, shook hands with us both, and introduced me to his assistant, Jacques Langlois.

Sensing that something of real moment was going on in their midst, a temporary hush spread over the gathering as it made way for the V.I.P.'s. I could not help overhearing my name being passed round the outlying circle.

I suppressed a groan—the first of many to come—at the thought that, only a few hours after my arrival, ten people, whom I should never have met, already knew my name and description.

"Quoi de neuf?" smiled Carte, looking from me to Pierrot.

"Just had a message to say that the felucca's due tonight," said the latter. "Bit of luck that Michel's got here or I might have had to wait for the next moon period."

"I'll have the reception committee stand by as from tonight. Come and dine at my house in Antibes and you can then leave by train with Claude Dauphin and his sister. Perhaps you'd like to come along too, Michel. There's a lot for us to discuss."

"I'd like to," I replied before asking, "Any news about Laurent's movements?"

"Full details, but they'll keep until tonight."

Shaking hands with us he turned his attention to a nearby group.

"Well, there you are," said Pierrot as we unlocked our bicycles. "Once you've been to Antibes you'll know it all. I've got a few things to see to before packing and you have to meet Antoine, so I'll see you later on at the villa."

Turning up my trouser leg on the chainwheel side, I cycled gently along the avenue beside the port. How peaceful it all looked under the sweltering sun. Not a ripple stirred the water as far as the eye could see, and a heat haze obliterated the horizon. I looked at the few customers already seated at tables outside the Café des Allées, but it was too early for Antoine to be there, so I moved slowly on past the Prefecture and turned left along the western side of the port. Here the medium-sized yachts floated side by side, like graceful swans. Through their masts I saw the mass of larger steam, diesel, and sailing craft on the casino side.

I pedaled on for a mile or so, past the stunted palms with the tempting sea on my left. I would have a swim when the opportunity arose. On the right was the main line by which I had come. Before me stretched the road to la Napoule. A smell of hot tar rose up to my nostrils and I could hardly believe that I had wearily ploughed along this same road, in the opposite direction, through three inches of water after the snowstorms in January of that year.

There was no motor traffic about owing to the absence of petrol, but cyclists were plentiful. Presently I ran across Antoine cycling toward me.

"I always take the coast road in preference to the interior way," he said when I had circled round and come alongside him. "One never gets tired of this gorgeous view."

"You're lucky it's not spoiled by the Wehrmacht and all their shouting."

"It's bound to come one day."

"You think so?"

"It's more certain than the fall of the sword of Damocles."

We cycled round the port and followed the Croisette up to the Miramar Hotel. There we turned up the Rue Pasteur and stopped before a small block of flats nearly opposite a garage.

Antoine pulled out a key and walked toward the far ground-floor flat. Opening the front door he led me in. Behind the door ran a passage at the end of which lay a furnished bedroom with a writing desk and chair. The window led out into a courtyard and the drop was negligible. Beside the bedroom was a private bathroom and beyond that a small kitchen. In the front door I noticed a contraption that could be moved so as to permit the occupier to see who was outside.

"This place is perfect, Antoine. How did you do it?"

"Well, I took it on a six-months' lease and paid in advance. I told the landlord that it was for a friend of a woman living in Lyon who actually doesn't exist. The landlord won't bother you, since he's been paid and he's not a nosey type. As for anyone else, nobody except myself knows about the place, and no one shall know from me."

"Antoine, this is the first clever thing that I've seen in this town today, and it really is clever. I'll refund you the rent at the villa. And now"—I smiled—"would you do something else for me?"

"What?"

"Find me a second flat somewhere else."

"What the dickens for?"

"If something should happen that forced me to leave by the window it would be too late to start hunting then. So let's do it now."

"I see what you mean," nodded the other. "I think I've got an idea, too. When would you want it for?"

"There's no particular panic rush," I said. "If I had to give this up suddenly I've got friends in the Californie district who will hide me away until things cool off, or I get another place, and Julien tells me that I can always count on his friend Audouard, the croupier, for a bed in case of trouble. Let's say the second place should be available within six weeks of today, and you take it on the same conditions, paying an advance rent of six months."

"The girl who had this place before you is a beauty specialist. She now has a flat where she works and sleeps, in the Rue du Canada—only two hundred yards from here. She knows of another flat in a quiet part of the Croisette which was left empty by American friends of hers at the beginning of the war. She might be able to get that for you."

"Sounds almost too good to be true," I said.

"There's another thing I wanted to mention to you," went on Antoine. "This girl, Suzanne, met Laurent on several occasions and she's been seriously toying with the idea of making herself useful to people on our side. One of her rooms at the beauty salon ought to make an excellent H.Q. for you. No one would suspect that such an establishment was being used for clandestine purposes."

"Splendid!" I said: "What sort of a person is she?"

"Discreet, quiet, fortyish, and most intelligent."

"I'd like to meet her."

"Come over now. We'll see if she's free. I'll bring your case over this afternoon in my little trailer."

We walked our bicycles round to the Rue du Canada and chained them to the railings outside the house.

A quarter of an hour's conversation with Suzanne was sufficient for me to engage her as a part-time assistant. Having lived in Cannes most of her life, she knew many of the town's officials and said that she could deal with such questions as renewals of ration cards and so forth with the greatest of ease. I decided that Antoine's previous comment on her intelligence was an understatement. I found Suzanne to be shrewd to the *nth* degree. It was arranged that the largest bedroom in the flat would be kept as an underground office or meeting place for the organization. Suzanne said she would attend to the matter of the second flat in the block known as Les Dunes.

After lunch with Antoine at his villa, I went to my rendezvous with Julien. This was in the Jardins Fleuries beside the Majestic Hotel in Roger Renaudi's shop. It had an entrance into the gardens and another leading to the street behind, an ideal spot with views both ways through a dividing curtain. Here, besides the legitimate and normally thriving business of selling fancy goods and exhibiting the large range of modern buttons which he himself designed and manufactured in his own factory, Roger kept open house for the Carte group, of which he was one of the chief members. His pretty young wife, Germaine, was the principal saleswoman and also acted as courier to the organization.

Julien was waiting for me and handed me the day's decoded messages written in neat block letters on a small piece of paper. I read them:

NUMBER 57.
FOR MICHEL.
REPEAT STAND BY TONIGHT WATCHMAN* BRINGING SIX AGENTS INDEPENDENT STOP ONE TON MATERIALS TO BE SUNK WITH LINE TO BUOY POINTE DE LESQUILLON COLLECT ONE TON TINNED FOOD STOP MAXIMUM PASSENGERS RETURN PIERROT AND TWO OTHERS TO LEAVE SPACE R.A.F. MEN EMBARKING ELSEWHERE STOP SIGNAL BOAT TO SHORE RED M FOR MOTHER SHORE TO BOAT WHITE O FOR OSCAR ENDS.

* Felucca operation.

NUMBER 58.

FOR MICHEL.

WELL DONE HALIFAX REAR GUNNER SAW YOU SPINNING. KEEP W/T MESSAGES YOUR LENGTH GOOD LUCK LOVE AND KISSES ENDS.

"What the devil's all that soppy stuff about?" I asked.

"They claim that it puts off possible enemy decoders."

"Have they got any radio-detector vans here?"

"Not so far."

"Send them this," I said scribbling on a small pece of paper: YOUR 57/8 O.K. STOP NUTS ENDS.

"Shall I really send that?" asked Julien.

"Yes. Perhaps they'll sack me and give me a job in the Cabinet."

I noticed that there was a constant coming and going in Roger's shop and that precious few of the people seemed to buy anything. After I had shaken hands with half a dozen resistance "customers" I turned to Julien with a hopeless shrug:

"Security just doesn't exist here, does it?"

"No. But the very naturalness of these people seems to take its place. You never see any hole-and-corner whispering that gives the show away. The cloak-and-dagger stuff they taught us in the schools might work among the impenetrable Chinese, but here it simply doesn't wash."

"The trouble is that any one of the people one meets might get caught, and just look at what they know and who they know."

"It's unavoidable. One becomes like them in the end."

I decided I must immediately find another meeting place as an alternative to the beauty salon. I simply must try and control this crazy comedy somehow.

It was now time to go to Antibes. The nine kilometers along the coast road, past the house where the Duke of Windsor used to stay, over the railway bridge, and circling round the Golphe Juan was a sight for sore eyes. The late-afternoon sun beating down on my exposed skin made a whoop of joy well up in my throat and my resilient nature wiped out all the complications of this crazy life. By the long empty stretch of sand before Juan-les-Pins I would have a swim and clear my mind and refresh my body. Perhaps the salt water would do my groin some good. My right leg was doing all the work on the pedals.

I had put on a skimpy cotton triangle below my clothes after lunch and a towel lay rolled up in one of the two panniers over the back wheel.

A handful of people lay scattered along the sand on the long circular beach. I picked a quiet spot, threw my clothes in a heap, and entered the tepid water. I swam around for a quarter of an hour, exercising gently and finding the most comfortable action to strengthen my leg.

I continued my ride in a tingling, salty glow.

Carte lived with his wife and four daughters on the top floor of a modest four-storey house, not three hundred yards from the circular gardens where Julien had landed in March.

His paintings hung in every room, and the flat was already teeming with humanity at six o'clock as though a cocktail party were in full swing, the only real difference being that there was not a glass in sight, either empty or full. The hum of conversation was simply due to Latin exuberance.

In one group stood Carte, Claude Dauphin, his sister, Pierrot and an imposing-looking, middle-aged man of military bearing. On being introduced to him, I learned that this was Colonel Vautrin, one of the senior officers of the Deuxième Bureau.* In another group two handsome, sun-tanned British officers—Gervais and Robert—were talking to Jacques Langlois, Carte's eighteen-year-old daughter, and a Commissaire de Police from the Préfecture de Marseille.

A host of couriers and lesser fry stood about in the corridor. I shook hands with them all, thus knocking up the number of men I should never have met to something over two dozen in one single day.

Among the people I was glad to meet were Captain Frager—a distinguished gray-haired Artillery Officer of both wars—known as Paul, and a young man called Marsac who was known by the odd French war name of End. Both these men acted as

* French Secret Service.

Lieutenants for Carte on an equal footing. There were plenty of other Lieutenants about, but happily not on parade that day.

A small, powerfully built youth with thick, fair hair, who had been a sergeant in the French Air Force, turned out to be the chief courier, by name, Riquet. His quiet, serene manner caught my eye amid all the hubbub. I felt that with a dozen men like him I could undertake almost anything. Nor was my judgment wrong over Riquet, for later I was to recommend him for the Military Cross

At seven o'clock, Carte ushered his supper guests into the dining room, where a frugal meal appeared out of nowhere. The stuffed tomatoes, fish, and cheese did not take long to eat. Nobody spoke about food; the subject was taboo, for all meals were the same in this poorly provided sector of France, and nobody ate their fill except on the black market. The guests were also very abstemious with the *vin ordinaire.*

At about seven thirty those who had to go off to the boat took their leave and I remained alone with Carte.

Without any preliminaries about my means of arrival in the country, Carte got down to business.

"Laurent is being taken to Lyon tomorrow morning. My rescue squad will board the same train and get him away from the gendarmes at the moment they think best. He will be hidden away on a farm. We thought of snatching him in Nice, on the way to the station, but that's a bit risky."

"He'll have to go back to England afterwards as he's blown sky high now," I said

"Certainly. I shall be sorry not to have him, as we got on well, but I'm very glad you are to replace him. I'm having some difficulty in my relationship with Julien. It's not that he doesn't send my messages, but he openly complains of their length. I am confident that you will have a salutary influence on your rather undisciplined compatriot. He is not in the same street as Robert or Gervais."

"It's not quite the same sort of job," I said as tactfully as possible, smiling. "Moreover, they're trained to send only short, urgent messages."

"All my messages are urgent."

"I'm afraid this is going to be a problem. Surely the couriers can take everything that does not concern immediate operations."

"There are two couriers for Switzerland and Portugal every week, and I promise you they don't travel empty-handed. But if Julien can't or won't handle the stuff, I must request that a private radio operator be placed entirely at my disposal."

"I shall put your suggestion to the Section."

"Good. Then you keep Julien."

I refrained from saying how glad I would be to do that.

"Tomorrow at three P.M. there will be a meeting in Renaudi's private flat above the button factory. I hope to have some news for you by then about Laurent and the felucca. We will also discuss other matters. I will tell you where our next rendezvous is to be, then. I hope you will not forget what I said about the radio operator. Everything depends on a state of harmony between us."

"It shouldn't be hard to maintain," I said, feeling incapable of making an issue of the radio impasse on my very first day, although I feared I would have to put it bluntly before long.

The night ride back to Cannes seemed considerably longer to me than my afternoon run to Antibes. There was no curfew, and in the breathless night I was accompanied all the way by the whirring of the dynamo turning against the front wheel of Antoine's machine.

I wondered how Major B. would have tackled this radio problem; how he would have tackled all the other problems In fact, I wondered what Major B. would have thought of the whole bag of tricks. Not much, I fancied. These deliberations did not bring me any closer to a solution. I was certain that no radio operator would stand for more than twelve hours of almost steady transmitting, even if there were no radio-detector cars about. They just weren't meant to work that way. I wondered why I took it all so seriously. Here I was, a thousand miles from home, in the heat of the south where people were supposed to go native, and yet the heat made my mind function better than ever, and the trouble was that these things did worry me.

I let myself into my flat and wheeled the bicycle inside. My bag was there and, in the kitchen, a loaf of bread, a pot of honey, and some tomatoes lay on the dresser. Good old Antoine, I thought, as I tore off a welcome hunk of bread and dipped it into the honey.

The flat looked cozy by electric light, and that front door with the peephole on the inside was a boon for the solitary saboteur. I tried it several times, reducing the aperture to a mere slit, then walked over to the bedroom window and satisfied myself that it opened and closed soundlessly. I then laid out my things, undressed, and went to bed. But try as I might, sleep would not come. Nor was this really surprising, for much had happened that day, and despite the speed with which each successive event had dovetailed into the next, they had nevertheless all left first impressions on me, and I now began to analyze and elaborate those happenings which had not taken their right perspective in the haphazard existence I had accepted.

My first thoughts revolved around Pierrot. What a frigid manner he had shown throughout the handing-over process. A few impersonal instructions had been the order of the day. To my questions he had made curt, impatient replies. Then there was the rather unseemly haste over his departure with a handshake for me that one might confer upon some crashing bore met at a cocktail party and at whose separation one is showing rather too much delight. It semed odd to say the least of it that an officer of H.Q. staff handing over a somewhat tricky assignment to a new man, whose predecessor was in prison, should behave in this way. Maybe I was being oversensitive about the whole thing. Maybe Pierrot was simply one of those cold, impersonal, and unattractive beings with whom it was the occasional unhappy lot of humans to be thrown in contact.

Having dismissed this matter, I turned next to the Carte problem. Undoubtedly Carte was a shrewd man and born leader, capable of making decisions. I had seen all that on my first visit to Antibes during the winter. On my return to the office I had made my favorable recommendation and, as a result, Carte had received the spiritual blessing and financial backing of the War Office. With this power behind him, I now realized what I had not foreseen: that beneath his bland manner lay a will of iron that would brook no opposition, and I feared that behind the skirmish over Julien lay an ultimate, implacable rupture.

Finally, I thought of some of the people I had met that day. Antoine, Suzanne, Louis le Belge, Francine, Julien, George, Paul, End, Riquet, Jacques, Colonel Vautrin, Gervais, and Robert. What did fate hold in store for these people? Who would be captured, who killed, who betrayed?

At length the turmoil of this living nightmare was stilled by blessed sleep.

After a shave and a refreshing cold shower, I went across to the Rue du Canada to see Suzanne. I made arrangements with her to call at my flat every morning at 9 A.M. before starting her cover work. Having lived in the flat before me, her presence would tend to dispel rather than arouse any suspicions in the mind of the landlord. Whatever relationship he might attribute to the pair of us was immaterial to me. All I knew was that the closer the assumed relationship might be, the kinder would be the eye turned toward me. I showed my appreciation for the food I had found in the kitchen and asked if some coffee could be organized. It could, at one thousand francs per kilo.

Then I met Julien and gave him the Rue du Canada address. The house was called l'Augusta.

After discussing various radio matters and taking down the address of a house whose proprietors were prepared to permit transmissions, Julien took me to a further rendezvous in order to meet Porthos—Laurent's and now my lieutenant.

I had heard that Porthos was a fearless and resourceful agent and that he was a Jew. Rumor had it that he had been chased out of Paris by the Gestapo and that the price on his head was one million francs. As far as the racial question was concerned, it meant nothing to me provided Porthos were only half the man that Louis of Antibes was. If he was as clever and useful as Julien—likewise a Jew—all would be well. It was therefore with an open mind that I first shook hands with my "number two." Julien excused himself and Porthos and I cycled off to a quiet spot near the beach where we could talk.

Porthos required no encouragement to talk, and he spent the

better part of an hour elucidating the situation as seen through his own eyes. It seemed a pity to me that he prefaced so many of his remarks by saying, "You, who have no experience in these matters, will find it difficult to understand that. . . ." I listened patiently to all that my lieutenant had to say, but all the time I felt how regrettable it was that I must one day be forced to haul this young man severely over the coals so that he would know who was the boss. I also thought it a little steep that I must inherit someone else's lieutenant rather than pick up and form my own. Riquet was the right type. Quiet, not flashy. Or else Raymond, who had been through the training schools with me at home. I could have asked for him. I might still do so. The human relationship was so important. The whole thing was easy where comradeship and mutual respect and reliance existed. I did not feel that anything like that could now result between myself and Porthos after this bad start, which was rapidly deteriorating into such a conceited monologue that I felt sorely tempted to smack the man down.

I was glad of the necessity to bring the interview to an end because Gisèle's train was shortly due in. I decided that I would handle the courier business myself and give her lunch for her trouble. I began to excuse myself.

"Well, I must go now. See you at three in the button factory."

"Where are you going?"

"As a matter of fact, I'm meeting Gisèle. It's her visiting day."

"So it is. With all my work and tearing about, it slipped my mind. I'll come along with you."

"Sorry. As I said before I want you to stand by at the Jardins Fleuries in case they bring in anyone from the Pierrot Watchman."

"But I've got to see Gisèle," insisted Porthos.

"Why?" I inquired, hiding my determination to put a full stop to this nonsense here and now, with some difficulty.

"I've got some important information for her."

"Give it to me. I'll pass it on."

"Why don't *you* go to the Jardins Fleuries and I'll attend to Gisèle?" said Porthos with all the confidence of someone so convinced of his own superiority that he was quickly going to show his chief who was running the show.

"No," I said quietly. "You do as I say."

"But I always see Gisèle," he went on with a condescending smile at my futile ignorance.

"Today you won't."

"I don't understand you."

"It's quite simple, Porthos. As long as I run Laurent's circuit, I give the orders. If you don't feel inclined to accept them, just let me know. There's plenty of work to be done here without having to be my number two."

"O.K." said Porthos, with no little surprise.

"What about that information for Gisèle?" I pursued, hopefully.

"Oh. It'll keep," replied the slightly punctured Porthos.

My hope had been fully realized. I shook hands with my puzzled lieutenant and was not altogether displeased, as I pedaled gently toward the Café des Allées, with the thought that Porthos' last expression was the kind of look one might expect to see on someone's face who had just seen a rabbit produce a conjurer out of a hat.

Such, for the time being—with added complications—was my daily lot. Some of the additional complications came in the form of two radio operators who appeared out of nowhere. Both had been dropped by parachute and neither ought really to have been in Cannes. But Cannes, at that time, was the haven of all lost agents, for the news soon spread through Gisèle that Julien's radio set was working and that Julien knew how to work it—and radio sets meant contact with H.Q. The first of these stray operators was Ulysse and the second Hilaire. Hilaire had broken a leg by his parachute only half opening.

On the credit side was Catherine. This lady, who was an artist by the name of Mademoiselle Odette des Garets, was a friend of Suzanne. Having frequently voiced the desire to strike a blow for the Allied Cause, her opportunity came with my arrival. We met and she unreservedly placed her apartment at my disposal for any purpose for which I might require it.

Number 20, Quai St. Pierre became, henceforth, my second H.Q. It was to serve as more than that as time went by. Catherine's quiet, firm nature was to be a source of constant inspiration to all who entered her house.

Practically all the "independent" agents from the Pierrot Watchman, who were supposed to go off under their own steam, passed through the Jardins Fleuries and were issued with correct ration books by Suzanne and helped in various other ways. Some of them were even housed before adequate arrangements had been organized. But let the actual entries from my situation reports describe some of these events.

CHAPTER VI

REPORT NUMBER ONE. *September 10, 1942*

1. So far we do not know why the Pierrot Watchman is so late. The reception mob is there every night and I understand these characters carry on like a Bank Holiday crowd on Derby Day, for they cannot fathom what is so secret about landing rods and strange Joes on their soil, nor do they see any particular reason for putting a sock in it just because a felucca is pulling into one of their coves. As a result I am not very surprised to learn that when the intrepid Poles bring in the sampan, the entire operation is watched with considerable interest by constables sitting in grandstand seats and also by the guys in the semaphore. I also learn that the youth camps are since dredging for the stores they sink and mark with a buoy. It is a lucky thing that the chief constable of the department where this comic opera takes place is a great friend of England. He knows all about this particular performance and last night in a friend's house he is seen beating his hands

against the wall and crying, "I close my peepers to what the Albions do right under my very nose, but in the name of the Holy Virgin why do they not help me and themselves by picking any one or all of the seventeen to twenty nights in the month when there is no moon whatever." *Verbum sap.*

2. Porthos* is a full-time Jew with a death sentence and a million-slug shake hanging over his loaf. He talks too much, too often, and too loud. Now with the Jewish question rampant as it is here, with hundreds of foreign Jews being snatched off to the pen at three bells and the night made ugly with the screaming of dolls being torn from their ever-loving husbands, it is even money that the next purge goes against French Jews. Porthos has a Jewish identity card which he openly waves around the waterfront cafés. Confidentially, I will have no part of this guy, and my advice is that he is not fit to continue handling Laurent's business, even if the bulls do not put the arm on him. The last purge takes place three nights after Pierrot's departure and the heat is on everywhere in this town.

Added to this, Porthos takes Ulysse to the Marseille ghetto where, of course, Porthos is a very big potato, owing to the death sentence hanging over his head and this and that. But these members of the Big Family will have no part of Ulysse whatever, as he is not on the run, not a Jew, and not ostensibly on the rocks. This is no kind of a setting for piano study† whatever, so after many changes of residence and no appearance of the piano, it is not so surprising that Ulysse returns to this town. What kind of work is this?

In the train with Gisèle, Porthos is openly bandying Pierrot's real name and discussing submarines and parachutes and other strange goings-on, much to the delight of all the citizens in his compartment. One of these characters happens to know Gisèle and asks her afterwards who this Porthos is. Then Porthos declares to one and all in Gisèle's home town that he now runs Laurent's racket. Gisèle, who is not one to carry a torch for anyone, goes out of her way to claim that Porthos makes a

* All names of people and places were concealed in these reports by means of my personal code with the War Office. For simplicity's sake the full names are given here.

† Radio operating.

very bad impression anywhere around and about outside the ghetto bounds, all of which goes to show what a bright course this Gisèle is But I will eat my old school tie if I understand what I do to inherit this palooka.

3. S.O.S. We are in a sorry state without the *feuilles semestrielles* (multiple forgeries promised for parts of the ration books).

4. Olivier of Marseille has two full tankers leaving 18th—see my 97th piano concerto (W/T message No 97). Instead of heading Whitehouse (Casablanca) skippers are prepared to hug the Gibroute. If R.N. collect these prizes this simple proposition will pay all S.O.E. (Special Operations Executive) expenses for the duration and even show a profit. The Treasury ought to offer Olivier a job after this scramble is over.

5. There is an old level-crossing tomato at Arles who attends to the permanent drag (railway lines). This is no ordinary crow by all accounts. Her humble scatter is like a René Clair studio with teams of comic guys jostling around for fresh orders. As she knows the complete menu (timetable) she tips off these joskins when a real lulu is taking off for the Third and Last (Germany) and without a tremor these acrobats get cracking. Of course they are losing out on hostages, but it is nice to know there are some hard potatoes around; and all this, mark you, with the Schlocks (Germans) running the Z.N.O. (unoccupied Zone) network. I send this sweet-pea a letter with a few modest tips Ord gives us on that special transport course and I go out of my way to include a kiss.

6. I have two new bikes up my sleeve—one up for Porthos. One new tire costs 1,000 francs plus one kilo of sugar and one kilo of noodles.

7. Have copied your photostats "Targets for tonight" and sent one on to Marie of Lyon for her crowd.

8. Eugène of Toulouse temporarily out of touch.

9. Julien is out for the count after Pierrot's departure as he is on the job nightly due to the Watchman chaos. He has a fever and even turns down offers of food, which is almost unheard of in his case. Ulysse is now helping with the coding and so Julien is back in circulation on alternate days. Suzanne is attending to the housing question for U.

10. This will leave tomorrow, Friday 11th, through the new

Hoareland (Spanish) post boxes which I recently tried out successfully with a few sheets of toilet blat.

11. Paul and a strong posse accompany Laurent in the train from Nice to Lyon, so as to snatch him from the dicks. The rescue boys elbow the customers away from his window and run through the bookie signs with Laurent, but for some strange reason he does not appear to wish to be snatched, so these heroes beat it at Arles without quite understanding what is coming off except that if they keep up this signaling nonsense all the way to Lyon it is even money, or anyway nine to ten on, that they are all put in the sack. So now Laurent is nothing but a gone gosling but I will suggest to Marie that she gets him into the pen infirmary and snatches him out of there, because Marie is more than a raw hand on these transactions and this will keep her in practice. However, if he gets out I still maintain he must beat it for home as he is blown wide open and if I am in his shoes I will be pleased to scram out of this mess.

REPORT NUMBER TWO. *September 17, 1942*

Gisèle tells me Olivier has a new dodge for shunting Joes out of the country which consists of dolling them up as Franciscan monks and passing them from one monastery to the next. I must say, I confess to Gisèle, this Olivier is always full of fresh stunts and I consider it a great courtesy on his part to share them with his neighbors, particularly when they are escape stunts, because anyone along this coast will tell you they are very pleased indeed to dress up as nuns or anything; in fact, they will go so far as to dress up as Gendarmes or even Frids (Germans) if it will help to get them out of the country. I tell Gisèle I have a customer in mind for this prospect. Gisèle says why am I laughing and I say because this customer happens to be a Jew and I cannot think of a better person to be wandering around between the monasteries with an old rope around his brown horse blanket testing out this exit Well, anyway, this guy is the rich harmless one I mention in a previous tap dance (W/T message) and if you accept him I will send his full monicker so that Barcelona may expect him.

2. Hilaire with the broken shank who is now here from a

clinic requires special food and attention so his bone will set. It is all laid on very carefully for him to go to Carte's clinic for an overhaul where Carte has a great pull on a fifteen carat sawbones and where they do not ask silly questions. Carte gives me a solemn oath that Hilaire can arrive at ten bells.

The second part of this plot is that Hilaire is being installed after this trala in a house in Carte's district where the red carpet is down and there are so many flowers around you will think there is a wedding coming off. Well I take a big hand in all this paraphernalia because I figure any jerk who wants a private pianist badly enough is wise to treat such merchandise just like it is his ever-loving sweet-pea and I ought to know.

Well, Hilaire gets there at ten bells in a short (taxi). The clinic is never wised up and the poor guy sits around waiting for five solid hours for the medic. They then put him on a spot with all that stuff I wish to avoid. How is this accident happening and where, and what is your name and where are your ration cards and what else. In the end he musters his remaining strength and jumps a hack back to where he comes from.

This trap stings him 800 slugs and he writes me a letter that nearly gives me a hemorrhage. Well, I pedal this headache over to Antibes. It is the third trip that day and all the way I am hopping mad, and working up a clutter of rich phrases I intend to launch upon this uncrowned ace of clots. The road is very hot but I do not notice it because I am so inflamed that you can fry an egg on any part me and I do not cool off even when I reach Carte's door, in fact I am very angry indeed.

When I finally bust into his stooge-ridden dive, I say Carte I have something private to tell you and we go next door where I say my piece and all he says is, Pish! I forget the whole proposition. Well, I fume, you will not get Hilaire back if you offer him the crown jewels and confidentially I do not think you have a hope in hell of getting anyone else either. Now Carte sees I am very annoyed and in no condition to be challenged with anything whatever and he is more than somewhat surprised because he figures, like Porthos, that I am a guy who will always step off the sidewalk and so he lays on the old mush.

But what am I to say to Hilare? What would you say, chums?

CHAPTER VII

AT THE HEIGHT of all this chaos Porthos brought off a coup. Neither he nor I had the slightest inkling of its importance.

Bursting into the Augusta flat one early afternoon, he announced with all the exuberance of a fanatical butterfly collector who has just pulled off the catch of a lifetime:

"I picked up a stray musician near Grenoble when I was doing my rounds. This chap was dropped twenty miles away from his landing ground by the R.A.F. and went to a nearby farm where I heard he was hiding. I told him he'd better come and see you."

"What, another D.P.?" I groaned. "Where is he?"

"At the button factory."

"I'll go and take a look at him," I said.

A ten-minute cycle ride brought me to the factory. As I climbed the stairs to the Renaudis' private quarters above the factory, I wondered what sort of a specimen this was going to be.

On entering the room I encountered the hard, even gaze of a pair of dark gray eyes. I smiled and he withdrew his hand from the region of his shoulder holster and got up with the ease of a panther.

Taking in the wide shoulders and powerful hands at a glance, I addressed the sulky young Hercules:

"What's your name?"

"Arnaud," growled a deep voice.

"Where do you come from?"

"Who the hell are you, first?" challenged the stranger.

"Michel," I replied.

"One can never be too sure," said Arnaud, "although you do fit the description," he added grudgingly.

"Well, where do you come from?" I went on.

"London."

"Who are your bosses?"

"Major B. . . . Major de G. . . ." He began listing them.

"O.K., O.K. How did you come out?"

"Through the hole in the floor of a Halifax four-engined bomber with a Polish crew."

"All right " I smiled Arnaud passed a huge hand through his mop of brown hair.

"Where were you supposed to work, Arnaud?" was my next question.

"Paris!" snarled the young giant, raising a bushy eyebrow to indicate the full irony of his plight.

"Yes," I said, agreeing with the implication. "You couldn't very well be much further away."

"You're telling me!"

Stroking my chin, I looked at this handsome, scowling savage for a few moments. I supposed he might be twenty-five years of age

"Arnaud," I said suddenly, "I've got an idea."

"Well?" he inquired unhopefully.

"My present operator is going home on leave shortly. Why don't you stay and work for me?"

"Not on your life!"

"Why not?"

"What, in this hole?"

"What's the matter with it?"

"It stinks. There's no war going on here and the people are a lot of jelly-bellied baskets "

"Oh, don't think I'm trying to sell you the proposition," I said indifferently.

"In any case," he went on more moderately, "London would never wear it because they've promised Paris that I was coming."

"Arnaud, if you'd consider working for me . . . I could fix it."

"I might consider it . . ." said Arnaud slowly, "but London would never play on that one."

"Like to put a small bet on it?" I asked, raising my eyebrows.

"Certainly."

"How much?"

"Fifty thousand."

"It's a deal! Where's your piano?"

"Porthos has got it."

My brain began to race with renewed hope. "Stay here," I said "I've got a doctor who's willing to allow concerts in his house on the Route de Fréjus. No one's ever worked there before. It's all yours and fifty cycles* into the bargain. I'll fix you up with a place to live in before tonight. When's your sked?"

"Eighteen hundred hours."

"All right. Stay here for an hour, then go to the Jardins Fleuries—Roger will tell you where that is—and you'll find Porthos, who'll take you to your workshop and introduce you to the doctor. Your piano will already be there. When they hear your call sign, send this." I took out a piece of paper and rapidly scribbled the words: FROM ARNAUD MISSED RECEPTION CONTACTED CANNES MAY I WORK FOR MICHEL REPLY SPECIAL SKED 0600 TOMORROW ENDS.

Handing this to Arnaud I said, "Porthos will take you out for dinner and show you where to stay the night. Personally, I think the doctor won't mind your staying with him in view of the morning 'do.' If London says no I'll arrange for you to cross the 'demarcation zone' and proceed to your lovely Paris."

"Fair enough, Michel," said Arnaud, allowing the vestige of a smile, that I fancied sprang from a suspicion that he was being talked into a trap, to reveal a row of faultless white teeth.

We shook hands and, as I was about to go down the stairs, I turned and said, "Porthos will help you fix the aerial and he'll be at the morning sked so as to bring me the result. Don't forget the difference in the hour with G.M.T. I'll see you tomorrow and let you know where."

The rest of that day passed quickly enough with all the things that required my attention, but not quickly enough for

* An electrical term, like A.C. and D.C.

me. That night I offered up a fervent prayer to the Goddess of Good Fortune, asking her to smile upon this project.

Next morning at five minutes to eight, I was already seated at a table on the terrace of a tiny café waiting for Porthos. I vaguely sipped at a cup of artificial, milkless coffee, almost unconscious of its filthy taste, for I was concentrating all my attention on the bend in the road around which Porthos was due to appear at any moment. I would know by his expression if it was yes or no.

Here he came now, on the dot—well done! With my elbows on the table, I scanned the approaching face over my coffee cup, but there was nothing to be gleaned from it.

"*Bonjour,* Porthos," I said, reaching up my hand and pointing to a chair beside me. "*Un café?*"

"*Volontiers,*" he replied, sitting down deliberately.

I ordered the coffee and watched two workmen get up and leave. Then, turning my head slowly toward Porthos, I said, "*Alors?*"

Porthos pushed a tiny piece of paper toward my saucer and I opened it slowly, with one hand, where it lay. I read the single miraculous word: CERTAINLY.

The question of the fifty thousand francs was never raised or mentioned by either of us. I very well knew that it was not going to be plain sailing with Arnaud. He was a tough who clearly believed nothing and nobody. It was my aim to grapple Arnaud to myself with hoops of steel, even if it took me months to do it. As individuals we were diametrically opposed in character, and the only way to earn Arnaud's confidence and regard was to prove, time and time again, that when I promised something it came off. I hoped that the Section's generous, cooperative gesture in allowing him to stay would act as the first milestone in this game, and I equally hoped that Arnaud would not consider it a weakness on my part to have waived the fifty thousand francs.

After his first contact with London, Arnaud for some unaccountable reason was unable to get through any more. By the time Julien had left, several fresh houses in Cannes, Antibes, and up in the hills had been placed at his disposal. With

Julien's set as a spare he tried everything he knew—but to no avail.

Each day when he met me it was the same grim story with only slight variations in Arnaud's fruity language.

"Well, Arnaud. Any luck last night?"

"Not a ruddy squeak. I bet those ——— sons of ——— aren't even listening."

"Of course they are, Arnaud. Anyway, they're daughters of ———, as you well know. Those girls are twisting the dial all day and all night. They're just as anxious to hear you as you are to contact them."

"Those ——— glamorpants are only dreaming about the dressed-up sissies they're going to spend the night with."

"I know exactly how you feel, Arnaud. You just keep hammering away. You're sure to get through soon. I'm positive about that."

"Wish I could feel so sure."

"Have you got the aerial facing north?"

"Of course I have."

"Are your crystals O.K.?"

"Must be. They're the ones I used when I did get through."

"Have you remembered the difference in the hour?"

"Yes."

"Are you sure the houses are fifty cycles?"

"Carte says so."

"What about Julien's set?"

"I can't even get that to work."

"There's a White Russian in a wireless shop who might be able to give you a hand. Shall I get him to have a look at the pianos?"

"———! No. I'll be damned if anyone touches my piccolos."

"O.K. Arnaud. Have it your own way. Get weaving."

Seventeen nerve-racking days passed in this manner, and all the time things were happening and urgent messages were piling up.

Couriers were kept on the run day and night to make up for the absence of the vital radio link. Three times a week men with seemingly charmed lives crossed and recrossed the Swiss, Spanish, and Portuguese frontiers, leaving Cannes and Antibes every two days. But the answers were the snag, for they only trickled through very slowly. Certain senior French officers in the southeast zone's resistance movement were not long in realizing at whose door to place the blame for this situation, due to the folly of having made Julien's life impossible.

Doubts as to Carte's efficacy as a leader began to form themselves in certain minds, but so great were his zest, his optimism, personality, and driving power that, as in the case of Hitler's entourage, all such disloyal thoughts and open criticisms among themselves simply vanished into thin air under the spell of his dynamic presence.

At this time Carte was at the pinnacle of his power; power that he wielded as though born to it. And, unlike Hitler, he was a man of considerable charm and his powers of persuasion were not those of a raving maniac, but those of a man who talked people intelligently around to his own way of thinking.

At long last Arnaud burst into Catherine's flat with something different from his usual morose curses. With trouser legs clipped at the bottom, his handsome face wreathed with smiles that no one had previously seen, he held out a large oil-smeared hand toward me containing some crumpled bits of paper. All of us present knew what this meant, for all had shared some of the tension of the battle of the W/T.

Catherine went out of the room as I avidly read three urgent messages, and returned with four glasses and a bottle of treasured nectar from her modest cellar. We raised our glasses to Arnaud's triumph, and his shy acceptance of our toast showed that he was not altogether displeased at suddenly feeling himself to be accepted as a part of our team.

The messages concerned, in the main, a dozen or so parachutings for the coming moon period and ran along these lines:

> FOR CARTE AIX-EN-PROVENCE O K. B.B.C. LE RENARD PERD SES POILS STOP SIGNALS GROUND R FOR ROBERT AIR F FOR FREDDY STOP. MANOSQUE B.B C. SONNEZ LES MATINES STOP. SIGNALS GROUND P FOR PETER AIR V FOR VICTORY STOP.

And so forth.

These cryptic messages were the result of the following activity in France.

In the seventeen subsectors of the southeast zone were an equal number of local resistance leaders with their parachute reception teams, sabotage cells trained by Gervais, and local talent of every description, such as demobilized officers of the French Army, friendly mayors and sous-préfets, safe houses, etc., etc. All the sectors were in constant touch with Carte, thanks to the relays of couriers.

On learning that the railways in their sectors had to be sabotaged at a future date which would be given them in due course, and that this was part of a concerted plan for D-day, the local leader, who knew his district inside out, would select a suitable spot on the main line—such as a curve with a bad drop beside it—and make plans to blow up the line just there. The next step was to find a suitable landing ground on which to receive the explosive—preferably near a friendly farmer who would be prepared to hide the material until it was required. This spot was then plotted on the Michelin map of the district and sent to Carte by courier.

By means of a special code and a squared mica protractor I, like all the other organizers, reduced the pinpoint positions on the various Michelin maps to a minimum to facilitate the radio-operator's work. For Aix-en-Provence my request for explosives would be: 84 AIX N 13 RAILWAYS. On receipt of this decoded message at H.Q. Major B. would ask an assistant to bring out Michelin map number 84. Aix being as well-known to people like Major B. as the whereabouts of Birmingham to the average Englishman, he would slide an identical squared mica protractor over the right squares and mark N 13 with a pencil point. Then, consulting the R.A.F. liaison officer as to the feasibility of performing a drop at this point, he would know if the operation was on or not. If it was, the next step was to arrange a B.B.C. message with the person handling that department and then transmit that message to France.

Everyone dealing with this work in the Resistance knew that these operations took place during the moon period—a period lasting fourteen days in every month—i.e., from the time the moon was half full, up to full, and back to half full. They also knew that the aircraft were scheduled to arrive between the hours of 10 P.M. and 2 A.M. on the night when the

B.B.C. message came through and they listened for their particular message on the seven-thirty program from Bush House over the European wave-length. Fog, flak, and shortage of aircraft could delay these messages, and Resisters all over occupied Europe, as well as in France, often found it difficult to believe that weather conditions in England could be so different from the peerless nights they usually experienced on the Continent.

When the conditions were favorable for any particular operation, the B.B.C. was advised to send out the specific message dealing with that flight and, once it was heard in France, nothing short of a crash would stop that aircraft from dropping its parachutes on the agreed pinpoint. The accuracy of the R.A.F. navigators soon became a legend in France.

With Julien and Porthos on the high seas, Arnaud living with Monsieur and Madame Glise on the heights of the outskirts of Cannes and working the two sets in different houses every day, it seemed to me, from the comparative safety of my ever-changing headquarters, that things were slowly getting organized for whatever lay ahead.

The next problem was not long in making itself felt. Fortunately it came with plenty of forewarning, and this was due to information from Colonel Vautrin.

One day at a meeting convened by Carte, this high official of the Deuxième Bureau announced that thirty-six German radio-detector cars had been sent to Marseille to pick up the sets along the coast. So detailed was his information that I was put in possession of the registration numbers of those cars assigned to the Cannes-Antibes district. I was advised that each car had a driver, a machine gunner, and an expert sound detector; that the cars worked in couples throughout the day and night; and that from the instant they heard the operator tap on his key until they picked him up was only a matter of a few minutes.

With this information I reduced Arnaud's transmitting to a limit of six consecutive minutes per day and only once a day. I also told him to advise all householders that they would be provided with two lookout men placed at such positions in relation to their houses that if the householder stood guard at a window during the six perilous minutes, he or she would be advised of the approach of such a car from the time it was one kilometer away from the house. By warning Arnaud to stop tapping immediately, hide his set, and vanish by the back entrance, the chances of the guilty house being suspect were reduced to a minimum.

These measures proved an ample safeguard for his continued work, and no householder in any of the forty-eight houses in which Arnaud was to perform in six different towns was ever apprehended. In time the radio-detector cars became part and parcel of our underground lives, and I was glad of their presence in the sense that the enemy was now visible and kept everybody on his toes.

Soon after this came news from Colonel Vautrin that a certain General de Lattre de Tassigny—then practically unknown—was in command of a Division stationed at Montpellier and, thanks to a conversation with the Colonel, was made aware that British officers working in the French Resistance were on the lookout to arm groups of French guerrillas prepared to make a stand in the mountains. As Commander of one of the sole French Divisions still in existence under the Armistice terms between Hitler and Vichy France, the General was prepared to move his Division to the Pyrenees entirely at his own risk and responsibility, on condition that the War Office would supply it with provisions, tanks, transport, etc., from the air.

"The General would like to know," concluded Colonel Vautrin, looking at me, "if you would put this proposal to London and, subject to their approval, if you and Arnaud would be prepared to join his staff."

"I can tell you the answer to the second part straight away," I said, seeing the war being shortened by the pinning down of at least a dozen German divisions to face this new challenge.

The H.Q. reply to this question read:

> WAR OFFICE APPROVAL 100 PERCENT STOP ALL SUPPLIES BY AIR STOP YOU AND ARNAUD MAY JOIN DE LATTRE SECOND MUSICIAN WILL DROP LATER STOP

I could hardly contain myself. All the stupid wrangling of the past two months, the struggle to make people security-minded, the radio complications, the endless cover stories that had to fit one's every moment, and the constant tension of an existence that showed no tangible results, all seemed to lose their cumulative effect at the prospects of serious action.

The good news was rushed to Montpellier and the waiting began. I would know when to move from Colonel Vautrin.

Resistance activities in no way diminished because of this new possibility and, if anything, they increased. Gervais continued to give endless sabotage courses in various private homes to large classes of Frenchmen; Robert went up into the Alps and taught groups of Corps Franc (French Commandos) the technique of ambush, bridge, and rail sabotage; couriers still crossed the frontiers and journeyed about France; R.A.F. crews had still to be got out and money had to be found to finance it all.

It was Suzanne who inadvertently discovered the method that was in future to obviate the need for parachuting money into this zone. She overheard a wealthy client complaining bitterly that her husband had not placed large sums of his money in England at the time of the "phony-war" when it would still have been possible. After probing this woman's politics for quite a while and then checking up elsewhere, she asked me what I thought of the idea of collecting francs in France and making a sterling exchange possible by means of the radio.

I put it to London and they intimated their willingness to arrange for such transactions. A favorable exchange rate was agreed upon for French people willing to make such deals; and proof that an account had been opened for them at the bank of their choice and the equivalent amount placed to their credit would come to them over the air on three successive nights when the B.B.C. European wavelength would broadcast a message only known to them and to me.

The first of these transactions was executed for a sum of two million francs with Suzanne's "find." I was introduced to him and the conversation we had was typical of others of a similar nature.

"Although I understand you're a British officer," began the would-be investor, with some diffidence, "I find it a little hard to believe."

"Well, I am," I said, feeling as though I were standing naked at a public auction.

"And is it a fact that you can open an account for me at Barclay's Head Office in Lombard Street with sterling, equivalent to two million francs, at 225 to the pound?"

"It is."

"And how do I know if and when this transaction has been completed?"

"Just give me a short message—anything you like—and you will hear it at seven thirty on the French program of the B.B.C. tomorrow night and on the two succeeding nights."

"How is that message going to reach the B.B.C. so fast?"

"I'm afraid that must remain my secret."

"Well, it sounds like magic to me. When I hear my message for the third successive time, I shall pass the money over to Suzanne."

"What is your message?"

"Ma fille va faire sa première communion demain."

"Very well. Au revoir, Monsieur."

Only one man refused to proceed with such a deal without a certificate signed by me and he missed his opportunity, for I would not sign. There was never a slip over any of these transactions, and I handled something like fifteen millions in this manner.

CHAPTER VIII

Among the messages that came in during this busy second half of October, Arnaud thrust a poser under my nose. It ran:

> W/T SILENCE IN MARSEILLE ARLES AND TOULOUSE PLEASE REPAIR.

"Well, fan my brow with a pickax!" I said, throwing it down

on the table and looking at Arnaud. "Remember all those cute instructions we had some time back telling us on no account to go crashing into neighboring territory if we found ourselves on a spot?"

"As though I could forget . . ." concurred Arnaud with grinding sarcasm. "But when Tom, Dick, and Harry find themselves in a hole, it's quite a different story. *Please repair,*" Arnaud mouthed the words, "the God-damn cheek!"

"But, Arnaud," I continued, tickled pink that we had this thing in common and realizing with pride the high regard in which my tough operator was now held at Headquarters, "they did say *please.*"

"Trying to soft-soap me into repairing their ruddy sets."

"That's what you get, Arnaud, when the generals start asking the colonels why the majors can't keep the captains playing their flutes."

"Just imagine those lousy ———s in Marseille, Arles and Toulouse—"

"Arnaud, don't let's imagine. Let's remember that we went through a rotten patch together once," I pacified.

"I refuse to look at their sets," he said flatly.

I had rather hoped to avoid quite such a categorical rejection of what I was slowly working around to. I would never have dreamed of giving Arnaud a direct order for such a mission. To begin with, it was a dangerous task to tamper with other people's keys where security was problematical (nine radio operators had already fallen to the detector cars), and then Arnaud was still an unpredictable quantity. There was quite a long way to go before I could feel sure of him. Although I was no milksop, I knew that Arnaud could have picked me up with one hand and thrown me out of the window.

"Just think, Arnaud, what a feather it would be in your cap if you were to fix those three sets," I said. "Why, you could do it on your head." I looked out of the window affecting boredom.

"What, and leave all the important stuff that's going on here for God knows how long?" he snapped.

"You could send our stuff on the sets you repair, and get the answers."

"Sets?" bawled Arnaud. "You sound as if you imagine I could fix them all."

"To tell you the truth, Arnaud, I know you could," I said, with all sincerity.

"You're crazy, Michel! I always knew it," said Arnaud. But I knew by his tone that I had won the battle.

"If you were to come here at nine fifteen tomorrow morning," I said, "I could have a second-class through ticket to Marseille, Arles, and Toulouse with a return by sleeper. I could arrange for a courier who knows the addresses of the three operators to take you to their houses and you would still have time to send a couple of messages tonight. Tomorrow's morning express leaves at nine forty-seven."

"Got it all organized, Michel. You never give up, do you?" He rose, looking at me with a mixture of uncertainty and disapproval.

When he had left the room I looked for quite a while at the door through which he had passed, then called for Suzanne to make all the necessary arrangements.

Next day, shortly after 9 A.M Arnaud entered the flat. In a brisk and businesslike way he handed me four messages, two of which required answers. He placed his tickets in his wallet, tapped his hip pocket where he preferred to keep his Colt automatic, and ran his fingers along the top pockets of his waistcoat to make sure they were stuffed with spare clips. Suzanne handed him a large bowl of coffee with an equally large smile, for although, like most people, she was terrified of his evil humor and bad language, she was quick to see the change and, underneath it all, she knew that he was the key and right hand of all our work.

His pockets stuffed with wire, string, screwdrivers, a piece of bread, and garlic sausage, Arnaud was ready for the fray. Slipping on his shiny mackintosh and pulling down his green hat, he waved good-bye to Suzanne and me and left the flat with Riquet.

There was no time for any anxiety about Arnaud. The day's work had to proceed and, as always, it was a full day.

There was a constant coming and going at Suzanne's flat. Bernard of Clermont-Ferrand had been in the town for the past few days, making arrangements with me to have his wife —due on the next felucca—sent on to a certain address. During his short stay he had found fit to give my name and address to the head of the Communist resistance group of Cannes, and now this man was insisting on a meeting with me for the purpose of soliciting arms. I told Bernard that it might have been a good idea to have asked me first if I wished to be in touch with this group. I had no objection to any group engaged in the general struggle, but there were limits to my already heavy commitments.

Suzanne had to handle this awkward situation and try to explain that my hands were full, but the Communist chief felt slighted and wrote me a note demanding an interview— or else! I ignored the note and told Bernard to clear out and mind his own business.

Hubert was in trouble because he suspected an address he had been given by London was being shadowed by the Gestapo in Sainte Etienne. Having also heard that Cannes was a good place to come to in times of stress, he had lost no time in getting there. Arnaud was in possession of a message asking for instructions for this man and, until his return, I would have Hubert on my hands. My next meeting with Carte was at a doctor's house just off the Route de Fréjus.

I showed him the latest messages, one of which read:

> FOR CARTE BOMBER WILL PICK UP THE FIVE GENERALS YOURSELF AND MICHEL AT VINON SUBJECT MICHEL CHECKS UP ON GROUND STOP DETAILS LATER.

"There's no need for you to check up on our grounds," said Carte, as though insulted by such a proposal. "Our men are quite capable of doing it themselves, and besides, I've had a team of French airmen living beside this particular field for two weeks. They ought to know what they're at."

"It's not a question of lack of faith, Carte," I said. "It's simply that I underwent training with the R.A.F. so as to learn their exact requirements."

"Well, if you want to look at the place, you must get there under your own steam. I've got no petrol for such unnecessary journeys."

I controlled the rage that mounted in me. Here I was, an expert simply because I had been trained to do these operations, trying to make arrangements to send five French generals to swell de Gaulle's staff, and this was the attitude of the man I had personally recommended and whom I only wanted to help.

My hands were now tied. I was trapped. If I went to see the ground, Carte would soon find out and consider himself slighted; if I did not go and the operation was a flop, Headquarters would be entitled to court-martial me.

Before I had time to slide any further down the road of my ultimate fate, Colonel Vautrin broke in on my thoughts.

"I don't know if you've noticed the papers lately, Michel," he opened.

"No," I confessed, wondering what calamity was now in store.

"Well, there's a new law being passed shortly whereby anyone between the ages of sixteen and sixty who has not got a job is obliged to go to Germany on forced labor."

"Holy smoke!" I said.

"I shouldn't worry too much," went on the Colonel, "but that rather flimsy free-lance journalist cover story of yours will hardly do in the circumstances."

"Have you got any suggestions?" I asked, ruefully.

"Yes, one that I believe will suit you and your purpose admirably," he pursued.

"Yes . . . ?"

"The Agence Taylor on the Croisette is run by a friend of mine called Madame Rondet. She is a chemist by profession. I have told her that I have a friend called Pierre Chauvet and she is expecting a telephone call at the Agency or your visit at her shop. It is the big one on the left at the end of the Rue d'Antibes. If she were to engage you—which I think she may—you would be in a position to rent villas in out-of-the-way spots for Arnaud's use."

"Has she any idea as to who I really am and what we do?"

"Not a clue. The only thing I hinted at was that I believed you had an English great-grandmother."

"Well, I'm most obliged to you, Colonel," I said. "I'll drop in at the shop this afternoon."

I was as good as my word; in fact, I called at her shop on the way to lunch. I introduced myself and she accepted my invitation to dine *chez* Robert—my favorite restaurant—that night.

To make doubly sure that there was no hitch, I went to the restaurant, booked a table, ordered a bottle of 1911 Château Chambord, and settled for hors d'oeuvres, an herb omelette, and roast chicken. It was not for nothing that I had been a regular customer for nearly eight weeks, during the first month of which I had had to put up with the standard fare, until the manager had decided it was safe to tell his staff that Monsieur Chauvet was certainly not a snooper from the Food Office and therefore the time had come to lower the drawbridge and wave me through to the "black-market" tables.

The stage was now set. If I were not an estate agent within a very short time, it would not be through any fault of the dinner!

I cycled back to the Augusta flat, but everyone had left for lunch. I returned to my own flat, picked up my bathing costume and a towel, and, grabbing a hunk of bread off the dresser, I went out and cycled off to a quiet portion of the beach, munching my bread on the way.

After my swim I had a Pernod with Roger and the beautiful Germaine and then returned to my flat, where I washed off the salty flakes from my earlier swim and got into my only suit—a fairly well-fitting light-brown herringbone affair that Suzanne had unearthed from her American friend's wardrobe.

I walked round to the Agence Taylor and rang at Madame Rondet's flat. I escorted my guest on foot through the streets of Cannes to the restaurant. A freshness in the evening air pointed to the close of a long and stifling summer.

It was a new experience for me to spend an evening in the society of a person who had not the foggiest notion of the complications of my underground life, and I made it my business to see that nothing I either said or did should arouse her faintest suspicion.

We had walked through the town in an unhurried manner, touching lightly on a variety of commonplace topics, and now one excellent course followed smoothly upon the last with a decorum that always soothed my jagged nerves after a long and tiring day. The sommelier—also named Michel—brought forth his vintage treasure at the precise moment when it was required, poured the first offering for my approval, discussed its merits with me at just sufficient length to show mastery of his subject, deference to people of good taste, and the impeccable tone of the house. After pouring just the right quantity into each glass, he laid the bottle carefully down with its cradle and silently moved away.

Looking across at me, with my tanned face and ready smile which might have been those of any carefree parasite who had spent the summer lolling in the sun, she said, "What a lovely dinner, Monsieur Chauvet, and what a charming evening you are giving me."

"I am so happy to hear it, Madame. It is so nice that such things still exist."

"Colonel Vautrin tells me that you might like to join my staff of estate agents."

"That is so, Madame."

"Things are rather quiet just now. What with the war and now the close of the summer season."

"I realize that, Madame. Yet people of means are still pouring out of the Occupied Zone, and I know quite a few who are looking for homes and still others who would come if they were sure of finding a vacant villa."

"These contacts sound interesting, Monsieur."

"I think I am safe in saying that I could find tenants for at least four houses in a very short time."

"I will give this question my serious consideration, Monsieur Chauvet. But," added Madame Rondet, proceeding in a rather breathless haste, "there is a question I have wished to ask all day. . . ."

"Please ask, Madame," I said suavely, wondering what was coming up.

"A young man like you . . . in the prime of life. . . ."

I raised my eyebrows and my guest dabbed her lips with

her napkin as though embarrassed as to how to phrase her thought. She returned to the charge:

"Bluntly, Monsieur, I am wondering whether it is wise to engage someone who might one day feel the call to join the Free French Forces in London."

I broke into silent laughter with relief. After all, my guest had not taken me entirely at my assumed playboy face-value. I must now leave her in no doubt.

"Have no fear, Madame. I have a horror of war and, besides, to answer your question as frankly as you put it, I must confess that a certain blonde in the neighborhood is my sole interest in life," I lied with a glibness that even surprised myself.

"Tiens!" said Madame Rondet in a noncommittal manner, as though her own relief at this information were somewhat dulled at having her shrewd assumption proved wrong and now seeing her host in his true colors—those of an ordinary, self-indulgent, unpatriotic egoist.

The conversation for the rest of the meal was inclined to hang fire, and when at last I got back to the welcome peace of my flat I was gratified at the success I felt I had at least achieved in keeping my guest off the scent. A word from Colonel Vautrin would now unfailingly clinch the job.

Before going to bed, I considered whether or not I would prepare a further report on the ever-changing situation in my zone, but in view of the possibility of my return by aircraft during the coming moon period, I decided that I could give a clearer picture by word of mouth. One thing was sure; I would never return here if Carte was to remain in command. I wondered how Major B. would unravel the knot.

Next morning at 9.30 I cycled along the Quai St. Pierre to handle the morning's work.

To my utter amazement I found Arnaud already there, dipping a huge hunk of bread into a bowl of coffee. Catherine was sitting beside him. With his mouth full, his tired eyes looked up out of an unshaven face as he mumbled a greeting.

A wave of thankfulness swept over me at the sight of my friend. I sat down opposite Arnaud and waited until he had reached the stage of wiping his greasy hands on his jacket. Then I handed him a cigarette and said, "Well . . . ?"

"You were right, Michel. I was able to fix the whole lot."

"What, all three in one day?" I gasped incredulously.

"Yes, the whole ——— lot."

"But it's six hundred kilometers to Toulouse and you had to catch four trains. How the devil did you do it?"

"If you'll give me a chance, I'll try and tell you."

Catherine and I shrugged knowingly at each other and then looked back at Arnaud.

"I got to Marseille at around twelve forty and we went straight to the first house. There wasn't much wrong with this piano—a mere trifle—and I was through to London in four and a half minutes. I sent your two messages and told the girl to stand by to pick up the Arles set. Then she had to waste my time coming back to me."

"What did she say?" asked Catherine.

"Some poppycock about crossing her fingers," said Arnaud disgustedly.

"Ever meet this poppet?" I asked.

"Don't be a sap, Michel."

Catherine suppressed a gurgle.

"Go on, Arnaud. What happened then?" I said.

"Riquet and I just managed to get on to the one thirty-seven express for Arles and, of course, we were there in no time. Ulysse works his set in the back room of a druggist's shop in the middle of the town. Well, it was in a ——— state and it took me all of seventeen minutes to get through."

I had it on the tip of my tongue to ask what the girl had said this time, but Catherine frowned at me just in time.

"I got the replies to the messages I sent from Marseille and also from Cannes the night before. I've got them here somewhere," said Arnaud tapping his pocket. "Well," he continued, seeing that he had his audience eating out of his hand. "I gave Ulysse a few tips that I learned from that bad patch I went through myself and, as we had quite a wait before the next train, we went and had a bite to eat. Then we caught the four something and eventually pulled into Toulouse well after nightfall. There we picked up the connection for Montréjeau. We were met at the station and driven in a trap to the farm where Urbain works. God knows when we got there, but they certainly looked after us. Hell of a meal—hams as big as elephants and wine in buckets. Never saw such a thing. Dream place to work in—at least that's what I thought at that moment."

"What d'you mean by that?" I asked handing across another Gauloise.

"I'll tell you if you'll only give me time," said Arnaud puffing at his cigarette. He then took up his story. "I told them that I had to catch the two A.M. sleeper—Riquet had found out the time—so they took me up to have a look at the set immediately after eating. It was in a ——— state! You never saw such a ——— sight in all your ——— life! Everything was loose, rusted up, stuck in upside down and the aerial all to ———. Must have taken me a good half hour to sort it out before I ever got round to the buzzer. Well, then I started buzzing and I buzzed and buzzed but nothing happened. Then, suddenly, I heard the approaching roar of engines and then I knew who I was getting through to."

Arnaud took another draw on his cigarette and saw by our expressions that we, too, knew who was on his trail.

"My first reaction was to pull out my gun and go over to the window, but the farmer saw what I was up to and grabbed me by the arm and told me we'd just enough time to hide. I picked up the set and Urbain gathered up the heavy battery and together we bundled out of the room and followed the farmer down to the kitchen. Just as he was opening a trap door that led to the cellar there was a hell of a bang on the front door. Telling his wife to attend to the matter—slowly—he pushed us down the steep stairs and closed the trap behind. I was just beginning to wonder what the big idea was of getting us into this hole where they were bound to find us, rather than let me pip them through the bedroom window."

Catherine and I leaned forward with much the same query in mind.

"Before I had time to speak, the farmer had another mysterious door open and we found ourselves inside a damp tunnel.

He closed the door behind us, lit a match and said, 'I wondered when this old underground passage would serve some useful purpose. This farm's about four hundred years old and the people who built it must have known what they were about. Perhaps they were having trouble with the Germans, too. They seem to have been annoying us as far back as I can remember.' "

"Et alors?" urged Catherine.

"We seemed to walk for quite a while and then emerged in a dilapidated old ruin. From here we had a perfect view of the farm. It was about one thousand yards away and the farmer went back to it over the fields saying he would return when the Schlocks had gone. I stuck the set down on a slab of rock so that I could see the farm over the top of it and got on with the repairs."

"You didn't work the buzzer, Arnaud?" I asked anxiously.

"God, no!" sang out Arnaud. "Those ———s were sure to have left a man listening on the D/F in case the tapping were coming from somewhere other than the farm."

"How long did they stay?" asked Catherine.

"Must have been a good hour before Urbain and I heard steps coming along the passage. I put my Colt away when we saw the farmer emerge. He told us in a rather flat voice that both cars had gone."

"Two cars?" said Catherine.

"Yes. The old game of working in couples for a double check; just as they do here, dear Catherine," came the rather bored explanation.

"How could you try the set out with these so-and-so's about?" I asked.

"I haven't got the ruddy thing repaired yet!" cried Arnaud, raising his arms to heaven as though appealing to the Doyen of all Referees to blow a whistle on these off-side interruptions.

"All right, Arnaud," I said in pacifying tones. "We won't interrupt you any more, but please watch your language in front of Catherine."

"Go ahead, Arnaud," chimed in that lady rapidly. "Don't mind me. I wouldn't miss this for anything."

"Pardon, Catherine," said Arnaud, waving his head from

side to side like a repentant bear. Then he got back to his tale.

"I asked the farmer how he could be sure they'd gone and he told me he'd watched them from the roof until they'd disappeared from view miles away. I asked him if he thought they'd come back and he said that when we'd had a look at the wreckage of his home we'd understand that there was precious little to come back for. We didn't talk much on the way to the farm and then we understood what he'd meant. They were so certain that a piano was hidden somewhere in the building that they'd torn the place to bits. You never saw such a ——— shambles—sorry, Catherine—in your life. I won't go into the details, but by now I hoped they'd return, the God-damned bastards; I'd've gladly shot them all. By the time I was ready to plug in the set on the battery and have a go, the farmer was on guard at the window with a French light machine gun and Urbain was hunched grimly over some other useful-looking rod from the rich assortment that Eugène seems to be collecting. As for me, my automatic was all cocked and ready within reach and Riquet was on the roof with a basketful of hand grenades. I gave the call sign and listened. . . . *Clickety-click* came back the opening bars of the sweetest music you ever heard. . . . I recognized the same girl's touch from London and cut in in clear with CHRIS-SAKE STEP ON IT PLACE RED HOT. Well, I've got the messages here. They somehow got me onto the last train for Toulouse." Arnaud checked himself. He was suddenly bored with his recital. "Got any more of that coffee, Catherine?" he ended lamely, pulling out twelve messages and dropping them casually in front of me.

"All the coffee in the world is yours, Arnaud," said this gracious lady, rising to oblige.

I lit a cigarette and threw the packet across the table. For a little while I watched my companion in silence, then I picked up the pile of decoded messages and glanced rapidly through them. I would look at them more closely later on. For the moment I was hunting for something. . . . Ah, there it was . . . FOR ARNAUD WELL DONE FINEST HAT TRICK IN W/T HISTORY ENDS. So after all, I thought, Major B. had also been at the receiving station and had shared something of this epic feat.

I dropped the piece of paper back on the pile, wondering if they would ever really know what a horse of a man this operator was.

CHAPTER IX

THE MOUNTING crescendo of our lives was now to be temporarily muted by the tiresome arrival of four new men and three women, all of whom were merely passing through. I knew exactly who was coming and roughly how they would behave; it had happened so often before. But the women were something new to my district. I hoped that the arrangements Suzanne and I had so painstakingly devised would insure that their short stay would pass in comfort and safety and prove a minimum of hindrance to my manifold activities.

Antoine had agreed to take the four men and, since Suzanne lived at the Augusta flat, it seemed eminently fitting that the women should come under her wing. There was sure to be plenty of washing and ironing to do after ten days and ten nights in Jan's open felucca, and Suzanne would know all about hairdressers and the hundred and one other things essential to women's comfort.

By ten fifteen on November 2, the decks were clear for action. If they came, as expected, on the morning express from Marseille they would be arriving at any moment. Suzanne had economized her gas so as to cater for at least two baths, and I had done the same in my flat, lest there be a scream from all three women to jump in the tank at once.

On the sideboard lay a large plate bearing succulent French gingerbreads, on which a great number of bread coupons had been expended, and nearby stood two bottles of red wine. A table for four had already been reserved at a quiet restaurant where I would entertain the three women after they had had a bath and change, and three beds were ready to rest their weary limbs after the fatigue of their appalling sea journey.

"Here they come!" announced Suzanne, who was looking through the window. "Why don't you relax, Michel? You look like an anxious headwaiter about to receive royalty."

"I don't know," I said. "This whole business gives me the berries."

Suzanne went to open the front door, and I stood some way behind.

Led by the tall Marsac, there then entered the scruffiest bunch of tramps that I had ever laid eyes on. The women were not so bad, as they had clearly succeeded in repairing the worst ravages of the journey with the implements in their handbags.

Shaking hands with Marsac, I said, "Bravo. Do you mind taking these men up to Antoine's now? He's expecting them." Then, taking in the four men with a sweep of my eyes, "You'll be very comfortable where you're going. It's one of the best villas in the neighborhood. I'll come up and see you late this afternoon, after you've had lunch and a sleep."

Marsac took off his troupe to their destination and I turned to welcome the women. "This is Suzanne," I said. "She is your hostess and this is her flat."

Each woman then introduced herself, thus enabling me to see which name applied to which, since I already knew their names from a W/T message.

"You must be terribly hungry and tired," I said, "and probably longing for a bath. Suzanne and I thought you might like a light snack first. Then we can fix you up with baths and perhaps you'd come and lunch with me afterwards. Then, in the afternoon, you can all have a well-deserved rest."

The program met with a chorus of approval, and soon the whole party was munching gaily away and I was filling up the glasses.

The eldest of the group was a gray-haired lady of considerable character and gaiety. I put her at fifty-two years of age. She was inclined to break into English rather too often for my liking and I warned her gently to beware of this tendency. Undaunted by her adventure in an open boat, she declared that within a very short space of time her requirements would be reduced to a visit to the hairdresser and then she would catch her train to join her husband near Clermont-Ferrand.

The next was about twenty-seven years of age and seemed about as suitable for this sort of life as my refined friend, Eugène of Toulouse. But there it was; the outward and visible show was no indication to go by. Time alone would show if she had the hidden depths of a Eugène or not.

As for the third, I put her down at about twenty-five. Her name was Lise, and from her mop of light-brown hair, swept back to reveal a rounded forehead, down to a pair of discerning eyes, there emanated a distinct aura of challenge that was only intensified by the determined set of her chin below a somewhat colorless face. A fearless look suggested that not even the thought of the prisons held any terrors for this girl; so much so that, in the flash of time I gave to my snap judgment of her, it even occurred to me that she might not bother to take all the precautions she should to avoid capture.

But what took and held my gaze above all else were the hands; hands such as I had never seen before in my life. They were long with slim, capable fingers and, as the left one held the wineglass and the other broke off pieces of cake, I observed the telltale expanse between thumb and forefinger, denoting extravagance, generosity, impetuosity; the ambition in the index fingers; the unusually wide gap between them and the second fingers, showing independence of thought only matched by the independence of action that almost cried out from the gaping valleys that lay between the third and little fingers. At the moment, the second and third fingers on the left hand were overlapped in a shy gesture, as though seeking each other's company—or was it to hide the platinum wedding ring that had not escaped my eagle eye? If the occasion arose I would take a surreptitious look at the lines on her palm and see whether or not they confirmed the already extensive disclosures of the general view.

Although these observations impinged themselves on my mind in about the space of time required for a picture to reflect onto the film of a camera, it was not fast enough to pass unobserved by Lise, for when my eyes returned to her face a slightly pouting mouth suggested that my impact upon this young lady was not of an order that inspired either approval or any promise of harmony.

The morning's arrangements passed without a hitch, and at lunch the three women were looking as elegant as possible in the rather austere outfits provided for them by the Section.

It was after lunch that the challenge broke into words. With her two companions comfortably resting on their beds, she tackled me.

"This reception's all very nice and in keeping with what I expected from the endless remarks I've heard about you from the Office, Gibraltar, and even Jan Buchowski, who sends you his compliments, but I'm anxious to get on with the job and I'm supposed to go to Auxerre," she said.

"I know you're going to Auxerre, Lise," I said patiently, "but you'll need a guide to take you across the Demarcation Line and for a day or so everyone's tied up. In the meantime the best thing you can do is to relax and get yourself acclimated to the atmosphere of the country. I suggest you start off by having a good rest this afternoon."

"I don't need any rest, thank you," she replied.

"Well, I'm afraid I have one or two things to attend to, Lise, so you'll have to excuse me," I said.

I left her with Suzanne and went out for the various meetings I had to attend before calling on the four men up at Antoine's villa. Here I found no difficulty whatever in persuading the new intake to sit back for a couple of days or so, until proceeding to their respective zones. I acceded to their request for a courier to shepherd them as far as Marseille and get them on their various trains at that dangerous terminus.

Returning to the Augusta flat toward five-thirty, the door was opened to me by Suzanne, who warned me with a finger to her lips not to disturb her sleeping charges. I tiptoed along the corridor, stopped and listened at the first closed door, then, satisfied by the regular breathing, moved to the next which I found ajar. Pushing it slightly more open, I peered in and smiled. Lise was sound asleep, with a look of childlike peace upon her face.

During the following day, Lise's two companions left for their destinations, the four men were comfortably installed and resting or swimming until their courier materialized, and, in the meantime, my attempts to get a guide from Carte's personnel for Lise had failed.

When I arrived at the Augusta flat I would have to announce a further delay. My surmise as to Lise's reception of this news was fairly accurate. After I had explained that they were inclined to be up to their eyes in work owing to the coming moon period, she said:

"Well, if I've got to hang around here any longer, you give me a job. I don't mind what it is."

"Lise, I've got a thousand jobs. Do you really want one?"

"Of course I do," she said.

"Can you ride a bicycle?" I asked.

"Certainly! What do you want me to do?"

"I want you to go to Juan-les-Pins. When you get there, leave the Provençal Hotel on your right and go straight up to the top of the hill. Just over the brow you'll find a sharp right-hand turn. Take it, and four hundred yards down on the left you'll see a villa called 'Les Jonquilles.' Ask to see Carte, tell him who you are—he'll recognize you from my description. . . ."

"What description?" asked her surprised voice.

"Don't interrupt, Lise!" I said evenly. "Give him these messages which you must hide on you and wait for the answers. It's about seven kilometers each way. All right?"

"Yes," said Lise rather timidly.

"Then repeat the directions," I said.

Lise complied and got them off word-perfect. So they did teach the women something, I thought. I said, rather more kindly, "Lise, you'll find a blue bicycle downstairs Here's the key for the chain lock, and Suzanne will tell you the best way out of the town."

She took the proffered key and left the room in search of Suzanne. Riquet came in a few minutes later and said he had heard Lise was going to Juan and that he could save her the trouble.

"Nice of you," I said, "but I'm only sending her on a sort of trial trip. I want to see how long it takes her."

"Oh, I see," said Riquet. "New-Agent-Goes-Through-Hoop." He walked over to the window to watch her departure as I spread out a Michelin map on the table to pinpoint another dropping zone.

Presently a resounding crash of metal came up to us from the street, ending up with the shrill note of a bell that has been done grave injury.

"What was that?" I inquired, without looking round.

"That," announced Riquet, "was Lise and her hoop." He then proceeded to give a running commentary. "She's looking most annoyed. She's dusting herself off. She's inspecting a rather attractive knee. Oh, my best stockings," he clowned, "she's dabbing her knee with a handkerchief . . . Blood! Oh mother, look what that nasty man's made me do . . . She's gripping the handlebars sternly . . . Her leg's through the gap . . . Her foot's on the pedal . . . We're off! We're on . . . ! We're off! We're on again. She's swaying . . . she's just missed a dog . . . she's round the bend."

"She certainly must be 'round the bend,'" I said without moving, "to say she can ride a grid if she can't. Sounds as if she'd never been on one before in her life."

"Attractive, though, in an odd way," mused Riquet.

"Very odd way," I said, reminding myself to have another look at her when she got back.

Some three hours later, toward twelve thirty, after I had concluded my business with Arnaud and we were both smoking and talking, with Arnaud standing by the window, I looked at my friend and said, "Very restless today, aren't you, Arnaud?"

"Why?" he asked.

"You've been hanging around that window as though you expected the Queen of Sheba to pass."

"And so I do. I can hardly wait to see this Lise."

"You may have to wait several days if I'm any judge of trick cyclists."

"Is she staying with us?"

"You know very well she's going to Auxerre."

"I seem to remember I was going to Paris, once. . . ." said Arnaud, smiling sardonically.

"That was different. . . . *You* were indispensable."

"My God!" suddenly exclaimed Arnaud. "There's a walking dead coming through the gate and trailing a heap of scrap iron. Come and have a look."

I got up and went over to the window.

"The Queen of Sheba herself," I announced. "Look out for squalls . . . and Arnaud, don't go all goosey when she comes in I tell you, this girl's dynamite. One moment of weakness and she'd have any man climbing Everest for a sprig of edelweiss."

"Be a change from this God-forsaken life."

"Put a stop to it completely, I should say."

As Lise entered the room I had my hand up to my forehead as though concentrating deeply on some papers before me. I did not wish to appear conscious of the ladders in her stockings, on which my eyes were accurately focused through a gap in my fingers.

Only when the girl was close to the table opposite me did I look up with perfectly feigned surprise, and say: "Ah, Lise . . . You're back all right, then."

"Of course I am!" she replied.

Turning my head toward Arnaud and back again to the girl, I introduced them casually.

"Lise, this is Arnaud. . . . He works the radio."

Arnaud walked over to the girl and held out his hand. He put on a smile that would have melted an iceberg to accompany his greeting: *"Enchanté,* Lise."

Her return smile was the first I had seen. I thought it well worth waiting for, even though it was for someone else's benefit.

She quickly froze it at my next remark:

"Took you rather a time to do the double journey, Lise."

"My compatriots at Carte's headquarters haven't entirely lost the old world courtesies yet," she smacked back.

"Sorry, Lise."

"Oh, that's all right. Is there anything else that you'd like me to do now?"

"Plenty. . . . But first of all I think lunch is called for. As a rule we go our separate ways, as no doubt they still advocate in the Schools, but since it's rather a special occasion let's all go to one of Arnaud's little spots just off the Boulevard de Lorraine."

"Good idea!" echoed Arnaud.

"And then we can fête the return of a very talented cyclist. . . ." I ended on a teasing note.

Lise laughed. "By the way," she said, pulling out a letter from her blouse, "Carte asked me to deliver this to you."

I took it from her and hid it away. I would read it later. It could hardly contain anything conducive to the sort of atmosphere I hoped would prevail at lunch; in fact, unless things had radically changed, it was more likely to spoil my appetite altogether.

Lise went off to change her torn garments and Arnaud and I were left together.

"That girl's got guts, as well as knowing all the answers," said Arnaud.

"I told you she was dynamite," I said.

"Auxerre . . ." mouthed Arnaud sarcastically. "Hmmmm. . . ."

After a pleasant if meager lunch, Lise and I returned to the flat.

"What do I do now?" asked the girl, fearing that I would be tied up for the rest of the afternoon and wanting to receive her instructions first.

"Lise, I've got a tricky one for you and you needn't do it if you don't feel up to it," I said.

"What do you think couriers are sent out for? To ride bicycles up and down this artificial coastline . . . or is that all you think they can do?" came her reply.

I looked at her and realized that she would take me up on anything Well, she might just as well drop in from the deep end right at the start I would give her the works and see if she still came up for more.

"I want you to listen carefully, Lise . . ." I began.

"I'm all ears," she said.

"I want you to take those four new men to Marseille tomorrow and see them on to their connections. Three of them are

English and naturally they feel a bit strange out here. The first few days are always a jittery business, but in the presence of a Frenchwoman they'd rather die than show it. Go up to Antoine's villa and find out each man's destination, then come back here and study the nearest departure times from Marseille to coincide with your arrival there at about twelve forty—you leave Cannes at nine forty-seven A M Book all the seats in advance—second class—and get yourself a return.

"Now, Lise," I said, looking at her intently. "Marseille at the moment is an ugly town, full of traps, raids, and other disagreeable surprises. You'll find the Gare St. Charles swarming with whole companies of the Afrika Korps, but you needn't pay any attention to them. They stand around under the eagle eye of their officers and all they're thinking about is how quickly they can jump the transport that will get them out to their hero, Rommel, in the desert. The people you must be on your guard against are the armed Vichy troops in blue uniforms who stand by the exits with German uniformed soldiers of the Security and R.T.O. Units. However, these uniformed men fade into insignificance beside the glowering gentlemen in civilian clothes who are liable to be checking papers. These are the Gestapo. I need hardly tell you that with the sort of papers with which we're provided by the Office, you can pass these men with your nose in the air.

"There are dining cars on all the trains, so you needn't bother about that. Just get them away from Marseille and that part of the job is done. O.K.?"

"Fine," said Lise.

"Having got rid of your charges," I went on, "you then leave the station by the Buffet exit. Strangely enough, there is no check point there yet.

"When you get out, walk along the side of the station until you come to a vast flight of steps leading down to the town. Go down them on the left side and stay on the left-hand pavement so as to avoid the Hôtel Splendide opposite. It's the H.Q. of the Gestapo. Go down to the Canebière—the main street—and turn right. Then right again at the next tram crossing and you're in the Cours Belsunce—one of the largest squares in the town. Stay on the right-hand pavement, and after passing some stalls where they sell everything, from peanuts to perambulators, you'll find the Hôtel Moderne Go up to the first floor where there's a fat, blowsy woman sitting inside a glass cubicle. She's the reception clerk. Ask her if Monsieur Vidal is in. If he is, so much the better. He's an inch smaller than I am in height and width, and he's fair. Give him this password. . . ."

"But I know him, don't I? . . . He was at the felucca reception. . . His name's Olivier, isn't it?" she asked in one breath.

"Good for you, Lise. . . . That's quite right. . . . I'd forgotten he was on that job," I said. "Well, then . . . if he's not in the hotel you can bow yourself out, go back the way you came, turn right in the Canebière, and go up the Rue St. Ferréol, which is the first on your left. Olivier works at No. 47 on the right-hand side as you go up, and he's on the first floor of an import-export business. When you've run him to earth ask him where they put that suitcase that came off the felucca for me. You might bring it back. It contains clothes they've been promising me for the last two months. Have you got it all so far, Lise?" I asked.

"Yes. Nothing to it," answered Lise.

"Now, when you ve got all that tied up, I want you to go back into the Canebière, turn left along it, if you come from the Rue St. Ferréol, until you reach the Vieux Port and then right, where you'll find a glass tram terminus. Catch the No. 3 tram. It goes to Aix-en-Provence, twenty-nine kilometers away. When you get there, you go to the Boulevard Zola which is road 96, and almost on the corner is a blue-painted garage. Ask for Monsieur Gontrand. He's always there, as he lives on the premises. Tell him you come from me and give him this." I drew out my wallet and counted out fifty thousand francs. "Ask him to hold five hundred liters of petrol at our disposal. The agreed rate is one hundred francs per liter. We shall be needing some of that very soon, Lise, and an advance payment will show Gontrand that we mean business. He's a splendid person; very dark, with thick black hair and about five years older than I. When you've done this, come back. If you have any trouble, Olivier will be only too glad to help you. Have you got it, Lise?"

"Yes, I think so," replied the girl.

"Repeat it, then," I said.

I was flabbergasted by the speed of Lise's recital. I had a suspicion that she was trying to imitate my style of delivery; but the impetuous flow was not entirely accurate, and I supposed I must make allowances, for, after all, Lise was a human being and not a machine. I corrected the discrepancies and told her to go and repeat the details to herself in the next room until it was absolutely correct. I told her to come back in a quarter of an hour, to be sure that it had all sunk in.

Her final rehearsal proved flawless She made the train reservations and, next day, the convoy departed.

CHAPTER X

NOW THAT the new intake had been disposed of, I had to work at double pressure to catch up with lost time. I cycled over to the Gomez farm near the gas works at La Bocca to check up on the material that had been hidden there after a complicated transport job from the spot where it had been landed by the felucca. There were seventeen interurban shortwave transmitting and receiving sets to be disposed of. First of all, these had to be taken to a central safe house in Antibes, where constant comings and goings would not attract the same attention as at the farm. The sets were intended to serve as a speed-up in communications between the various districts in the southeast zone, and they would also come in very handy in warning couriers not to call at certain houses that were temporarily "burnt" or under Gestapo supervision. Arnaud was to have the added task of showing local operators how to work them.

There was a huge barrel of sausage bombs for aircraft sabotage and quantities of tinned food.

The radio sets were in a sorry state, for their packing had come adrift on board the felucca and the sea water had done its deadly work. The majority were rusted; others had a coating of mildew. It pained me to discover so much damage to this expensive and useful material. I hoped that much of it could be saved by experts. At the same time I imagined the look that would come over Arnaud's face when he saw this waste, and I could almost hear the torrents of evil language that were sure to follow. All the sets lay higgledy-piggledy beside and on top of a heap of turnips on the damp floor of one of the farm's outbuildings. How could these simple farm people or, for that matter, those who had risked their lives bringing the sets through miles of police checkpoints, realize that they were handling stuff that could not be replaced for a ton of diamonds?

I got the farmer's son to pile them all up in a neat square on a foundation of dry sacks and brown paper and the pile, in turn, covered up until such time as they were removed from the farm.

"You realize what this means if there's a police raid on the farm. . . ." said the farmer's son.

"Friend," I said, "I promise to have it all out within twenty-four hours."

"Very well . . . but after that, if they don't come, I shall have to mix the pile up with some turnips and spuds, or we may not survive to be of future service to you," said the young man.

"Fair enough," I said.

I then did the long trek to Carte's hide-out and extracted a promise that the sets, aero-sausages, and tinned foods would be taken away the next morning and carefully stowed and serviced by experts. Carte agreed heartily—an inland route, avoiding the coast road, a cart, some hay. It would all be attended to. Yes, I thought, it would all be attended to, if it was not forgotten. There was nothing wrong with the young men who handled these assignments. They loved this sort of thing and would pull it off without a qualm. The trouble was that the

P.C. (Poste de Contrôle) or H.Q. of the southeast zone was one of those hives of industry where it would never occur to its chief to say: "This is your route. Fifteen kilometers with quite a climb at the beginning. It'll take you at least three hours what with loading and so forth. See to it that the garage below X's flat is swept out before the stuff arrives and have plenty of grease, oil, and brown paper ready, because the stuff's got badly rusted in transit."

No. The order would simply be: "Dumont—(or whoever was on tap)—get a hay cart from somewhere and bring a load of stuff that's parked at Gomez' farm and stick it in Rochefort's garage. Better take an interior road so as not to walk into anything, and be careful how you handle the stuff. Some of it's rather valuable." He would then get on with the next item. But neither type of order was given in my presence, for the right man was not available at the time. Instead, Carte tackled me on the letter he had given Lise for delivery.

"I hope you agree with what I said in my note, Michel."

"I'm afraid I haven't had time to read it," I said.

"I should be glad if you would. It's rather an urgent matter. It's about Arnaud."

"I'll have a look at it as soon as I get back," I said, sore at having been caught on the wrong foot and not wishing to explain the reasons for the delay.

I cycled back to Cannes and arranged with Suzanne to go with Antoine and collect some of the tins of food from the farm to be shared between the three of them and Catherine There was a ton of the stuff, so at least seven-eighths of it would be left over for the Carte group. I had already given some to Gomez.

One of Arnaud's messages asked that a French aircraft specialist known to be on the run from the Vichy authorities should be traced and offered a passage to the United Kingdom where his services would be of great assistance to the Aircraft Industry. I gave Suzanne his last-known address and asked her to tackle the matter for me. I also intimated that I would shortly be running out of money and that if she could rustle up two to three millions from her previous or similar sources it would be a great help. Suzanne undertook to take care of these matters in her usual helpful manner and began thinking out loud as to the best method of handling each.

Having left these problems in her capable hands, I went off for an early dinner chez Robert.

Here, as ever, the smooth style of the place, the excellent food, and the courtesy of the waiters helped to bring back a state of comparative equanimity to my fraying nerves.

During the course of this particular dinner my mind was shaken out of its temporary depression by the substance of a most unusual conversation.

The wine waiter, who had little to do owing to the earliness of the hour and consequent lack of customers, remained talking rather longer at my table than was his normal custom.

For some reason we got around to the war, and, after plainly manifesting his dislike for the Germans, the sommelier proceeded to say:

"You know, Monsieur Chauvet, all sorts of things are being prepared to help a future Allied landing."

"Is that so?" I said with unfeigned surprise.

"It is, Monsieur . . . and this coast is simply teeming with British Officers who are organizing that work."

"You astonish me!" I lied. "Have you ever met any of them?"

"I haven't personally, but I've heard a great deal about them, and it appears that the Head Man around here goes by the name of Michel."

"Tiens, tiens!" I exclaimed, hiding a shudder that involuntarily went through me.

After the sommelier had left my side, I wondered how on earth this sort of thing could be public property, but it was only three weeks later that I found the solution. Jean, the dapper head waiter, belonged to one of Louis' cells in Antibes. Naturally he would talk to those members of the staff whose politics were known, and just as naturally Louis would have mentioned me and the others as part of his "sales talk" to get more and more local adherents for a movement consisting of trained officers who had gone to all the trouble of coming out from Britain. It was only through the fortunate coincidence that I had never met Jean at Louis' house that neither Jean nor the wine waiter ever suspected that their regular customer, Monsieur Chauvet, was Michel.

Reversing the roles, I could see what a strong incentive such knowledge would be, even if it were only as nebulous as the tale of the snow that had been seen on the Russians' boots who, the rumor went, had passed through England by train during a grim period of the 1914–18 war.

Back at my flat, I tore open Carte's note. It turned out to be a long letter. Unable to believe its contents on the first reading, I read it through a second time.

It ran:

DEAR MICHEL,

I have received a note from Paderewski [Arnaud] telling me of his wish to risk a concert at ———.

It is not for me to assess this risk—it only concerns you and him—but I would ask you to consider my inability to impose a risk that I judge to be grave as well as unnecessary on my men. Consequently, if he wishes to run this risk I must cut the contacts between the danger that he represents and our houses and men.

Let us then be agreed (and do not think that I am upset or annoyed—I understand his impatience—only—I do not approve of it and wish to dissociate myself from a foolhardy action):

1. That he will not live in a house provided by us.

2. That he does not give concerts in places furnished by us *or any of our people,* i.e., nothing coming from X and Y—in order to avoid the danger of getting them, through him—if he were caught—*which is what I fear.*

3 That he also cuts all contact with our friends, simply for reasons of security. In a word—I would ask you to strengthen all security measures between you and myself—and that we adopt the military regulations governing a fighting army.

Here they are:

When one asks for subsistence or help from a unit one accepts its security and disciplinary rules, unless one is given "carte blanche" in this respect for each individual instance when a man or material is used belonging to that Unit.

Dear Michel, these regulations are all the more imperative to both of us at this moment when strict Police measures are announced. The battle will begin very soon. Discipline must therefore be severe to avoid the worst.

I have just learned that the denunciation responsible for the order to frame an arrest warrant for me was due to a great extent to Julien's intrigues and this will explain my wish to be very strict.

It goes without saying that we are at your disposal—but on condition that we are in a position to protect ourselves against any breach of discipline or any recklessness on the part of any of your men.

I count on you . . . you can count on me . . . there is so much to be done.

Yours ever,

CARTE

I threw the letter disgustedly onto the table with a hollow laugh. I repeated the first two phrases of the last sentence to myself, mockingly: "I count on you. You can count on me." "Perfidious Albion . . ." went the saying. How the roles were reversed! Security! Why, I had been preaching security ever since I arrived. I thought of the recent happy-go-lucky meetings on park benches with anything up to half a dozen of the local top Resistance men sitting around and scribbling their orders and instructions under the public gaze. This was the man who had expected Julien to transmit all day without listening to the holdups, the raids, and other difficulties of the job. It was not a fortnight back since I had strongly opposed the idea of Arnaud's working in one of Carte's Antibes houses where submachine guns were stored. Carte had roared with laughter as though I were a little schoolgirl frightened of a mouse. It was not a week since I had dissuaded this man, who was rapidly becoming the textbook example of a reckless lunatic, from sending a team of his best men to practice blowing up the Antibes Radio Station at night with "live" plastic. The place was strongly guarded and the normally fearless head of this hand-picked squad—for whom I had nothing but the highest admiration—had implored me to countermand Carte's order. The memory of my embarrassment at having to arbitrate between these men and their Chief, as an outsider—a foreigner —made me wince.

Picking up the letter again, I scanned the penultimate paragraph. "We are at your disposal." I thought of the Vinon airfield. Then there was that fiasco of Hilaire's pathetic arrival at the clinic. It gave me a bitter twinge to think how he and Julien had been disposed of. It was hardly surprising that either should have complained of their treatment to anyone within earshot. To expect utter loyalty in these circumstances was really asking for the moon. Nor was it only Julien who voiced his disapproval. Frenchmen at the top of the hierarchy were beginning to scratch their heads and make polite excuses to me. They knew that my heart was in my job, that I was their friend and no mere paid hireling of the British Government.

I wondered where Carte had dug up the French Army Regulations and, considering the Treasury's generous subsidy for the movement, I rather relished the bit that began, "When one asks for subsistence or help from a Unit . . ." Not that I grudged the subsidies; they were only too natural. Neither Paul nor End would have penned such drivel. Nor would Bartoli or Roger or any one of half a dozen other responsible men who were always prepared to take part in any risky enterprise.

But the cream of it all was that Carte had written a thesis on "security" as though he had just invented the subject.

I consoled myself that if Carte's compatriots were unable to solve this growing problem of their own chief, my own inability to do so was excusable. But the waste of time irked me, nevertheless. I was not looking for excuses; I was looking for a solution.

I was no genius myself, but I was doing the best I could. I wondered what had motivated London recently to send me a message out of the blue that asked: WHAT SABOTAGE HAS YOUR CIRCUIT EFFECTED SINCE ITS INCEPTION. Remembering my instructions not to blow up anything until specifically told to do so, I had seen red. I chuckled to myself when I remembered my answer to that one: WHO THE HELL WAS RESPONSIBLE FOR YOUR NUMBER 139—and how London had never followed up the matter. I thought of Arnaud's unprintable comments on the subject with gratification: bless him . . . It was his way of showing that the first rivets of our friendship were also being driven home on his side.

I then let my mind wander off to Lise. I wondered how she was getting on. She ought to be back tomorrow. So regular were the movements of couriers that it never entered my mind that anything could stop her.

And so, reflecting on these and other problems, another day drew to a close.

The fifth of November dawned bright and sunny with the promise of continued warm weather.

I went over to Catherine's flat for the day's normal routine meetings. Catherine agreed with alacrity to my request that Arnaud might transmit from her bathroom, which faced north.

When by ten thirty and again at eleven o'clock Lise had not shown up, I made arrangements for all trains from Marseille to be met, and those assigned to this task were instructed either to bring her to the flat, or return and report that she was not on the train.

At two thirty Lise had still not returned, and I began to get worried. I had to attend a rendezvous at Antoine's house, billed for 3 P.M., so I set off to get there early.

This turned out to be a mammoth meeting—much to the embarrassment of Antoine, who saw his house and garden invaded by a veritable army of resisters. I thought it was more like a garden party than a clandestine gathering. Despite the security letter, there were absolutely no measures taken against possible intruders and, throughout its long sitting, I felt as though I were on the edge of a volcano. Above and away from it all sat the raging figure of Antoine, on his private balcony, with despair in his heart. No one paid him the slightest attention.

Behind the desk in the library sat Carte. Facing him sat row upon row of his minions with paper and pencil at the ready, like a class taking notes at a lecture. The overflow, of couriers awaiting orders and others seeking an audience, sat sunning themselves on the terrace and the noise of their merry babble made it difficult to catch what their chief was saying.

They were all in their places when I arrived. No doubt I had been given the wrong time. At my entrance, Carte's soft musical voice broke off to greet me, and then the real business got under way.

"Michel," began Carte, "Colonel Vautrin has just informed me that this zone is to be occupied by the Italian Army. The occupation will be headed by three Divisions who will arrive by train at 1 A.M. on November the eleventh. A motorized Division will make its appearance along the coast road during the morning of that day and certain light mountain batteries will take up their positions to defend the coast from the frontier up to Marseille."

"Where do the trains cross the Franco-Italian frontier?" I inquired.

"Through the three tunnels that exist between the Mediterranean and Switzerland," answered Carte.

"It seems to me that it might be quite an idea to blow up those tunnels just as they go through them," I suggested.

"Exactly what I was going to propose," said Carte.

"If you'll give me the co-ordinates of those tunnels and pinpoint a vulnerable spot where the three Corniche roads join, I'll get Gervais to handle the tunnels and ask London to invite the R.A.F. to attend to the road," I said.

"I invited Gervais here with that idea in view," said Carte.

"Will you let Gervais pick nine men for the operation?" I asked.

"With the greatest of pleasure," said Carte.

With rings marked round the three tunnels on the Michelin map of the area, I took Gervais outside and found a quiet spot.

"Now, Gervais," I said, "pick nine of the best men you like and form them into three teams of three. Designate a leader for each team and take them all to a quiet place just outside Nice. Carte will provide the spot. Get them all rigged out as campers or hikers, with rucksacks, and have each team take one pound of plastic, some instantaneous fuse wire, and a fog signal for the job. Better double the order in case of a slip. There are bound to be sentries on the French side of the tunnels, so these hikers must make a careful reconnaissance and find out (a) if there are sentries, (b) how often and when they change guard, and (c) how far away they stand from the mouths of the tunnels. If they're obviously going to be a nuisance on the night, they'll have to be taken care of. No need to bump them off; just give them the one-two-three and tie them up with the string routine they gave us, and gag them. Hide their rifles, if there's time. Get Aramis to provide you with plenty of bread coupons and I'll fix you up with money. All right?"

"Why Nice?" asked Gervais.

"Because they should see the ground after you've given them their instructions and some 'close-combat' stuff, and report back to you at a forward base before the job is done. They've got to know that ground backwards and in the dark."

"Can I join one of these teams?"

"It's a French job really. We provide the wherewithal and their men carry it out. But if you can't bear yourself, join the party on the tunnel nearest Nice. Don't forget to organize the retreat. Pop the plastic one hundred yards inside each tunnel at twelve fifteen on the eleventh and scram. . . . But remember this, Gervais: don't blow those tunnels unless you get confirmation from me in my writing on blue paper. It won't be a long screed; just *Go ahead.*"

"O.K.," said Gervais.

I watched the young instructor walk down the path smoking his pipe, and thought to myself "It's in the bag." I looked round the group and then caught Antoine's eye. The man on the balcony shrugged his shoulders hopelessly.

I returned to the library and informed Carte of my arrangements with Gervais. Then, as I was leaving I was buttonholed by my friend, Commandant F. of the Deuxième Bureau.

"I've got a rather embarrassing matter to discuss with you, Michel," he said.

"Fire away, *mon Commandant,*" I said, feeling that embarrassment could be faced lightly in view of the more important developments.

"Do you happen to know a compatriot of yours by the name of Monsieur Gavot?" he asked.

"If he's a fairly recent arrival I wouldn't know the name on his identity card. What does he look like?" I asked.

Commandant F.'s description left no doubt that the gentleman in question was Grégoire—the "professional."

"I think I do know this man," I admitted, now fully prepared for anything.

"Well, he's got himself into a peck of trouble. Two nights ago he signed a check at the Casino for losses of thirty-eight thousand francs. He's done the same thing at a hotel and both checks bounced."

"Judas!" I exclaimed. "What am I supposed to do?"

"If you feel inclined to cover these sums—about fifty thousand in all—there'll be no repercussions."

"What . . . and have it happen again tomorrow or the next day?"

"Couldn't you ship him home?"

"I could. . . . But look at the trouble he'd cause before the boat left; and anyway, I'd rather keep the space for an R.A.F. type any day."

"Bit of a teaser, isn't it?"

"It is . . . I'll think it over tonight and let you know tomorrow morning."

On this dismal note, I detached myself from the meeting. On my way down the drive I met Colonel Vautrin. I congratulated him on his masterly information about the Italians, then told him what had been done to meet the eventuality. Then Vautrin said:

"I'm afraid I have a piece of bad—indeed tragic—news for you, Michel."

"What?" I asked, aghast.

"General de Lattre de Tassigny was picked up on his way to the Pyrenees by a Company of the Garde Mobile. His entire division has been disarmed and he's in the Riom Prison."

"Holy Mother of God!" I exclaimed "What happened?'

"We don't know yet," shrugged the Colonel.

As I cycled home I wondered if this was not another "Dakar" —another of those hush-hush missions discussed as freely as the weather and then passed from mouth to mouth at the speed of a bush fire. I hoped that I was wrong; but it had happened so often that there were no real grounds for this hope. The French were brilliant conversationalists, brilliant talkers, and to expect them to clamp down on the subject uppermost in their minds was to expect them to stop breathing.

I held the entire nation in high regard, indeed in deep affection. I knew the valor of its soldiers, sailors, and airmen. I also knew that the word *motus*—mum's the word—appeared in their dictionaries. But I fancied its inclusion was purely an indication of the country's culture; some sort of translation had to be found for what others sometimes did. They certainly understood its significance, but by their patent abhorrence of ever putting it into practice I could only conclude that they were not ideally suited for keeping secrets or prosecuting clandestine warfare. But in view of the Grégoire incident, I could only pray that the French did not tar all British agents with the same brush.

If only the tunnels could work, I thought, then all our combined shortcomings would be expiated I wondered if Lise was back yet and accelerated my pace in order to find out.

Lise was not back, and Arnaud and Catherine were looking concerned.

I told them there was nothing to worry about and tried to interest them with all the latest news They perked up considerably on hearing about the Italians and Catherine served us tea as we discussed the chances of blowing the tunnels.

I got out some paper and wrote down the day's messages. I had to make several corrections before they were clear and concise. I carefully printed the final copy, which ran:

> PYRENEES VENTURE OFF GENERAL CAPTURED STOP ITALIANS DUE START OCCUPY THIS ZONE ARMISTICE DAY STOP COMING BY ROAD AND RAIL STOP AM ATTENDING TO RAILWAYS PLEASE ASK R A.F. PLASTER CORNICHE AT NICE—M FOR MOTHER 12—REPEAT 12—AT MIDNIGHT 10 REPEAT 10 NOVEMBER ENDS.

"There you are, Arnaud," I said, pushing the slip of paper across the table.

"Yes, there I am, and there you are, but where's Lise?" said Arnaud.

"Search me," I said, suddenly aware of slight thunder in the air.

"Where did you send her?"

"Marseille."

"Fancy sending her to that ——— ——— pit of Sodomy before she's had time to catch her breath."

"What d'you expect me to do with her? Stick her in a glass case . . . ? If she were my courier she'd have to go wherever I sent her."

"May the Lord protect her from such a dreadful fate!" flamed up Arnaud. "I hope she clears off fast!"

"You're a liar."

"And you're a callous bastard . . . I always knew it."

Arnaud stormed out of the room, slamming the door so hard that one of the pictures fell off the wall.

Catherine walked over without a word to pick it up, and as I jumped up to help her, she told me politely, but coolly, that she did not require my help.

I walked slowly over to the door and, turning, said, "*Bonsoir,* Catherine."

"*Bonsoir,* Michel," she replied without turning her head.

I closed the door silently behind me and walked down the steps and out into the street. I automatically unchained my bicycle and rode back to my flat.

Once inside I went into the kitchen and poured myself out a glass of wine which I drank off at one go. I then lit a cigarette and lay on my bed.

That Arnaud should go off his rocker was one thing; he was unpredictable and frequently got steamed up. But that Catherine, of all people, should support him was quite another. What was the matter with them? What was so terrible about Marseille? . . . True, I had warned Lise of what to expect, but after all. . . .

I tried to talk myself out of it, but a little voice kept nagging at me: Remember, it kept saying, when you were there last January . . . Remember that raid when they cordoned off the street . . . Remember all those women and children they hustled off to Germany . . . Remember the French police they trapped at the Stadium and sent off, as well . . . Remember how those spivs shook you down for twenty-five thousand in a back street. . . . This is the gay resort from which Lise has not yet returned.

I jumped off the bed and walked over to the window. I went hot and cold all over. I looked at my watch. Six twenty-five. "Two more trains," I said to myself, "the seven fifty-three which George is looking after, and the eleven thirty-seven." I decided to meet them both myself. I would send George off to his dinner when I found him.

Five minutes before the seven fifty-three was due in, I joined the crowd waiting outside the gate. Four minutes later I spotted George. I went over and told him not to wait.

Presently the train came in and the passengers began streaming toward the exit. I waited until they had all passed the gate, but Lise was not among them. I walked away so as not to be conspicuous, looking back for stragglers from the busy road. But the girl had not come by that train.

Dinner was out of the question and the thought of the three-and-a-half hours' wait until the last train was due and how I was to get through the time, lay like a lump of lead in my stomach.

I cycled slowly back to my flat and wrote a report to London. I made it as long as possible and told them in detail about Vinon, de Lattre, the Italians, and Carte's recent discovery of the meaning of Security. I took my time over it and wrote it very carefully, even including Carte's letter about Arnaud—word for word—in Runyonese. I told them about the new intake, my chances of getting a job as an estate agent, and about Grégoire's outrageous behavior. I poured out all the bitterness of my soul in the last sentence concerning that crook: "Is this your answer to my earnest request for 'sword-of-honor' men?" I told of my disappointment on learning from one of their W/T messages that no naval unit in Gibraltar had been available at the time to collect the tanker prizes I had sent for Olivier because they were so busy elsewhere. I bluntly suggested that this was utter nonsense, since a rowing boat could have guided them in. I gave them the details of Arnaud's hat-trick repair mission and recommended him for the Distinguished Service Order. If ever they had the time and the inclination to read it all, I hoped it might help them to follow the ever-changing situation out here. I finished up by suggesting that they engage an intelligence officer for the sole purpose of reading all reports and framing replies to urgent matters by wireless, and the word wireless automatically led me on to the dismal subject of the rusted interurban sets. I concluded by apologizing for sending this report and explained that the reason for my doing so was that I feared I was robbing all takers at six to one that Vinon would be a flop in view of Carte's attitude to my checking up the ground.

At last it was time to meet the eleven thirty-seven. I hid the report and made my way to the station.

Below the dim street lighting I joined the small silent crowd waiting for the last train. I walked slowly up and down by the wall of the advance luggage office, smoking the umpteenth Gauloise of that evil day. With my head slightly bowed and my hands thrust deep into my trouser pockets—it was still too warm for a coat—I was as inconspicuous in that gathering as one grain of sand beside the next.

A murmur from the crowd told me that the train had been signaled. A distant rumble then heralded its approach, and presently the hissing locomotive came in sight, with the driver and fireman shimmering in the red light from the open furnace. As the blacked-out coaches drew up, I knew that the passengers, getting out on the far side of platform two, would only come into view when they emerged through the subway. My heart began to beat faster and my mouth went dry as the first hurrying passengers reached the gate.

I stood back near the wall, away from the others, and had an uninterrupted view of the subway exit. In my anxiety I found my eyes veering off to the gate as well, lest I had missed her at the first point. Then, realizing my folly, I looked back; but then I was sure I must have missed her in between the two points.

And now they were coming thick and fast and spreading out beyond the gate like lava. I forced myself to remain cool and alert. It would never do to focus so much attention on one spot as to become unaware of what was going on around me. That was the sort of moment when an unexpected hand on my shoulder or a voice close to my ear would make me jump out of my skin.

The bulk of the passengers were now past and the rest were thinning out. Gradually I saw that I was almost alone, as the remaining few advanced in dribs and drabs. Soon the gaps grew wider between the last to come.

My heart sank into my boots. I put my hand against the wall to steady myself, for I had had little to eat during the past twelve hours. From my strangled throat came the words: "Oh, God, give me strength. . . ." when—lo and behold!—there, like a miracle, struggling with a huge suitcase, came Lise.

Swallowing down the lump that had come into my throat, I stood stock still watching the girl. My delight at seeing her was almost spoiled by my feeling of guilt at having so thoughtlessly omitted to consider the weight of the case.

As she gave up her ticket and walked out into the yard I observed the proud tilt of her head, the look of independence, the absence of self-pity. Staggering under the weight of the enormous case, she still managed to launch her aura of challenge into the unseeing night. But I had seen it, even if she had not spotted me.

I walked out of the shadows toward her, surprised that she did not turn her head. In one movement I took the case from her hand and slipped my arm through hers.

The sudden shock reflected on her face was slowly replaced by a tired smile. Lise had certainly not expected to be met by anyone at this late hour, and that it should be me of all people, whose veins she clearly thought were clogged with sawdust, only served to increase the stupefaction she must have felt at this odd twist at the tail end of her first real mission.

Conscious of all this, I was at some pains to say all that was in my mind. I squeezed her arm lightly to show my pleasure at her return and said, "Well done, Lise! We were beginning to get worried about you . . . you must be very tired."

"I am rather," smiled the girl, "and I feel as if I could eat a small horse."

"Well, that can be attended to, at least," I said. "But it won't be a horse, exactly. I think I can promise you a piece of cow, though."

I led her gaily to my private sanctuary—chez Robert—and the 250-yards' walk was sufficient to shed a greater load of anxiety from my mind than could ever have been counteracted by my suitcase, had it been filled with blocks of granite.

Sensing that we wanted to talk, the waiters tactfully left us alone and stood out of earshot, discussing their own affairs.

At first in snatches—as course followed course—and then in longer bursts, Lise unfolded her adventures.

All had gone well as far as Marseille, and then the fun had started.

One of the four men—an Englishman—had lost his nerve at the spectacle of the Gare St. Charles crowded with German soldiers. "It was as though he suddenly felt conspicuous on encountering the enemy at such close quarters that you could touch them," explained Lise.

"I know the feeling," I sympathized. "You almost imagine that neon lights are blinking from your forehead and proclaiming, on and off, *Made in England.*"

"Well, he started getting nervous at Toulon when the train pulled in and the loudspeakers announced, 'Hier ist Toulon. . . .' and a lot more that I couldn't understand," said Lise.

"What did he do in Marseille?" I asked.

"Got onto the first train back to Cannes," she replied. Then, "Haven't you seen him?"

"No," I said. "Must have gone to Antibes. Reminds me of a chap in a bomber who panicked at the last moment and refused to parachute over his dropping zone. When it was too late to jump he got them to circle the area and give him a second chance. Although he'd asked the dispatcher to kick him out when the light turned green, he held on so tight that there was nothing doing Can you magine his feelings during the three-hours' return flight to England? He finally came out by boat and is now a very capable agent." *

* The officer who returned from Marseille eventually rose to the rank of Lieutenant-Colonel. He was one of the few to escape capture and he welcomed General Patton's troops at the head of his own private army of some 5,000 armed Frenchmen during the August, 1944 landings in the South of France. This officer's culminating action was instrumental in paving the way for the swift advance whereby these regular troops joined their D-day comrades in the north For his gallantry he was awarded the D.S.O. and the Croix de Guerre with a citation in the Orders of the French nation.

After dispatching the three other men Lise had successfully contacted Monsieur Vidal.

By the time the suitcase had been located, with the help of Dr. Bernard—one of Olivier's associates—it was too late to do the double journey to Aix-en-Provence.

After giving her dinner, Bernard had fixed her up with a private room in one of the only safe places in the town—a brothel—and she had spent a nerve-racking and sleepless night because the place had been raided by German Military Police in search of deserters. The only reason they had not searched her room was that the woman who ran the place—a patriot—told the M.P.'s that her niece was sleeping in it and that she had scarlet fever.

Lise gave me these bare outlines with about as much emotion as one might employ in describing an afternoon's shopping excursion.

"This morning," she concluded, "I attended to the garage business, and here I am."

"Lise . . ." I said, "you've done a top-line job, and I congratulate you."

"Thank you, sir," she said, in a tone suggesting she had only done it to fill in time until she could go to Auxerre and get down to some serious work.

"Lise . . ." I said presently, "this Auxerre business . . . Why don't you drop it and stay here?"

"If I stayed anywhere it would more likely be in Marseille where things are happening, and not in this one-eyed hole. In any case," she went on, as though to soften the blow, "London would never hear of it."

"Of course, it's up to you, Lise, but I've got no courier and I'd be simply delighted if you'd stay. . . . With you and Arnaud, there'd be no stopping us."

"Michel, I appreciate the suggestion, but . . ." she said, walking into the trap, "I'm willing to bet anything you like that London would never play."

"I'll take you up on that, Lise," I said promptly.

"How much?" asked Lise, reflecting the Rue de la Paix in one eye, and Bond Street in the other.

"Fifty thousand," I said softly.

"Make it one hundred thousand," said Lise. still more softly. "I shall be in Antibes tomorrow morning, so when you see Arnaud at the Augusta flat, ask him to send this simple message: MAY I KEEP LISE."

"All right," she said, "but you're wasting your time."

"And if London should comply, Lise, and you still feel as you do now after, say, a month, you'll be free to go—and no hard feelings."

"Agreed," said Lise.

Within twenty-four hours of his message to London, Arnaud presented me with their reply. Apart from a rather distasteful look which he had affected for my benefit ever since Lise had passed him the four-word request, his expression was noncommittal. I read the words:

> SEND LISE TO AUXERRE AS ORIGINALLY PLANNED STOP SURELY CARTE CAN PROVIDE MEANS OF CROSSING DEMARCATION LINE.

Without a word I wrote on a piece of cigarette paper the two words: LISE INDISPENSABLE and handed this to Arnaud.

During the course of the day I met Lise. Her crowing jubilation at the result of our bet was not at all flattering, to say the least.

"Will you give me another twenty-four hours?" I asked her.

"If it can give you any pleasure to have it rubbed in," she bubbled gaily.

Next day, the still inscrutable Arnaud brought me my fate.

Among three other messages I found what I was looking for: YOUR 196 OH VERY WELL ENDS.

Among the three other messages that came with this humorous permission for me to keep Lise was a baffling instruction that left me entirely nonplussed. It read: ON NO ACCOUNT ARE YOU TO IMPEDE ITALIAN OCCUPATION.

After the initial shock of this order, it seemed to me that the War Office must have gone off its head. This was no private ruling from the French Section alone; it was a matter of Supreme Command policy, and no doubt Winston Churchill had been consulted over it.

What an iniquitous waste! I thought. Instead of the monumental all-round effects of blocking the tunnels and bombing the road, the Italians were now to be allowed their second triumphant entry into France in the course of one war.*

When Carte saw the message, his reactions were very much like mine, but now I had to defend the unreasonable order. My "There must be some very good reason for these instructions," sounded about as convincing to me as it clearly did to Carte.

CHAPTER XI

It was a lucky thing that I had got Lise to deliver the money to Gontrand in Aix-en-Provence for black-market petrol. When, the day before the operation was due, I was left to my own devices to reach the field, I was able to arrange for motor transport from Marseille.

Having been assured that every detail had been taken care of by Carte and that all I would have to do was place the nine flashlight bearers at the correct intervals for the flare-path and signal the aircraft down, my only problem was to make my way as far as Marseille by train and then proceed by car to the rendezvous at a farm beside the field which lay in a bend of the Durance, some eight kilometers southwest of Manosque.

Fearing that there might be a slipup over such trifling details as torches for the human flare-path, or food for the large party attending this operation that might last anything up to five hours in the freezing night, I saw to it that Lise filled my rucksack with a spare set of torches, spare bulbs, and two bottles of Armagnac. We would get fresh bread in Marseille and take plenty of bread tickets to spare.

* Colonel Vautrin's forecast of the Italian occupation was accurate to the very hour. The added work entailed by their presence in this zone prevented me from joining Madame Rondet's staff and I simply had to trust to luck and constant moves to avoid deportation to Germany on forced labor.

Wearing our thickest clothes and carrying heavy coats we set off on the first lap.

At Marseille we contacted End, who was taking a separate carload to the rendezvous, and then found Gontrand at a prearranged café.

Our drive took us through Aix and then some thirty kilometers further inland.

On one stretch of the road we ran straight into a French Control. When I spotted the two hefty gendarmes standing in the middle of the road signaling the car to halt, I wondered how Gontrand would get out of this mess. He had no papers for this journey, having been too busy to bother over such a trifle. I had had the jitters ever since I had inquired as to this detail. To be caught through such slovenliness would have been criminal. And now, as the car slowed down, the butterflies began to flutter in earnest in my stomach. Lise did not appear overanxious and, as for the driver, he was quite unconcerned. He simply looked out of his window and waited for it.

"Your papers!" challenged the larger of the two State policemen.

Gontrand produced his driving license.

"I don't mean that," said the man sternly, "I want your permit for this journey."

"I'm afraid I haven't got one," said Gontrand.

"In that case I want to see all your identity cards," said the man, suspiciously. ". . . and I shall require you to come along with me to the station."

"Oh, Officer," began Gontrand, "this is a perfectly innocent journey. I'm only obliging this young couple by driving them to Manosque for private reasons. You know how long it takes to get these permits. I told them I'd take them at my own responsibility. You'll see us coming back presently. . . . You simply must trust me."

There was a moment's deadly silence during which our fate hung in the balance, and then the big gendarme shrugged his shoulders and said:

"All right. You may proceed this time."

As the car moved off, I chalked this incident up as one of my lives gone and I felt a little older. Neither of us was armed, so what chance had we? Our only defense in the Underground was to avoid such unnecessary risks. The days of careering around in German military vehicles with Sten guns under the seats were not yet at hand. I only wished they were. At least one would know where one stood.

Once the danger was past, Lise and Gontrand forgot all about it, like animals.

Road 96 now joined up with the Durance and the car swept through some rocky landscape as the sun was setting.

Presently we drew up in a clearing beside the main road where the farm was located. At least three other cars were already parked there for all to see.

We joined the large group that anxiously awaited us in the bedroom upstairs. There was much handshaking all round and several new people to meet.

An indescribable atmosphere reigned in this poor homestead. By the light of two oil lamps I was struck by the unreality of the scene. Lying on the large family bed was a wretched lunatic girl of about thirteen, babbling her unintelligible madness, while her mother—the farmer's wife—held her hand and spoke soothingly to her with all the endless love that only a mother can give. She shook my hand with the faraway look of someone whose troubles cannot be increased by an invasion of twenty people waiting in her pitiful home for an aircraft to land within two-hundred yards of it, any more than they could if a herd of elephants had used her bedroom as a thoroughfare.

All around this centerpiece stood groups of people, busily engaged in their own conversations and seemingly unconscious of their incongruity The only person who seemed affected was Lise. I could almost feel the current running between her and the mother.

Carte, Vautrin, the Cannes police chief, and Paul stood in one group. Next to them were the five chosen generals. Carte had wanted to return with seven and had been very rude to me when the Section had sent its final instructions in a telegram ending a long wrangle on that point. There was no getting round their message which had said: ABSOLUTE LIMIT FOR AIRCRAFT YOU CARTE AND FIVE OTHERS.

The Generals appeared highly elated at the prospect of flying off to England, but I wondered what the Section would think of Carte when they saw these aged Blimps, for not one of them looked a day under seventy and I feared that if ever the aircraft took off with this ancient cargo, there might be some severe casualties on the way through sheer fright.

Next to this happy group was the flare-path crowd under the command of End. It consisted of Jacques Langlois, Riquet, Gontrand, a young farmer with his shotgun, a French pilot, Jacques Latour (Curator of the Musée Réattu in Arles), Dr. Bernard, and Jaboun the well-known French artiste and music hall compère.

Taking this crowd into a quiet corner, I showed each man where he would be placed on the flare-path and what he had to do at a given signal. I drew the positions on a large piece of paper and, when I had concluded, I asked if there were any questions. As there were none, I singled out two or three of the men and put various searching questions to them to see that they were not merely being polite. When I was satisfied that the picture was clear, I said:

"I shall give each one of you your position and nobody must move from it until the aircraft is airborne and out of sight. If it should develop engine trouble and want to land, we must be in a position to guide it down again. The operation will start at 10 P.M., but I doubt if the plane will arrive before midnight. It may even come as late as 2 A.M., but that is the outside limit. There must be no smoking and no flashing of lamps or noise throughout."

I then asked End if he had the torches. He said that he had not got them, but that Carte might possibly have entrusted them to someone else.

I made a point of asking Carte the same question in front of Vautrin Carte had to confess that nobody had any torches.

"You'll forgive me for saying this, Carte," I said in a clear voice, "but you assured me that this detail would be taken care of. Fortunately, I've brought a spare set."

By now it was nine thirty and time to be going. Everyone left the farmhouse and moved slowly across the moonlit fields toward the landing ground. The French airman who, according to Carte's previous assertion, knew all about this field was in the lead. Lise and I followed with the others.

The airman stopped at one end of a field and waited for me. It was a queer-looking field, lying in a hollow, and I hardly expected this to be it; but perhaps my eyes were not yet accustomed to the dark.

"Well, here we are," said the ex-pilot.

"All right," I said. "If the flare-path men will follow me I shall count out the 150 meter intervals."

Paul and the police chief remained at what was to be the first lamp position, which I was to occupy, but as no one wanted to miss the fun, the rest followed. I counted out 150 paces and placed my second man; 150 more and the third was in position; at the 450-yard mark I posted number four. All along I noticed with satisfaction that the surface was excellent even if the field did look narrow.

It was between the fourth and fifth man that my fears were realized. Halfway to the fifth lamp position the party had to climb a bank five feet high that ran diagonally across the entire field. It was a bank that would have upset a motor car doing thirty m.p.h. What it would do to an aircraft at ninety m.p.h. was so clear to me that the first four lamp positions must now be scrapped out of hand. I only hoped there might be sufficient length beyond the rise to use the rise, or a spot just beyond it, as the first lamp position and start the whole thing over again from there.

But, on looking beyond this hazard in any direction, I saw to my horror that the ground sloped downhill to a boundary of high trees not four hundred yards away; the hundred-yard mark being crossed by a deep eighteen-inch ditch, sufficient to knock the tail skid off any aircraft.

With murder in my eyes, I looked at Carte, who had not yet grasped the enormity of his folly in preventing me from inspecting the field as the War Office and I had wished. Instead he was purring away under the compliments of the five generals beside him.

"Where are the 1,600 meters of length and 800 meters of width which I explained were the minimum essentials and that you promised were here? . . . And who is the expert who considers this death-trap suitable for a bomber to land on?"

Carte pointed out the tall young man wearing a leather coat, and said:

"He did; and since he's an airman he ought to know!"

I turned to this madman and said, "What planes have you flown?"

"Potez 43's," came the answer.

On hearing the name of this archaic flying machine, I nearly collapsed, for everyone who took any interest in aviation knew that these obsolete aircraft were able to land at twenty-five m.p.h. in a following wind and only required a tiny space, quite incomparable to that of a fast heavy bomber, in which to land.

As I argued with the French airman, who swore that he could bring anything down in this "magnificent" field, I overheard Carte telling the generals how fussy British officers were, and if I wished to be so difficult, why had I not made a proper reconnaissance of the place myself; particularly in view of the importance of the passengers.

I was beside myself with impotent rage. My language surpassed anything that Arnaud had ever used. The more I felt Lise's presence, the more I thought she might as well know once and for all—as well as everyone else within range—just what I thought of this scandalous fiasco.

As I peered anxiously round for a solution to my impossible dilemma—any reasonable patch of ground where my friends could squeeze in a landing and take-off—the final crowning blow put paid to all my hopes. There, distinctly, came the approaching drone of the Hudson. It *would* have to come at ten fifteen into the bargain.

Carte, backed up by the crazy Potez pilot, shouted at me to line up the torchbearers, saying that the R.A.F. could land anywhere.

With a prodigious effort, I controlled my murderous rage and concentrated all my faculties. Everyone looked at me in dead silence. What was I going to do? I thought of the pilot and his crew, up there, and knew that this was the zero hour of their operation. They had certainly been told that the ground signals would only be given if all was in order below. And yet they had come a long way and I knew how keen were the men who went in for these dangerous missions. They would face almost any hazard and hardly ever expected these ops. to come off according to the book. However, there were limits. . . . I thought of my friends of the French Section waiting on the airport in England and laying odds with each other that everything would be all right, because of my past successes in other fields. There was no doubt in my mind that the general disappointment and unanimous blame for a failure would be laid at my door, instead of at Carte's. But even that was better than the certain loss of an aircraft and possibly most of its crew.

I looked round the group and said with finality: "I refuse to signal the plane!"

But the torment of seeing one of my own aircraft so near and yet so unattainable was not over by a long way. The roaring plane came down low over our heads and began to circle the field as though imploring me to do something. It spent some twenty minutes hurtling round and kicking up a noise to wake the dead. Each time it passed over our heads was added death for me.

Finally it headed for home, and the party, with Carte and the airman still piling recriminations on my hapless head, moved out of the bowl and up the side of a nearby ridge. When they reached the top, still mumbling with their remaining breath, a deadly hush came over the assembly and all stood still as statues looking in the same direction. I followed their gaze and wondered at myself that tears of blood did not spout from my eyes. There, stretching out before me, lay an abandoned two thousand-meter-long airfield. . . .

The next question was how to get the Hudson back onto the abandoned airfield which the crew must have seen and where they had probably been as amazed as I and so many others at not finding the reception committee waiting for them.

A prearranged telephone code existed between me and Suzanne that a morning call to the Augusta flat would announce whether or not the previous night's operation had worked. Lise was to attend to this. To expand on the theme of Uncle John's difficulty in finding the house and to insist he try again the very next night, was child's play for her. She left the telephone number of the Pascal Hotel, Manosque, with Suzanne so that after discussing the matter with Arnaud she could ring back

A later phone call brought the vague suggestion that an attempt would be made by Uncle John, but without any guarantee that he would be free that night.

In the early afternoon Lise, Paul, Riquet, and I walked the eight kilometers to the airport and sat on a bank inspecting the field. There was no need to pace it out for, with the naked eye, it was clearly longer and wider than the required measurements. Its surface was also in good condition. The trees at one end were well back and, in my mind, I fixed the spot where I would operate the principal lamp. This was at least three hundred yards from the trees and still gave ample space for the plane to pull up. At the far end of the take-off stood a low-built farm that would be a simple matter to clear.

We returned to Manosque in the later afternoon and were somewhat put out at the sight of two gendarmes cycling toward us in silence. Hiding in a thicket, we watched their movements and were relieved to see that they were going from farm to farm as though delivering official documents There were no Italians in the district whatsoever, and our only fear was that the noise of the previous night's attempt and the unusually heavy motor traffic must have aroused police suspicions and that they would be on the alert for any repetition of this sort.

After dinner, four cars picked up the twenty-odd persons who had attended the previous night's dress rehearsal and for whom lodging had somehow been found, and the convoy set out in the usual gay, carefree, noisy style of a charabanc load of football supporters returning after the victory of their side in the Cup Final. It was a style that was rapidly becoming the hallmark of the Resistance in the southeast, but I never quite managed to rise to the exuberant heights of my comrades' form.

Three of the four cars stopped near the airport and tucked themselves out of sight on a shrubby hummock, while Carte's machine roared gaily round the airport in search of the others with headlamps full on. As at the felucca receptions, a good attempt was being made to facilitate police surveillance of the new "pick-up" technique.

I placed my nine men; seven in a straight line at 150-yard intervals and the remaining two at right angles to the seventh flashlight bearer at 50-yard intervals, forming the letter L with the baseline inverted, thus:

. . . .
.
.

They fitted easily into this perfect field. The Generals with Carte and one or two others stood behind me, just out of the way of the aircraft's line of travel.

And now all we had to do was wait. The night grew steadily colder and I noted that two of the men were in ordinary lounge suits, without any coats, and suffering badly from the cold. One of these was End. On inquiring why he had come without a coat, I discovered that this young man simply did not have such a thing. I told him to buy himself one, saying that the Treasury would be delighted to pay for it.

We waited from 10 P.M for four solid hours, and the temperature sank well below zero. The two bottles of Armagnac saved the situation, and the loaves of bread were also a blessing.

It was a still, clear night and, after the earlier floodlighting effects of Carte's arrival, the party sobered down into an uncanny silence. None of the men moved from his position; none spoke, and no light was shone.

But it was all in vain. The unearthly silence remained unbroken and Uncle John did not oblige.

At 2.15 A.M. I scrubbed the operation, and the frozen score returned dejectedly to their hide-outs.

Despite the lateness of the hour, the Pascal Hotel party beat on the hotel door until the proprietor opened up the shutters of his bedroom on the first floor. Looking out and recognizing the authors of all this rumpus, he said:

"Well, for people who have paid their bill and said they were not coming back, this is a fair lark."

For me, the remaining hours of that night were a battle between fatigue and fear. Our good luck could not hold forever. An early peremptory knock on a bedroom door and the staccato words: "Police! Open up!" was well within the realms of possibility in a village whose quiet ways had been stirred up by twenty-four hours of a kind of "boat-race night" treatment. All, except me, slept like logs.

The next day the large party scattered to the four winds, unmolested, to await the next summons to another ground. Lise and I returned by train to Cannes to get on with routine business and to prepare the next attempt.

Arnaud gave me the strong impression that I had not been very clever in handling the Vinon affair. He hinted that he ought to bring his transmitter to the next one to insure its success.

The French Section's message: WHAT ON EARTH WENT WRONG AT VINON? did nothing to help my morale. I wrote a full report on the matter to H.Q. and sent it through Switzerland.

Meanwhile, Arnaud was kept busy with the railway sabotage program.

During this short period of comparative respite, I made a stupid mistake by cycling the wrong way up a one-way street. Before I could turn round I was stopped by a policeman, who took full particulars. As usual, I gave Antoine's address as my domicile.

On the following day a message from London said·

> OPERATION WILL BE CARRIED OUT DECEMBER MOON AT CHANOINES ARLES T FOR TOMMY 12 SUBJECT YOU CHECK ON GROUND IN PERSON SOONEST

I brought out the Michelin map covering the Arles area and pinpointed the code position of T 12. Then I called for Lise.

"Tomorrow," I said, "I want you to go to Arles and contact Jacques Latour at this address (I wrote it down). Go with him to a spot called Chanoines which is just here on this map. You —and not he—will be responsible for finding this exact spot, measuring out the field with long steps and seeing that it not only adds up to 1,600 meters in length, that it has the same width as the Vinon airport, but also a good hard surface and no trees or telegraph poles that would reduce the effective length of the runway. Is this all clear, Lise?"

"Perfectly," she said.

"Now, Lise, from this message you can see that I am held responsible for the fitness of this field. If something goes wrong this time, we're sunk. However, after the Vinon affair, I really feel that you could handle this for me. Do you think you can?"

"Certainly," she replied.

"Well, repeat to me every single detail that you must look out for," I said.

Lise complied to my entire satisfaction.

"Very well, then," I said. "You start off tomorrow morning and tonight perhaps you'd like to join me for dinner."

We went to Robert's restaurant for the first time since Lise's late return from Marseille some two weeks previously.

In quiet tones we discussed the events of the past few days. Toward the end of the meal as Lise had successively turned down my offer of a liqueur and a cigarette, I said:

"You're an odd one, Lise . . . you don't smoke, you don't drink, and you don't swear. All that'll have to change, you know. You can't belong to this crazy racket without even biting your nails."

"None of these things will ever change, Michel," she said firmly. "I simply don't like alcohol or tobacco and the word *zut* has served me well for many years."

"Careful, Lise," I warned. "One must not say 'Fountain of thy waters I will never drink.' "

"And yet that is what I do say about these three things," said Lise. "Nor do I blame you in the least for making a hobby of them yourself," she said, smiling at me.

"You make it sound very bad, Lise," I said.

"Not at all. I know you're one of the old hands in this business and I judged you harshly on our first meeting. It was because you looked so spruce and I so disheveled from the felucca trip, I suppose."

"Yet despite your handicap I judged you then as I do today," I said.

"A real Frenchman might have put that in another way." She suggested teasingly.

"You know what I meant," I said.

"Tell me, Michel, what makes you come back here time and time again?" she inquired.

"I've always hankered after Mediterranean cruises," I said, "and it's taken a war for me to be able to winter in the south of France." I watched Lise's expression as I spoke all this nonsense, then added, "How about you . . . tell me something about yourself, Lise."

"There's nothing to tell," she said.

"Come off it, Lise. Let your hair down . . . it won't do you any harm."

"Well, since you ask," she replied with a faraway look, "I am the mother of three little girls "

"Good God!" I exclaimed, with no mean surprise. "How on earth could you have left them?"

"It's a long story, Michel."

"Lise, it's going to be a long war, so get weaving with the first instalment."

"When France fell," she began, "French people in England (she used the term *chez nous,* an underground habit) had to put up with some nasty remarks. Of course, one got over that stage and afterwards all became kindness and sympathy."

Lise stopped momentarily, as though thinking of those times. I waited.

"After a good share of the London raids I went down to Somerset with the girls. The bombers occasionally passed overhead, but they were not for us. I was happy and very busy and yet there was plenty of time to think. . . . It suddenly struck me how very easy it all was for me to spend the rest of the war behind the comfortable barricade of motherhood, while others in similar circumstances over here were putting up with the occupation. . . . That's really how it all started."

"I see," I mused, studying her hands as she spoke. I said, "Where did you park the infants?"

"In a convent at Brentwood. They've got two splendid aunts and a devoted uncle who'll share them in the holidays and they'll never know I'm not doing a job in Scotland, as I said I was."

"How old are they?" I asked.

"Marianne's seven, Lily nine, and Françoise ten."

"And where is their father?" I inquired.

"He's in the Army. . . . But don't imagine he could have stopped me doing this job . . . I'm inclined to arrange these things on my own."

"That doesn't surprise me in the least, Lise. And now you come under the command of a complete stranger."

"No one's a complete stranger who's doing this job."

"Well, there are some queer cookies engaged on it, but I must say I rather admire your motives, Lise. . . . Three girls . . ." I repeated slowly.

"Yes . . . And a lovely trio, if I say it myself," she said with a sad little smile.

"I'll bet they are," I said.

Lise set off next day on her mission and I remained at Cannes. I would have liked to do the Chanoines reconnaissance myself. Besides the instruction from London to do so, it was my job, but a critical state of friction existed between Arnaud and Carte—not to be surprised at—and I felt it essential to remain and act as a buffer between the two. I was determined not to lose a second radio operator. The Vinon fiasco had made Arnaud even more furious than me. He felt that all his efforts were being wasted and, instead of looking at the whole picture objectively and simply getting on with his own work as a telegraphist would on a submarine or other unit in the armed forces, there was an understandable tendency for him and other operators in the Resistance to feel that if they, with all their handicaps, could keep the communications open, it was up to the others to succeed in what had only been made possible for them by the wireless. Arnaud, like most of them, was an individualist. The thought of his meager pay never entered his head; pride in his craft was the kernel of the matter. Even if he had known of my admiration for him, or discovered that I had already recommended him for high distinction, it would have made not the slightest difference to his nature which did not suffer fools gladly.

During the afternoon, Antoine called and informed me that two police inspectors had called at his villa asking if I lived there. Having said that this was so, they then asked if I was in. Antoine had replied that I was absent in Paris on business but that I was expected back in four days' time. The inspectors had then left.

"Well, they'll be back," I said.

"I wouldn't be surprised," said Antoine.

"A good moment to move to the second flat in the Dunes, I think. It'll just keep me one jump ahead of them."

"Well, let's wait until they do call back and that'll give Suzanne a chance to look over the new place and get it in order."

"All right," I said. "Let's leave it like that—and thanks, Antoine."

"Don't mention it. I can easily find excuses for any further visits from these gentlemen."

During the evening when I was back at my flat there was a ring at my door. I was not expecting anyone. Suzanne normally went straight home after the day's work. It was only in the mornings that she called for the day's orders.

Sliding the gadget in my front door gently to one side, I saw that it was Suzanne. Closing the slot, I opened the door.

"Michel," she said in a hitherto unknown conspiratorial whisper, "I don't think it's safe for you to stay here any longer."

"Why, what's up?" I asked.

"Two inspectors from the Préfecture called at the Augusta only half an hour ago. I was just finishing up before going home and fortunately none of our people was there. They asked a lot of awkward questions about the purposes for which the flat was used. I played the injured innocent role quite easily and they pretended to swallow it; however, my intuition tells me there may be a tie-up in their minds between these two places. There's something very queer in the air."

"Good for you, Suzanne," I said. "After what Antoine told me earlier on I begin to feel it myself. No chance of their having followed you, was there?"

"What do you take me for?" said Suzanne scornfully. "I watched them go from behind the curtain and saw them turn round and have a good look at the place from the opposite pavement before walking away. I then slipped downstairs and followed them until they were out of sight along the Rue d'Antibes."

"Well done, Suzanne!" I said, beginning to pack my belongings. I spoke to her as I moved around the flat. "I'll have everyone tipped off not to use your place any more for the time being and tomorrow you can describe those two men to the chief of police and we'll find out what it's all about."

After her departure, I strapped my case onto the back of my bicycle, filled the panniers with odds and ends, and, after a last look round the flat that had served me so well for almost three months, I closed the door upon it for the last time.

Catherine was only too pleased to offer me temporary or permanent hospitality. She already had a Hungarian refugee composer in one of her bedrooms, besides Lise and herself. The atmosphere of this flat was one of dignity and repose. The Hungarian pianist, a delightful person, knew that I was English, and we had occasionally conversed together. It was a pleasure for me to hear him play the piano while our underground plans were being hatched in another room. The Hungarian had told me that he was a friend of Sir Paul Dukes and how the latter had bet him that he would spend an entire year of his life earning his living as a circus acrobat—and had done so. For my part, I only knew one story about this well-known man, and it concerned his visit to Debden airport where he was to give a talk to the men during the war. My brother, the then station commander, who had never heard of their distinguished guest, had him clapped into the "cooler" until some intelligence officer told him what a mistake he had made.

Catherine offered me Lise's room, saying, "She won't be back for some time, I imagine."

I turned in early and slept like a log. Despite the constant dread of nocturnal arrest, I was always a good sleeper. Never able to wake myself up at any specific hour and, indeed, happy to wake at all, I tried hard—but with erratic results—to be fully alert at the moment of waking. Here, in Catherine's flat, an unjustifiable feeling of security gave me a record-breaking quality of sleep.

I awoke to find Lise looking into my face.

"Where the devil am I?" I managed a bleary smile.

"While I talk my way through half a dozen Italian Control Posts, in the curfew, you're sleeping in my bed, *mon cher,*" she said good-naturedly.

"Good heavens, Lise—I didn't expect you back as soon as this."

"The London message you read me out distinctly said that the Chanoines reconnaissance was an urgent matter," she said.

"The moon period doesn't begin until December fourteenth and we're only the second today. . . ."

"Well, I'll be. . . ."

"Go ahead and say it, Lise."

"Zut, alors!" came Lise's shocking expletive.

"I'm frightfully sorry that you've had this dreadful chase, Lise. But it will give the R.A.F. plenty of time to photograph the field. By the way—was it all right?"

"Perfect."

"Well, come and tell me about it at ten o'clock. We've got a lot to do."

"Ten o'clock!" gasped Lise. "Why, I've been up all night. . . ."

"All right. I'll bet you'd like to clean up and then you can sleep all day afterwards," I said.

Lise did not sleep all day or any part of the day. She was indefatigable, and I never saw her tired or yawning then or at any other time during the many months we worked together.

After breakfast we discussed Chanoines together.

"It's a peach of a field," said Lise. "If it's a trifle narrower than Vinon, it's easily the same length and the surface is perfect. Jacques Latour and a local man drove me out there and they said there was hardly ever any wind in the place except when the mistral blew, and then its direction was in line with its length."

"How about trees?" I asked.

"None in the way at all," she replied, adding, "They showed me two other fields as well. They were somewhat smaller and might do for a Lysander."

"I'll have a look at them when we all go there for this operation," I said. Then, turning to the question of her return I asked, "What's all this night drive about?"

"Gontrand had a permit which was no good after eleven P.M. but I said I would chance it and do the talking. There was only one really stiff control where the sergeant brought out the duty officer. I pulled a big yarn about tearing through the night in order to see my very sick child in a Cannes nursing home. When I saw him still hesitate I turned on a few tears and that fixed him."

"Congratulations, Lise! A man could never have got away with it."

"What's the matter with your flat that caused you to spend the night here?" she asked, curious in her turn.

I told her what had happened since her absence from Cannes.

CHAPTER XII

ON DECEMBER 12, Lise and I, with a small company of couriers, set off for Arles. The B.B.C. message transmitted to Arnaud for the Chanoines operation was *"Deux et trois font cinq."* All they would have to do was listen for this message on several* radio sets every evening and, if it came up, that would mean the aircraft was due between 10 P.M. and 2 A.M. that night. Arnaud remained behind and Suzanne was to bring me the daily messages every other day.

* The reason for listening in on several sets was that, owing to German jamming of the BBC European wave length, the chances of hearing the messages were increased by listening to sets in different houses, since some of them were less affected by jamming than others.

Riquet booked four tickets for lunch in the dining car on the Cannes platform before we all took our seats in a second-class compartment.

When the lunch attendant eventually fought his way up to us through the crowded corridors, ringing his little bell, we rose and made our way to the restaurant car. Lise and I sat with our backs against a glass compartment, with Riquet and Jacques Langlois facing us. The car had its customary proportion of German and Italian officers seated at various tables to whom the rest of the people paid little heed.

The Anglo-French table was a very gay affair, for all four of us were good friends. When the bill arrived I settled it and put down the usual two francs per diner on the little brown tickets placed at each table by the waiter. These represented the "Winter Relief Fund" for children and Lise knew all about them from her own abundant experience of train travel.

On this particular day she was in an impish and impudent mood, and looking at the brown tickets, she picked up one of them, saying, "I know the very person who should be paying this slight offering."

"Now, Lise," I said, "for goodness' sake don't start anything stupid."

Of course, I could not have found anything worse to say. If I had ignored her, the chances were that she would not have felt goaded into doing anything.

As I stood up to let her pass and follow Jacques and Riquet who were leading on, Lise followed in line until she reached a table at which was seated an elderly, bemonocled German general. She stopped dead at his side and placed the brown ticket in front of him on the table.

In a quiet voice she said, "I think that you, who are instrumental in bringing about the need for this fund, should pay for this ticket."

All eyes in the restaurant car turned toward the scene, and there was dead silence except for the clanking of the wheels over the gaps in the lines. The general screwed his monocle more tightly into his eye, looked down at the tiny slip of paper and, without a moment's hesitation, looked over his shoulder and beckoned the waiter toward him. When this flabbergasted servant of the French National Railway Company perceived his "error" in having placed a Relief ticket before such an august personage, he began to rub his hands in anguish to the accompaniment of abject apologies. Without a word, the general drew forth a two-franc piece and, placing it upon the ticket, gave the wretched steward an unambiguous order, with a mere gesture of the hand, to take it away. Having done so, the general drew himself up to his full height on his seat and looked Lise firmly in the eye.

There was nothing more to be said. It was a draw. Lise walked on, while all eyes followed her with open admiration as she sailed out of the car. Any reflected glory that came my way was of a kind I desired no part of whatsoever.

As we crossed the first swaying platform between the coaches, I said, "An admirable performance, Lise, and I understand your feelings, but for God's sake lay off that kind of thing. It's quite dangerous enough as it is."

We got out at Arles and walked to our hotel—the Grand Hôtel Nord Pinus. Only four rooms were available here, as the rest of the hotel was full of the senior German officers of the troops occupying the district. My companions and I were the only non-Germans there.

At the far end of the hall stood the bar and behind it was the proprietress—Madame Bessières, a gay and ebullient Frenchwoman. Monsieur Bessières was not about and, during the whole of our stay, was seldom seen, as he spent most of his time in his private sitting room.

It being mid-December, the sight of seven or eight young French people seated on stools before the bar excited no particular attention. These gay people were obviously enjoying their Christmas vacation and had not a care in the world. Their regular disappearances at about 7 P.M. every day merely indicated that they were dining early—probably with friends. Everything was perfectly in order and each night the personal messages were listened to in different houses.

The following day, Lise, Jacques Langlois, Jacques Latour, and I drove out to inspect the Chanoines field. It proved as good as Lise had claimed it to be. The other two fields, somewhat smaller, but with excellent flat surfaces, were ideal for

Lysanders, and I sent their co-ordinates via Suzanne to Arnaud for transmission to London.

Every evening we listened for the B.B.C. message, but the days rolled by and none came.

Toward Christmas it grew colder, with several degrees of frost at night. Three inches of snow lay in the streets and we, who had already visited and revisited the famous Roman ruins of the town in these wintry conditions, were somewhat bored with the lack of activity. It was all very well to visit the St. Trophime Church with its beautifully carved doors and its lovely cloisters once, twice, or even three times, but in winter some of the charm of these places was lacking. To me, being in this tourists' paradise in the circumstances that brought me to this town, with German troops at every turn, it all seemed quite incongruous. A glance at the Alyscamps, the Arena, and the Theatre were sufficient for me. Lise, on the other hand, enjoyed it all, and there were plenty of willing escorts prepared to show her the marvels of the place and to talk intelligently about any of the spots she wished to visit. There was hardly a single member of our group who could not discourse at length on Van Gogh's life and paintings in a manner that left me gaping. They appeared equally versed in Cézanne and other famous painters.

Carte finally decided that things were becoming too hot for him in Cannes and Antibes and therefore settled his large family into a tiny house in some picturesque narrow street in Arles. His wife and four daughters, ranging from two to eighteen years of age, accepted their nomadic lot with admirable philosophy. Both the elder girls helped their charming mother as well as acting as couriers for their father, the fifteen-year-old daughter being a most intelligent and capable aid in this respect. I thought a great deal of this girl. She hoped, one day, to become an actress, and there seemed little doubt that she would make a success of almost any career.

Paul left his Russian wife in Cannes and followed his chief. The small town was thus teeming with agents; so much so that they had to be farmed out on local patriots for meals in order that the same large group should not always be seen together in the few restaurants still open. Even this precaution did not sufficiently reduce the numbers that did foregather. However, as the Germans suspected nothing and the general gaiety of the gatherings seemed natural at this festive season, all went well.

Lise occasionally slipped away on her own to pay a visit to the church and light a candle to Sainte Thérèse, or to be alone to think about her children and pray for their well-being She was not a churchgoer as Catholics usually are, but I soon discovered that her faith was boundless, and that she was one of those people who liked to enter a church alone and was likewise quite able to pray in a field or in a wood or wherever she happened to be, when she felt inclined to do so. Her roots being in the soil of Picardy, she was always happiest among the marvels of nature, and her love of trees was quite remarkable. During the moments that she retired inside her shell of solitude to commune with nature and eternity, I felt myself cut off from her like a complete stranger. At such times it was as though she came from another world; as though she had a secret which I could never share. It was as if she had lived for centuries and was much older than I. Then I would leave her to her own devices. But just as she entered these moods she would emerge from them, to become once more her usual gay and impish self, with the rapidity of a small cloud revealing the sun after temporarily hiding its warmth.

The days passed by and every night was clear, crisp, and dry, with the moon coming up to full and then slowly waning. The fifteen-days' limit of each moon, from its being half full until it sank back to the half-moon—fourteen days in every month—was the keystone of all night operations, and the dates of these periods were more firmly implanted in my mind than the date of my own birthday. There were still two days to go before Christmas, and the last possible day for the operation was December 28.

Owing to the clarity of the moon it was difficult to understand why the message was so slow in coming. It seemed inconceivable that England should be fogbound. Yet the group had attended so many successful parachutings that all of us were confident that our B.B.C. message would come before the twenty-eighth.

Lise, whose constant gaiety and lively pranks made it hard

for anyone to believe that she was the mother of three children, became more and more sought after. Always prepared to join in on any expedition at all hours of the day or night, she gave the general impression of being nearer twenty-one than her real age. To me she seemed tireless, and her willing help made her an admirable, fearless, and resourceful courier. I soon forgot about the initial setbacks of our first encounters and, as she settled down to the regular routine, she too, forgot all about Auxerre or the idea of settling in Marseille. It was as though we had worked together as a team for years.

A regular morning feature of her stay in Arles was the arrival of a small bunch of violets from one of her admirers. She started each day by bringing this down with her to breakfast. Despite the war, the Germans, and the constant nagging fear that Nemesis might catch up with us at any moment during this cheeky enterprise going on under the very noses of the enemy, these simple violets, which gave her as much pleasure as a galaxy of expensive flowers wrapped up in cellophane paper, made Arles one of the high spots of Lise's underground career. I would have liked to have thought of the idea myself, but I had to give the palm for this delicate attention to one of my friends; indeed, I had to confess, one of my many rivals, for the flowers were not the only stab to my *amour propre* as her commanding officer. There were two poets to be contended with, as well. I hoped, perhaps unreasonably, that the tie between myself, Arnaud and Lise was something that could not be undone with flowers, scent, or poems.

On Christmas Eve information was brought to me of the latest flak and night-fighter dispositions throughout France. Although somewhat late in the day, this was a brilliant piece of work on the part of Carte's organization. I noted the new situation and sent it posthaste to Arnaud. Even if it were already known in London, it would act as a confirmation. One ack-ack battery had taken up its position not twelve hundred yards away from the Chanoines field and many of the new positions covered the general direction that the Hudson bomber would normally take. However, once this information reached London it would be a simple matter to alter the aircraft's course. The main snag lay in the proximity of the local battery.

A party of the southeast group had passed this post on bicycles and the 88-millimeter guns seemed to me to strike out all hopes for the operation. I wondered if the R.A.F. would still perform in the light of this knowledge.

Even if the battery mistook the Hudson for one of its own aircraft as it glided in to land, a telephone call to the officer-in-charge of the post would very soon elicit what was going on, and then the aircraft and everyone attending the operation would be surrounded and captured; or, at best, since the whole operation only took three minutes, there was still plenty of time to shoot down the plane as it took off and, as the ten-odd men who were due to land from the Hudson had to vanish into thin air with all their luggage, there was little hope of their ever reaching safety in the noisy, ramshackle cars the organization had at its disposal.

The whole thing had suddenly become extremely dangerous, and my telegram to the French Section giving them and the R.A.F. a clear picture of the new situation, would only reach them on Christmas Day. The trouble was that the B.B.C. message might come over the air that very night. Viewed from the ground the position, in my judgment, was hopeless. But now it was too late for either good or bad judgment. If the B.B.C. message came there was nothing I or anyone else could do to stop the wretched aircraft from finding the ground, as it unquestionably would with that uncanny accuracy of the R.A.F., and making itself a sitting target to the local flak post by circling round in search of the flare-path. As far as the aircraft was concerned, it simply made no difference whether the reception committee stayed in the town or went to the field; it could only affect the reception committee's survival or capture.

As we waited for the 7:30 messages that night, many a silent prayer was offered that a pea-soup fog would delay matters until London could take the full responsibility for this now most precarious operation. My limited responsibility was bad enough, for I would have to accept or reject the whole affair if the B.B.C. announced that the plane was on its way. I was trapped. The Arles radio operator had gone elsewhere for some very good reason, and Arnaud could not be reached in time.

Seeing the fatal results of the impossible quandary in which

I now found myself, I suffered the torments of the damned. Lise and the others tried to tell me that it was not my fault and that some eleventh-hour reprieve would save the situation, but it was of no avail. The whole weight of the thing was on me, and I cursed my fate and the clumsiness of the radio sets that had made me decide against Arnaud coming to Arles and doing his work on the spot. I had thought of it, but what with the Germans occupying the area, their radio detector equipment, the housing difficulty, and the question of the fifty cycles, I had abandoned the idea.

Each minute of each hour of waiting was an agony that only increased as 7:30 drew nearer.

Along with a small party I listened in at Doctor Béraud's house. We had to glue our heads to the loudspeaker so as to penetrate the jamming effects that the Germans applied daily to the wave length issuing these unfathomable messages. Through the harsh sounds, similar to a German fire-engine's alarm notes, we faintly picked up each twice-repeated message and, by the time they had all been transmitted, I was damp all over with perspiration. To my unutterable relief, I had heard nothing faintly resembling *"Deux et trois font cinq."*

December 26 was also a blank day as far as our B.B.C. message was concerned, but on the twenty-seventh Suzanne brought in a message from London acknowledging my warning telegram and announcing that the R.A.F. would probably come that night and that speed must be the keynote of the "pick-up" operation.

At 7:30 we overheard the faint sounds of *"Deux et trois font cinq"* on two of the three receiving sets where we were listening. There was a concerted rush to Carte's abode. We had all put on our thickest clothes and heaviest boots. Outside his door stood the two cars that were to take us to Chanoines. Lise had filled my rucksack with a dozen written reports from all over the south which I had kept hidden away under the flooring of her room. As she was not able to attend the operation through shortage of transport, we made our farewells at the hotel.

"You won't forget to call on my aunt and deliver the presents for my daughters, will you?" she said.

"Of course not," I replied.

". . . and you will come back, as you promised, won't you, Michel?" she went on.

"Yes. I shall come back all right if tonight's business comes off successfully," I said.

"You're always so cautious, Michel. Of course it'll be successful," she smiled.

"There are so many contingencies that go to make up a successful operation of this sort. Maybe I'm cautious by nature. It doesn't mean to say we won't do everything possible to make it a success, but my approach to all these things prevents too great a disappointment when they don't work."

"Well, I always believe everything's going to work," said Lise.

"You're an optimist, Lise, and I hope you'll always remain one, but with the endless bashings one gets in this trade, one invaiiably ends up as a realist."

"The only realism I shall understand is when I see you return and not stay at home as most of them do, once they go," she said.

"I'll be back," I said quietly, "you'll see . . . and Lise . . . if the aircraft does perform, take good care of yourself. I want to find you here when I get back, so don't go out of your way looking for trouble, there's a good girl."

"I promise you that, Pierre," she replied in a submissive tone I had never yet heard, and using the French translation of my Christian name for the first time.

I kissed her hand and walked rapidly out of the room, swinging my rucksack up to my shoulder by one strap.

I walked thoughtfully through the dark streets of Arles toward Carte's house. At my entry a silence fell on the assembly and Paul said:

"We've just discovered that a German motorcycle unit of forty men and machines has camped down within two kilometers of Chanoines. My advice is that the operation should be canceled, as this news, which we have confirmed, added to the flak post, now makes this venture far too dangerous, in my view."

"I still think that the speed of the 'pick-up' will catch them all on the wrong foot," said Captain Roland, a Zouave officer of our group. "Besides, our line of retreat, whether this business is successful or not, takes us away from the motorcycle unit and deep into the Camargue, where we spend the remainder of the night on a bull-breeder's farm."

"What is your opinion, Michel?" asked Carte.

"I can't risk the aircraft in these new circumstances," I said, "and now I honestly believe our chances on the ground, getting ten men and their luggage away, will prove impossible."

"Well," said Carte, "I have listened to all the points of view and my decision, despite all the dangers, is that we must tackle these heavy odds. We can't expect to glide through this war with all the cards in our favor: so will all those who agree raise their hands?"

All hands except that of the more experienced soldier, Paul (Captain Frager, Chevalier and Commander of the Legion of Honor, and Croix de Guerre with Palme) shot up without hesitation. Paul shrugged his shoulders and added his to the rest.

I could not subdue a wave of admiration for all these foolhardy men, and my hand rose, more in salute than in acquiescence.

As the group walked toward the cars there were no farewell scenes between Carte and his family. We piled into the cars and those who found seats took the others on their knees.

The crazy convoy ground its way noisily through the dark, narrow streets of Arles on flattened tires, and soon the trees were swishing by as we gained speed along the main road to Salon. The distance to Chanoines was only a matter of eight to nine kilometers, and presently we left the main road and went bumping down a narrow side lane toward our destination. We were not challenged on any part of the run.

The two cars pulled up in a quiet ravine near the foot of the field and everyone tumbled out. I had cramps in one leg from the weight of the person who had been bumping on my knees for the last part of the ride, and was unable to move for fully five minutes. This held up the proceedings in an aggravating way, for it was 10 P.M. and everyone remembered the 10.20 arrival at Vinon and feared the flare-path could not be organized in time.

At length we all walked onto the field. I had no difficulty in placing the men, for I had already determined their positions during my previous daylight visit.

By 10:20 the flare-path had been set up and the passengers had assembled around my controlling lamp.

A new regulation had come into being since the Vinon affair, entailing the addition of a tenth torch-holder, who had to take up his post five hundred yards beyond the base line of the flare-path, and his lamp gave a red light. This was, no doubt, a double indication to the pilot and navigator as to the wind direction. In this instance, the tenth man was a postman from Arles and his lonely position took him close by a thicket, away on his own. As he took a pull from my Armagnac bottle I looked back to make sure that the other lights were visible and promised to send someone along if matters were delayed, for periodical drinks to keep out the cold. I then returned to my own position and the waiting began.

The large field was bathed in the bright light of the waning half-moon, which was still strong enough to make most of the stars invisible.

All was still and the passengers talked together quietly or remained silent in the little group. As the night advanced and the calories of our early evening meal began to dwindle, the cold made itself felt more and more. By midnight the temperature was several degrees below zero and the second bottle of Armagnac had been opened.

It was an eerie thought for me that not three-quarters of a mile away stood a German gun crew, quite as wide-awake as we and, just over a mile off, in another direction, were the sleeping motorcyclists, with someone standing guard beside their quarters.

One o'clock came and went without any change and the time dragged slowly on toward 2 A.M.—the outside limit for the operation. By now the moon had moved through a considerable arc and the temperature dropped to ten degrees below, centigrade.

At 2 A.M. the same frigid silence reigned while the men stood steadfastly at their posts. It looked like another disappointment.

"I suggest we give them half an hour's grace," I said to Carte, "before packing up."

The last half hour seemed as long as the previous hour and it brought no sounds of aircraft.

At 2:30 all stood still for five minutes and listened for the distant drone which—if it came—would come to us from over ten miles away on such a night; but nothing was heard.

"Well, it's too bad," I said. "Maybe they met with some flak on the way. I don't think there's much point in staying here any longer."

"Doesn't look like it," said Carte.

I fetched the men in and we moved slowly off in a group toward our hide-out. The two cars were driven off to a nearby farm where the aircraft's would-be passengers were to spend the night.

When we had moved some two kilometers from the field a distant drone made us all freeze in our tracks. The plane was flying high and coming from the southeast and not from the north. It might be a German aircraft. We all peered upwards and listened. Closer and closer it came and then went straight toward the field we had just left. Presently it began to lose height and, as it passed below the moon, I recognized it as our Hudson.

A burning rage filled me. It was too late now to return and re-form the men. A dozen good reasons came to my mind to explain the late arrival and queer line of approach of the aircraft; the most feasible being that, owing to the new flak positions, she had had to make a considerable detour—even possibly following the Rhone Valley—and then returned along a prearranged course from some such easily recognizable landmark as the Etang de Berre, from which it seemed, in fact, to have come.

I felt painfully disappointed. Three times now we had made our way to fields, at no little risk, and this was the second occasion that an aircraft had shown up and that I had dismally failed in my purpose when, with a tiny piece of luck, I might so easily have succeeded. This time, however, the gnawing agony of Vinon was not there and, on account of the closeness of the Germans, I hoped that the aircraft would not hang around Chanoines as it had done before.

We watched it in silence and with heavy hearts as it sailed over the field we had only just abandoned after a four-and-a-half hours' freezing wait. It neither paused nor circled, but went straight on in a northerly direction toward England. I wondered if it might not be running short of petrol after its lengthy approach detour. I would not know the answer until I met the pilot, for London was not likely to waste time giving detailed explanations

The despondent crowd shrugged its shoulders and moved on its way. They tramped along in small groups of twos and threes and were soon chattering away merrily. After being cold for so long, they were glad of the exercise that was keeping them warm and were really too exhausted to bother over this latest jug of spilled milk. I, however, cursed myself bitterly for not having hung about until three in the morning. Little did I know what a grave error I had committed in this. When, later, I was to discover it I found small consolation in the thought of what might have been the fate of the aircraft had I been there to signal it down.

Lise did not grieve overmuch at this failure that could in no way be placed at Carte's door and which had prevented her C.O.'s departure.

We waited for the messages of December 28—the very last day of the moon period—just in case London should decide to try it again. Nobody really expected them to do so and, when I had satisfied my conscience, the party split up and returned to their bases for further instructions.

Carte was angry with me for this near miss. He had now attended enough of these operations to know how to handle them himself. All he required was a radio operator of his own and some co-operation from London. Convinced that I was a Jonah on these pick-ups, he began to hatch a little plot of his own. His followers, however, did not see eye to eye with him. Under the leadership of Paul and End, the majority of the "movement" considered Carte's latest decision to attend an operation under the very noses of the enemy as an unnecessary risk. Nor had they forgotten several previous incidents of a similar nature. They were also annoyed with him because he was not practicing what he preached when he advocated the separation of his men from their families so as better to fight the solitary battle of the underground.

The culmination of their dissatisfaction with their chief came about as a result of his openly telling me of his hearty dislike for the English and his wish that he could be doing this work with the Americans. Paul had attended this astonishing conversation which had started through Carte's rage at my defense and countercharge over the Vinon affair and my remarks concerning the way Arnaud's work had been made well-nigh impossible by his boycotting of all the houses.

In his rage Carte had thrown a wad of notes to the value of some 650,000 francs (about £3,250) onto the table and shouted, "Here's your filthy British subsidy. Do what you want with it. I'm through!"

At this point I made one of the gravest errors in the whole of my career in the Resistance. My natural impulse was to grab the money and tell Carte that he had been a pain in the neck quite long enough and that I could get on very well without his help. It was my golden opportunity to put an end to the situation and offer the leadership, plus my hearty blessing and the French Section's co-operation, to Paul. Instead of this, however, I remembered the endless string of things to which I had put a sudden end in my life through listening to the instincts of a violent disposition, and I counted slowly up to ten. During the count I heard my chief's words before I left London: "This is a kind of diplomatic post, Michel. Above all you must keep the peace. Harmony is an essential to this job."

Swallowing my own rage and drawing a curtain over the warning signs from my instinct and intuition, I wooed Carte back, as no doubt Carte's psychological and dramatic gesture meant me to do, like a lover after an angry quarrel.

I wondered afterwards what Paul had thought of it all. I need not have wondered, for Paul considered my position as a solitary foreigner being treated in this manner as quite intolerable. He thought that I had acted correctly, and so indignant was he at this final outrage that he instigated a court of honor —a kind of court martial—where Carte was indicted, before a French general, as being unfit to retain his post.

All this took place while I was back in Cannes and Carte had stayed on at his new H.Q in Arles. I was to hear about this and much else, besides, at a later date.

CHAPTER XIII

Along with the two members of my team, I settled down to a further month's waiting for the following moon period. The next attempt was to take place on a small abandoned airfield that had once belonged to a local flying club at Tournus, just north of Mâcon. There was no need to reconnoiter this field, as the R.A.F. had recently photographed it and it passed their requirements for a Lysander pick-up. A young Frenchman by the name of Roger (no connection with the Roger at S.E. H.Q.), who belonged to our movement and lived in the town, was keeping an eye on it. All we would have to do was to make our way to Tournus a day or so before the moon period began and, once more, simply wait for the B.B.C. message for the operation. This time, however, there would be no room for the generals, and only Carte and I were to take the plane.

While similar operations were being carried out successfully by other organizations all over occupied France, I simply had to resign myself to getting on with the usual Resistance activities At this rate it was in the cards that I might fluff several more. I felt galled by my failures and began to wonder if I had just been lucky with my submarine missions.

The telegrams between London and myself about Arles had run as follows:

From London:

WHAT STOPPED YOU AT ARLES.

From me:

AIRCRAFT ARRIVED AT 0250 HRS WE LEFT AT 0235 HOURS THUS 35 MINUTES GRACE BEYOND OUTSIDE LIMIT STOP IMAGINE OUR FEELINGS ENDS.

From London:

AIRCRAFT ARRIVED 0150 HOURS GMT AND SAW ONE FLASHING RED LAMP ONLY IMAGINE THEIR FEELINGS ENDS.

From me:

CULPA MEA STOP PROFOUND APOLOGIES ENDS.

For me, usually so accurate and painstaking over the minutest details, to make a mistake—indeed to forget entirely—about the difference between French time and G.M.T. was a blow to my self-confidence that took me a very long time to get over. If I raged at others' carelessness I simply fumed at the realization that I was capable of such a grotesque lapse. I wondered if I was becoming stale, but tossed the idea aside as nonsense; I was simply a blithering imbecile and had better wake up. I thought of Mars and the terrifying patrol we shared after the landing operations. Like Mars, I must rapidly make up for this with as many major operations as possible so that it would be forgotten, or at least canceled out, in the ultimate balance sheet. If only the gods would smile on me—just a little. I did not expect to do anything as sensational as Mars' sinking of two Italian cruisers with one salvo (about which I had heard soon after the event, which had taken place in August, 1942 before I had come out to Cannes), but I was sure that if I only kept pressing the right buttons the opportunities would avail themselves.

There was plenty to be done. The railway sabotage program was going well and during the months of January and February, 1943, Arnaud sent messages making forty such parachutings possible during each moon period.

It was in January that the Carte affair came to a head. At the court of honor before which he appeared, Carte was dismissed as head of the southeast zone. In his place, Paul and End were made Joint-Commanders. I could not have been more pleased at the outcome, for these men were friends of mine and men with whom I got on extremely well. End was a tireless, dashing type of man who was respected by all. He was about thirty-five years of age. Paul, the veteran of both wars, brought wisdom and a sobering influence to the pair. Both listened to each other's counsel and both conferred with me. A perfect understanding now reigned and was to continue for the rest of our time together. But my rejoicing at the outcome of the court of honor was short-lived, for quite another reason. Carte simply refused to obey the "sentence" and straightaway rallied all those who remained loyal to him.

When Ulysse—the Arles radio operator—returned to his post, Carte managed to enlist his services. He already knew all the B.B.C. messages for the January parachutings, and forthwith sent his own teams of men to collect the containers as they came down onto our allotted fields. He continued recruiting patriots who were totally unaware of the cleavage that existed in the southeast command, and in this manner the numbers of men normally required for such reception committees were easily obtained for all the drops.

While it was perfectly legitimate for Carte to continue resistance activities on his own account, the "kidnapping" of Ulysse was another matter, and the sending of men to fields which were now precluded from his private patriotic designs was bound to bring about a situation which can well be imagined.

Carte's men found the fields, on which they had no right to be, occupied by the reception committees of the newly accredited Leaders of the movement. The ensuing tugs-of-war quickly degenerated into unpleasantness. As a result of these experiences, both sides increased the numbers of their reception committees, until moonlight scraps between the two French factions became a regular feature of the southeast's resistance work. While both groups consisted of staunch Frenchmen who, at the best of times, paid little heed to the enemy, now no heed was paid to the Germans whatsoever, and the moonlit feud raged fierce and fast, and the hatred which might have helped both sides in their mutual aim of getting rid of the enemy was turned against each other, so that both were consumed in the madness of this fresh folly.

When I learned of the first of these incidents from Paul, we considered our next move very carefully. London was clearly unaware of what was going on and some means must be found of informing those who belonged to the Carte clique that they were backing the wrong horse.

We sent a joint telegram to London which read:

> CARTE REFUSES ACCEPT DISMISSAL AND SENDS HIS OWN MEN TO OUR PARACHUTINGS STOP TO END TROUBLE PLEASE SEND THREE NIGHTS RUNNING BBC MESSAGE MEN MAY COME AND MEN MAY GO BUT THE CAUSE GOES ON FOREVER (LES HOMMES PASSENT: LA CAUSE DEMEURE) ENDS.

The word was spread far and wide that all should listen in to London so as to realize that Paul and End were the accepted Chiefs of the movement.

London agreed and the message was broadcast as requested. However, it did not succeed in diminishing the nightly battles that took place in January to any appreciable extent. All looked forward to February and the comparative ease with which these droppings would be handled, for then Carte would not know the co-ordinates of the chosen fields.

In due course, the Tournus pick-up fell due and I took Lise along to act as one of the three torch-holders for the tiny flare-path required by Lysanders.

In place of Carte, Paul was now the second passenger and I was most anxious that we should return to London so as to clear up the confusion over the Carte question and have a definite ruling on the matter from H.Q.

The tiny town of Tournus on the Saône with its 4,500 inhabitants was not the best of places in which to await an aircraft. Arles, with its 20,000 inhabitants, had been bad enough, for the smaller the place the sooner were strangers recognized. It was an undisputed fact that large towns were the best in which to operate: the only trouble about them was that most of the cafés which one was bound to frequent sooner or later were clustered together in one district, and this facilitated Gestapo supervision. The ideal setup was to meet only in private houses, but the tempo of underground work did not always permit one to function according to the book.

The café where Roger took Paul, Lise, and me was an ancient building of no pretentions standing within a stone's throw of the lovely old Abbey made of rose-colored stone quarried from a nearby village. It was called the Café Thomas, and Monsieur Thomas, a member of the local organization, welcomed us with open arms. He was a cheerful man of the French working classes, and his short, witty comments were the exact replica of the Cockney. I took to him immediately

Our small party of visiting saboteurs filled all the available rooms of his inn. Most of our meals were eaten either in the kitchen, which Madame Thomas and her small daughter seldom left, or in a small cubicle intended as the proprietors' private dining room.

In the afternoon, Roger produced a van with an open back and we drove off to inspect the field. After a ten-minute run the van pulled up two or three kilometers short of Cuisery at the side of the main road and some twenty yards from a small farmstead.

"Here we are," announced Roger proudly, with a sweeping proprietary gesture, like an estate agent showing an unworthy client a property far too good for him. The driver opened the bonnet of his van and pretended to fiddle with his motor, as a camouflage for our stopping at this point.

I looked across at an open space that I would never have given a second glance, had it not been for Roger's outstretched hand. An expression of pained surprise spread over my face. Three months back I would have been horror-struck at the amazing sight that met my eyes; but now I was growing accustomed to my friends' queer conception of what was suitable for a landing strip. The sinking feeling that gripped my entrails with tolerable despair was the vision of a fairly large field, the whole of which had been systematically strewn with mounds of bricks three feet high, each neat pile looking as though it must weigh roughly a ton. This precise handiwork was clearly that of the Gestapo or German Security Forces, with the intention of thwarting the very sort of job I hoped to perform.

I shifted my staggered gaze back to Roger, reflecting all the weariness and impatience of my soul. I said: "What's the big idea?"

"I don't know," said the young man, a trifle crestfallen. "These bricks weren't here three days ago, when I last came along this road."

"Is that the way you keep an eye on local affairs?" I said, in a hard tone of voice. "I've come six hundred kilometers and you show me a brickfield," I added, without waiting for the young man's answer.

Roger, who was hardly more than twenty-one and who could not possibly know anything about the sort of work upon which he had embarked with so much patriotic enthusiasm, remained silent.

"Can you read a Michelin map?" I asked.

"Yes," he replied.

I unfolded the map of this region on the floor of the van and said, "Tell me where we are now."

With happy impetuosity the young leader of Tournus picked a spot at random only fifteen kilometers away from where we were now standing.

I shook my head and said, more indulgently, "Roger, I had to learn before I knew anything about these things. Look . . . it's simple. We're here," I pointed with a pencil, "and where you get deep slow-moving rivers like the Saône you're bound to find enormous flat meadows. You can tell by the shading. Without ever having seen the country, you can see from this map that there are at least four giant fields, capable of holding anything up to three airborne divisions each, all of them within a radius of six kilometers from this spot. We'll go and have a look at them now on bicycles."

The car was turned round and we went back to the town.

Lise and Paul remained in Tournus, as Lise wanted to do some shopping and get some more presents for her daughters, which she hoped I would, one day, succeed in delivering.

Roger dug up three men's bicycles and, accompanied by Thomas, we set off for the first of the fields.

We cycled along highway N 6—the well-worn route of holiday-makers going south—toward Mâcon. Four or five kilometers brought us to a narrow road on the left that crossed the railway line. It then went over a rickety bridge across the Saône.

On the far slope of the bridge there stretched before our eyes a prodigious field over which we walked our bicycles so as to test the surface. It proved to be almost as flat as a bowling green along its entire length of roughly four kilometers. There was not a stream or ditch crossing it at any point, and in width it exceeded two kilometers. At the far side was a wood in which we found, as marked on the map, a small road.

As we stood in the shelter of the trees and looked back across the vast expanse we had just covered, I said: "This lane leads back to Tournus through the village of Préty. The van could bring us here by that roundabout route and then remain hidden under these trees. From here N 6 is out of sight, which means that nobody could watch a night operation from anywhere except a helicopter. You could land ten bombers in parallel lines simultaneously on this one field and have the full band of the Garde Républicaine playing the Marseillaise in the very center without anyone hearing a sound or realizing what was going on."

"I begin to grasp the general idea," said Roger.

"The trouble is," I said, "that it's too late now to get a message to Arnaud in Cannes and have this used instead. It'll have to do for another time. If the message we're expecting—*'La tour de Pise penche de plus en plus'*—should come over the air tonight I daren't risk coming here—only five kilometers as the crow flies, away from the Cuisery field—and start flashing the lamps in the hope that the pilot would see them. If he didn't it would break my heart. So you see, Roger, we must use that old brick patch right on the main road—number 75—and take pot luck that the cops or the Schloks don't come and spoil the whole show."

"What shall we do with the bricks?" asked Roger.

"If the message comes at seven thirty it'll only take us a quarter of an hour to reach the field, so we'll want at least ten men to help clear a reasonable runway as far from the road as possible."

"I can get five men," put in Thomas.

"And I the rest," said Roger.

"I hope they don't belong to any union," I cracked.

"Have no fear!" came Thomas's reassuring reply.

Before six o'clock we had inspected the three other fields, all of which proved equally satisfactory, if on a slightly smaller scale, and I plotted all their positions.

Back at the café, we found End, Paul, Lise, and seven or eight leaders of an equal number of towns belonging to our group. They had all gathered on End's instructions so that matters of mutual interest could be discussed while Paul was still in the country. I shook hands with the bosses of Toulouse, Agen, Montauban, Aix-en-Provence, Mâcon, Lyon, St. Etienne, and Valence. I was staggered by the din of the conversation as we stood around in the public bar of Thomas's tiny café.

With the door closed to keep out the cold of the January night, a cloud of smoke that stung the eyes hung around the low ceiling.

Oblivious, as usual, of the sensation that this "Old Boys" Convention was causing amongst the local citizenry—accustomed to meeting their usual cronies for a quiet noggin and a game of belotte before dinner—the pandemonium was kept up without any restraint.

When the door opened to produce a policeman, they ignored him entirely and continued to discuss their plans at the tops of their voices. Brushing his way past the outlying members of the assembly, with a courteous *"Pardon, Monsieur,"* and an equally polite salute, he made his way toward Thomas, who was leaning against the bar with the cold, disfigured end of a homemade cigarette drooping from his mouth.

Holding out his left hand he shook the policeman's, while propping himself nonchalantly against the marble slab of his sanctum. He looked quizzically at his old friend and pushed the hotel forms across a puddle of Pernod toward him. These men had grown up together, had played on the same football team. They knew every intimate secret of every family in the place over the last hundred years or so.

The deadpan look on Thomas's immobile face was sufficient warning for the other to turn down his offer of a drink and beat a hasty retreat. Why get mixed up in other people's business? Thomas knew what he was doing; he was a good scout.

I watched it all, overheard their short, clipped phrases, and caught the looks that had passed between them.

As the policeman walked out, saluting the "Terrorists" politely and mouthing the one word *Messieurs,* Thomas relit the tattered, stained butt of his cigarette with the long flame of a cheap but effective lighter. The corners of his drooping mouth that blended with the heavy jowls and the bored look of his beady eyes, accustomed to looking at the drab monotony of his life, did not alter perceptibly, but the dullness of the eyes was only affected. Thomas saw everything. Shrewd and alert, he knew what he was doing.

With the suspicion of a twinkle in his eye he spoke to me out of the corner of his mouth: *"C't'un copain, c'ui-là."*

Lucky as it was that the policeman was a friend of Thomas, I decided that if the Lysander did not appear that night I would not remain in Tournus if the others were to stay.

We dined early and then split up into several gay parties to listen to the messages.

Lise, Paul, Roger, and I went to one private house where several bottles of wine and a tray bearing some twenty glasses indicated that the clans were to gather there in force.

We listened to the personal messages, but the Tower of Pisa's increasing lean was not hinted at. Shortly thereafter the listening teams from other houses joined us and the sort of party that I simply abhorred, for reasons already stated, got under way. This sort of thing was all right on the *Maidstone* after a patrol, but all wrong here.

Paul, Lise, and I escaped from it all and went up to the Abbey where Les Petits Chanteurs à la Croix de Bois were due to give a concert under their talented musical director, brilliant showman, and generous fairy godfather, l'Abbé Maillet.

In the cold nave of the dim-lit Abbey we took our places among the overcoated throng and waited.

Presently Father Maillet announced the first song and, turning to his large white surpliced choir, each member of whose happy face looked straight into the eyes of their Master who had trained their voices and fashioned their lives, he hummed one note.

The choir broke into the harmonized chord of their first unaccompanied part song, attacking the notes with the precision of polished artists. Now their rich voices pursued their theme of praise, swirling round the sturdy columns and surging up to the heights of the arched vault with as joyful a promise of Paradise as had surely ever been heard within these walls. Their warm crescendos sent an ecstatic shiver down my spine and, during the soft stream of silvery notes in the pianissimo passages, it almost seemed that the sweet face of Sainte Thérèse tilted a little more in her private chapel to smile her approval at the purity of tone, devoid of any huskiness.

When the song was over it was all I could do to refrain from applauding.

Moving from one song to the next the congregation was treated to the whole varied scale of the choir's prowess, and when it was over Father Maillet floated majestically up the steps of the pulpit to address us all.

"These boys," he said, "who have just returned from a triumphant tour of South America, were each brought to me in their infancy by poor parents who hoped they had voices. You are the judges of what the Great Potter has enabled me to do with them.

"We are not paid for these concerts, but come to each separate town after the insertion of a small notice in the local paper openly asking for hospitality in your homes. This kindness allows us to bring you something that has nothing to do with wars and all the folly of man.

"Our journeys between towns are done in a hired coach and your generosity in the collection will meet that expense, any surplus going to the fund that maintains our Paris establishment so that boys who have voices may continue to bring joy to a troubled world so long as I am given strength to perform this happy and heaven-sent task."

I opened my wallet and withdrew a 500-franc note. On a piece of paper I scribbled the words. *Thank you for the unutterable joy you have brought to a British officer.* Pinning the two together I slid them into the passing box, knowing full well that a man like Father Maillet had no time for politics and, at the same time, that my action was that of an incorrigible sentimentalist.

The next night we listened for our B.B.C message in the same house as before, but again it failed to pass.

Toward 9:30 I beckoned Roger over and said I wanted to see the Cuisery field at night and study the traffic on road 75. Roger was game and we excused ourselves, returning to Thomas's café for the bicycles.

It was a cold night and the moon made visibility excellent, the brick piles looking very sinister in this light. As we skirted the far end of the field, we came upon two men cycling in the opposite direction without lights. When they had passed I said: "Is this a local custom?"

"No, it certainly isn't," replied Roger.

On reaching the main road entrance to the field by the corner of the wood we heard a man calling out the name of Albert. Slowing down, we again heard the voice, calling toward us more urgently:

"Hey, Albert! Where the hell have you been?"

"Neither of us is Albert," I said. "What's the trouble?"

"Oh, nothing much," said the youth who was now taking shape. "One of the wheels of my trailer has a puncture and I hoped one of you was my friend Albert, because he's around here somewhere and he knows how to fix the tire. When we were riding without lights just now we thought you must be the police. I'm relieved to see that you aren't, because we're running a black market in potatoes."

"Well, I'm sorry we can't oblige, but if Albert's within earshot of this conversation he shouldn't be long," I said, and with that we moved off somewhat perplexed, for we had seen no trailer anywhere.

About one hundred yards down the road we came across a man pretending to repair his upturned bicycle on the grass verge. I gave him a friendly greeting as we passed, but he made no reply. If this was Albert, he was more cautious than his friend.

As we looked across the brick-ridden field from behind the hedge our attention was attracted by a distant hullaballoo of voices. Peering over the hedge we saw lights flashing about all over the place. Several men who began to take shape were throwing bricks around and talking at the tops of their voices as though they were the advance party of a traveling circus clearing a space for the big tent. Roger and I did not have to take great pains to keep out of sight of this crazy gang, since they were obviously deaf and blind to anything outside the sphere of their prodigious activities.

"What do you suppose they're doing? Taking the bricks away or changing their position?" I asked.

"Haven't the foggiest notion," Roger replied.

We stood gaping at the scene for half an hour or so, when suddenly we heard the distinct sounds of an approaching bomber. There should have been nothing very surprising about this, for the Germans flew at night over the countries they occupied; but the shouting on the ground was increased and all the lamps were extinguished.

So that was it, I thought; it had happened at last. Another organization—goodness knew which—was using my field for precisely the same purpose. It was only a happy coincidence that the Lysander had not been announced for the very same night. What a lark that would have been!

The approaching drone of the bomber now clinched the matter. It was a Hudson, without any shadow of doubt. This was the third time I had heard their motors in the night sky of France, and the famous silhouette was as unmistakable as the Nelson monument.

"Who the devil are these acrobats?" I asked.

"Search me," said Roger.

"Seems a little odd that two organizations should exist in a one-eyed hole like Tournus, without anyone knowing about it," I said suspiciously. "I've still got to see one of these operations come off and I'll be damned if this one has a hope in hell with all these bricks lying around. . . . A Lysander might have been possible, but a bomber . . ."

The brick-heaving efforts were now redoubled. I had reckoned on being able to clear a short Lysander path in three hours, but these optimists had to clear 1,600 meters and had only been at it for just over half an hour.

The bomber circled the field patiently, the pilot could have no notion of what was waiting for him but, like all these pilots, he would stay as long as the petrol held out.

Half an hour passed in this manner. I drew out my flask and shared a pull with Roger. I knew I was about to witness something that few eyes in the world would ever see

The drama about to be enacted was already giving me the creeps. This operation was pure murder. From the road I had seen that the field was barely long enough and the trees of the wood that ran along one side, plus those beyond the telegraph poles following the road, would hamper a take-off still further.

For forty full minutes the hectic heaving of bricks continued unabated. Occasionally a howl of anguish pierced the deafening roar from the Hudson's low circling, as a brick went astray, striking a hapless worker in its dangerous flight.

"Pas sur mes pieds, nom de Dieu!" "Attention, bon sang!" and short, heartfelt cries of *"Merde!"* added to the cacophony of this crazy night.

And now, at a signal, the line of torches was lit up and the circling Hudson came down in a long sweep. Lower and lower it came, its touching-down point being not two hundred yards from where we stood watching.

A high thicket close to the first lamp brought a burst from the engines so as to clear the obstacle and made the plane sail past and over the first lamp. Its wheels were now aimed with professional skill at a spot just on the right of the second lampholder—a hundred and fifty yards beyond the first.

There was a pregnant swishing of air as the heavy plane passed in front of them and I waited for its first impact with mother earth, feeling that this was going to be a very sticky moment. By now the piles of bricks must have been visible to the pilot, but the state of the surface was, for a few seconds yet, an unknown quantity.

As the wheels touched down there was a tremendous splash, and the man holding the second torch simply vanished in a wave of mud. Squirting up huge waves on either side, like a destroyer, the pilot squelched his way through to drier ground, miraculously keeping his aircraft level. There was a banging and clattering as the machine ran up to the end of the strip and pulled up between the sixth and seventh lamps. It taxied on and turned on one motor through the eighth and ninth lamps to return to lamp A for the take-off into the wind.

The reception committee had forgotten all about this return route, parallel to the flare-path, and none of the bricks had been removed from there. However, a little thing like this was nothing to such a pilot, and Roger and I were treated to the unusual sight of a bomber slaloming nimbly between the piles until it was snorting round on one engine within a few yards of us, as it turned round into the original flare-path by the first lamp. When it came to a halt it began to sink into the worst of the quagmire.

The door of the plane was opened from the inside and ten men stepped out. Ten others, waiting to return to the U.K. by this shuttle service, clambered in. The door closed behind them; the whole thing had been done in less than two minutes.

The pilot now opened the throttles to full bore and gently released the brakes; but nothing happened. They were stuck in the bog. A second attempt met with no better results. The door was then reopened and the ten passengers climbed out, placing themselves around one of the wheels and the left wing, while the newly arrived ten disposed themselves similarly on the other side.

When the pilot accelerated they all pushed with a will, but to no avail. The pilot closed the throttles and switched off his engines. A deathly silence spread itself where so much noise had existed.

Normally the whole affair should have been over in a matter of minutes, but now the ever-increasing gallery was treated to something quite out of the usual.

The cockpit cabin door swung open and the pilot stepped out onto the top rung of his ladder to address the reception committee in these terms, with a strong English accent flavoring each carefully pronounced and hard-sought word: *"QUI-EST-LE-CHEF-DE-CETTE-BANDE-DE-SAUVAGES?"*

A young Frenchman sailed happily up to the pilot and said that he was in charge.

The pilot looked down at him and said, "Well, you've got nothing to be proud about. Not only have you landed me in the back yard of a brick factory, but in the center of a bog into the bargain."

"We knew that the R.A.F. could land anywhere, Monsieur," said this Gallic flatterer, with some truth.

"Land maybe," said the pilot, "but I'll be damned if I know how we shall ever take off. Besides, your flare-path stinks. Just have a look at those trees. They're not fifteen hundred meters away. I'll never clear them with this load. You get your chaps to fix me a new one running diagonally across the field and then, if the gods are willing, I might just manage to clear that corner over there."

The nine torch-bearers and twenty passengers all set to work on this new task, and the sounds of crashing bricks went on for fully an hour. My eyes kept wandering toward the road. At any moment I expected to see the headlights and hear the throaty exhausts of official Citroens belonging to the police or the arrival of a convoy of German troop carriers bearing down upon the scene.

If this were to happen I would definitely go out and yell for the British crew to come along with me. Standing around supervising the new line of the flare-path—as most of them now were—they were sitting birds if anything went wrong.

While working out several alternative plans, I saw the pilot and two others returning to the aircraft. Presently the rest of the gang followed—the lamp-holders included. Thirty-odd men now stood beside the machine receiving their orders. Dividing themselves into two lots, they arrayed themselves for the great push. It looked as though the co-pilot and navigator had also joined them, for only one person entered by the cockpit door.

Just as the second motor burst into life, both were suddenly left to idle and the tiny door opened once more, showing the pilot leaning out and pointing toward the road.

All eyes flew in that direction, and one man separated himself from the ground party and began running that way as fast as he could. Peering hard into the distance, I beheld a farmhand leading two horses along at a gentle pace

When the runner reached them they began to change direction, coming across the field toward the aircraft with the farmhand and Resistance man in the lead. Coming up close, one of the horses neighed at the sight of the mighty bird. They were turned round and placed one behind the other, a length of chain being attached to a strong upright beside one of the wheels. The yokel got his team to take the strain while waiting, with his whip at the ready, for the concerted effort of men, engines, and his decisive beasts.

Both motors now began to bite the air and the pushers to take their grips. There was no need for the whip, as the roar of the engines was sufficient to frighten the horses into trying to break away from their ghastly din. But the chain held and the great plane slowly moved forward. The strange caravan advanced in this manner until the wheels were on dry ground, then the brakes were applied and the horses released from the most unusual rescue work they had ever performed. With a wave to the pilot, the farmhand led them off to their more gentle duties.

The pilot now turned his machine and ran it over to the far corner of the field, turning once again for the take-off that would bring it across the wide arc of our field of vision.

The flare-path men took up their new positions, their bicycle lamps all pointing toward the aircraft. The ten departing passengers got in, and the door closed finally behind them.

Now the Hudson's engines were opened up to within a notch of their full power and, with flames shooting from her exhaust pipes, she lay there, quivering and straining to be off for the grand finale. I knew that all the passengers would be huddled up at the front of the cabin to get the weight forward. This was going to be their bad moment of blacked-out uncertainty.

Now the brakes were released and all the pent-up energy got under way. From where we were standing it looked impossible that a lane existed between those piles of bricks, yet the pilot managed to avoid any obstacles on this run of runs. Both inside and outside the plane, all must have held their breath to make the aircraft lighter.

At the halfway mark I put his speed at eighty miles an hour and I realized that he simply must get off the ground soon or it would be curtains for them all; there was not enough space before those trees to say Hallelujah! But still the nose was down. Only at the three-quarter mark did the plane bounce up to become airborne. A gasp of relief issued from every throat behind the hedge.

All leaned forward peering toward the trees in order to catch sight of the black silhouette of the wings rising above the topmost branches. Slowly one wing came into sight against the lighter background of the sky, but the rest of the plane did not rise until the very last moment. The right wing appeared to graze the top and there was an ominous sound of a snapping branch mixed up with the roar of the engines.

I held my breath and then, hearing the steady drone of the twin engines receding beyond the wood, I fumbled weakly for my hip flask. Drawing it out I raised it in the direction of the departing Hudson. In my silent toast to the unknown pilot I said, half to him, half to myself: "To a Victoria Cross: for succeeding in accomplishing the impossible!"

I was up early the next day and took Paul along to the field to inspect the marks of the tires in the mud and look for evidence of what had sounded like a broken branch.

The wheels had sunk eighteen inches into the bog and the ground was ploughed up in every direction as though by a tank. I ran my hand along the tire marks with a certain nostalgia, for it was five months since I had left England and this was the nearest I had got to one of its aircraft.

As for Paul, he wandered about in open amazement, saying, "How they ever got out of this defeats me!"

Together we walked over to the corner of the field, but it was not a branch that we found, but thirty inches off the end of the Hudson's wing.

"My God!" muttered Paul.

"Yes," I agreed, "you can say that again." I did not discover the rest of the story until some time later.

On our way back across the field we met two men. Paul, still bubbling with admiration, could not refrain from saying to the first of them: "Just have a look at those tracks in the mud. Those R.A.F. boys are unbeatable!"

"I heartily agree," said the man, in a stage whisper. "But don't say it so loud. This chap behind me is the Head of the Gestapo from Lyon!"

CHAPTER XIV

LISE AND I returned to Cannes for the last time. Messages exchanged with London showed that the Tournus affair had been handled by one of De Gaulle's agents, and the fact that the same field was used as that accepted for the Lysander was not elucidated. De Gaulle's rival show, run from Duke Street and known as "Our friends across the road," was apparently not working in close co-operation with S.O.E., although the R.A.F. served them both.

I was now urgently required to try for a fifth time to get a Lysander to land on another disused airfield passed by the R.A F Photographic Reconnaissance Unit, at Basillac, ten kilometers from Périgueux, during the same existing moon period —subject to its not being in use.

This meant a journey of over eight hundred kilometers, changing trains at Marseille and again at Toulouse. It would mean staying in a hotel at Périgueux and making a reconnaissance of the ground, getting there by any available means of transport.

Lise and I had hardly time to pack a bag before we were off once more. Again we made advance code arrangements with Arnaud for a telephone call that would be necessary to indicate whether the field was free or otherwise.

At Marseille we met End who passed Lise a small portable radio receiving set essential for picking up the B.B.C. message for this mission. *"Les femmes sont parfois volages,"* for we had no contacts in Périgueux, it being outside our already large area.

It was a long and tiring journey. Paul and Jacques Latour would only be arriving one day later, owing to urgent business in Lyon, and our rendezvous in the town could only be a chance meeting in the largest café in the main square of this place with its 37,000 inhabitants. No time could be stipulated for this vague encounter, as we did not know by what train they would be coming, nor could they be certain that Lise and I would be back from our reconnaissance of the airfield. As for hotel accommodation, no one knew if there would be any available as the town, like Arles, was full of Germans.

The whole thing was a pure gamble, our only hope of success lying in our combined desire to meet and succeed in our purpose.

Dead tired, we traipsed our bags from the station toward the center of the town and walked confidently up to the reception desk of the largest hotel in the place—the Domino.

Yes, the two last rooms in the attic were still free if we would consider such modest quarters. More than delighted to find anything, we settled for these rooms. I explained that we would be staying for two or three nights while waiting for friends who were shortly due back in town and in whose house we had been invited to stay.

After cleaning up from our journey, we went to the dining room to see if the town's reputation for truffles and foie gras was being maintained despite the war.

We were happy to be together. This shared meal was one of the better moments, made still better through the sharing of so many more moments of cold, fear, frustration, and the knowledge that we were outlaws. The three months in which Lise had been my courier had given me every opportunity of studying her character and assessing her worth. More than ever, I knew I could count on her in any circumstances. Although she had been an accepted and fully-fledged member of the team for quite a time, I was always conscious of my good fortune. Besides, she was a most attractive girl. She may have been thirty, as she said, but nobody—man or woman—of our considerable Resistance entourage, between the ages of twenty-one and sixty, would have put her at a day over twenty-three. Not that age has anything to do with charm; it was simply that she represented eternal youth.

Lise had a flair for clothes and dressed herself with tasteful simplicity. Since she had settled down and come to know everyone, she had found the new life, with its swiftly alternating spells of solitude and gregariousness, to her liking. The change from the regular routine of being a mother, occupying her entire day with the endless needs of three small children, deep in the countryside of Somerset, seemed to suit her well and showed her to be adaptable. Married at nineteen, she had had little experience of living among other people of her own age, or indeed, of knowing very much about her fellow creatures. Delicate and timid as a child, her own accounts of her early youth dwelt mostly on the fawnlike solitary existence she had led in the wooded country of Saint-Sens.

Having accompanied me through the stress of so many thwarting disappointments in the scale of underground activities, and seen the sparks fly to the accompaniment of some of my shocking language, I supposed she could not think very much of me. As for my own feelings toward my enigmatic courier, my singleness of purpose in regard to the war was such that I could only betray them by the merest hint.

After lunch we hired two single-seater vélo-taxis and were transported to the village of Basillac. Along the latter part of our run through this pleasant corner of the Dordogne, we had seen the airport below us on the left. A hangar and some office buildings beneath a watchtower with a well-kept drive inside the ground suggested that if there were no life in the place the last tenants could not have left so long ago The sudden appearance of two individuals emerging from the buildings warned us that this hope had been in vain and that the place was occupied, even if only by a small holding force. From the road the men seemed to be wearing blue French Air Force uniforms.

"A curse upon them!" I muttered. "I wonder how many they are in there and whose side they're on. This is the trouble of working in an unknown place without local contacts."

"Not that the local contacts are always so hot when we have them," said Lise.

Having paid the taxi-cyclists, we ambled gently down through the village following the lane that ran round three-quarters of the airport's perimeter. Sauntering along, arm-in-arm like lovers on a country walk, we carefully studied every foot of the ground, its surface, its three approaches (one on either side of the buildings, and a third that led over a bridge across a river and back to Périgueux by a parallel route).

The field was small—perhaps a thousand yards in length and not more than four hundred in width—but adequate. Yet the best place in which to wait for the aircraft, out of sight below the far bank, was merely the distance of the width from the buildings.

Apart from two or three airmen in the vicinity of these buildings there was no local aircraft activity whatsoever. If it were not for these men the place would have been ideal. It was now Friday and I hoped that the message would come through on Saturday so that the business could be effected that night as late as possible when the personnel would be asleep after an evening of belotte and red wine. This was the best I could hope for, always supposing I decided to risk it.

Although a speedy landing and take-off could be guaranteed, the danger still existed for those who were left behind. Then there was a passenger to be landed into the bargain, if not two. Getting them away was always a problem. Lise and Jacques could vanish over the bridge and probably get away with it, but not if they were handicapped by two stiff newcomers, plus their luggage.

The tasks for the following day consisted of finding a plug in which to insert the radio lead into the bedroom-lamp socket, getting permission to use the radio, finding Paul and Jacques, and finally listening in to the B.B.C. messages.

The first part of the program was the most complicated, since the purchase of radio parts was strictly forbidden by a recent law. The presence of the occupying troops was sufficient to see that this regulation was adhered to. However, after trying several shops in search of the requisite part, Lise soon shamed the shopkeeper who had it into letting her buy it. I fixed it to the wire and, having obtained the necessary permission to use the set, we tried it out. All was in order.

At the apéritif hour and again after lunch we combed the cafés in the main square in search of our two friends. On returning to the hotel with the long faces of disappointment, we found Jacques Latour walking down the steps of the hotel just as we were about to enter it. Leading us gaily to his chief, the four of us held a council of war.

Jacques informed us that he had already cycled over to have a look at the field and had gone so far as to enter the grounds leading up to the watchtower. He had then sounded out one of the men, but had not received very reassuring comments as to their loyalties. I suggested that this forthright move was a mistake, submitting that if the conversation was discussed among the Basillac men, they would now be on the alert. I refrained from telling my friend that he ought never to have done such a foolhardy thing, for Jacques was one of the best men of the entire group, his courage and resource being of the first order.

Somehow this fresh complication did not seem so important under the spell of Paul's distinguished canonical aura. His calm was contagious to me, and his presence brought a feeling of normality to the most frightening exploits.

Lise had prepared a picnic in case the message came over that night, and this had been packed away in my rucksack. Her own small bag was likewise packed and ready for a swift getaway. Jacques would take care of her case and I would carry my pack which, as usual, was crammed with reports for London.

It was agreed that we all should dine in the nearby Fénélon Hôtel, where Paul was staying, and that I would run across and either advise them that they could not stay, or join them, as the case might be.

In my room I now plugged in the set and tuned in to London. The reception was appalling and sounded as though I were getting three stations at once. Time was running out; only two minutes to go and I was very conscious of the flimsy walls around my tiny room and the noise that must be reverberating through the entire attic. My nerves were not improved by the memory of the man who had been yanked off by the police at 6 A.M. that day. For a moment, on waking up, I had thought they were knocking at my door. The illegal business of listening to London in this hotel was not my idea of fun.

Toning down the volume to a mere whisper, I walked across to the door and opened it casually. There was nobody there; all were dining. Returning to the set I suddenly remembered an alternative wave length on another band. Using both hands I switched rapidly across to the new position.

Just in time. The first sounds that reached my ears were: "I repeat: '*Les femmes sont parfois volages. . . .*' "

"God! What luck!" I gasped, switching off the set.

Within a matter of seconds I was on my way downstairs, my rucksack over one shoulder and the wireless set tucked under my arm and snugly encased in its cardboard box

Asking for my bill at the desk, I explained that my friends had just arrived and that I was quite prepared to pay for the two rooms, including the charge for the night we would not be using them. I said that someone would be along to collect a case that was still upstairs, in a few moments.

There were no awkward questions, and two minutes later I was sitting beside my friends in the Fénélon restaurant, quietly telling them that our meal must be canceled

Having disposed of Lise's bag and settled the question of Paul's room at the Fénélon—Jacques being installed elsewhere in a modest café—we were on the road to Basillac by 8 P.M., traversing the wooded countryside bathed in the light of a gigantic full moon. Whatever fate held in store for the four of us, we were not likely to forget the exquisite beauty of the ten-kilometers' walk through that fairyland. Pale and black shafts of light stabbed downwards through the trees, lighting up the white patches of ground mist like soft wads of cotton wool, as they formed here and there with the increasing cold of the bitter night.

By 9:45 we had reached the turn in the road, down to the left, leading to one of the airport's accesses. Looking at our field below us we saw that it, too, was covered with mist to a depth that could not be accurately gauged from our level.

I asked Paul and Jacques to follow Lise and me at a distance of twenty yards and then went ahead slowly along the road that skirted the field beneath the cover of some trees.

Walking silently side by side, we reached the cutting that was to hide the party both from the road and anyone in the watchtower. On looking back we perceived that our friends were nowhere in sight. They had succeeded in vanishing during the short approach walk.

"Incredible how they manage to talk even with zero hour approaching!" I said, annoyed that my friends could not keep closed up. "I bet we shall see them walking calmly straight across the airport toward us through the mist."

With our heads just above the embankment, we could see that the entire field was covered to the height of four feet. If it remained like this it was going to be an eerie experience for any pilot to land and feel his way down to earth.

Presently two heads came in sight bobbing up and down on two sets of shoulders that seemed to be floating toward us on top of the mist, as though walking through a gigantic foam bath. I got up and bobbed my way toward my companions. Each party eyed the other with considerable distrust until we had recognized one another. My friends admitted that my truncated advance had scared them out of their wits.

"Serves you right for dithering about instead of keeping close behind us," I said.

Once back behind the shelter of the bank the mist, as if by a miracle, began to scatter, leaving clear patches that grew imperceptibly over the field. This phenomenon was all the more astounding as there was simply no wind whatsoever.

I spaced out the three lamp positions near the edge of the field farthest away from the buildings. The two main lamps were one hundred and fifty yards apart, allowing an unhindered flat approach devoid of trees; the third lamp being placed at right angles to the second and only fifty yards away from it. The Lysander could pull up in this short space, turn to the right, and return to the guiding lamp I held before turning once more for his take-off through the two others.

Placing white handkerchiefs on sticks at the chosen spots, so that they could easily be found later on, I carefully explained the procedure that Lise and Jacques must perform. We then returned to the bank and had our picnic.

It was 10:30 and complete silence reigned over the buildings below the watchtower. Perhaps the men were already asleep; perhaps they did not spend the night there, after all. Maybe they were in Périgueux at the cinema. There was no knowing.

We ate our picnic as though this were a nightly performance that we enjoyed, and while it went on I gave Lise my ration book so that she could have the use of two during my absence. The hands of my luminous watch moved slowly on toward the next hour.

"I hope to goodness they don't come before midnight," I said. But I had hardly got out the words before the distant drone of a single-engined aircraft made us all sit up with a start.

"Blast the thing!" I said. "I spoke too soon."

Lise hurriedly wrapped up the remains of the picnic and stowed it in the rucksack, doing up the strap.

We went to our respective positions and Paul accompanied me to my place.

From half a mile away the Lysander came straight at us over the airport at perhaps eight hundred feet. I had ample time to flash him the *Q* sign several times; each time, saying to myself, as I had been taught, "Here comes the Queen."

But there was no recognition Morse signal from the pilot—the agreed letter being *R*.

With a roar that echoed back from the hill above the village it shot over our heads and vanished in a straight line into the night.

Leaving Paul for a minute, I went across to Lise and said: "I simply don't understand it. He must have seen the signal and I'm sure he'll be back soon. Take off that white mac. It's visible for miles. Sit on it and lie low, in case anyone comes. If you sit quite still you won't be seen."

"All right, Michel," she said, taking off her mackintosh.

I moved over to Jacques and told him to stand by for the almost certain return of the aircraft.

"Keep an eye on those buildings, Jacques, I have a feeling we're in for an unwelcome interruption from that quarter. If you see me wave my torch from side to side, go and grab Lise and make yourselves scarce over the bridge and back to the town that way."

"Right!" said Jacques.

I returned to my own position. Several wisps of mist still hung over the field. I looked at Paul and said: "Queer, isn't it?"

"I confess I don't understand it either," he said. "It's not as though he were circling round; he seems to have gone off due south for some unaccountable reason."

"Look out, Paul!" I whispered, tugging my friend by the arm. "There's someone coming! Lie flat on the ground!"

We now saw that two men were coming straight toward us from the direction of the watchtower. Protected to some extent by the patches of mist, we lay there waiting, our hearts beating against our ribs. Looking round, I saw with satisfaction that Lise and Jacques were lying as still as felled trees.

The two men were talking in what seemed a very natural manner, and I thought that if they had been coming in our direction with any ulterior motive they would not have been conversing in this way.

Closer and closer they came. I feared that the thumping of my heart must surely give our position away as clearly as the beating of a drum. Their line now led them ten yards away from us, and I silently prayed that the Lysander would not choose this particular moment to return. Trying to project my hearing into the distance through their conversation, I missed what they were saying.

And now they were passing, their footsteps barely perceptible on the spongy turf. "Get a move on!" I urged within myself.

Why the dickens did this crate have to come so soon? It was only 11:10 and the Chanoines aircraft had arrived almost four hours later.

When the sounds of the two men's footsteps had dwindled to nothing along the road, we rose to our feet. I went over to have a word with Lise. As I came up to her she said: "I thought they were going to walk slap into you. I can't think how they missed you."

"The plane ought to be back at any moment," I said hurriedly. "If there's any danger from those buildings I shall wave my torch sideways and Jacques will come over to you and you're both to beat it over the bridge. Paul and I will make a separate retreat; better to be in two groups."

"All right, Michel. But I can't see any lights coming from those buildings."

"Nor can I. Let's hope there's no one there."

"Listen!" said Lise, whose ears were as sharp as a Zulu's, "I can hear the plane coming back."

"You're right! Well, here goes . . ." I put my hand lightly on her shoulder, smiled, and then ran back toward Paul.

Holding my flashlamp at the ready, we both peered into the sky toward the increasing sound that came from the south.

Over the top of the hill roared the aircraft. My thumb was just going to press the first "dash" of my *Q* sign when, from three hundred yards away on the line of the Lysander's approach, a large aldis lamp began to flash an urgent message with its blazing light toward the tower.

The spot from which this endless warning emanated was one that had slipped my attention during my daylight visit with Lise. That someone had picked up the signal in the tower was instantly clear, for the buildings sprang into life with a sudden blaze of light.

As soon as these lights came on, a voice rang out that was audible above the roar of the low-flying plane, and it was shouting: "Put out those lights, you imbeciles! Wait for the plane to land and we'll grab them all."

This was quite enough for me. Waving my torch from side to side I gave the signal to abandon the field. Jacques did not require a second bidding and, within a matter of seconds, he and Lise were lost in the trees that ran along their prearranged escape route. To make sure that Lise got away, I had instinctively moved a few yards in her direction; but there was no need for anxiety on that score. As I watched the two of them run off, I heard Paul coming up behind me and we, in our turn, began to run across the field through the remaining patches of mist toward our chosen line of retreat.

Seeing Paul's arms moving like pistons, I said: "Where's the sack?"

A look of dismay crossed my companion's serene face and, without a word, he stopped running and turned to fetch what he had forgotten through sheer absentmindedness.

"No!" I ordered. "Keep going as you were . . . I'll catch up with you."

I dashed back to where the rucksack lay with all its incriminating papers, snatched it up and, within half a minute, was back, urging my companion to abandon his cardinal's gait and run for his life.

Paul seemed mesmerized by the Lysander's odd behavior and kept following it with his eyes instead of looking for possible pursuers whom I expected to see pouring out from below the tower. However, the building remained in darkened silence while its inmates were, in all likelihood, also watching the nocturnal antics of an inquisitive and enraged pilot who, having come so far, failed to understand why the antlike forms below him were running away instead of lighting up his landing strip.

The highly maneuverable plane was being put through its paces in a style that made me positive that its pilot must be the tall, dark young Irishman who had instructed me in the Lysander course held in Bedfordshire. (Later events were to confirm this assumption.)

Aiming at Paul and me as though we were targets to be obliterated, he dived down onto our heads with a plaintive whine coming from the wind in his struts. Then, soaring on at a height of six feet, he suddenly rose almost vertically into the sky, turned, and grazed the watchtower on his next sweep round. On and on he went, up and down the field in its length and breadth, intimately nosing out each nook and cranny of this field that was made to measure. I expected him to land at any moment, without any guiding lights, and come up behind us to bawl out the question that his aerobatics already asked so plainly: "What in hell is the matter with you clots?"

If only I could tell him! But all these men were slightly "round the bend" or else they would not volunteer for this type of night work. The pilot ought to have known that if the lamps were not lighted, it spelled danger on the ground.

The crazy nightmare could not have lasted three minutes in all before I had pushed Paul through a thick hedge and away from the scene of yet another ghastly rout and heartbreaking disappointment.

As we followed the hedgerows parallel to the road back to Périgueux and were in comparative safety, the Lysander kept up its mad whirl like an angry wasp until, disgusted, it finally turned for home, its sounds fading away into the distance.

I kept Paul relentlessly on the move. Now that there was no fear of being machine-gunned from the air, the defenders would quickly realize that a German inquiry was inevitable and that lame excuses on their part would not go down as well as live captives.

Perspiring freely because of all the clothes we wore to keep out the cold, and puffing away from these exertions, we only slowed up—still under cover—after five kilometers.

"I wonder how Lise and Jacques got on," I said.

"They'll be all right," reassured Paul. "Jacques is as smart as a barrel of monkeys. Anyhow, they had a start on us owing to your rucksack. I'm so sorry about that."

"Don't give it a thought, *mon cher,*" I said.

We walked on in silence, our thoughts running parallel and needing no expression. As we came to the last bend leading down a gentle incline to Périgueux, I called a halt.

"We musn't go into that Boche-ridden town at this time of night, Paul. If the buzz has got round, they'll have every street blocked against us. Better sleep here and return at first light."

"I agree," said Paul.

We entered a vast thicket, well hidden from the road and, pressing down some brambles with our feet, we sat down and opened the rucksack. There was still plenty to eat, though neither of us was hungry.

"The only way to get any sleep in this cold is to drown yourself in Armagnac," I said, handing over the bottle.

Paul took a modest pull and handed it back

"That's no good!" I said. "Let it slide down until it starts a fire—like this!" I gave a full-scale demonstration and passed back the bottle.

Paul took another little sip and smiled at me. We put back the cork and lay down, huddled up together for warmth.

It was ten degrees below—centigrade—and I, who was well accustomed to these frosty outings, was dressed for the part. Below my shirt I wore two vests and a complete set of flannel pajamas. Over this were two sweaters, a sports jacket, and a "Canadienne."

Worn out through nervous exhaustion more than anything else, I fell asleep almost immediately.

On waking up some four hours later, I saw that dawn was breaking. All around me the ground was white with frost. Paul was no longer beside me and I must have wakened because of the cold that had seeped in where Paul had kept me warm. I pushed myself up on one elbow so that my eyes were on a level with the top of the thicket

With his arms behind his back, Paul was walking slowly round a small clearing Catching sight of me, he came over and explained that he had risen two hours before in order to get his circulation going.

"You didn't drink enough, old dear," I said.

We gathered up our belongings, smoothed our hair into reasonable shape, and made off for the town.

By 7·30 we had begun to do the rounds of all the main cafés, looking for our friends Everywhere we took a cup of poisonous synthetic coffee to get ourselves warm and by 9 A.M. we were still at it—tired and rather silent.

A sixth sense told me that Lise would presently appear. It never entered my head that she might have been caught. She simply must appear, for she had my ration book. It was as simple as that.

Having tried the smaller cafés, we now returned to the main square and were sitting in the glass-enclosed veranda of the Domino Hôtel with an uninterrupted view of the whole square, sipping our umpteenth cup of coffee, when Lise and Jacques came into view.

At the sight of Lise's gay walk, her fresh look and polished shoes, all our fatigue vanished in a flash. Jacques was there beside her. We waved at each other through the window and were soon united in a smiling glow of warmth and affection around the same table.

Another black page was suddenly wiped out and life began again.

Now we must get out of this town, but it was Sunday and the express only left in the afternoon.

Like most small towns in wartime France, restaurants worked on a rota on certain days, like chemists'. This meant that those who were not lunching in private houses were sure to meet one another.

Thus the Montaigne restaurant unwittingly served, that day, at neighboring tables, both friend and foe; for beside the innocent-looking party of saboteurs sat four members of the Gestapo, one of whom was in uniform.

The waiter, only conscious that he was serving a party of French folk, said to us, winking, his back to the enemy: "I have a wine for you that is not for everyone."

We had a most enjoyable lunch Afterwards Paul, who came from Alsace, told us what he had overheard in German from the next table. It appeared that cordons were out surrounding the area within a radius of five kilometers of the airport and that before nightfall they were certain to discover the terrorists, either alive or frozen to death.

CHAPTER XV

THE INCREASING speed of the Toulouse express was not fast enough for Lise and me after our nerve-racking wait on the icy platform in Périgueux station. There had been too many Germans about, too many well-fed people who did not look French, and our wearing experiences of the previous packed hours gave us a feeling that the sands were running out. Our incredible luck could not last, like this, forever.

In the course of the afternoon Lise had related the gist of her own return from the airport. They had been chased by an Alsatian dog and she had automatically taken to the river instead of crossing the bridge; Jacques had vainly tried to call the dog in his direction.

Wading through the water had not made the eight-kilometers' return, by that route, any more comfortable although it had put the dog off their scent. They had gone straight back into the town, since, wet as they were, the only alternative was freezing to death. They had made good time, running some part of the way to keep warm, and Jacques had succeeded in waking up the café proprietor before 1:30 A.M.

We broke our journey in Toulouse. Contacting Eugène, I discussed our plight with him. Eugène's position at the time was fairly stable and he quickly and gladly found quarters for us in one of his many safe houses.

I was struck by the efficiency of my young colleague—not more than twenty-two years of age. It was amazing to see this slim scholarly, sensitive, and artistic youth on his own home ground. His quiet assurance and the way both men and women twice his age accepted his calm orders left a profound impression on me. Having considered my young friend almost as my protégé, I observed the development and growth of his stature with the pleasure of an affectionate elder brother. In the normal hierarchy of a regiment, Eugène—Captain Maurice Pertschuk—would probably have been a colonel by now—so large was his command and so great the respect in which he was held.

I suspected that the situation in Cannes could not very well have improved since last I was there. Fearing the contrary, Lise and I remained until Gisèle's return from another of her endless trips. It was well that we did, not that Toulouse was exactly the saboteurs' paradise. The Marseille train that had pulled in during the morning before our evening arrival from Périgueux had been met by the Gestapo and all the passengers herded into ambulances, Black Marias, and other transport, to be taken to Headquarters for questioning. Everyone had had to prove his identity and give reasons for his journey. These had then been checked and many had failed to return from this trap. If they ever got out they would be lucky if it was only to go to Germany as a member of a forced-labor gang. In the course of 1943, a member of S.O.E. was to end his underground activities in this very manner and he was lucky to survive to tell the tale.

Gisèle's arrival did not bring reassuring news. Colonel Vautrin, having seen the writing on the wall, had slipped across the Spanish frontier. His Number Two, the Major of the Deuxième Bureau, had likewise made his getaway, paying a fabulous sum to do the thing in style, being met by a car. (One million francs was the sum quoted.) The days of paying a guide a mere twelve thousand francs were long past, for the whole Franco-Spanish frontier was now guarded by German troops from a mountain division and night crossings were difficult and hazardous in the extreme.

My flat had been raided and only Catherine's place overlooking the port remained intact. Arnaud was still active, but strongly counseled a change of scenery, a thing with which I was inclined to agree.

The commando instructor in Antibes had been captured, Gervais was carrying on in Marseille and the rest of the birds had wisely flown.

Antoine still held on grimly at his villa and had received further inquiries from police inspectors, now no longer under Vautrin's control, as to my whereabouts. Gisèle intimated that his life was about as attractive as that of somebody sitting on a barrel of gunpowder and wondering when the sizzling fuse would put an end to it all. As for Suzanne, she was apparently keeping her head and still slapping elderly women's faces into shape in the beauty parlor with her secret lotions.

Cannes was thus clearly no place to return to for a rest cure. There were, nevertheless, things to be settled, people to be paid, and clothes to be rescued before the final break. It had also to be decided where to instal the new headquarters.

Paul and Jacques had remained behind in Périgueux with some friends of theirs to tie up certain contacts which they felt were worth the risk and they only joined me two days later to discuss the future.

No sooner had they arrived than their own local branch H.Q. was raided, and although the majority of the trapped men managed to escape, two men were caught.

Paul was very upset at this first loss, a loss that I had expected to happen some months ago, owing to the outsize gatherings they held without any security measures. Further arrests were reported from the Marseille branch and, in this state of mounting alarm, an attempt was made to set up the main control post in Montauban. This lasted for two days, before another raid resulted in the capture of Captain Ruffiol—a great loss.

It was now clear that a complete break was imperative if the show was to survive at all, and Paul and End proposed that they should move as far north as the Haute Savoie. It appeared that a quiet village, nine kilometers away from Annecy and only forty-three from Geneva, called St. Jorioz, was the answer to their prayers.

"I'll join you there with Lise and Arnaud on condition that Arnaud's transmitting houses and living quarters are at least ten kilometers from yours," I said, "and that Lise and I are housed in rooms at least five kilometers from your H.Q. There must be no more of this living on top of each other, or else we shall all be surrounded and grabbed together."

"Agreed," said End. "We already have our feelers out in that part of the world. There's an excellent group of patriots in Faverges—sixteen kilometers from St. Jorioz—and Arnaud can be housed there. As for you and Lise, the Hotel de la Poste will be left entirely at your disposal and we shall rent a house nearby."

"That sounds a fair arrangement," I said, "but while we're on the subject, I must insist that no one ever calls at the hotel for us, and that we meet elsewhere. If the hotel bar is used by your chaps, it'll just be Tournus, Toulouse, or Montauban all over again."

"You're quite right!" said Paul with feeling.

The next thing was to get the all-important Arnaud and his equally indispensable radio sets away from Cannes to a less troubled zone where he could have a comparative rest until he took up his duties in one or other of the promised houses in

Faverges which I had decided to check personally. Every detail must be worked out before he arrived. There could be no haphazardness over that.

Riquet was detailed to share the dangerous mission of traveling with Arnaud and his compromising transmitters, and he readily agreed to do this.

Within forty-eight hours the two men were back in Toulouse without any mishaps. Before catching my train to the peaceful retreat of a well-known brewer and his charming wife's private house in Montréjeau, the four members of S.O.E.—Lise, Eugène, Arnaud, and I—had a two-hours' interval in which to exchange news.

"Where do we go now?" asked Arnaud.

"To the Savoy mountains," I said.

"Good God!" blurted out Arnaud, "from the Maritime Alps to the Alps of Savoy. Always these bloody mountains! How I hate them!"

"This time you'll be working right up on an Alp and there'll be no detector cars."

"But I shall never get through the blasted blocks of granite!"

"Yes, you will, Arnaud," I said patiently, "I shall find you a spot with an empty gap running north and there'll be no interference. Furthermore, the distance to London will be reduced by about three hundred fifty miles."

"It had better be good," grunted Arnaud.

"I won't have you fetched unless it's perfect."

The others smiled and Arnaud looked at me dubiously.

Having disposed of this problem, Lise and I said our last farewells to Eugène. We were never to see our friend again.*

Returning to Cannes, I decided not to get out at the station

* Betrayed shortly afterwards by his Number Two, a Frenchman, Captain Maurice Pertschuk ended his life in the infamous extermination camp of Buchenwald where his Calvary was shared by a handful of more fortunate Resistance survivors, including Lt.-Cmdr. Patrick O'Leary, G.C., Wing-Cmdr. Yeo-Thomas, G.C., Christopher Burney, the Newton Brothers, Maurice Southgate, etc., not to mention the tens of thousands from all walks of life and every European country, with the exception of Portugal and Finland, who did not survive. Christopher Burney's first book *The Dungeon Democracy* is dedicated: "To the memory of Maurice Pertschuk, hanged in Buchenwald Crematorium on the 29th of March, 1945, who fought more gallantly than any of us and died more sadly."

but to go on to Antibes and enter the town by bus. It was a wise precaution that I then followed up by going to stay with my farmer friends at la Bocca. Lise, who could safely stay with Catherine, handled all my business, doing the double journey to and from the farm on an average of twice a day. As always, she was indefatigable, optimistic, and elegant. No one would ever suspect that her cycle rides were taking her from one clandestine house to another with important messages, tying up the loose ends of a large concern whose head office was shifting elsewhere.

It was with a feeling of intense relief that she and I finally shook the dust of Cannes from our feet. What with the ten-days' delay in Toulouse and as many in Cannes, we were well on into February now. As our train rumbled along the rain-drenched Côte d'Azur where I had spent nearly six months and Lise four, heavy forebodings took the place of the hopeful projects I had entertained when the sun had shone upon my arrival. But for Lise's presence this journey would have been a painful antithesis. Never had so much been packed into a mere six months; never so little accomplished. Would the gods allow me at least one successful coup before it was too late? I counted my blessings; they began with Arnaud and ended with Lise. It was a rich, consoling thought. We were still a going concern. With this pair I could undertake anything—if only for them. The war had reduced itself to this. It had centered itself around the deep-seated loyalty between the three of us—a Frenchwoman, a Russo-Egyptian, and an Englishman. But we never thought of each other under these headings of different nationalities, for we were as one. There was no time to hate the enemy, nor were we impelled by the patriotic motives that had fired our enthusiasm before coming out to France. It had become our own private war now.

Glancing at the resolute face of half my assets, sitting by my side, I drew strength from her in my hour of gloom. When the train slowed up to enter the Gare St. Charles at Marseille, I woke up to find that my head was resting on her shoulder.

CHAPTER XVI

MADAME MARSAC—End's wife—met us at Annecy station and led us to the bus that took us out to St. Jorioz.

The Hotel de la Poste with its old brown wood, white paint, and chalet appearance was a far cry from the busy centers we had left with all their dangerous associations. At least, so it seemed.

The main building at the crossroads of a tiny village of one hundred souls, it was the hub of local activity and the bus pulled up beside it.

It was February, 1943, and yet the sun was shining so that our first glimpse of the vertical block of Mont Veyrier across the still black lake, with the snow-clad Dents de Lanfon and La Tournette beside it, made an indelible and beautiful impression on us tired travelers.

The atmosphere of the place filled me with fresh hope. Up here in the mountains I felt that something might be done. Breathing in deep draughts of the cool morning air I took on with them a fresh lease of life.

End was there to meet the bus and lead us into the hotel. We sat down at a table and had an excellent cup of coffee—one of the first we had ever tasted. End passed me an identity card, saying:

"We thought you had better start here under a new name, since Pierre Chauvet has figured rather too long in the police files."

I opened up my new card and saw below a photograph that I had given End in Toulouse, the name *Pierre Chambrun*. At sight of the surname of Pierre Laval's son-in-law, I said smilingly: "Well, if this gets me by with the Germans, I shall probably be shot out of hand by the Patriots as a Collaborator —still, thanks very much."

They all laughed, for the choice of names, simple and easy as it was to remember, could not have been more paradoxical.

Seeing his opportunity, End now took us into a private room just behind the bar. Here he introduced us to Jean Cottet, the proprietor.

"Although you might never think so," he said, looking at me, "Monsieur Chambrun is a British Officer."

I was as staggered by this statement as by the hôtelier's instant counter-remark:

"How did you know that you were safe in bringing him under my roof?"

"Oh, we have ways and means of checking up on people's loyalties and we know that you think as we do," came the other's reply.

I shook hands with Jean Cottet and took in his powerful build, his comparative youth—for the twenty-eight or twenty-nine years I gave him seemed young to be the owner of such a hotel—and the hidden depths of the inscrutable brown eyes that looked at me squarely through horn-rimmed glasses I did not know that this moment was one that fate had kept in store for Jean Cottet for almost three years to enable him, at last, to strike a blow for the freedom of his country. Nor did Jean or Lise or I know that this was the beginning of a lifelong friendship.

Presently we were joined by a beautiful girl of twenty-five, Jean's wife, Simone, who was introduced all around.

We then took our leave and returned to the main lounge. Here we found Jacques Langlois and Jacques Latour who swelled our party, looking very massive in their fur-collared Canadiennes.

"We hunted all round for a suitable house," said End, "and the only place anything like large enough is that house over there." He pointed through the window to a square, boxlike building standing on its own opposite the tiny village station and not three hundred yards away.

"I see," I said, thinking that it could not very well have been much closer.

"Paul's staying with his wife in a little place across the lake and rows over to see us at the 'Tilleuls' twice a day."

"Who's with you at the 'Tilleuls'?" I asked.

"There's my wife, my secretary—Suzanne—, Roger (my Number Two), a Colonel Lambert, Madame Lelong who's doing the cooking while waiting for our 'camp breakers' to rescue her husband, and a constant flow of anything up to half a dozen couriers of whom the two Jacques, Louis 'le Belge', and Riquet are there at the moment: Gervais is staying on his own in a little village called Duingt, three kilometers away."

"Good old Gervais," I thought, "at least he'll have a chance of survival as well as Arnaud, even if Lise and I are trapped in this tiny ring." I said: "Do you think Riquet could dig up two bicycles before ours follow us by train from Cannes, and show me the Faverges setup this afternoon?"

"Certainly. He's here entirely at your disposal."

"Thanks," I said. "I'll be over to pick him up at one forty-five if that's all right."

Lise and I unpacked and put our things away. We then lunched together amongst the twenty-five or thirty other guests. The hotel was a friendly family affair with the Cottets' small children chattering and playing about among the tables and stopping momentarily while their heads were affectionately patted as they passed.

In her bag Lise had an "authentic" medical certificate stating that, for reasons of health, she had to live at an altitude of at least twelve hundred feet—St. Jorioz being in the region of fourteen hundred. Jean and Simone Cottet were glad of this cover, since curiosity as to the new couple was inevitable and this answer solved more than half the problem. Whatever my connection may have been to Lise was of less interest to a French gathering than in any residential hotel inhabited by a similar section of retired persons or evacuees in England. I assumed, with the greatest of ease, the attitude of someone who is putting up a good show in face of his companion's advanced state of consumption, and we were soon accepted as an aloof couple whose passionate hobby was cycling.

Lise had plenty to attend to that afternoon, sorting out her clothes, washing and ironing, while Riquet and I cycled over to Faverges. We found the village nestling at the foot of high wooded mountains and went straight to the private house of a sawmill owner, Monsieur Favre. He turned out to be a small, unassuming, quiet, bespectacled man.

Leading me round to the front of his house, he pointed out a tree, suggesting that it might be suitable for Arnaud's aerial. I looked up at the house, back at the tree, and beyond it along the open valley stretching away to the north.

It was all too easy. Favre indicated his willingness for Arnaud both to live and transmit from his house, as though he were a boardinghouse keeper clinching a satisfactory deal for his last vacant room.

After some of the struggles and sales talk I had had to put up to get Arnaud accepted in certain other establishments, I was flabbergasted by this attitude. Favre's amiable and comely wife then showed us the room that they had set aside for his use. I thanked them both as though I were quite accustomed to this kind of co-operation, and we went off to call on the next man.

Milleau owned a minute bar with a separate counter where cigarettes, postcards, and the sort of stationery found in small villages were on sale. The place was empty except for his wife, who received us with a pretty smile and the information that her husband was in the back room.

Opening the frosted-glass door, she showed us in and returned to her duties.

Milleau was a square hunk of a man in his early thirties, with a thatch of uncontrollable straw-colored hair rising above a straight forehead, a pair of frank blue eyes, and a determined chin. The captain of the local contingent of the Secret Army was reading the paper at his ease, for he wore neither collar nor tie.

He welcomed me in a booming jovial voice and crushed my hand in a gorilla's grip. I inadvertently raised an eyebrow at the agreeable pain of my first contact with this healthy specimen

Yes, Arnaud could transmit from an alternative spot two thousand feet up the mountain in the forest guard's house. Wasting no time, Milleau fetched his Renault "302" and drove us up the mountain road past Seythenex and up the narrowing lane through the snow to the first house of a tiny agglomeration of farm buildings known as Les Tissots.

The place was perfect. With its open northern aspect there was nothing to hinder radio contact with London. From the security point of view it was equally ideal, for no one could reach the spot without being heard or seen while still a long way off. Here Arnaud could work with impunity and, if ever hunted, escape in three directions.

The afternoon's work seemed entirely satisfactory to me, as Riquet and I were raced down to the valley at Milleau's breakneck speed.

As Riquet and I cycled back to St. Jorioz, I wished I could spend the rest of my Underground days in this part of the world. The men of this district were all right and so were their wives.

That evening, when I was relating these happenings to Lise across our small dinner table, with a bottle of Jean's remaining Poret already half gone, Riquet was well on his way to Montréjeau to bring the second member of our team into the fresh and hopeful setting where the three of us were to live the next page of our many lives.

Within forty-eight hours, Riquet was back once more reporting, in his phlegmatic style, that Arnaud was not only installed, but that he had already contacted London from his eagle's eyrie where he had decided he would always work in preference to the valley. He was now waiting for me on the jetty at Bout du Lac.

Ten minutes on my bicycle took me to the post and, when I caught sight of my friend's powerful frame that could not be concealed by the easy fit of his gray tweed suit, a great wave of affection and relief came over me. Nor was Arnaud unaffected, as we shook hands. Though he made no mention of his long and dangerous journey with Riquet and the two radio sets, and did not comment on his new installation, so carefully prepared for him in advance, yet the warmth of his greeting and the smile on his handsome face told me that the trust and friendship, which had for so long been one-sided, were, at last, mutually established.

"Eugène sends you his best wishes," he began. "I was able to do quite a lot of sending for him because of more trouble with Urbain's set. However, it's all right now. As I knew your views about the Scharnhorst and Gneisenau, I sent them the dope about their departure from Brest in plenty of time for the night of February eleventh, but you know how it is. They light their bloody pipes with our messages. I don't know why we bother to send the God-damned stuff! Why don't we b——— off and go skiing somewhere? Another little trick they tried on me recently was putting on a new pancake last Sunday who couldn't receive at more than twelve. Just imagine, Michel, twelve ——— words a ——— minute while I sit there sweating with the 'cars' closing in on me like hornets!"

"What did you say to her?" I asked.

"Nothing. But I've got a message here for H.Q. about it that I want you to see before it goes." Arnaud handed over the usual filthy scrap of paper on which I read the amazing words: IF YOU PUT THAT BITCH ON AGAIN NEXT SUNDAY I QUIT ENDS.

Handing back the scruffy bit of paper, I said: "You can send that with my blessings, Arnaud."

We went on discussing such matters for another ten minutes, and after fixing a rendezvous at a different spot for the following day, where Lise would take up the liaison, we parted.

The next day Roger got our bicycles for us from the station and handed them over in one of the streets of Annecy. When he had gone, Lise said to me:

"I don't like that man; he's got shifty eyes."

"What d' you want me to do?" I said. "Drop him in the lake?"

"Mark my words, Michel. That man's no good."

"Well, maybe you're right. But so far he hasn't put a foot wrong; and if ever he does, it'll be up to the French to attend to him. They've got their own professional killers here. I was introduced to two of them by End in the Avenue d'Albigny yesterday. In any case, one must have proof before indiscriminately knocking off people who are only guilty of having shifty eyes."

"Maybe it'll be too late when the proof comes," said Lise.

"Well, as a foreigner, I can't tip off Paul or End to keep an eye on him; besides, they're just as impressed by his intelligence and the way he's behaved in recent night operations as I am."

We dropped the matter there. If only Lise had said to me: "I implore you to tip off Paul and ask that he should be followed wherever he goes and his telephone conversations tapped," or if I had understood it without her saying more, many things might have been different.

We were now at the beginning of the second week in March, 1943. More than two weeks had elapsed since we had settled into our new H.Q., and it seemed at last that we had succeeded in putting the Gestapo off the scent.

The parachutings increased and the railway program was going ahead once more quite satisfactorily.

It was at this moment that Paul informed me that Carte had succeeded in getting away from Chanoines on a Hudson he had landed himself. The report was that seventeen men had subsequently been arrested in Arles and that most of the Carte family were also in prison. I was never able to confirm this information, except with regard to Carte's departure; but there seemed no reason to doubt its truth, in the light of what we had already seen of the situation in Arles, which could hardly have improved with the passing of time.

Carte's arrival at Headquarters in London must have set an embarrassing problem to the Command of the French Section of the War Office. On the one hand they had their own man in France liaising with Carte's successors, of whom they had already shown their approval, including B.B.C. messages openly proclaiming their attitude to all patriots concerned in the cleavage and, on the other, here was the dethroned leader whom they had previously helped and now brought out of the country

Paul also said that at the time of Carte's departure their listeners had picked up B.B C. messages patently refuting the substance of the three previous messages and saying that Carte was back in favor again. It seemed clear to me that Carte's seductive manner had not only won over my superiors, but even succeeded in making them stab me—their personal representative—in the back If that was really so, then the bottom had fallen out of the bag. But I was not downcast by this; instead I fumed with rage. What a row I would cause at Headquarters! I would tear the place apart, and particularly the gentlemen responsible for this betrayal. My God! I thought, how I would attend to them! At no time had my feelings toward the enemy reached half the hatred I suddenly felt against my own folk at home. It would be a pleasure to do a couple of years in the Tower of London or Wormwood Scrubs for what I planned to do to the party, or parties, responsible for this affair. With these and similar thoughts floating on top of the adrenalin that sprang from my glands in reaction to the staggering news, my feet hardly touched the ground for several hours.

When I had simmered down, I wisely decided not to share this news with Arnaud. The struggle must go on, even if the ground was taken away from below my feet by our own side. I must get back now with Paul, at all costs, so that this nonsense could be cleared up. There were messages to be sent, one, in particular, became urgent that very night.

Jean Cottet, upon whose time and privacy I never imposed myself, invited me to have a cognac in his private den. There he informed me that two thousand men had gathered on the Plateau of Glières—not four miles distant as the crow flew—where they intended to stay rather than go to Germany on forced labor.

"There are half a dozen officers among these men," said Jean, "and their leader is a determined young lieutenant called Tom Morel. This man has an excellent cover for this work, as he is the director of the Annecy Office of Voluntary Recruitment for Labor in Germany."

"You interest me strangely," I said, leaning forward. "But tell me, this name Tom Morel doesn't sound French to me."

"Perhaps not. Nevertheless, he is a Frenchman and these men, Monsieur Chambrun, mean business. But to transact such business they must have arms."

"I see what you mean," I said, stroking my chin. "I will give this matter some serious consideration."

"Rumor has it," added Jean, "that a strong force of the Vichy troops is assembling with a view to surrounding the Plateau on March eighteenth."

I swallowed the rest of my drink and got up.

"I'll do what I can," I said.

In my room, I tore off a piece of paper and prepared the longest message I had ever asked Arnaud to send. When I had crossed out all unnecessary words I read it over to myself. It ran:

> MOST URGENT 2000 DETERMINED WELL OFFICERED MAQUISARDS STATIONED ANNECY M16 EXPECTING LARGE VICHY ATTACK MARCH 18 STOP BESEECH YOU ARM THESE MEN SOONEST STOP RESISTANCE INCENTIVE TO OTHER MAQUIS THROUGH THEIR VICTORY WITH OUR ARMS INCALCULABLE ENDS.

As there were other messages to be sent, and since I required Arnaud's assurance that he would not reduce one single word of this one, or tamper with it in any way, I took Lise's place at the next meeting.

Handing it over to Arnaud I watched his expression as he read it.

"My God!" he said. "This is the real thing! I'll try and get a special sked for tomorrow morning so that you can have the answer when we meet tomorrow."

"Good for you, Arnaud," I said. We shook hands and went our separate ways.

I could hardly sleep that night, and on the following afternoon, as I made my way to a spot in the reeds just past the end of the lake, I did not really expect London to have made up its mind so quickly.

Arnaud was waiting for me, punctual as usual, and handed me three small scraps of paper. He did not say a word beyond the customary handshake we were in the habit of exchanging.

I read the top message. It ran.

> WELL DONE—THIS IS WHAT WE HAVE BEEN WAITING FOR STOP WARN MAQUISARDS PREPARE THREE LARGE BONFIRES AT HUNDRED YARD INTERVALS IN LINE OF WIND AND LIGHT THESE ONLY AT SOUND OF SQUADRONS APPROACH STOP EXPECT DELIVERY OF ONE HUNDRED AND TWENTY SIX CONTAINERS BETWEEN MIDNIGHT AND 0200 HOURS MARCH 13 RPT 13 RAIN HAIL OR FLAK STOP NO BBC MESSAGE STOP TALLYHO STOP ENDS.

"This is something I don't want to miss," I said, watching the paper curl up under the flame of my lighter.

"Read on," said Arnaud casually.

Looking at the message I saw:

> LYSANDER WILL PICK YOU UP GIANT FIELD TOURNUS AS FROM MARCH 14 RPT 14 B B.C. BETTER LATE THAN NEVER ENDS.

"Hell's teeth!" I groaned. "Seven ruddy months and I'm going to miss the only thing we've ever brought off. . . ."

"You've had a good run, Michel, whereas I've seen absolutely nothing so far. This is going to be my big reward."

"And how you deserve it, *mon vieux*," I said, putting my hand on his arm and forgetting my own disappointment as I shared my friend's satisfaction. "Right on your doorstep, too," I added, almost visualizing the scene.

"Yes. I shall be up on an Alp with the Faverges boys waving a flag as they go over . . . And Lise will open her window and see them zooming across the lake."

We both remained silent for a while. Then Arnaud said grimly: "Better have a look at the third message."

I read

> LYSANDER BRINGING ROGER* REPLACE YOUR ABSENCE STOP PLEASE HAVE HIM MET AND ALL LAID ON ENDS.

I did not have to look at my friend to know that he was glowering like a bull that has just entered the ring. I knew exactly what was in his mind. As I burned the two last messages, it was Arnaud who broke the silence.

"If they think they can send out raw recruits to give me orders they've got another think coming!"

"Don't be a chump, Arnaud," I said.

"The —— cheek of sending someone out to take your place! As though we needed somebody to teach us how to suck eggs! I refuse to send his messages, and that's flat! Besides . . . I know Lise feels just the same as I do."

"Now, Arnaud," I said, drawing on all the patience and

* Lt. Francis Cammaerts, later to become Lt.-Col., D.S.O., Croix de Guerre.

persuasiveness that the situation demanded, "you know very well that this man, Roger, will come out fully briefed with the very latest instructions from London. He will have read all our messages since the year dot, and just imagine his feelings at the thought of meeting you after what they'll have told him at home. As for Lise agreeing with this tough attitude, it's as clear as the Tournette who will put her up to it."

"Lise is quite capable of making up her own mind," said Arnaud with a great deal of truth.

"During my absence, Arnaud, I shall put Lise in charge and you'll kindly do what she says and also take great care of her."

After the full impact of this fresh prospect had been digested in his mind, Arnaud said, "All right, Michel . . . but you'll never come back."

"Oh yes I shall."

"I shall believe it when I see it."

"You'll see it . . . and Arnaud, don't forget what I said, and don't be prejudiced against Roger. Remember, it's not very funny the first days."

I held out my hand, which was swallowed in a giant's grip, and said, *"Au revoir, mon cher vieux."*

"Adieu," said Arnaud, simply.

On my ride back to St. Jorioz, I stopped at Duingt on the offchance of finding Gervais. He was in.

Telling him what was about to take place at Glières and of my own departure, I said·

"Here's something for you to get your teeth into at last. I want you to go up to Glières the day after the stuff arrives and show these boys how to work the Stens. Report to Tom Morel, who's running the show and give him my compliments; he'll be expecting you. They'll be in a bit of a mess, so give them an idea of how to store those guns and ammo in a dry place and how to grease them. Put them through the firing routine and go easy on the rounds. The noise will be very salutary to one and all, particularly the gentlemen in Vichy who'll hear about it very soon through their spies. You'll find the usual instructions in French in each container. Stay as long as they want you; but my advice, which is not an order, is to leave them before the battle begins, because it's a French show and a kind of civil war.* Furthermore, I shall want you for other things when I come back."

Puffing gently on his pipe and nodding his head as he took it all in, Gervais held out his hand to me and said, unemotionally: "All right, Michel. *Bon voyage* and *bon retour.*"

There was great excitement at H.Q. over the Glières news and even greater excitement up in the mountains when the Annecy ambulance driver delivered the message the same evening. Now they could defend themselves against the Militia and strike a blow that would echo all over France.

The news that I was to try for another Lysander came as no particular surprise to Lise; she was getting accustomed to the routine. It was I who got a surprise from her attitude in regard to my successor, for it was identical with Arnaud's. In a way I was flattered that my two friends should react in this manner, but I persuaded her—as I had done Arnaud—that this was no help to anyone and not a very nice way of behaving.

I told her she was in charge and that Arnaud was already aware of this, that I would return, and that I would like her to take care of herself and keep her eyes wide open in the meantime.

Lise said: "This time you'll get away."

"What makes you say that?" I asked.

"I just know it," she replied.

I slipped away that night through the Cottets' bedroom

* The Maquis of the Plateau des Glières were the first to fight a pitched battle against the Germans

Whittling down his numbers to 450 picked men of whom 50 were Spaniards, Tom Morel made them all take an oath to fight for their freedom. His motto *"Vivre Libre ou mourir"* stands today, carved in stone, on the monument inside the Morette Cemetery—on the Annecy-Thones road—where 112 men, including their commanding officer, lie as a constant reminder of their epic battle of March, 1944.

Surrounded by 10,000 soldiers of a German Mountain Division, with 88-millimeter guns and three-inch mortars and battered in advance by two squadrons of Stuka Dive Bombers, this handful of men fought against 22 times their number. They killed 300 Germans and lost 12 men before escaping over a snowbound pass. The other hundred in the cemetery were betrayed by the French Militia who recognized them later in the valley. All the 100 were tortured before being put to death.

window, and as my foot was on the window sill Josette woke up and said to her mother, *"Où va-t'il, Monsieur Chambrun?"*
I smiled and looked at Simone. "Tell her I'm going butterfly hunting." Then I vanished in the dark street.

CHAPTER XVII

THE AIRCRAFT never came to Tournus, and I spent seven days hiding away in the village of Préty from the inevitable mob of Resistance Chiefs who had learned nothing from the heavy losses they had so recently sustained, and gaily foregathered in ever-increasing numbers. Against his better judgment, Paul had to stay with them.

On the seventh day a courier brought the news from Arnaud that the aircraft would pick us up in a field seventeen kilometers away from the town of Compiègne and that we must get there for March 23. It was then March 20. A hurried council of war settled all details.

In no time an old car came chugging up to Thomas's door and Paul, Riquet, Jacques Latour, and I bundled into it, throwing our gear onto the roof rack. For this operation only Riquet was required, as we would place the torches on the ends of sticks, merely lighting them at the last moment. When the job was over, he would collect the torches and lead the passenger away to a hide-out for the rest of the night. This was still to be found, whereas in Tournus it would all have been so simple. Jacques was only coming as far as Paris.

The car rattled slowly along N 6, the great highway leading toward Châlons-sur-Saône, where we would entrain for Paris. It seemed that it would never get there at this rate.

As we approached the Demarcation Line, the driver looked nervously at the small attaché case that I was nursing on my knees and asked what was in it. I told him that it was full of correspondence.

"I can't take you through with any letters," said the man, "that's just what the Jerries are after on the Line."

He pulled up his car and we discussed the problem.

On hearing that there was a branch road a few kilometers further along that led to the Saône, Riquet volunteered to walk along it with the case and meet us in Châlons after crossing the river.

"How do you intend to cross that wide river?" I inquired.

"I'll pinch a boat. There are sure to be some lying about," said that intrepid youth.

"Nice work," I said, and the car got under way.

At the agreed spot, Riquet took off to the right, saying, *"A bientôt"*—and was off.

Presently the car came round a gentle bend and there was the barrier across the road.

A solitary, middle-aged Wehrmacht soldier came up to the car and inquired:

"Wo gehen-Sie?"

"Châlons," said the driver.

"Haben Sie Briefkarten?" was the sound of the next question.

"Keine Briefkarten," replied Paul.

And that was all.

The driver deposited his passengers at the station, was paid and drove away as though leaving a bunch of lepers.

Jacques bought the tickets, while the rest of us waited about on the platform for the train. It was due in fifteen minutes and there seemed little chance of Riquet's getting there in time. However, Paul and Jacques seemed in no way worried by this and said that he would catch us up in Paris. We still had a day's grace.

As the train steamed up to the flatform, Riquet appeared simultaneously through the subway, walking casually toward us. None of us made any fuss as he joined us, thus giving the impression that he had only fallen behind a few paces. As we took our stand at the end of the corridor in the crowded train, I grabbed Riquet's arm and gave him a smiling wink. If ever a man had earned a comprehensive M.C. for a series of acts in the face of danger, this was that man. If he never got it, I would always consider that he had earned it.

Arriving in Paris late the same night, I telephoned my friend Charles Fol, whom I had not seen for four years.

Hearing his wife pick up the receiver, I said:

"Hallo, Biche. Don't be too surprised. It's me, Pierre. I should have got into touch ages ago, but I've been taking it easy in the south of France."

I said all this to give her plenty of time to collect her thoughts.

There was silence for a moment; then I overheard a whispered *"C'est Pierre!"* to her husband in the next bed.

"Give it to me," said a firm voice, grabbing the instrument.

"Hallo, old boy," came the clear, lightning reactions of this man of the world. "How's life and where are you?"

"Life's not so dusty and I'm speaking from the P.L.M. Métro," I said.

"Well, come over. I'll be downstairs to see you past the concierge You ought to be here in twenty minutes."

It all went off like clockwork. Within half an hour I was drinking a glass of old brandy with my friends. They were a little taken aback by my wintry getup and rucksack, but I soon put them at ease by telling them I could not stay more than two nights and that, as far as the concierge was concerned, I was simply an old friend who had been up in the mountains on holiday.

The following day was memorable for several reasons. I spent a very pleasant hour with my hostess's charming mother, paid a surprise visit to my friend Louis Chevalier, who nearly jumped out of his skin, stood beside a U-boat crew as they saluted the unknown soldier's tomb below the Arc de Triomphe, and wound up the day by listening to a rousing speech by Mr. Winston Churchill.

After this pleasant interlude, we re-formed—minus Jacques —and entrained for Compiègne.

We took rooms in a tiny hotel near the station and set about looking for means of transport to get us to Estrées-St.-Denis. From there we would discover the whereabouts of the Sainte-

Beuve hop farm where, according to the London message, Madame Sainte-Beuve would solve all our problems.

As there were no bicycles to be had, Riquet unearthed a horse and trap and we jogged along to carry out our reconnaissance in this old-world manner.

Our gay spirits were dampened early at the sight of the Compiègne Concentration Camp where patriots—including some of our own friends—were held before the last lap into Germany. Passing right beside its walls was a horribly close reminder of what lay in store for us if things went wrong.

Within two hours we were entering the drive of the place we sought.

Madame Sainte-Beuve, an aristocratic Frenchwoman with prematurely gray hair, wasted no time once she had recognized the password. Taking me in her private trap, she drove me over her grounds and up to a small field that might have been designed by a fussy Lysander pilot—if such a person had ever existed.

"I hope your message comes tonight," said Madame Sainte-Beuve, "because tomorrow those tractors over there are going to plough all this up and there is nothing I can do to stop it. The people who work for us are unaware of my sympathies."

"Would you allow us to stay and listen to the message so as to save us all that distance?" I asked.

"Not even that can I do"—and the sad look in her proud, handsome eyes told me the rest—"however much I should like to."

We went back to the farm, and we reached Compiègne in darkness. As we passed the Camp, the sweeping searchlights lit up the wretched hutments in a terrifying manner.

It was a sober couple who sat down to dine in a "prefab" restaurant as we waited for Riquet's return from listening for our message. To sit in the shadow of so much misery, that might one day be ours, was not conducive to merriment.

At last he came back. When he had sat down, he said, "Sorry, nothing doing."

"Well," I said, "as the field will be ploughed up tomorrow, we might as well catch the seven-fifty and get back to Paris. I shall be glad to get out of this place, anyway. It gives me the creeps."

We paid our bill and went to fetch our bags.

Entering the blacked-out station, Riquet led us along the platform beside a darkened train. Opening a door we bundled in. We lit cigarettes and smoked silently in the dark. Presently a train at another platform started moving off in a direction that I thought led to Paris.

"Hey!" I said, "that's our train . . . what's the idea?"

My remarks were met by a suppressed giggle from Riquet and a happy chuckle from Paul.

"Well," I laughed rather weakly, catching on, "of all the so-and-so's I ever met. . . ."

When we detrained at the halt before St. Just-en-Chaussée, I hung back to allow Paul to get his bearings undisturbed. But we never reached first base, for Paul had forgotten the minor detail as to whether the trap had turned left or right on leaving the station yard when he had studied the route that afternoon.

Like a burning flash the thought of the one thousand kilometers and more that had been covered, at some risk, since leaving Annecy, the knowledge that it was 8:40 P.M. and that a mere five kilometers or so separated us from an ideal field, where my seventh desperate attempt to connect with an aircraft seemed to have had an even chance of success, rushed through my mind. Now the whole project had suddenly frittered away into a two hundred to one shot.

Feeling my entrails writhing into knots I said, with passable control: "I bet you were so busy exchanging old-world courtesies with Madame Sainte-Beuve that you never saw much beyond her handsome gray eyes."

"I'm almost sure we went to the right," said Paul lamely.

Fortunately for us all, Riquet's sense of direction was so good that he led us like a bloodhound to our goal. At 9:45 P.M. we topped the final rise and there, in the distance, lay the huge farm, ringed round like a fortress with its high walls.

Pointing at the railway line that flanked the Sainte-Beuve property, Riquet said: "At that level crossing I understand there are two Frenchmen on duty. Moreover, all crossings and bridges in the whole country are now guarded from dusk to dawn in this way to stop sabotage."

"A cunning device," added Paul. "If anything goes wrong on their stretch, the men are taken as hostages. Everyone knows what will happen to them if there's further trouble at the same spot. This diabolic stunt, supposed to act as a deterrent, has little effect, for in war one mustn't consider the fate of hostages."

"I hope they won't be blamed for whatever happens tonight," I said.

"Only they will know what happens tonight, and they're not likely to talk about it. It's a blessing, too, that the field is to be ploughed up tomorrow."

As we descended the gentle incline toward our clearly outlined field, a persistent whistling of the V-sign—dot, dot, dot, dash—the opening bars of the Fifth Symphony and the musical call-sign of the European wave length from Bush House to France during the war, came to our ears.

"That's End," I said to the others. "I wonder what the devil he's doing here, frightening us out of our wits."

Riquet ran over and presently returned with End and a new man, whom he introduced as a member of the Paris group. We all shook hands as though we had just bumped into each other at the Rond Point des Champs Elysées. I thought I would never get used to my friends' odd behavior.

"Nice to see you," I lied to End. "But why did you bother?"

"I thought it would be so much easier to take Riquet and the passenger straight back to Paris in my friend's car rather than let them shiver through the night in a haystack."

"What about the curfew and all those barriers around the gates of Paris?"

"Our papers are good for the whole night. The Paris group is well organized and has German permits and Ausweises as well as an excellent forger of the Kommandantur's various signatures."

"Well, good for them!" I said, admiring their cheek.

With the additional help of the two unexpected men, there was now no need to attach the lamps to sticks. I instructed the whole party in its simple individual tasks and, leaving the usual white handkerchiefs at the appointed spots to be replaced by lamp-holders, we settled down to wait for events in one group.

The night advanced and the half moon's surprising clarity lit up the scene. In the silence we could hear the distant coughing of one of the men at the level crossing. The last light went out in a bedroom at the farm and only fourteen kilometers away thousands of Frenchmen behind the electric wire lay tossing on hard prison bunks, praying for blessed sleep and oblivion.

An aircraft droned its approach and we leaped to our positions. I waited, my torch at the ready, all else forgotten.

As it roared overhead I gave the ground signal, repeating it over and over again. It paid no attention, heading straight along its course. We reassembled to await its return. This was Basillac again, but this time, we hoped, without interference. We knew all the tricks, all the snags. We had seen it all. Nothing would stop this operation from being a success if the plane spotted us. If need be, we would stay out all night and to blazes with G.M.T., double summer time, and all the rest of it.

There it came, blasting its way back toward us and advertising its presence like the trump of doom. All ran to their posts and stood tensely waiting for my warning to click on their lamps.

I flashed up the code sign, repeating it as before, my bright light visible up to twenty thousand feet. What was the matter with this man sailing by at a mere two thousand and ignoring my signal?

"Wake up, chum!" I implored, seeing it go by once more and realizing that there were simply no landmarks here to help a pilot. Once across the Channel, he might have to zigzag past the Flak posts and find them by dead reckoning.

However, the pilot did not hear my anxious call and, if he had, the chances are that he would not have understood, for he was a German, minding his own business, in a Junkers 88.

This went on for hours and, up to 1:30 A.M., the aerial traffic was so heavy that my battery was beginning to wear out and I feared my ears had become so mithered by the sounds of aircraft engines of the Luftwaffe, that I might let the Lysander pass, mistaking it for the Fieseler Storch I had already buzzed, besides nine others.

We sat down and shared some cold rabbit and a bottle of wine. Another plane drew us to our feet.

"Don't bother," I said, eating a bone in my fingers, "I'm not going to give our position away for any more Germans to plot, and I shan't signal again until I see the peculiar cut of the Lysander's wings right over us."

"Curious thing," said Riquet, "that they manage to get as far as the south of France by ten-fifteen and yet here, where we're so close to England, they hang on so late."

"D'you think he'll come, Michel?" asked End.

"All I know is that once the B.B.C. message has passed they've never failed us so far," I said, wiping my fingers and looking into the western sky.

We finished the bottle and looked at our watches. One fifty-eight.

And now the silence was rent once more; this time by the brittle bite of a low-flying aircraft coming straight toward us. Closer, closer. This was surely it. We all stood up and tried to pierce the poor visibility.

As it came in, low and fast, my eyes focused and held the well-known shape. Instantly my torch flickered on the ground signal. As quickly came the pilot's recognition from a small lamp below the fuselage which he operated with slow, well-spaced dots and dashes as he rushed by.

"Here we go!" I said, *"au revoir, mes amis!"*—as they dashed to light their lamps.

Following the triangle that gave him his line of approach, the pilot circled down, throttling back his engine. His wheels touched down in a perfect landing not twenty feet from me and Paul, and he pulled up hard by the second lamp. A quick turnabout and I saw Riquet duck below his wing as he revved back—a trifle close—to the controlling lamp. A quick flick and he was around again, facing the two end lamps, the tip of his wing by my face.

Running up to the pilot who had already pushed back his sliding roof, I shouted, "You can let her idle, there's no one around for miles."

Throttling down, he turned his head and said, in drawing-room tones:

"Congratulations on a perfect field. This is a piece of cake."

Paul and I now waited for Roger to alight. He was followed by a second man who was handing down their luggage. As soon as they were both clear, I nudged Paul, saying:

"Watch your step up that small ladder . . . I'll follow you."

I shook hands with Roger.

"Welcome, friend. . . . There's a car laid on. Good luck!" Then I turned to the other. "Why, Charles! It's you!" I greeted my old friend from Lyon.

Climbing up the ladder—for there was not time for small talk—Paul and I waved to the two passengers on the field who were giving the "thumbs up" sign to show the pilot they were in.

Pulling the roof to and sliding on the safety catch to hold it shut, I felt the powerful motor surge us forward. In sixty yards we were airborne, and below stood the waving figures of the two end-lamp men, clearly visible through the mica hood.

A feeling of triumph swept over me as we soared higher and higher into the enemy's sky. I had done it at last! Five thousand kilometers on the ground and one hundred fifty days of waiting were the price for this three hundred-kilometer hop that would not take two hours. My part of the job was over, and if we were brought down by flak or night-fighters it was not my concern any longer. I gave Paul a big slap on the knee and grinned happily into his face. My friend placed a hand over mine and nodded his calm contentment.

The aircraft twisted and turned like a fast car on a winding road before finally setting a straight course for home.

Presently we were over the Channel where we soon ran into a pea-soup fog. This was not so funny, and I began to wonder how we would ever land in such a solid blanket. On and on droned the Lysander, its pilot knowing his business, while the damp cold seeped into the back compartment.

Now we began to lose height. I looked forward and there, less than a mile ahead, were the concentrated beams of twenty searchlights in a ring, all crossing above the airport.

The pilot threw his machine down like a toy and landed in the center of the blaze. In an instant he had switched off his engine and the searchlights fluttered out.

CHAPTER XVIII

It was all over. We were safely down on the soil of blacked-out England. In dazed silence we listened to the ticking of the hot cylinders, already complaining at the change of temperature; then English voices came to us across the tarmac.

We were led off to the sergeants' mess like cargo that must be treated with care. Inside, two plates of steaming bacon and eggs were placed before us.

As soon as the buzz got round, all the Lysander pilots came crowding in around us offering us whiskeys and soda. Plied with questions by my friends, I was in a state of high excitement.

"What the hell were you running away from at Basillac?"

"Say when."

"I knew it was you, you big black devil, chasing us up and down."

"Say when."

"WHEN! For God's sake! I can't drink all that." Then turning, "I only saved your life by not signaling. They were waiting to grab us all. . . ."

"Lay off my passengers They gave me a field out of the book."

"You always get the jammy ones!"

And so on. . . .

Finally they simmered down and left us to gulp down a mouthful or two. I found my plate resting on the front page of the *Evening Standard,* a glass of neat whiskey at each elbow. The thick black type of the right-hand column of the paper, just visible, caught my eye.

D.S.O. FOR R.A.F. MAN.

I read on:

"Squadron Leader Picard has just been awarded a bar to his D.S.O. for an act of gallantry, the details of which cannot be divulged for reasons of security. . . ."

"My God!" I said, dropping my knife and looking round at the pilots. "Surely that's the Tournus job! I watched it all. He should have got the V.C.!"

"Goodness knows, old boy," said one of them. "Might be anywhere. . . . Someone's out every night. Most of the places we get aren't much better than a cemetery."

I knew I was back in England, right enough; back home where the standards were high, where no one was particularly impressed, because anything less would have been unusual. Yet I was glad I had seen that epic and, as I sipped the strong whiskey, I imagined the navigator's or wireless operator's sober and carefully worded report of the proceedings· "After some delay due to the settlement of the aircraft in the somewhat soggy surface and the rearrangement of the flare-path to give a longer runway across a field littered with foreign bodies, the Captain made a good take-off, only slightly grazing a tree which the heavy load of passengers prevented his clearing. He returned to the U.K. without further mishap." *

Warmed and restored by our friendly reception, Paul and I were then whisked off by car through the misty dawn of March 24 to London. After breakfasting on the way, the car drew up outside Orchard Court at about 9 A.M.

* Years later the full story came to my knowledge With his undercarriage jammed in the down position by the top of the tree he had snapped off, his speed was so reduced that he passed over the Normandy Flak posts in full daylight at low level looking so like a lame duck carrying a large twig to build its nest that the gaping Germans let him pass and he landed safely on his own airport.

It was Picard who later led the squadron that blew in the wall of the Amiens prison, thus enabling 72 condemned French patriots to escape. Coming round for a second time in order to make sure that the job had been accurately done, he came in line with the now-alerted flak. A direct hit put an end to the brilliant career of this very brave pilot.

Major B. was there and several other Headquarters officers, many of them new to me. After being introduced to Paul, Major B. took me aside and said:

"Well, Michel, it's good to see you back after all these false starts. We've got a lot of catching up to do, so if you've got any queries, just fire away."

"The first question I should like to ask, sir, is what made you decide to let the Italians in through the tunnels, when I could so easily have stopped them?"

"That was a simple question of the overall view. When you gave us the information about which divisions were to occupy the south we knew where they came from. Now either the place they left was weakened and therefore inviting an invasion by us, or, if the divisions that left were replaced by others, some other spot was left weak. We were in a position to obtain that necessary information from other sources. We also knew that you would be able to carry on your activities just as well with the Italians in the zone, and the longer we kept the Germans out, the better it suited the general war aims."

"I get it, Buck," I said, using my chief's nickname. "But what a frustration that sort of thing causes to the individual in the field."

"I can well understand that," replied Major B. "Wars are like that and there's simply no time to go into long explanations over the air."

"The tankers not being picked up at Gibraltar was another pain in the neck," I went on.

"That," said Major B., "was an Admiralty decision What with the Madagascar show and the general shipping situation in the Mediterranean, the Naval Authorities must have had some severe headaches. You know yourself how short they were of submarines. It's been a long defensive war, but the tide is turning."

The final question was the all-important matter of Carte. After I had outlined my view of the affair, my superior explained:

"This is Paul's second visit here, so we know him. We also like him and recognize him. As for the B.B C. messages which you suggest were aimed against you, they were merely sent out to enable Carte's people to arrange for his pick-up by a Hudson. We have our reasons for wanting to see Carte and none of them is for the purpose of getting a report on your activities."

From this conversation I realized how wrongly I had judged my own people at home and how my rages had been wasted. I began to see the complications faced by Head Office. They must have dozens of similar situations coming from scores of agents, causing misunderstandings so easily unraveled once the agent returned to thrash it out with his too-often-maligned superiors. From my own C.O.'s lips the words—"We don't claim to be infallible but believe me, on our side there is no bad faith or conscious negligence"—clearly showed how conscientious and patient they were in handling the ever-increasing work of the Section and doing everything in their power to give their men in the field the co-operation to which they were entitled.

"Where is Carte, now?" I inquired.

"He's in London at present, but he's going to the States shortly."

"Then all his dreams will come true," I said.

"What do you mean by that?" asked Major B.

"He told me he preferred working with our friends to us."

I found that the original small happy family concern of private enterprise which I had previously known had altered and grown to such an extent that I almost felt like a stranger. I longed to get back to my private war which had nothing to do with what seemed to have been turned into a large state-owned company.

One event took place that caused me a smile of satisfaction at the Office. Called into the presence of a young man of high rank—one of the newcomers I had never seen before—I was put on the carpet for Arnaud's disgraceful language over the air. This cynosure of the French Section looked at me with justifiable indignation, waving copies of the shameful evidence before my face.

"Can't you control your radio operator's language any better than this?" came his toffee-nosed and deeply pained voice.

"I'm sorry about the language," I answered, "but I associate myself entirely with Arnaud in this matter and I challenge anyone to control him any better. In fact, you are at liberty to try someone else."

"I think there's hardly any need for you to tell me what I can do," came the other's reasonable reply.

The interview was over, and any satisfaction that I got out of it was immediately canceled by the certainty that my written recommendation for Arnaud's D.S.O. or M.C. would now go straight into the waste-paper basket.

However, my first recommendation for Arnaud had been agreed by Major B., and the message to Lise announcing Paul's and my safe arrival included another which ran: FOR ARNAUD STOP CONGRATULATIONS YOUR CAPTAINCY ENDS.

On my way home for a short visit to my parents, I ran over my new impressions of H.Q., comparing my recent reception with my first triumphant return from France more than a year ago, when I had been fêted as though I had just brought back the "Ashes."

However, I told myself that I must not be too hasty in my judgment. Perhaps I was altogether mistaken and that what I took for an atmosphere of soullessness was only due to my possible state of jumpiness resulting from the many shocks and frights I had suffered over so long a period, to which had been added the crippling blow received on the day of my return, when the news was broken to me that my fighter-pilot brother had been dead for seven months, killed in action on the day I had first entered Cannes.

Having to leave my grief-stricken mother, whom I hardly recognized, and whose third son had been absent—operating with the Italian partisans—for a year, was not conducive to that state of alertness essential for the quick thinking and cool snap decisions that I would have to make as soon as I set foot in my troubled sector again. My determination to go back was now no longer anything but a confused part of my numbed senses and I shuffled through the motions leading up to my return like an automaton. My excellent physical condition was such that no one realized at H.Q. that they were only talking to an empty shell—like that of a locust, still flying with the swarm though its inside was eaten away by insects, and which would suddenly crumble and drop for no apparent reason. It was therefore not their fault that they did not take matters out of my hands, instruct my friends to make a clean break and go into hiding, while they kept me in England.

In the meantime the information that I did receive was not very encouraging. End and Suzanne had been captured in Paris soon after their return from Éstrées-St.-Denis, fortunately, Roger had got clear and made his way to St. Jorioz.

One day I was called to the office and Major B. passed a decoded telegram across the table, saying to me ominously:

"Have a look at that!"

I read.

FROM LISE STOP ABWEHR OFFICER BY NAME HENRI CONTACTED ME ST JORIOZ SUGGESTED IF YOU PROVIDE HUDSON HE WILL RELEASE MARSAC AND SUZANNE RETURNING WITH ME AND THEM DISCUSS MEANS OF ENDING WAR STOP ENDS

"Phew!"

"What do you think of it?" asked my chief.

"I think it means Marsac gave Lise's address and that Henri is hoping to earn a Ritterkreuz by capturing a bomber and that the whole thing is so dangerous it should not be touched with a barge pole. I think Lise should be told to buzz off to the other side of the lake and Arnaud to leave Faverges and stay up at Les Tissots beside his set."

"That's just about how it strikes me," said Major B. "You know, Michel," he went on, "there's absolutely no need for you to go back and clear this up. We can have Lise and Arnaud picked up by Lysander and you can eventually start another circuit elsewhere, or have a home posting."

"Oh, I want to go back; and now that the Glières men have been armed I should like to join them and end the war with a gun in my hands instead of fighting the eternal unarmed duel of wits where you stand so little chance if you're caught."

"Well, it's up to you, Michel. You've been in it long enough to know where you fit in best. I think there's still time for you to catch the April moon. . . . Any particular preference of landing ground?"

"I should imagine that if the Hotel de la Poste is known to Henri and that there's been talk of bomber landings, his men are probably waiting for me on all our choice fields. Let Lise and Arnaud decide. I'm not fussy."

Major B. sent out the following message:

> HENRI HIGHLY DANGEROUS STOP YOU ARE TO HIDE ACROSS LAKE AND CUT CONTACTS WITH ALL SAVE ARNAUD WHO MUST QUIT FAVERGES AND LIVE BESIDE HIS MOUNTAIN SET STOP FIX DROPPING GROUND YOUR OWN CHOICE FOR MICHEL WHO WILL LAND ANYWHERE SOONEST STOP ENDS.

Twenty-four hours later came the reply:

> STUDYING SEMNOZ ANNECY P 14 STAND BY ALL NIGHT SPECIAL SKED

On the following day Major B. announced that a 3 A.M. message had confirmed the spot and that the B.B.C. message had been sent them for the operation on the same sked, plus the news that five containers would be dropped as well. Then, pulling out Michelin Map No. 92, we had a look at it together.

The co-ordinates indicated that they had chosen a spot starred for its beautiful all-round views and beside it, the figure 1704—showing its altitude of something over 5,500 feet—was something like a slap in the face that brought me out of my groggy condition to survey this staggering picture of reality.

"'Struth!" I said, rubbing my face with one hand. "They certainly took you at your word when you said I'd land anywhere."

"Seems like it," chuckled Major B., puffing at his pipe and taking a closer look. "An Alp all to yourself."

As the moon period had only three days to run, I was driven out to Station 61 forthwith. Paul was to return by Lysander in due course.

There was no waiting this time, and I was whisked off to the Halifax bays before any boredom could set in with its attendant nervousness.

At the briefing hut I was introduced to the navigator, whose graying curly hair, rows of decorations, and dilapidated blue battle-dress showed him to be an old stager whom I supposed had sneaked into the R.A.F. by marking down his age to the tune of anything up to twenty years.

"This mountain top," he said in the French of a Frenchman, tapping the spot with a pencil on a large-scale map, "there's nothing to it . . . I've dropped fifty-seven customers already, and if you go out when I give you the green light, I'll drop you on a six-penny bit."

I smiled, "I'm glad someone's pleased about this whole thing."

I entered the aircraft and, after the usual take-off routine which I knew by heart and followed in its successive stages, we were airborne.

It was 10:30 P.M. of April 15.

CHAPTER XIX

AT PRECISELY the same time Lise, Arnaud, Jean, and Simone Cottet were putting their best foot forward on the Sevrier-Leschaux road—No. 512—and they still had three kilometers to go before their twenty-five hundred-foot climb began up the steep wooded path that led to the spot they hoped to reach before the Halifax got there.

They could not console themselves that their chances were practically even in this vital race against time, for they did not know that the aircraft had only just left its base and still had over seven hundred and fifty miles to fly along the route it had to follow. Past experience had shown that planes could arrive at any and all hours between 10 P.M. and 2 A.M. and that these times were quite unrelated to the distances from their base.

Reckoning on a conservative daylight climbing speed of one thousand feet per hour on dry ground, the best they could possibly hope for was to reach the summit in three hours, namely by 1:30 A.M. If, handicapped by darkness and thick snow, they could maintain that rate, then they would enter the class of those whose accomplishments are worth recording.

Goaded on by the knowledge that even then the odds of success stood at about four to one against them, the four friends did not waste their strength with idle conversation.

The reasons for their being on road No. 512 instead of on the St. Jorioz-Leschaux road require some explanation.

On receipt of the message instructing them to find a dropping ground for their C.O.'s. return, Lise and Arnaud put their heads together Shaken by the speed of recent events, what with End's surprising capture, the subsequent baffling visit from Henri, and strong suspicions of betrayal by Roger Bardet (Arnaud was only dissuaded from shooting him out of hand in an Annecy café by Lise cycling beside him for twenty kilometers and using all her powers of dissuasion) the two friends laid aside their knowledge that the net was closing in to choose my ground.

Leaving at 4 P.M. they set out on their reconnaisance. The first eleven kilometers up to the pass were easy enough. An inquiry then led them to their stony mountain path. Up they went. Presently they entered the snow belt, yet, thanks to the daylight, they could follow the winding tracks of the path through the trees. In under two hours they came to a clearing and there, nine hundred yards above them, lay the white outline of their goal.

It was indeed ideally suited for their purpose. The best portion of the hog's back was a dome-shaped area close to an abandoned hotel and it measured some 300 yards by 80; the flattest part of this was roughly 100 by 80. The flanks of the hog's back were not too steep for snow to have settled upon them, so a reasonable deviation in either of those directions would still mean a soft drop. A bad mistake on the west flank would not be quite so healthy owing to a precipice. But they were not expecting bad mistakes, knowing that I—whatever else I might or might not be—was an instantaneous jumper. As for the R.A.F.'s accuracy, they did not give it a thought—its reputation having become legendary.

To make doubly certain that the navigator's dropping point should be clear beyond all possible doubt, they decided to guide him in with a huge bonfire instead of the usual torches.

Gathering vast quantities of branches from nearby trees and dragging them to a disused chalet for protection against possible rain or further snowfalls, they pinpointed their chosen spot for the fire and left all in readiness for the night when the B.B.C. message came through. A bottle of petrol and some matches would set it off in style.

All this took them some time, and they did not get back to the Hotel de la Poste until 11 P.M. that night.

While Lise had a well-deserved sleep in her room (she had decided to close a blind eye to the instructions about moving across the lake because of the time it took to meet and convince all her French colleagues to go into hiding, the difficulties of paying them all separately when she did find them, and her intuitive certainty that Henri would not move until the eighteenth), Arnaud cycled the sixteen kilometers to Faverges and then pushed his bicycle two thousand feet up the mountain road leading to his radio hide-out. It was thus only at 3 A.M. that he put through his message confirming the Semnoz as my landing point. The girl who was his opposite number in the London Receiving Station immediately sent him the B.B.C. message: *"Le carabe d'or fait sa toilette de printemps."*

All Arnaud had to do now was to make his way to the Hotel de la Poste by 7 P.M. that day, tell Lise what the message was, and himself listen in on Jean's set to see if I was coming. If not, he would repeat this process every night.

But Arnaud had seen so many operations go wrong for one reason or another and, distrusting all radio sets except his own, he closed the powerful transmitter in its suitcase and strapped it to the back of his bicycle. With the earphones inside and other parphernalia disposed upon his person, he attacked a hunk of bread and a piece of garlic sausage before taking a few hours' rest.

At 7 P.M. on the fifteenth he was already installed in one of the hotel bedrooms (it being Easter-time the place was empty, the guests only due back on the sixteenth).

At 7:15 he heard the news in French; at 7·25 the rich, powerful voice of Monsieur Schuman, the London "mouthpiece" of Free French thought and propaganda. At 7:30 came the daily announcement for which he was waiting.

. . . *Voici maintenant quelques messages personnels* . . .

In tense excitement, both hands delicately holding the dials, Arnaud listened.

At this precise moment the German jamming apparatus came into play, making rapid noises on three notes, thus: aou-eou-aou-eou and so on throughout the messages.

With silent oaths Arnaud gave the dials the merest fractional movements in a desperate attempt to get between the noise and the messages. Dim distant mouthings that seemed to have nothing to do with the spring toilet of his golden beetle vaguely reached his anxious ears. He pulled off the earphones in disgust. Surely the drop could not have been laid on already. Perhaps it would come off tomorrow.

Jean Cottet, likewise, stood baffled beside his 12-tube receiver. He kept this set beside the hotel boiler in the basement so that none of the guests could be in a position to inform on his illegal practice of listening-in to the news from London. (Madame Finaly, one of the guests, simply listened-in to the same program on a private set in her bedroom; but as the saboteurs had no time to go into the sympathies of the various guests, they never knew they had an ally, nor did this lady ever suspect what they were up to.)

Lise was listening for the messages on the same portable set which had served us both in Périgueux. She had plugged it into the lamp standard in her room and, despite interference, her sharp ears picked up the message.

Imagining that if she could hear it Arnaud must also have done so, she spent a moment getting herself ready for the climb before going downstairs.

In the bar she found Arnaud and Jean celebrating the fact that they did not have to climb the Semnoz a second time two days running.

"Why aren't you ready?" she said, impatiently.

"Ready for what?" asked Arnaud.

"He's coming! Hurry up!"

"What d'you mean, he's coming?"

"Didn't you hear the message?" she said, getting annoyed.

Two blank faces looked at her in stony silence. Then Arnaud said, in a rather superior tone of voice:

"If the message had passed I should have heard it."

"Well, it did pass and it was repeated. I heard it both times and on each occasion they said *'le scarabe'* instead of *'le carabe.'* "

"You're imagining things, Lise," said Arnaud, none the less shaken that she should have noticed the error of entomology—a subject which, like the radio, he considered his private domain.

"Well, I don't know what *you're* doing," she said, "but I'm off!"

"Just a moment," said Jean. "Since time is so important I'll take you as far as the Col de Leschaux in the car; that'll save you an eleven-kilometer walk."

"I'll come too," said Simone.

"Chic!" exclaimed Lise with delight, "and thanks, Jean. Let's hurry and get ready."

Jean ran down to the garage and began to fiddle with the taps and light up the stove in his charcoal-burning V-8 Ford. It had lain there so long, unused, that it proved a slow and difficult performance to instil the damp motor with the spark of life.

At last some splutterings announced that the little flame of hope had filtered through the pipe from the stern-burner; with wild jabs on the accelerator, Jean soon had the garage full of black smoke and throaty sounds.

It was 8:20 before the party—all wearing studded boots and heavy sweaters—took to the road. Realizing that the charcoal-gas device on his car reduced its power by thirty per cent, Jean decided on the easier gradient of Road 512. Consequently he drove them toward Annecy with a view to picking it up at le Crêt—four kilometers away.

They reached this first objective not without mechanical

misgivings and turned off to the left. A few hundred yards of the slight gradient of road 512 were enough for the engine. It petered out and no amount of coaxing would bring it back to life.

By the time they had given up hope of doing the twelve kilometers to the Col de Leschaux in ease and comfort, it was getting on for 9 P.M.

That was why the breathless party still had three kilometers to go at 10:30 that night and had no inclination to waste their ebbing strength on conversation. Had they walked up the steeper road, leading straight up from the hotel, they would have reached the pass by 9:45. The realization of this fact only added to Lise's determination to maintain a speed dictated by her mind and far beyond her normal physical capacity, already used up by the previous day's exertions.

On leaving the road for the stony path, more time was wasted in the sleeping village of Leschaux looking for the gap in the houses where the track began.

Jean Cottet finally led them to it and the stiff climb began.

Owing to the blackness of the night—the moon was rising on the far side of the mountain—they could not even see the the tracks they had previously left in the snow. Torches were of no avail and it meant retracing their steps.

A near-panic seized the anxious climbers. Should they go back? Should they go on?

Pointing up to the left Arnaud said, with his customary assurance: "I swear there's a short cut to the top if we climb up that way."

Looking in that direction Lise, depending on instinct rather than on her somewhat hazy sense of direction, said, "Never! That's simply miles off our line!"

"What do you say, Jean?" asked Arnaud, turning to their friend who had lived his entire life in the district.

"I confess I don't know," said he.

"Look!" said Lise, pointing to a telegraph pole. "I remember those poles go straight up the side of the mountain and end up on the top. Why, there's even one by the very spot we chose for him to land on. Don't you remember, Arnaud?"

"I seem to remember the one at the top, but frankly I don't connect the rest with it. . . ."

As this statement was one of the closest things to an admission that Arnaud had ever made, it was now mere child's play for Lise to persuade her friends that by following these poles they would reach their goal by the surest and swiftest route.

Leading them on, sometimes from boulder to boulder, Lise was now tackling an approach to the top that averaged one in two.

At midnight they stopped for a few seconds to catch their breath and listen for the possible sounds of a distant bomber. With their bodies soaked in sweat they could hear nothing but the pounding of their hearts.

At 12:30 and again at 1 A.M. they repeated this process with identical results.

By now the pace was too hot for Simone, and after assuring her husband that she would find the way following the telegraph poles, she fell behind.

Arnaud was the next to lose heart. Turning to Lise in the snow, he gasped. "This is hopeless! We're not getting anywhere. Just look at the time. Are you sure you heard that message, Lise?"

"Of course I did," she replied.

"We'll never get to the top in time. . . . When they see no lights they'll turn back and he'll be fast asleep in England before we get to the top."

"Come on, Arnaud! Don't waste your breath! We'll get there all right. . . . You'll see. . . . Besides, we've got GMT on our side."

On they climbed, their ears pounding with the strain and altitude.

It was nearly half past one when Arnaud heard Lise's triumphant voice just ahead of him crying: "Look, Arnaud! Look!"

Coming up he saw that the long forest belt was over and in front, rising steeply before them, lay the snowclad hog's back —a mere nine hundred yards away. The rising moon lit the silvery crest, casting its rays beyond and onto the tops of the pines under which they now stood.

The three friends scrambled up the last slippery stretch with only one aim in view; to get those branches out of the chalet in double-quick time.

As the red specks of strain burned her sore eyes, Lise prayed: "Oh, God, let me get there before the plane!"

The last nine hundred yards can be a very long way, especially when you already have so many miles weighing down your weary legs. My words kept coming back to her: "When you have ten paces to make and nine are done, only then can you say that you are halfway." She knew this was not original; she knew it was Chinese, but she also began to realize that it was very true.

Buoyed up by the vision of their goal, they accomplished the final spurt and mounted the rise abreast.

And now the exhausted climbers dashed for the hut and snatched up armfuls of branches, staggering out and piling them up on a foundation of straw in the center of their little pitch that looked so much smaller by moonlight.

Back and forth they ran, Arnaud doing double the work of Lise to make up for his moment of weakness and to save her from complete collapse.

The giant bonfire was no sooner ready than Lise flopped down panting beside it in the snow.

Pulling out a match which he held at one end of the striking board, with the open bottle of petrol stuck into the snow between his feet, Arnaud glanced at his companion's fragile form, lying half dead beside him. Never had he admired her so profoundly.

What was that sound in the distance? He peered into the northern sky and listened hard. Were his wishful ears playing him another trick? Jean was now kneeling beside Lise holding up her head and making her drink some brandy from his flask. In the deathly stillness their black shapes stood out vividly against the moonlit snow Lucky Michel, thought Arnaud.

Yes! It was an aircraft all right. An involuntary thrill of excitement ran through him. He remembered how I had said I would come back and there I was, inside that very plane. Soon he would see me come tumbling out toward them.

"Here it comes!" he cried, pouring the petrol over the

branches. Seeing that it was not pouring out fast enough he smashed the top of the bottle against his foot and dropped the lot onto the heap. Striking his match he threw it in while the sulphur still sizzled. With a small explosion the mighty fire caught light.

While Jean moved away slightly, looking for Simone whom he hoped would not miss the show, Lise and Arnaud stood side by side watching the thirty-ton bomber come in toward them. Every now and then he squeezed her affectionately with the arm he had placed around her shoulder. It was then that he decided that he would stand back and let her receive me first as I sailed earthward.

And here it came, cutting across the hog's back diagonally. Now it was almost straight above them.

With mouths wide open they anticipated the great moment; but nothing dropped from the aircraft's belly as it flashed over their heads. The Halifax flew off on a slow turn to port.

"Oh, God!" said Lise. "I can't bear it. . . . After all this sweat, they're taking him home again. . . ."

"Don't be a chump!" said Arnaud, "You can see this fire for a hundred miles except in the valley. . . . They're only turning round to come in along the length of the hog's back. Don't forget, they've got six 'chutes to drop on a mere three hundred yards. . . ."

Lying on his stomach in the glass nose of the four-engined bomber, Colonel Philippe Livry-Level, the French navigator, suddenly spotted the fire.

Speaking over the intercom he announced to the dispatcher and the others in general: "Bonfire ahead. . . . Action stations!"

The dispatcher pulled away the two semicircular boards covering the dropping hole, over which he switched on a maroon bulb. Groping his way carefully past the hole in the dim-lit fuselage, he tapped me on the shoulder and led me to the hole.

I sat down on the ledge, with my back to the engines. The dispatcher then pulled out the loose thong of my parachute and clipped it to the static line, pulling on it hard to show me that it was well and truly fixed.

The red warning light came on and I glanced rapidly down to see the snowclad mountain side rising until we were a mere three hundred feet above the trees.

A hand on my arm drew my attention away and the dispatcher shouted in my ear:

"We're going round once so as to make a better approach."

The warning lamp was switched off as the aircraft went into a slow turn. Looking down once again I saw the green murky waters of Lake Annecy, now some five thousand feet below. As I looked away I wondered if my reflection of that color was visible to the dispatcher.

And now the circle was being closed, and as the snow-covered trees flashed by the red light came on again.

The usual panic fear swept down from my mind and gripped my entrails in a vise. I felt the flaps go down and the variable-pitch propellers reducing our speed to something like 175 m.p.h.

Here it was again! I knew it all. . . . When the light turned green, the hand that would simultaneously flash down beside my face would be the hand of Destiny and the voice that shouted "Scram!" the voice of doom. If I did not go out at that precise second, I knew very well that I would land on the wrong Alp.

Gritting my teeth, I waited for it. . . .

As the red light gave way to green I was halfway down the chute before the dispatcher's shout died down

Closing my eyes and putting up my hands beside my face to keep the wind from snatching off my glasses, I was thrown back horizontally by the slipstream A violent jerk in my groin and below my armpits told me the 'chute was safely open.

I had swung round 180 degrees and was now facing the departing aircraft. It was only two hundred feet away and just above me, the full roar of its motors deafening my ears. Almost at once the sound dwindled to nothing, but my eyes remained glued to it, fascinated by the tongues of flame shooting out of the eight exhaust pipes of the four engines.

Now, one by one, the five other parachutes flapped open and hung, staggered, within a short space above my head.

From my right came the full brilliance of a five-eighths moon shining out of a peerless sky, and all around me lay the majestic scenery of the Alps cloaked in silvery snow.

It was a sight I would never forget. But, knowing that the drop would only take some fourteen seconds, I grudgingly looked away to see what lay below.

It was at this moment that I remembered the navigator's words: "I'll drop you on a sixpenny bit . . ." and fully understood them. . . . I was falling straight into the fire.

A swift pull on the forward set of nylon cords billowed out some air and made me move backwards. Lucky thing that this exercise was included in the parachute training. . . .

Now below me I saw two figures standing by the fire. The larger of the two then began running toward the second 'chute probably thinking it was I.

I was glad of this move, because it meant I would be dropping very close to the smaller form, which was peering anxiously into the sky, as though wondering which could be my 'chute.

As I came closer I saw that I was coming down straight onto her head. At the same time the air currents rising, from the flanks of the hog's back, caught and filled my parachute so that my normal descent at 20 m.p.h. was reduced to something nearer six.

It seemed, as I got lower, that I was no longer moving at all. But as I hovered over Lise's head, reaching down with my feet, as though this might speed things up, I refrained from saying anything to the upturned face that still did not see me.

Only at the very last moment did I speak.

"Hallo, Lise!" I said quite softly. "If you'll take a step backwards, I shan't land on your head."

With an ecstatic cry, Lise caught sight of me and, moving back out of the way she reached out her arms, as though to catch me.

I glided down, landing on my feet in the soft snow before her. I did not even have to bend my knees to take the shock.

As we embraced each other at this crowning moment of our

lives, the silk canopy fell lifeless on to the snow and, in the crackling of the fire, I heard her sweet voice repeating my name, "Pierre, Pierre," in tones that told me everything a man could ever wish to hear.

A huge form now came running up into the firelight, calling out, *"Sacré Michel!"* and, as I tore off my rubber helmet, Arnaud hugged me in a bear's grip, burying his face in my neck.

With an arm round my two companions, I smiled speechlessly from one to the other of these two beloved faces.

Catching sight of Jean Cottet, standing tactfully on the other side of the fire, I smacked the chrome buckle to climb out of the 'chute and moved toward him.

"Bonjour, Jean," I said, shaking his hand warmly. "Nice to see you here." I added, using the familiar form of speech. "I think the occasion calls for our dropping formalities."

"Nice to see you back, Michel," he replied, using the intimate 'thee' to show his agreement.

Presently we were joined by Simone and then, forgetting our fatigue, wandered over the snow, pulling in the huge cases that lay littered about the crest.

Lise stayed beside me, her arm through mine, relating the hundred and one complications of their lives during the past three weeks, at tremendous speed. My eyes on the lookout for parachutes, I was unable to take it all in.

Arnaud did most of the work, with Jean a good second. Between them they hauled up a square case, weighing several hundred-weight, from the bottom of a gulley down which it had slipped. Thanks to the snow it was like pulling a weight on smooth wheels or, at least, that was their gay claim.

It took all four of us to carry the huge steel container that had been dropped from the bomb-bay. After breaking into the hotel through some shutters and opening the main door from the inside, we hauled the quarter-ton object up the steep outside stairs and stored it within.

When all the cases had been stacked inside the hotel, we collected the six parachutes and threw them regretfully onto the fire, sitting around watching the necessary destruction and passing round a flask.

Finally it was time to go. It had taken us a full two hours to complete our work and it was now 4 A.M.

Arnaud was to stay at the hotel and guard the arms and equipment until relieved by Tom Morel's men, who would be due to collect most of the stuff in about twelve hours' time after Lise had warned the Glières Chief of its arrival.

Telling him to open up one of the cases in the meantime, we stood by to watch his reactions, a hint of which the others had already received from me.

Arnaud tore open the case in question and began pulling out one promised article after another. As he brought forth two new suits, a mackintosh, two pairs of thick brown walking shoes, two pairs of sheepskin gloves, two Colt automatics, a Belgian pistol, spare clips, radio parts, new crystals, batteries, and finally a personal Sten gun all to himself, hidden away in a log of wood with moss growing on the outside, he grunted his approval: *"Eh bien . . . Tout de même . . . Enfin! . . Nom de Dieu!"* and, having discovered the secret catch in the log that displayed the Sten, his joy knew no bounds.

We left him trying on this article and that, picking up one object and laying it down again so as to get his hands onto the next. It was a happy Arnaud who was required to spend the night on his own, surrounded by his most prized possessions. I felt sorry for anyone who might consider disturbing him in the center of his armory, and I felt warm inside at the thought that I had made Captain Alec Rabinowitch a happy man, even for a short while, for it was the fulfilment of a long-standing ambition.

CHAPTER XX

LISE, the Cottets, and I now began the downhill journey. It came as no surprise to me that we never found our way and merely floundered and slithered straight down into the valley through the snow. What amazed me was that they had ever found their way up.

The gradients of the slopes we took in the deep snow were in the region of one in one when they were not almost perpendicular. Lise, being one of those people who could not face the downhill slopes she could climb like a chamois, was obliged to hold onto my hand as I lit the snowy surface for each step with a torch held in the other. Being a downhill merchant myself, enjoying an equally keen dislike for any uphill work, I was in my element and, if slightly handicapped by having no free hand, I was only too delighted by her unstable proximity. Jean and Simone took everything straight without the least difficulty.

Lise did not help matters by talking twenty to the dozen in her justifiable anxiety to impress me with the full import of recent happenings. Mistakenly convinced that I could concentrate on three things at once, she divested herself of her thoughts while, at the same time, confidently leaning her full weight upon me in sudden lurches.

Under normal daylight conditions this precipitous descent in the snow was one that called for ropes. By torchlight it was a pure hazard.

It was at one of the worst points that she slipped out of my tight grip and slithered down a sheer bank. The horrible crashing of her body striking various objects in her thirty-foot fall, ending in a dreadful thud, made me sick with apprehension.

Skidding after her, like a skier, I was kneeling beside her where she lay sprawling, her back across the fallen trunk of a tree, within a matter of seconds

But Jean was there before me and already had her unconscious head cradled in his arm. The gray color of her face beneath the torchlight gave me the awful certainty that she had broken her back. Rubbing snow into her face and neck and alternately slapping her in the hopes of bringing her round, I became frantic at the realization that I might lose her.

"Lise, Lise, for God's sake say something!" I implored, close to her ear, as I continued rubbing snow all over her forehead.

"Doucement!" said Jean, pouring drops from his flask into her mouth.

With a choke Lise opened her eyes. She looked from one to the other and then at Simone who formed part of the horrified circle. Blinking her eyes, she said: "What are we waiting for?"

At that moment something told me that Lise had a charmed life.*

We reached the hotel at 8 A.M.

Lise went to her room, changed, washed, and came down at 8:25 for a cup of coffee. She then caught the 8:30 bus for Annecy where she went to call on Tom Morel and to see other people.

In the meantime I laid out my affairs, cleaned my shoes, and generally marked time until 12:30 when she returned for lunch. After that I rowed her across the lake where we called on Madame Frager—Paul's Russian wife—and gave her the latest news of her husband. We also took rooms in a small, quiet spot, well off the beaten track, which I wanted us to occupy that very evening. But Lise, who knew the situation more intimately than I, persuaded me that we still had thirty-six hours before Henri would make a move. I ought to have dissuaded her from following this line of intuition, but, as she had handled matters so successfully during my absence, I decided not to take the initiative out of her hands over this point.

* 1945 X-rays showed that Lise had smashed a vertebra in the middle of her back on this fall. It never healed. This item is not even mentioned in the list of ailments that still qualify her today—October 1953—ten years later, to a hundred per cent disability pension.

Lise made no mention of any pain in her back, nor did she show any abnormal fatigue from the last forty-eight hours of her strenuous exertions.

In the evening Arnaud, relieved of his watch, joined us at the hotel where we all dined together in a happy group.

I gave him a message running: R.A.F. AND RECEPTION PERFECT STOP ALL UNDER CONTROL.

Bearing these "famous last words," the tired Arnaud, much against his will, returned by cycle to his hide-out—nineteen kilometers away. We were to meet again the next day at a quiet spot by the roadside.

Lise retired to her room shortly afterwards and I was not long in following suit.

In the silent hotel only one light shone. It came from Jean Cottet's office, where he and Simone were doing the accounts.

Presently the front door opened and Louis "le Belge"—one of the couriers—came in. With a troubled look he told the proprietors that he was the bearer of bad news, that he had come as fast as possible to warn Lise, if she was still at the hotel, that Henri was about to strike.

As Louis "le Belge" was *persona grata,* Jean told him to sit down while Simone went upstairs to fetch Lise.

Knocking at her door, Simone said: "Louis 'le Belge' is downstairs. He's got something very urgent to tell you."

"I'll come right away," said Lise.

Suspecting nothing, she got into her dressing-gown and went downstairs. At the foot of the winding staircase she walked straight into Henri's gun.

"Don't try to warn Michel by shouting, Lise," he said suavely. "If you do, he's sure to jump out of the window and I think I should tell you that the hotel is surrounded by Alpini troops who have orders to shoot."

Lise was stunned by the turn of events. She gave Louis a look of utter contempt, so that that young man, working as an accomplice of the Gestapo and Roger Bardet, looked down at the ground in shame

The hall seemed full of large men.

Henri continued on a quiet, firm note: "You've played the

game well, Lise. But now it's over, so kindly lead us to Michel's room."

Realizing that if she did not comply with his wish there would be a room-to-room search, in which the Cottets' children would be awakened—as well as all the others who had returned that day—and given a fright they would not be likely to get over for a long time, and fearing that the sound of footsteps in the corridors would result in my jumping to my death, the unhappy Lise saw that the game was up.

With a heavy heart she took the enemy to the room of the man for whom she was then, and subsequently, prepared to lay down her life.

My door was opened and when the light was switched on I awoke to find Henri, a Gestapo man, and a member of the Italian Secret Police standing round my bed. I knew none of them, but realized full well what it all meant.

"What's your name?" asked their spokesman—a tall, dark young German—in fluent French.

"Chambrun," I replied, automatically giving my latest false name.

"Chambrun!" repeated the tough sarcastic voice, "or perhaps Chauvet. . . . They both mean Captain Peter Churchill, saboteur and filthy spy. . . . Put up your hands!"

Two automatics now pointed straight into my face. There was no possible argument. I was told to dress and did so, slowly and deliberately, all my faculties suddenly wide awake to everything, including the fact that this was the beginning of the last act. I cursed myself inwardly for having been caught fast asleep, for not having insisted on moving out, as reason and security had dictated in a clear voice. I cursed fate for not having let me pick the easy poison I could bear—that of paying for it all in the heat of battle with a gun in my hands—instead of making me die each dawn of an agent's dreaded and dreadful captivity. Of course I would have a stab at escaping, but even that thought had lost its urgency since success in that field would only add to Lise's torment. Unless we were rescued by Morel's men, what hope had she of breaking out? Moreover, I had a feeling that without me, she would never contemplate a solo attempt.

I did not notice that Lise, who had entered my room, was half dressed below her dressing-gown, nor that she was taking my wallet from my jacket hanging at the foot of my bed on a clothes hanger (it contained incriminating evidence and fresh radio codes for half a dozen operators, as well as some thirty thousand francs) while the men were keeping their eyes on me and searching every corner of the room for weapons and lethal tablets—neither of which they found.

Lise, thoughtful as ever for me, filled a small satchel with a change of linen and spare handkerchiefs that lay littered around the room after the men's fruitless search for other things.

When she came back, dressed and ready, to find me standing there with the handcuffs on, she picked up a second coat and put it through my hands to cover the telltale steel. She smiled a hundred thoughts and prayers into my eyes.

Turning my back on the twenty-ninth and last bedroom of my underground career, I walked slowly along the passage of the Hotel de la Poste with leaden steps. Lise was beside me, and close behind I felt the invisible automatics pointing at our backs through mackintosh pockets.

Slowly we descended the staircase to the ground floor. In the hall stood Jean Cottet, all the blood drained from his face.

Stopping the cortège at the foot of the steps, I looked at my friend—the instigator of the arming of the Maquis of Glières, the man who had helped us without questioning.

"Monsieur Cottet," I said, "I'm sorry to have caused such trouble in your hotel. You couldn't possibly know that I was a British Officer."

Jean shrugged his shoulders, thankfully taking the cue.

"With all the comings and goings in this place, it's a little difficult to know exactly who everyone is. . . ."

We were now taken to a waiting car. As we took our places, Henri asked me if I had any preference as to whose prisoner I wished to remain—German or Italian?

"It won't matter what I say," I replied. "You'll have us grabbed from your Italian allies in any case. But since you ask, the answer is that I prefer the Italians." The car moved off.

Lise, pretending to fasten one of her garters, tucked my

wallet out of sight below the seat. No one saw this clever move —not even I. It did not matter that Roger Bardet's betrayal already ran into ten typed sheets. The names of the men tucked away below the rear seat were unknown and would remain so, with any luck, forever. The man who found that wallet would be very pleased to transfer the thirty thousand francs to his own and consign any odd slips of paper to the fire.

Thus Lise and I, on our way to an endless Calvary, left things in order as far as it was in our power to do so.

As the door of my first filthy hovel slammed behind me in one of the guardroom cells of the Annecy barracks, my heart sank into my boots. I felt like a wild animal whose momentary unwariness has made him drop into a deep pit from which there is no getting out.

Lise, lying on a camp bed in one of the offices, found no sleep that night. Conscious that Henri had sprung the trap before the time her intuition had wrongly anticipated, she had now to pay the awful price for this miscalculation in the knowledge that her Commanding Officer had to share in what she was fully prepared to face alone.

Finding little consolation in the thought that if I ever managed to escape I was almost sure to contact Roger Bardet, whom I still hardly believed to be a traitor, she vowed she would shelter me and save my life by every available means.

Despite the heaviness of her soul Lise was determined—as I had forseen at our very first meeting—to bear the ignominy of it all with the same equanimity as that with which she had accepted her short moments of triumph. She was also to display such dignity of bearing throughout her long torment that she invested her captivity with a glory that even put her jailers to shame.

So Lise and I entered the long, dark, parallel tunnels of our solitary passage through the valley of the shadow—toward death or survival.

Biographical Index

André	Captured . . . Survived.
Antoine	Captured . . . Survived.
Aramis	Captured . . . Survived.
Arnaud	Captured 1944 . . . Executed.
Audouard family	Never captured.
B., Major (Colonel M. J. Buckmaster, O.B.E., Legion of Honour)	P.R.O. Ford Motor Co., Ltd. Author of *Specially Employed.*
Bardet, Roger	Captured by Allies after the war. Condemned to death as traitor by French Court . . . Subsequently reprieved and released.
Benson	Foreign Office.
Bessières	Never captured.
Buchowski	Killed in an accident.
Carte and family	Survived.
Catherine (Mlle. Odette des Garets)	Never captured.
Charles of Lyon	Captured . . . Executed.
Churchill, Group-Captain Walter	Killed in action.
Churchill, Major Oliver	Survived.
Cottets	Never captured.

Dauphin, Claude	French film star. Never captured.
Edmonds, Harry, R.N.	Killed in action.
End (Marsac)	Captured . . . Survived.
End, Madame	Captured . . . Survived.
Eugène	Captured . . . Executed.
Favre, M. and Mme.	Never captured
Frager, Capt. Paul	Captured . . . Executed.
Frager, Madame	Never captured.
Francine (Cannes)	Never captured.
G., Major de (Jacques de Guélis)	Killed in Germany in a motor accident.
George of Lyon	Captured . . . Executed.
Gérisse, Dr. A. (Lt.-Cdr. Pat O'Leary)	Captured . . . Survived.
Gervais (Capt. Hazan)	Captured in Spain; released, survived.
Gisèle	Captured . . . Executed.
Gomez	Never captured.
Gontrand	Captured . . . Executed.
Haddow, Lt.	Killed in an air accident.
Hilaire	Captured . . . Survived.
Jaboun	Never captured. Fought later with French tanks. Wounded.
Jean (radio operator)	Captured . . . Executed.
Julien (radio operator) (Captain I Newman)	Captured . . . Executed.
Langlois, Jacques	Never captured.
Latour, Jacques	Captured . . . Tortured . . . Survived.
Lattre (General de Lattre de Tassigny)	Captured . . . Escaped from Riom prison . . . Flown to U.K. . . . Led victorious French 1st Army in Allied advance . . . Died in Paris 1951.
Laurent (Capt. Basin)	Captured . . . Rescued . . . Survived.

Lise	Captured . . . Tortured . . . Survived.
Livry-Level	Survived.
Louis of Antibes	Captured . . . Died on evacuation march from Concentration Camp.
Louis "le Belge"	Captured by Allies after the war. Condemned to death as traitor by French Court . . . Subsequently reprieved and released.
Marie, alias Germaine, of Lyon (Miss Virginia Hall)	Never captured . . . U.S. Consular Service.
Matthieu (Capt. Edward Zeff)	Captured . . . Survived.
Milleau, Capt. and Madame	Never captured.
Morel, Lt. Tom	Killed by a Militia Colonel during a parley.
Olivier of Marseille	Captured . . . Executed.
Pasolé	Never captured.
Philip	Captured . . . Survived.
Pierrot	Never captured.
Porthos	Captured . . . Executed.
Renaudi, Roger	Captured . . . Escaped . . . Recaptured . . . Survived.
Renaudi, Madame	Never captured.
Riquet	Captured . . . Survived.
Roger (Lt. Col. Francis Cammaerts)	Captured . . . Condemned to death . . . Rescued . . . Survived . . . Headmaster of Alleyne's Grammar School, Stevenage
Roger of Tournus	Never captured.
S., Captain (Captain G. Voelcker, R.N.)	Killed in action.

Sainte-Beuves	Never captured.
Suzanne (End's Secretary)	Captured . . . Survived.
Suzanne of Cannes	Never captured
Taylor, Lt.-Cdr. "Buck"	Commanded his own submarine. Survived.
Thomas	Captured . . . Survived.
Ulysse	Captured . . . Executed.
Urbain	Captured . . . Executed
Vautrin, Colonel	Killed in an air accident.
Vigerie, Baron d'Astier de la	Never captured.
Women (two unnamed agents)	Never captured.

CPSIA information can be obtained
at www.ICGtesting.com
Printed in the USA
LVHW082247200519
618478LV00012B/333/P